MW01679375

So Much More for the Mind

Synthesis of Secondary School Theory and Practice

James Olesen

DETSELIG
ENTERPRISES LTD

Calgary, Alberta, Canada

So Much More For the Mind: Synthesis of Secondary School Theory and Practice
© 2007 James Olesen

Library and Archives Canada Cataloguing in Publication

Olesen, James

So much more for the mind : synthesis of secondary school theory and practice / James Olesen.

Includes bibliographical references.

ISBN 978-1-55059-335-8

1. Thought and thinking--Study and teaching (Secondary)

2. Education, Secondary--Curricula. 3. Teaching--Methodology.

4. Education, Secondary--Aims and objectives. 5. Critical pedagogy.

I. Title.

LB1628.O56 2007 373.01

C2007-903102-1

Detselig Enterprises Ltd.
210, 1220 Kensington Road NW
Calgary, Alberta
T2N 3P5

www.temerondetselig.com
temeron@telusplanet.net
Phone: (403) 283-0900
Fax: (403) 283-6947

All rights reserved. No part of this book may be reproduced in any form or by any means without permission in writing from the publisher.

We acknowledge the support of the Government of Canada through the Book Publishing Industry Development Program (BPIDP) for our publishing program.

We also acknowledge the support of the Alberta Foundation for the Arts for our publishing program.

SAN 113-0234
ISBN 978-1-55059-335-8
Printed in Canada

Cover Design by Alvin Choong

CONTENTS

I wish to thank my wife

MAVIS

for her continued support and encouragement.
Her wise counsel is deeply appreciated.

PREFACE

Rip Van Winkle awakens in the 21st century after a hundred-year snooze and is, of course, utterly bewildered by what he sees. Men and women dash about, talking to small metal devices pinned to their ears. Young people sit at home on sofas, moving miniature athletes around on electronic screens. Older folk defy death and disability with metronomes in their chests and with hips made of metal and plastic. Airports, hospitals, shopping malls - every place Rip goes just baffles him. But when he finally walks into a schoolroom, the old man knows exactly where he is. "This is a school," he declares. "We used to have these back in 1906. Only now the blackboards are green."

"How to Bring Our Schools Out of the 20th Century"
Time Magazine, December 18, 2006

The genesis of *So Much More for the Mind* stems from my work as a curriculum Developer for Saskatchewan Education during the 1980s and 1990s. Good curriculum writing attempts to encourage growth in what teachers teach and students learn. The challenge in curriculum writing is to be 'out in front' of the educational establishment, but not so far out that the curriculum becomes obscure. Change must proceed slowly and meaningfully if it is not to be dismissed out of hand by teachers, administrators, and parents. We pushed the envelope as much as we could for that time and place.

The basic objective for the 1980s round of curriculum development was to encourage teachers to increase their emphasis on critical and creative thinking, moral and ethical thinking, developing research skills, and improving student ability to communicate their ideas to others using a variety of media. Some gains were made, but a fundamental disagreement developed over the amount of time to be devoted to teaching process objectives (skills, activities, research, etc.) and the time devoted to teaching for content objectives (basic subject information).

Teachers were reluctant to give up content. Some teachers were prepared to compromise by including more emphasis on skills but felt they must continue to emphasize course content. They complained that the 'new' curriculum placed inordinate demands for time devoted to skills development, leaving a lack of time for covering content. Some asked what a reasonable balance between an emphasis on skills and an emphasis on content should be. When pressed for their balance, most teachers suggested a 10-20 percent emphasis on skills and an 80-90 per cent emphasis on content. Most were quite shocked when it was suggested the new curricula were calling for something much closer to a 50-50 division.

This balance is a profoundly critical issue for secondary schools, because it has a major effect on the kind of students we are likely to see at the end of 12 years of schooling. Are we to be satisfied with the status quo: the kind of student we have been producing for the past 30 years or so? Or, do we believe highly competitive, technological, and liberal democratic societies need some other kind of student: students who have the capacity to be self-starters, who have learned to be independent thinkers and life long learners, and who are able to cope with the technological nature of our society?

The Theoretical Framework for So Much More for the Mind

Secondary education in North America is chronically under attack. One of the most recent volleys comes from Margaret Wente in the October 15, 2005 issue of the *Globe and Mail.* She charges Ontario education with a failure to educate its young people effectively. She notes the drop out rate has grown to 31 per cent, indicating a profound unwillingness by young people to remain within the education process. She goes on to discuss how raising literacy standards have contributed to the rising dropout rate. Like many observers, she is torn between being in favour of higher literacy standards and being aghast at their consequences in terms of dropout rates. Her solution is to return to the streaming process that was once applied to students having difficulty with academic education.

In all of the critiques one hears, the teaching learning process in classrooms is almost never mentioned as a place for inquiry and analysis. For most observers, the classroom is like a black box where students go in one end and come out the other, presumably after something has happened to them that makes them successful at standardized tests. Whenever solutions are offered, the solutions tend to be some reversion of the good old days, as Wente does with her paean to the benefits of streaming. Wente has one thing right: there is a profound dislike among students for secondary education as it presently stands. Seldom offered by Wente and other commentators is a realistic discussion of the learning processes used in classrooms, and most importantly their effect on student attitudes toward learning. *So Much More for the Mind* has that as its central purpose.

The problem is that we - meaning society - are unclear about the direction secondary education ought to take. A good example of that can be seen in Bill Gates' comments on secondary schools in America. In his column for the *New*

York Times of September 4, 2005, Thomas L. Friedman quotes a portion of a speech Gates gave to the State Governors.

In his speech, Gates argued that:

> *American high schools are obsolete. By obsolete, I don't just mean that our high schools are broken, flawed and underfunded . . . by obsolete, I mean that our high schools - even when they are working exactly as designed - cannot teach our kids what they need to know today.*
>
> *Training the work force of tomorrow with the high schools of today is like trying to teach kids about today's computers on a 50-year-old mainframe . . . our high schools were designed 50 years ago to meet the needs of another age. Until we design them to meet the needs of the 21st century, we will keep limiting - even ruining - the lives of millions of Americans every year.*

Gates' dissatisfaction with the state of education in North America secondary schools resonates with a variety of commentators. In the statement above, he appears to be convinced that the teaching-learning process in high schools needs to change profoundly. Without significant change in their education, American students will not be able to compete in the global economy. But is that what he really thinks?

In a somewhat different context, when asked whether he believes the American emphasis on creativity over rote learning gives American students some kind of advantage over foreign students, he offers the following observation:

> *I have never met the guy who doesn't know how to multiply who created software . . . who has the most creative video games in the world? Japan! I never met these 'rote people' . . . some of my best software developers are Japanese. You need to understand things in order to invent beyond them.*[1]

What does Bill Gates consider to be the purpose and function of education? Looking at the first quote, one might conclude he believes that education needs to change so students do learn the kind of knowledge and skills that will prepare them to function in a technological world. The second quote suggests that he believes there is a strong need to return to the basics, as symbolized by memorizing the multiplication tables. Mr. Gates expresses a somewhat contradictory but typical frustration based on his sense that, for whatever reason, students are not learning the fundamentals they need. The important questions to be considered are what those fundamentals might be, and how they should be taught. *So Much More for the Mind* considers these questions in detail.

Critiques from people like Bill Gates are problematic, because their analysis of the problem is limited, and their solutions typically resort to a 'back to the basics' approach to education with built in accountability systems such as rigid curricula and standardized testing. They assume that more authority and less freedom will accomplish their broad goals for education. But will 'back to the basics' produce the educational change that people like Gates want?

Popular discussions of education miscast the debate. *So Much More for the Mind* demonstrates how this has happened. Conservatives see education withering under the mistaken thrall of progressivism, because they believe that 'progressive' educational policies condone and reward mediocrity in the name of freedom and creativity. 'Small l' liberals see 'back to the basics' school systems retreating into an authoritarian past where learning is simply a dreary round of rote learning in an authoritarian setting.

The remarkable feature of this debate is the lack of attention that both sides pay to what actually occurs in average classrooms across North America. *So Much More for the Mind* brings the discussion back to the classroom, and argues that teaching has actually shifted remarkably little over the past century despite what both sides believe. *So Much More for the Mind* brings the conversation back to the classroom by examining what is going on there, and - more importantly - what could be happening in classrooms. Based on that analysis, the book argues that it is time to radically rethink the assumptions governing our approach to teaching and learning.

What dispassionate observers of classrooms are likely to discover is a curious and unproductive mixture of progressivism and back to the basics. This 'compromise' has evolved over the past century. What they will almost certainly find is an overreliance on text books, which in turn results in an unhealthy emphasis on learning information to the exclusion of learning to think. At the same time, those progressive elements surviving in the classroom are theoretically aimed at independent thought and creativity, but actually do little to teach thinking, or to provide useful thought activities to stimulate and guide student learning about thought. Both phenomena are present in classrooms, but unfortunately the personal biases that observers select for the perception of one eliminates the perception of the other. This is the source of the confusion for people like Wente and Gates. It is also the source of frustration for high school students, and contributes to the problems that both Wente and Gates comment on.

Educational institutions are dominated by broadly accepted paradigms. Paradigms have the capacity to affect the basic assumptions people use to interpret the reality they perceive. Teachers, parents, students, and citizens all tend to share educational paradigms that appear to be common sense to all four groups. The prevailing educational paradigm (or common sense) holds that the major purpose of education is to teach information.

Traditional paradigmatic thinking prevails in education for a couple of reasons. Teachers model their teaching on the paradigm in which they were taught. That paradigm establishes the purpose of education and the methodologies to be used. The upshot is that teachers continue to teach as teachers have taught over the years; Bill Gates has got that right. And so despite what conservatives argue, 'modern' education in its fundamentals has changed very little from its inception in the nineteenth century. Education systems continue to be controlled by a prevailing educational paradigm that highly conserves traditional approaches to teaching and learning. Based on this paradigm, teachers believe that they know what 'good' teaching should look like, as do parents and society in general.

The second problem is that students rapidly learn the prevailing paradigm as well. They quickly discover their role is to learn information regardless of whether it has any meaning or purpose for them. Despite their lack of understanding of the information they are studying, they know that they must achieve good marks to earn certificates of performance. Given this situation, what do students who want to survive the system do?

Their dilemma is solved by memorization. Memorization is such an obvious solution for every one that it has become fundamental to the information-centric paradigm which controls education. It has become the narcotic of choice for educational systems. In the same sense that drugs divert from people from confronting a reality they really should face, memorization is a narcotic. School systems, as 'responsible' representatives of society, are afraid of independent thought because it comes with all sorts of issues that they would rather not face.

For school systems, especially those who espouse standards, an exam based on memorization appears neat and precise. If the student repeats a certain body of information accurately, then one can place an exact number (grade) on that performance. Students either know the material or they do not, and there is no middle ground. On the other hand, evaluation of thinking is seen as an equivocal process which is subjective, and as such subject to question and debate. School systems under pressure to deliver 'quality' education find the evaluation of thinking too fraught with uncertainty and thus too risky to pursue.

The narcotic is actually worse for students. As pointed out above, students find memorization eliminates their need to understand the material they study. Simply memorize it, and all will be well. Students who memorize well find they are rewarded for their effort. They are applauded for their success at remembering detail and few are seriously asked if they can thoughtfully and creatively discuss what they have learned. In the few cases students are asked to discuss something in a thoughtful, creative way, they often do not perform well. The upshot is failure, particularly if students have to think something through in an examination setting.

Marks plummet and students learn to associate independent thinking with failure. Many retreat firmly and permanently into memorization. The addiction is in place.

The fundamental thesis of *So Much More for the Mind* is the need in education to move from a focus on absorbing information to a focus on learning to think independently and creatively. Independent and creative thought can be applied to all aspects and walks of life, whether it is moral and ethical citizenry, artistic and athletic creation, spiritual living, as well as scientific, technical and business endeavours; all of these activities (and the preceding list is not exhaustive) require the capacity for thought. Not a simpleminded focus on information, thought is what people need to become successful life long learners. Information is merely the means to the end of being able to think about all of the multifaceted experiences of life. One does not memorize one's way to success in any of life's experiences.

This is not to argue that students should not learn information (or even memorization for a specific purpose, such as reciting poetry), but they need to learn information in the context of thinking about something in a way that has some kind of personal meaning. Learning cannot be meaningful until it is grounded in the reality of the student. Learning proceeds faster and lasts longer when it is meaningful and purposeful. Research indicates quite clearly the retention rate of memorized information is short, while retention of the gist of information can be permanent.

A paradox - actually a synergy - occurs when high schools emphasize independent thinking, often presented in the form of creative problem solving. Students learn and retain larger amounts of the information they encounter in their quest to solve problems than they would if they had just memorized it. It is possible to get the best of both worlds, but high schools must give up their emphasis on accumulating information in order to gain the benefit.

School systems will find switching from teaching for information to teaching for thought a difficult transition. School systems have evolved for so long under an information paradigm that educators find it difficult to implement another approach to learning. Before change is possible, a case will have to be made for a different approach to education.

Replacing the teaching of information with the teaching of thought (epistemology) is critical to the future success of students. Unless school systems are seriously prepared to make this change, high schools, "even when they are working exactly as designed" (Gates), will be unable to produce the kind of student needed in an information based society. This is the paradox: an information based society needs thinkers, not walking encyclopedias

The central issue to be considered is what constitutes an educated person. Is an educated person one who can parrot reams of information, or is an educated person one who can thoughtfully and wisely select and apply information to situations as needed? The latter answer seems obviously correct, but despite that, educational systems continue to choose to behave as if the former answer is what society wants.

Another reason that change is not made is because teachers have a very dim idea of alternative approaches to teaching. They simply do not have a background of experience in teaching thought to draw upon.

So Much More for the Mind devotes several chapters on how school systems can make the change from a memorization based learning system to a thought based system. A surprising number of teaching methodologies already exist which can be employed in the classroom to teach thought. All of these methodologies are based on sound research. The first chapters outline the situation high schools presently find themselves in. The development of the information paradigm is outlined and used as a basis for analysing the need for change in secondary school education. In the latter half of the book, the problem of creating thought based classrooms is discussed. Educators are supplied with practical classroom based approaches which make such a transition possible as well .

Many of the suggested teaching methodologies necessary to the teaching of thought already exist, and have been effectively used in a few classrooms for a couple of decades. Others are newer, but have been demonstrated to be highly effective in stimulating and teaching thought. The problem is not a lack of alternative approaches to teaching, but a willingness to enthusiastically adopt them.

The issue comes down to whether the public, schools and teachers are ready and willing to make a change. *So Much More for the Mind* provides a clear explanation of thought based teaching methodologies that educators could rapidly implement if they were willing to make the change. It is through the creation of thought based classrooms that the capacity to create a well educated public able to creatively adapt to the future will be found.

ENDNOTES

1. Thomas L. Friedman. *The World is Flat.* New York: Farrar, Straus and Giroux. 2005 p 264.

Chapter One: A Paradigmatic View of Educational History

The capacity for hope is the most significant fact of life.
It provides human beings with a sense of destination and the energy to get started.

Norman Cousins

Table of Contents

Traditionally, school begins the day after Labour Day. On a beautiful fall morning, young people walk to school dressed in their new school clothes. Everything about the day suggests hope and renewal. Consider a hypothetical class of 30 grade nine students on the first day of high school. They are restless and nervous. Some respond by withdrawing within themselves a little. Others, the extroverts, want to relieve their nervous tension by getting something going. You are their teacher and the moment of truth arrives as the first bell rings. A hush falls and a wary expectancy turns on you as you say some welcoming words.

You too are wary as you go about the bureaucratic functions of getting names and distributing forms. "What am I going to teach these people?" you think as you go about the opening day routine.

The students have concerns as well: "What is high school really going to be like?" "I hope it won't be as boring as some classes I've been in." At this point, two solitudes study each other across the social division of the teacher's desk.

Is it possible to cross that barrier in some meaningful way? The adolescents sitting in front of the desk have a powerful need to define their individuality. The strong ones are determined nothing - including parents, schools, teachers, and whatever else - will stand in their way. Behind the teacher's desk lies a powerful societal expectation, which demands that these young people be socialized into productive, law abiding citizens. Are these sets of expectations in conflict, or is there room for some kind of mutuality? Can both students and society come to feel satisfied with the education process? It is the teacher's task to make these two sets of needs mesh.

The Purpose of Education

What should the ultimate purpose of education be? The traditional point of view holds that education must preserve and pass on the culture. A more recent point of view believes that education is about the personal development of the individual. The point of view taken in this book will be that education should help people learn to live their lives successfully.

Young people want an education that gives them the ability to make sense of and give direction to their personal reality. First and foremost, they want to understand themselves. Then they want to understand how external reality relates to their lives. Many adolescents are unconsciously Socratic in the sense that they believe "the unexamined life is not worth living".[1] Adolescents are profoundly interested in discovering how their lives relate to the world outside family and school. They see this as the major task for their lives.

A teacher has to reconcile the tension between the legitimate needs of students and the legitimate needs of society. In one sense the gap is not so great, because democratic societies need people who are courageous, independent, creative, critical thinkers, and who are able to take a moral and ethical approach to life. This is simply a definition of good citizenship. In another sense, the gap may be very great: as the death of Socrates demonstrated. Certain power groups in society do not embrace critical thinkers. Parts of society strongly believe in conformity, especially for adolescents.[2]

Society can treat independent thinkers very harshly. Adolescents experience some of this. The conflict between advocates of critical thinking and advocates of conformity is a fundamental conflict in society, and it can make the classroom an uncomfortable place. Responding to conflict requires growth, change and risk for adolescents, teachers, and society as well. The teacher is caught in the middle. Unfortunately, the middle position has the potential to be unpopular.

The assumption underlying the approaches taken in this book is that to be effective, education must be meaningful to the student. Without meaning, there can be little learning. The notion of 'being meaningful' is a broad generalization that needs to be carefully defined. Creating such a definition is a major purpose of this book. An initial starting point is to say that meaning is always created within the mind of an individual.[3] Therefore, a major purpose of education is to help students become adept at discovering meaning already constructed within their minds, and using that discovered meaning as a basis for constructing more meaning. In effect, this is a definition of the purpose of education for this book.

The human mind is good at searching out meaning, because that is what it was created to do. It is not good at warehousing large amounts of information, especially if it cannot make the information meaningful in some way.[4] Storing information with little meaning requires memorization. Memorization is a struggle for most people because they find it so unfulfilling. Yet it is ironic that in spite of their dislike for memorization, students learn to rely on it as one of their most basic learning tactics.[5]

THE REALITY OF EXISTING EDUCATION

Many students regard high school classrooms as a long, dreary grind to be endured in return for a better life. They and their teachers have given up the possibility of classrooms as exciting and interesting learning environments. Both look outside the classroom for positive stimulation, whether it be social experiences or activities such as music and athletics. Teachers see their responsibility as 'covering' the course yet one more time. Classrooms are where people work, and if the work is drudgery then so be it. Extracurricular activities will have to provide the creative environment for students.

This is a description of high schools many would resist, but there are indicators of it everywhere in our society. One can do a personal perception check by engaging friends in reminiscence about the learning conditions they encountered as students. Telling horror stories about life in classrooms may be a joke thirty years after the fact, but it is no joke for students currently encountering their own horror stories. If one wishes to compare perceptions of past education with the current, find some students presently in high school and engage them in a discussion about their classroom life. Today's classrooms maybe appear friendlier and somewhat less overtly authoritarian. Despite that, the fundamental need to 'cover the course' and have students assimilate as much information as possible may actually have become more demanding under the pressure of the information explosion. Classrooms remain places where drudgery is seen as scholarship.

Problematic schools are a world wide phenomenon. American schools stagger from one disaster to another, depending on football and cheerleading as fragile social glue. Japanese students, who once had an international reputation for docility and obedience, have begun to rebel against the regimentation they find in their classrooms. Japanese students who receive grades of 'B' or less know their education careers have hit a dead end. Many 'B students' are no longer willing to do massive amounts of hard work for very little reward. They drop out in one way or another. Thai schools are running into similar difficulties.[6]

What has happened to a vision of education which claimed to want the best for young people? In a nutshell, the answer is that society has never seriously considered the views and needs of young people. Many adults would take serious exception to this statement, but that is the reality of the situation. A 'serious' consultation is one where young people feel free to offer their viewpoints without fear of censure and recrimination, and where they know their suggestions would be seriously considered and acted upon. In that sense, adolescents are seldom consulted; because they have not been consulted, we are left with groups of adolescents who have not been engaged by their education.

Adolescents have a variety of reasons for remaining associated with an unfulfilling school system. The attitude is 'grind it out' and then get on with your life. Others find alternatives like computers, music, drama, athletics which they use to carry them past the boredom. Others drop out. Some drop out permanently while a few are occasionally salvaged by special school programs which constructively and significantly revise the way a school system and its teaching processes interact with students.[7]

What is remarkable about the salvage programs is that few ask what seems like an obvious question. If school is not working for those who drop out or fail in some significant way, why should one assume it is working well for those students who have not physically dropped out? Simply because they are thicker skinned, more competitive, and motivated enough to stand the rigours of a system does not mean that the system is good for them. This situation is mindful of a time when miners used to take caged canaries with them into mines as an early detection system for poisonous gas. The highly sensitive canaries would quickly react to minute amounts of gas giving the less sensitive miners time to evacuate the mine. Are the young people who drop out the canaries of our educational systems?

For many, questioning the performance of school systems in this way will seem nonsensical. Of course schools are working, they will say. We are graduating thousands of students every year all around the world, and those graduates go on to do good things in society. For most people, it is difficult to imagine any feasible alternative to what we presently have. For others, it is the basic nature of students which determines the nature of schools. If students were different, then schools could be different. For traditionalists, school systems are institutions which have evolved over time to become what they are today. They have stood the test of time, and if 'they are not broken, don't fix them'.

Institutions like schools do not provide clear and unequivocal signals like dead canaries in a mine. Cause and effect in a mine can be very clear, but are less so in school systems. If school drop outs are signals of deeper problems, it is difficult to see the problems. Many alternative explanations are offered purporting to demonstrate dropouts as the anomaly rather than the rule. Drop outs are not an anomaly. Classrooms are filled with drop outs who, while they may be physically present, have dropped out of any serious intellectual activity related to their schooling. We perceive this reality, and yet we deny it because we do not want to see it. A convenient form of denial is to claim that high school students are too immature to know what is good for them. We adults, who are more mature, are in a better position to determine what they need. This is simply a convenient fiction allowing us to maintain the status quo.

Another reality complicating our thinking about the best approach to education is the complex nature of humanity. As we will see later in this book, humanity appears to have a dual nature. On one hand, human beings appear to be capable of great goodness and empathy for others. On the other, human behaviour is more perverse and destructive than it seems possible to imagine. How to approach this dichotomy often confounds policy makers as they attempt to create successful learning experiences. On top of this dichotomy sits another basic dilemma. Is the purpose of education the satisfaction of the needs of society, or should it be to satisfy the needs of individual students?

Over the years there have been a variety of balances drawn on these issues. Where the balance is drawn depends upon the prevailing paradigms governing society's perception of young people's humanity, and the development of an appropriate response by educational institutions based upon that humanity.

Paradigms Affect the Way We Think about Students and Schooling

This is where the problem of paradigms enters the discussion.[8] Paradigms may be defined as a set of coherent ideas, beliefs, and values broadly accepted within society as being the 'common sense' viewpoint on an issue. Paradigms govern how a majority of people in society perceive the reality they inhabit.[9] In *The Structure of Scientific Revolutions*, Thomas Kuhn describes the effect of paradigms on thinking. He explains how paradigms influence the perception of reality, and how that perception influences thought. In turn, perception and thought are powerful influences on behaviour. Kuhn states it this way: "All of us have undergone, from infancy, what has been called a prolonged apprenticeship in how to perceive reality."[10] He goes on to explain how we are trained to perceive reality in certain ways, and to respond to it with certain culturally prescribed behaviours. He calls this process "coming to possess an intelligent eye".

Kuhn demonstrates the influence paradigms have had on the history of science. He suggests that paradigms act as models whose purpose is to define reality. Models simplify reality by highlighting certain aspects of reality while ignoring others. Modeling reduces complexity to manageable levels. It does this by directing perception towards certain aspects of reality while screening out others.

In practice, the process works through the development of what an observer considers significant questions to be asked and explored. Since not all questions can be explored, this leaves many questions unasked and unexplored. The selected questions direct the observer toward certain observations which come to act as sources for the development of a 'reasonable' hypothesis. Only those hypotheses which seem to lead to reasonable conclusions are drawn from the observations made. 'Reasonable' is also determined by the researcher's prevailing paradigm. From acceptable hypotheses, basic lines of explanation are defined which lead the thinking of researchers in certain directions to the exclusion of others. It is a circular process.

A famous example of this process is Ptolemy's geocentric theory explaining the structure of the universe. This theory was accepted for centuries as a reasonable explanation for phenomena people could observe around them on a daily basis. Every day, if one cared to look, the motion of the sun passing overhead and the essential flatness of the earth could easily be observed. From an earthbound frame of reference, what could be clearer? And if it were so clear, then it was completely unnecessary (silly, really) to question an obvious reality. Thus, for example, the reality of ships slowly disappearing over the horizon was effectively screened from perception. Acceptable (reasonable) reality is perceived, and unacceptable reality is discarded.

Those simple observations formed a model of reality in which the earth was the centre of the universe. Based on such a model, it was nonsensical to reinterpret the behaviour of the earth as a tiny ball spinning at over 1000 miles per hour and at the same time revolving around the sun. Using a new frame of reference provided by telescope technology, Galileo made careful astronomical observations beyond the boundaries of the earth. He soon found other data which could only be explained by creating a new model of the universe. The Ptolemaic model was clearly inadequate to explain the reality Galileo was now observing. Galileo's work led to a new model of reality. Based on the work of Galileo and others, a new paradigm evolved that still guides the work of scientists.

The paradigm shift Galileo played a role in more than simply supplanted a new model of the universe for an old one. What is critical here is that Galileo's thinking represented a shift in metacognition; that is, how one should think about reality, how one should ask questions to find truth. Galileo rejected tradition in favour of actual observations and in favour of asking hard questions about what is happening in reality. Galileo's heliocentric model of the universe ran into trouble with Church authorities because they would not abandon traditional biblical interpretations. The Ptolemaic theory was acceptable in their eyes because it corresponded with their biblical paradigm. Galileo was rejected, despite his evidence, because his paradigm clashed with their paradigm.

There are many other examples of this process. Some Nineteenth and early Twentieth century researchers into human psychology brought a racist paradigm to their observations.[11] Their race based model of humanity assumed race was a real phenomena, leading them to accept that racial assumptions could offer significant observations and interpretations of human nature. These researchers set about to document human characteristics in ways which would prove their racist hypotheses. Unsurprisingly, they came up with data supporting their conclusions. It was only later researchers working under non-racist paradigms would discover major errors in the research supporting those conclusions. It soon became clear racist paradigms (models) were inadequate to explain the diversity of human behaviour researchers were discovering.

The power of paradigms to control peoples' perception has nothing to do with their humanity or their intelligence. Medieval people invented many of the concepts we take for granted today. They were highly perceptive and creative people, but they could imagine only so much that was new. Paradigms limit our ability to perceive and imagine realities very different from those provided by our 'trained eye'. What currently seems obvious may be found to be less than true some time in the future.

The Evolution of Educational Paradigms

Over several centuries, one can observe changes in the paradigms or models of childhood and their related educational practices. To understand those changes and their effect on modern paradigms of childhood, we need to look at the evolution of attitudes toward children and education from a couple of standpoints. The limitations and needs of society were (and remain) powerful influences on the perception of children. These social factors work in partnership with a philosophical view of the nature and behaviour of humanity.

Changes in education models do not occur in a simple progression. They leap forward in attitude and then regress to older attitudes as people change their assumptions about the reality of educating children. Philosophical beliefs retain the power through paradigms to affect peoples' perception and interpretation centuries after their inception. That is as true for the twenty-first century as it is for the fifteenth century.

Some examples of this process: By the Renaissance, Western European societies were evolving away from dominance by the Catholic Church to dominance by powerful kings. Monarchs were determined to centralize as much power as they could. Their public justification for centralizing power was the need to develop and maintain an orderly, peaceful society. They and their supporters argued for the development of virtuous citizenship among young people. Thinkers such as Machiavelli (1469-1527) began to discuss education from the standpoint of instilling morality and ethics in young people, mainly men. It seemed a reasonable proposition that the state should have a primary interest in the 'proper' schooling of young people. Therefore, morality and ethics should be concerned with loyalty and obedience to the state as personified by the King. Honour was very much seen in these terms.

Around the same time Northern Humanist thinkers were defining humanism as a new view of humanity. Northern Humanists accepted that human nature had been corrupted by sin, but they argued all was not lost. People were still fundamentally good and an education based on Christian virtues of love, faith, and hope could lead students to piety and an ethical way of life.

Thinkers such as Erasmus and Thomas More believed education could build a better world. Erasmus (1504) argued the core of any curriculum had to be based on the Gospels containing the teachings of Christ. In Erasmus' and More's opinion societies based on the philosophy of Christ would be more just and humane than existing societies. If children were educated to live by Christian principles, then society could be improved. More developed a new concept he called utopia, meaning 'no place' (1516), to define the kind of future he envisioned. More conceded that incipient utopian societies had to be protected from corrupting influences by placing them on isolated islands, until they became strong enough to resist outside influence.

By the sixteenth century one can see two competing visions of education. These visions pivoted around the issue of the nature of humanity and its effect on the general behaviour of society. There is the 'hard nosed' realism of Machiavelli who believed society had to be accepted as it is: people are neither good nor honourable; wealth and recognition are scarce and people violently compete for them; and, the supreme value in any society is order, because without order all other components of civilization are lost to chaos. The central responsibility of government (the Prince) is to control the anarchic tendencies of society as ruthlessly as necessary.

Northern Humanist thinkers believed Machiavelli was simply capitulating to the status quo. Rather than trying to do something about corrupt societies, Machiavelli accepted them. The central point for Erasmus and More was that children (people) can grow morally and ethically. Progress was possible, and education was the means to that end. By helping children learn to live a better life morally and ethically, society helps itself become more humane. This debate has not gone away. It continues on into our era as a fundamental heuristic defining how people approach education.

Events in the seventeenth century confirmed both points of view to some degree. The religious and civil wars in various European countries supported Machiavelli's view that societies without a powerful and effective Prince, capable of maintaining order, would be violent and bloody anarchies. At the same time the misbehaviour of powerful, unaccountable kings supported the Humanist's view that a better way of governing society had to be found. Two thinkers appeared who would carry the debate to a higher level and continue to affect modern educational paradigms.

John Locke (1632-1704) set out two related theories of human behaviour. The first examined political behaviour. Locke argued that people form societies and establish government to protect life, liberty, and property. If government does not protect life, liberty, and property, then by definition it becomes a tyranny. Reason tells people that they have the right to rebel against the unreasonable behaviour of a tyrannical government.[12] The ideas of Locke quickly appealed to a middle class paradigm which had been slowly evolving over the past century. The middle class saw Locke as legitimizing their social and political aspirations. However, it would be a while before it would become even marginally reasonable to apply these notions to children.

In another paper, *An Essay Concerning Human Understanding* (1690), Locke developed a second theory outlining his view of the learning process. Locke rejected theorists like Descartes who held that children are born with unchanging ideas and ways of thinking. Locke believed children come into the world as a blank slate (tabula rasa). Children are not born with instincts or predispositions - such as original sin - which control their future behaviour. Locke argued that every human characteristic is learned in response to the sensations people receive.[13] By 'sensation' he was referring to the information people receive through their senses. Everything we are and know we have learned through our senses. All life experience is written on the tabula rasa. What was written on an individual's slate (what moderns now call 'memory tapes') creates the character and knowledge of that person.

Based on his model of learning, Locke argued that the direction of human development is controlled by the kind of education and treatment children receive, and not through some hereditary, instinctual inheritance. Change the education and the treatment people receive and you will change people.

Locke's theories were revolutionary. They had the potential to change profoundly prevailing paradigms of governance and education. Despite that, Locke's ideas about education were not readily accepted. Traditional ideas about the nature of humanity and the nature of governance do not change easily.

At roughly the same historical period Thomas Hobbes (1588-1679) wrote what would be interpreted as something of a counter-theory to John Locke's. Hobbes argued the basic nature of humanity is defensive, selfish and power seeking. The human need for power ceases only at death. Hobbes implied that human character is much more individualistic than what Locke implied. Self-interest would always be more important than some kind of reasoned and mutually acceptable social contract as envisioned by Locke. In Hobbes' view, self-interest would have to be controlled by a powerful authority to prevent the evolution of corrupt, violent societies.[14]

Hobbes was a social contract theorist who believed that people originally formed societies for self-protection against anarchy and its violence. People surrendered their power to a central authority for order and security. Security for power was the deal (social contract), but once a social contract was established people could not be trusted with the right to overthrow it. It was simply too dangerous to release the individualistic, anarchic tendencies of humans within society for whatever reason.

Locke was also a social contract theorist. He theorized people originally came together voluntarily and agreed upon a social contract because by doing so they could create a better life for themselves. It was not that life was not so bad in a state of nature, but that it could be better in a cooperative, social venture. Hence the formation of societies. Locke believed the benefits of living and interacting together was what drew people to form societies rather than the fear of violent, anarchic societies as described by Hobbes.

These two views continue to be heuristic for the way schools and classrooms are envisioned. Are classroom/playground societies always teetering on the brink of violent anarchy, or are they places where adults and children come together to build a better life for themselves? This is a dialectic that has not gone away. School discipline centres on the issues raised by Hobbes and Locke. Are classrooms groups of power hungry adolescents whose only agenda is to 'get' the teacher? Or are classrooms primarily filled with people who see the classroom society as a route to the construction of a better life?

The complicating factor in all of this is the approach taken by the classroom society toward students and vice versa. Classroom discipline can be conducted so that students are unable to perceive anything constructive accruing to them in that situation. They conclude that rebellion and disengagement are the only outlets available to them. On the other hand, classroom discipline (leadership) can be applied so that students feel empowered and included in the management of the classroom society. It is possible in practice to create either a Hobbesian or a Lockean society within schools. Both have been done. Thus it becomes more of a choice to be made than a foregone reality. Yet as we shall see, the paradigms we have inherited continue to suggest that classroom societies should be viewed as being Hobbesian. The interesting question is why we opt for Hobbes over Locke.

Power is a central issue in all of this. How power is viewed and employed in social institutions determines whether a society is based on Hobbes' assumptions or on Locke's. Power can be viewed as self-aggrandizement. This is the zero-sum view of power, through which power is considered to be of a limited quantity within a society. Power comes in limited quantities and it is never equally shared. The point of the power game is to accumulate power by taking it from someone else. If someone gains power, then someone must lose power. Power cannot be created, it can only be distributed. This view of power matches the social realities described by Hobbes and Machiavelli.

Bullying within schools and playgrounds is currently a major problem for some school systems. Bullying is based on a zero sum view of power. The question for school systems is how to respond constructively to the bullying problem. Schools have the power to bully the bullies. The dilemma in that approach is the appearance of validating bullying as a solution for problematic social relations. A more Lockean approach is to discuss with the bullied and the bullies how, by changing behaviour in a constructive fashion, a more satisfactory society can be created.

That leads us to the view of power described by Locke. His view of power might be termed 'empowerment'. From this perspective, power can be shared, and by sharing it more power is created. People who come together and share their power (talents, energy, enthusiasm, etc.) are making each other more powerful.

This can be a response to the bullying problem. Students are helped to understand that respect and inclusion are powerful and satisfying approaches to human relationships. By learning to handle social relationships in this way, one comes close to Locke's view of society. Still, the problem remains of how to persuade people to buy into a socially constructive paradigm when a self-aggrandizing paradigm seems so much more satisfactory in the short run; remember that in terms of history, a lifetime is the short run.

For the next centuries the debate would waver between these two points of view. Life in the sixteenth, seventeenth, eighteenth and nineteenth centuries was hard. Contraception was crude, and many unwanted children were born. Over the course of those centuries society became more urban and mechanized, lessening the need for child labour. Infanticide and abandoned children were common, because desperate parents could not afford large families. The mortality rate for infants and children was very high: so much so that parents really did not consider children human - or lovable - until they were certain that a child would survive. Parents simply could not risk falling in love with a child who would, in all probability, die. Doctors refused to treat sick children because it seemed pointless. Children were neglected because they tended to die, and they died because they were neglected: a brutal trap for everyone.[15]

One area where adults were not indifferent to children was discipline. Their emotional response to childhood was to control it with harsh discipline. Children were seen in Hobbesian terms, and it was the responsibility of the parent to use their power to instill order among their children. Daniel Defoe (1660?-1731) coined the term "spare the rod and spoil the child". This was more than a maxim, people really believed it. Susannah Wesley, the mother of 25 children - including John Wesley, founder of Methodism - practiced a stern discipline. She believed the first task of a parent was "to conquer the will of the child and bring it to an obedient temper." Her babies were "...taught to fear the rod and to cry softly; by which means they escaped the abundance of correction they might otherwise have had, and that most odious noise of the crying of children was rarely heard in the house."[16] John Wesley (1703-1791) asked his mother to share her child rearing practices with him so that he could understand the reasons for her success. Wesley later would give his mother's child rearing practices a biblical interpretation.

Freedom for Children: Is it feasible given their nature?

John Wesley believed in original sin. Children come into the world as sinners and must choose to become holy. It is the responsibility of parents as members of the Christian church to raise their children in maners that encourage them to repent from their wrongful ways. Parents who fail in this responsibility are condemning their children to damnation. The child-rearing philosophy of people like Susannah and John Wesley - there were others spreading similar messages - came to define the beliefs of a critical mass of British society in the eighteenth and nineteenth centuries.

Freedom was considered by Wesley and others to be the great enemy of children. Any time a child is allowed freedom to make choices, those choices will be bad ones. Bad choices become bad habits, and those habits must instantly be broken by the use of corporal punishment. Children should never be left unsupervised, particularly in play. Correct habits are established when children play orderly games under adult supervision. It is folly to reason with children. They are incapable of reason, and will use it for their evil and self-serving purposes. Only honest punishment can establish and maintain the habits of obedience, self-control and self-discipline.

John Wesley is an important example of the influence a particular point of view can have because of deep respect for certain religious and philosophical views. This influence allowed leaders like Wesley to have a major impact on the child rearing and education paradigms that come to dominate society. Wesley was enormously energetic and organized. In his lifetime he traveled 250,000 miles and preached 40,000 sermons. He formed societies, examined and commissioned preachers, raised funds for schools, chapels, and charities, and superintended schools and orphanages. On top of all that, he wrote commentaries on many subjects and maintained a prodigious correspondence.

The teachings of Wesley and others like him came at a point when Western society needed to think about education on a mass scale. This was a time when Western European countries were establishing a variety of school systems. Many of the newly created schools were parish schools established to teach children how to read the Bible. Of course, parish schools would also wish to provide students with an acceptable theological interpretation of the Bible. People trusted Wesley's theology, and with that it was a short step to accepting Wesley's educational theories. Everything fit into the biblical paradigm Wesley was proclaiming

As noted above, life was hard and tragic. Life expectancy was still short, and the economic and social situation in Great Britain was changing profoundly as the economy moved toward the Industrial Revolution. At the same time, the general literacy of people - and by extension, their social expectations - was increasing. By the end of the eighteenth century, literacy rates had risen to 90 percent. Literate people began to look for explanations about the social realities they were facing. The Church and its related school system was one source of explanations that made sense. A paradigmatic reality about the purpose of education (reading and accepting the teachings of the Bible) had been established. A related and important phenomenon was that a definition of schooling had been established. Children who went through these school systems were learning what a 'normal' approach to schooling should be. In Kuhn's terms, an 'intelligent eye', concerning what one should expect from schools, had been established.

Paradigmatic Fundamentals of Education

These parish schools - and the assumptions they were based on - would have a powerful influence on the future direction of schooling. The debate about schooling was by no means over, but some fundamentals about discipline in schools were established at this time. The purpose of education was to impose social and religious obedience on children who are willfully ignorant and in need of civilizing by schools. To that end, a strict hierarchy between teacher and student must be established and maintained. Teachers had a duty to use corporal punishment as needed, and teachers had the right to stand *in loco parentis* while children were in school. The other major purpose of education was to make children literate and numerate, and train them to accept certain necessary 'fundamentals' of civilization. An educational paradigm had been established, and societies are still reacting to these fundamentals at the beginning of the twenty-first century.

Despite the widespread acceptance of an authoritarian education paradigm, there remained an ongoing debate about the democratization of schools. The debate would focus on the need for discipline tactics like corporal punishment and the capacity of children to make decisions about their own lives. This debate did not begin in the twentieth century; its roots can be found in the sixteenth and seventeenth centuries.

Some people remained dubious about the efficacy of treating children harshly, despite the widespread acceptance of the points of view of people like Wesley. Here and there, individuals and small groups of people felt intuitively there had to be a better way of disciplining children. One such person was a Puritan leader, John J. Robinson, who commented that it was still "much contraverted whether it be better, in the general, to bring up children under the severity of discipline and the rod or no."[17] It is interesting to note the bitter reaction of other Puritan writers to mild comments such as the one above. One commentator blasted:

> *'Foolish' parents who refer to their children as 'harmless creatures' 'pretty innocents' and other fond names ... which figuratively denote the same things, such as 'little doves', 'harmless birds', when in reality children really should be considered ... birds of evil omen if not birds of prey... who need to taken in ...the snare of the fowler.*[18]

Apparently many Puritans felt they had to react aggressively to this perceived threat. In their minds, the future of civilization hung in the balance.

It remained for Jean Jacques Rousseau to provide, in his novel Emile (1762), a rationale for allowing children a measure of freedom. Rousseau started from the premise that God had made all things good, which would include children: "Let us lay it down as an incontrovertible rule that the first impulses of nature are always right". He went on to argue "there was no original sin in the human heart, the how and why of the entrance of every vice can be traced to some human cause".[19]

Rousseau believed small children were basically amoral. By that he meant they were incapable of forming a deliberate intent, either good or evil. They would be able to form responsible intent only when their minds became capable of reason. Rousseau argued children from very early in their lives were innately capable of understanding principles of justice and virtue. Based on these premises, Rousseau developed a model of education which did not actively interfere in the lives of children. Rousseau believed non-interference was necessary because children would choose right only as long as they were not interfered with by authority figures who would model wrong behaviour to children. Children, if left to their own devices, would opt for justice and virtue.

Still, Rousseau had to deal with the problem of the origin of evil. If humans were born good, how did evil get into the world? Many children demonstrate bad behaviour from a very early age. Rousseau's response was that evil was a human creation caused by the pressures of civilized society. These pressures enslaved and depraved humanity. Children are taught by society to behave badly, beginning with the family. If children are given constructive models to learn from, they will willingly become virtuous people.

Freedom was the basis on which children could be protected from societal depravity. In Rousseauistic terms, freedom should be thought of as independence and not as license. Independent living means learning to accommodate consequences. License is the notion that one's behaviour is immune to consequences. Constructive education provides children with an environment where they are free to make choices and learn from the consequences of those choices. Legitimate consequences are those that derive from living within limits determined by health, safety, and those societal requirements which enable people to live together peacefully. Above all, children should be allowed to be happy.

Rousseau did not believe that virtue could be taught. Rather, he thought children could be provided with a non-corrupting childhood until the age of 18 years or so. A child's experiences should be carefully controlled by environmental manipulation, so that as the child's powers of reason develop he/she could learn to judge the worth of an experience. The adult in charge of a child's experiences had to learn to control the child without precepts: "let him always think he is master when you are really master."[20] By these means, children can be brought to virtuous behaviour.

The problem for Rousseau and his supporters was that societies were still highly invested in hierarchical social systems. By the end of the eighteenth century, the aristocratic societal paradigm was under attack in many western countries. Rousseau was only one voice - albeit an important - questioning the hierarchical assumptions of the aristocratic paradigm. The long-standing aristocratic social paradigm would continue to exert a powerful hold over the thinking of people who lived under it. Social change came with great difficulty, and was accompanied by a fierce debate about the proper balance between the poles of hierarchy and equality on one social continuum and freedom and order on another. Over the course of the nineteenth century, social systems would draw increasingly liberal balances between hierarchy and equality and freedom and order. As institutions, schools would eventually be forced to respond to peoples' opinions about the proper balance between those qualities.

A critical hierarchical assumption was the belief that people of the lower classes could never be intellectually equal to those of the upper classes. People who are born in the 'better' classes have superior breeding and education. These people have a duty and a responsibility to lead and set standards for society. Allowing people from the lower classes to have some kind of intellectual authority within society would be folly. They are simply unable to make the sophisticated decisions needed. That was the aristocratic side of the argument, but philosophical and economic forces of society were slowly but surely changing the social complexion of society.

At the same time, the middle class was growing in wealth and insisting that the concomitant power and influence be awarded to them as well. Thinkers such as Adam Smith provided a powerful intellectual basis for their claim to authority within society. Smith argued government control in the form of mercantilism was stifling progress. Governments needed to allow a free and open competitive system in which all citizens would have fair and equal opportunities to contribute to and profit from the economic well being of society.

Paradigms of Modernity

The economic realities described by Smith would continue to drive Western societies down the road toward economic and political equality, and also social equality to some degree. The direction and speed of change would vary from country to country, but by the end of the twentieth century the social paradigm would have changed to one more based on equality than hierarchy. Somewhere in the nineteenth century, a paradigm which came to be understood as modernity came to dominate the thinking of Western societies. Modernity - with its connotations of science, progress, liberalism, etc. - provided the fundamental assumptions of these societies. Over time the assumptions of modernity would extend into other parts of the world as the economic and political influence of the West expanded.

Education would play an important role in that process. One can trace the paradigmatic debate as education attempted to respond to the needs of society. It was increasingly recognized that children would have to be prepared to function in a decentralized, competitive, technological society. Such a society would demand a basic level of literacy and numeracy. But more than that, students would have to be instilled with the necessary conformity and self-discipline, which would make them productive citizens. Similar logic also applied to the question of how 'ordinary' people could be prepared to play a role in government, however tenuous that role might be. In these senses, it was clearly believed that the economic future of a nation depended on the ability of schools to prepare children to perform well in a changing adult economy. The third force operating here was that after an initial foray into child labor, most societies recognized children were unnecessary in the work force. Better to put them to work being educated than to use them unnecessarily in the work force. For all of these reasons, compulsory mass education grew quickly in the nineteenth century.

Returning to our original paradigmatic questioning of the purpose of education and the nature of children, we see that the limitations and needs of society still remain powerful influences on the perception of children. People (labour) are now perceived to be a factor of production in the same sense as land and capital. Children need to be socialized in ways that make them useful to the economy, and it is clearly the responsibility of schools to do that. In the twenty-first century little has changed. Economic success remains a powerful educational incentive among parents and students alike. It is so powerful that it remains paradigmatic, because for most people (parents and students alike) there really is no other purpose for attending schools as they are presently constituted. If the economic incentive did not exist, many students would simply withdraw from whatever schooling process they happen to be involved in.

Once the economic need for compulsory public education was established, then the mostly unspoken question revolved around the form mass education should take. It was an unspoken question because the dominating paradigm for planning a program of compulsory mass education was based on the maintenance of hierarchy and order. For most people, the notion of applying freedom and equality to children seemed far fetched at best. The Rousseauistic notion of allowing children freedom (independence) in their school lives did not conform with the dominant paradigm of hierarchy and order. In fact, that notion was not accuratefor parents either. Compulsory education laws took the option of freedom and independence away from parents as well. Most often the justification for compulsory education was couched in language that argued for the protection of children. The fact that the protection of children was also in the best interests of the state and the economy was not seen as something needing discussion. An authoritarian approach to education seemed both safe and sensible for all concerned.

Metanarratives of Progress

The late nineteenth and twentieth centuries saw the era of the modernism. From a post-modernist perspective, it seems clear that modernists accepted the possibility - if not the reality - of the existence of metanarratives. Metanarratives are the "grand, master, or sweeping narratives of a culture, people or society."[21] There were a number of sources of grand narratives in Western society. For centuries, Christianity had been the single greatest grand narrative. During the Enlightenment, Christianity was augmented by history and fledgling social thought. The narrative of nationalism became more influential as nation states grew and consolidated power both geographically and socially. Based on the success of the enlightenment project of the eighteenth and nineteenth centuries, science became another powerful grand narrative in Western societies. The discourse of these narratives contributed to a sense of the past marching through the present and on into the future. It gave people a sense of where they were and where they were going. The various narratives accepted by modernity were most often summarized as progress or as being progressive.

Nationalism and racism became powerful co-narratives. Nationalism became important to people because technology and industrialization had made the world global in ways that it had not been in previous centuries. People recognized their standard of living depended upon the ability of their nation's economy and military to compete successfully against other nations for markets and resources. If one's nation failed to compete, the consequence would be a fall in standard of living. Economic survival depended upon being loyal to one's nation above all else.

Racism during the eighteenth, nineteenth, and into the twentieth centuries would become an increasingly potent influence on the intellectual community, and ultimately would affect educational research and schooling. Social thought was permeated by the assumptions of determinism and its handmaiden racism.[22] Natural science, theology, psychological research, and the social sciences in general - to name a few - were all caught in its snare. Evolutionary theory was easily transformed into Social Darwinism. At that point, it could be used as an intellectual justification for racism, and was used as such. Locke and Rousseau had presented some tough questions for the determinist crowd, but despite their efforts, the forces of nationalism and racism would easily elbow them aside. For racists, it was simple, clear, and obvious: the nature of humanity was determined by one's race. Nationalism, racism, and economic power would join forces in the late Nineteenth century to justify the imperialistic control of other people.[23]

The debate in the nineteenth century was not one-sided. There was an ongoing dialectic around the nature of humanity and the nature of knowledge (epistemology). The problem was that it was not a nicely defined dialogue between well founded but competing points of view. It was more like a cacophony of developing philosophies competing for the attention of society. Burke had made a powerful case for conserving the best ideas and traditions of society. Liberals under the leadership of the Mills were successfully making a case for the development of liberal democratic societies. Marx hopefully predicted a class war which would ultimately create a classless society. At the same, time science and technology continued to transform the world in ways which would seem unimaginable a century earlier. People were ambivalent about change. It was difficult to argue with social and technological progress, but where was all of this heading? Societies were scrambling to catch up with all the change happening.

A variety of narratives gained wide spread discourse, some more than others. They, at least, gave people some sense of direction in their lives, albeit a narrow and incomplete direction. The language of a narrative, with its concepts and metaphors, has the power to make the hidden - and often confusing - forces working behind the scenes in society more explicit . With a perspective based on a narrative, people felt that they had something they could get a handle on. Narratives gave them ideas to share and work toward. Unfortunately, narratives can provide a false sense of certainty about issues which are at best ambiguous and inherently uncertain.

One institution heavily affected by these kinds of grand narratives were schools. Schools came to be seen as a concrete social mechanism which could be used to make grand narratives a reality. Parents believing in the notion of upward mobility were determined to create schools, and to provide their students with the best education possible under the circumstances. In Western Canada at the turn of the twentieth century (and also in the U.S., Australia, New Zealand), one of the first things immigrant families did in newly established farming communities was to create neighbourhood schools and churches. Discourse among parents living in those farm communities was about the potential future made possible by providing sons and daughters with educations their parents and grandparents could only dream about.

It fell to ideology to provide political grand narratives around which political power would coalesce. Ideology became significant for other areas of society because of its power to inform the narratives related to other institutions. As we shall see, ideology significantly informs education narratives. We have space here to consider only a few of the major ideologies. Capitalism, Communism, and Fascism became the most significant, because their followers were able to achieve the power necessary to establish societal models based on their respective ideologies. Each model society purported to lay out a blue-print of the kind of society that could be built by the ideological vision. Each ideological vision provided the sources of information and perspectives for what would be considered an acceptable narrative discussion within society.

Naturally, the basic visions of each ideological grand narrative clashed with the others; and just as naturally, their followers turned to violence as a means of imposing and defending their particular visions. There were obvious differences among the visions, but interestingly there were also underlying similarities. The assumptions of modernity pervaded all three. Each ideology accepted the assumption that a single narrative was capable of offering a single plan suitable for all of society. A further assumption was that everyone in society would have no choice but to accept the grand narrative.

The Establishment of Broadly Based Authoritarian Education

Modernists from each ideological persuasion accepted - to greater or lesser degrees - the necessity of the state as a vehicle for implementing the narrative. Nationalism was accepted and used as a means of ensuring loyalty and support for the state. It was further accepted that state security justified giving the state rights to coercive powers denied to ordinary citizens. Under the rubric of leadership, they all accepted hierarchical societies as being necessary. They all saw citizenship as bestowing special benefits on citizens to the exclusion of non-citizens. No supporters of various ideologies questioned the notion that science and technology offered salvation for the ills of society. Followers of each ideology saw industrialization as the means to progress. Each ideology defined progress as the increase of material wellbeing for the citizens of the state.

In all three systems, the role of schooling was to reproduce society as envisioned by the ideology. History, civics, literature, etc. were seen as vehicles for inculcating the values of the prevailing vision. Children would perform various patriotic exercises which were intended to teach them loyalty and conformity. Schools became *in loco parentis*, meaning that while the child was in school, the school stood in place of the parent. Schools had the power to impose corporal punishment as they saw fit. Schools had the right to define a child's performance and to use that performance as criteria in determining the course of a child's future life. Schools were hierarchical and elitist. Children were taught to accept their inferiority in the school social system, and to accept that certain children were superior to other children. In many of these societies, the race of a child determined whether she or he was eligible to attend school.

School subjects were hierarchical as well. Typically, there was a small cluster of significant subjects: literature, history, mathematics, and science were the usual candidates for this honour. A key component of nationalism was the national language and its related literature. People believed the successful transmission of the national language to the next generation was a significant contributor to the national well-being of the nation state. Nationalism is the belief that a people have done great things in the past, and on that basis they can expect to do more great things in the future. National literatures and histories were the 'proof' of past national greatness. Schools must be sure that young people catch the glory of the past so that they may carry it into the future. Mathematics and science were seen as being critical to the development of a numerate and scientifically literate population.

All ideologues feared their model society's future would be seriously compromised if schools were not firmly based on the fundamental beliefs of the ideology. The competitive international system had the effect of making them even more fearful. This was the basis for the educational paradigm which came to prevail in the early twentieth century, and remains more or less intact in the early twenty-first century. This paradigm did not prevail without a fight, and its opponents have ameliorated some of its worst effects.

Events in the twentieth century played havoc with ideological narratives. The staggering death toll of World War One - soon followed by the even worse record of World War Two - dealt a body blow to faith in most nineteenth century narratives. The perceived failures of Christianity to prevent war, the horrific consequences of racism in the holocaust and other places around the world, the co-option of capitalists and communists into military-industrial complexes, the complicity of 'big' science in weapons manufacture, and - to some extent - the suspicion of 'progress' as a narrative all cast doubt on the simple (naïve) nineteenth century prognostications of future progress. Somewhere in all of this, schools had to find their way. It is a struggle which continues into the twenty-first century. It provides an instructive context to consider the nature of present day schools.

Evolution of the Educational Debate

What was it that children needed to learn for their own protection? First and foremost were the famous three 'Rs'. Literacy and numeracy would be high on anyone's list. Following that would be a series of values that had much to do with teaching children their role within the state. Values like duty, obedience, loyalty, acceptance of authority, acceptance of the work ethic, the ability to compete, etc. were significant parts of the informal curriculum of schools. Schools as institutions were authoritarian, and punishments meted out to children would be seen as assault by any adult who received such treatment.

Conservatives believed the school's responsibility was to reproduce society. That responsibility could take several forms. Mostly it involved teaching nationalism in the form of loyalty to the state and respect for the national identity. Histories were mostly national histories, the lessons of which were to instill pride in the great events of the past and the potential of the future. National literatures were also used to instill pride. It would be unusual for schools to actively involve their students in critical thinking about past state policies and behaviours, particularly if they were disreputable. If nothing else, less than honourable behaviour would simply be omitted from school histories. Schools were expected to inculcate loyalty to the state. Athletics emphasized team work and loyalty to the team. A good team player simply did not 'let one's side down'. Young people were to exhibit patriotism and be prepared to fight for one's country as needed.

Liberals believed solutions to hierarchy-equality conflicts within society would be provided by education. Schools were seen as the social vehicle by which the poor would gain entry into the middle class. Schooling would provide the opportunity for social mobility. In Canada, Edgerton Ryerson and others fought for a public system of education available to students from all classes. Horace Mann played a similar role in the United States. While it was true that everyone was required to achieve a basic level of literacy and numeracy, it was not true that children would be educated to move beyond their class origins. Schools reproduced the existing class structure. For most ordinary people, a definite ceiling limited their educational progress. Such a ceiling was justified as being economically necessary, and - to some degree - an acceptable state of affairs. In this sense, order was more highly prized than freedom.

So far we have not discussed in any detail the broader intellectual landscape and its effect on education. There was a relationship between the dominant philosophical and scientific paradigms and the goals and purposes of education. The relationship was mixed in the sense that intellectual ideas would permeate the information to be taught in schools, but it would have very little effect on the conduct of classroom life. For example, in the Nineteenth century, intellectuals became highly enamoured with classicism. Greek thought in particular was held in very high esteem. University buildings were often built in the classical style to underscore the close relationship between classical studies and 'good' education. Children were systematically taught the achievements of the classical Greeks.

An unspoken objective was for schools to reproduce the glories of classical Greece in current society. It is notable, though, that the teachings of Socrates about critical thinking never became a reality in ordinary classrooms. The kind of independent thinking that Socrates died for was as much anathema in late nineteenth and early twentieth century classrooms as it was to the judges of

Socrates 2500 years earlier. Schools were much more comfortable with the authoritarianism of the mature Plato.

What did evolve in the nineteenth century was the typical classroom. Twenty to fifty students sitting in rows, facing a teacher in front of some kind of chalkboard under their firmly control. The slate board of the nineteenth century has evolved technologically over the past two centuries into chalkboards, overhead projectors, and now large computer screens able to show an array of technological marvels. Despite the technology, the basic composition and function of classrooms has not significantly changed in two centuries. The point of the classroom and the improved technology continues to be the transmission of received knowledge to minds considered to be incapable of determining for themselves what they might like to learn.

In the nineteenth and early twentieth centuries, several crunch issues were becoming clearer. Science and technology had been fused by the industrial revolution of the last century, and the benefits of industrialism were beginning to roll in. Transportation was making the world smaller and more unified. The power and reach of the Western world could be seen everywhere. Societies were becoming increasingly liberal. Social and economic progress seemed to be accelerating, and to many it seemed only a matter of time until poverty, disease, war, etc would be eliminated. Science replaced religion as the great intellectual anchor of society. Societies were becoming increasingly secular, and education replaced religion as the social glue to some extent. Hence, public education came to be seen as a critical social process in preserving and extending the goals of society.

There were a number of fundamental assumptions that would have a very large effect on the direction schooling would take in the twentieth century. Few nineteenth century thinkers would quarrel with the notion that science had the capacity to answer the serious questions facing humanity. The mysteries of physics, chemistry, and biology all appeared to be open to the processes of the scientific method. Prior to Einstein, it seemed only a matter of time until all the secrets of the universe would be unfolded. Einstein's work seriously challenged that notion, but despite that challenge, the scientific enterprise continued to roll along. A particular philosophy of science, Logical Positivism, became a fundamental approach to understand reality. Logical Positivists believed that reducing the material of the universe to its fundamental essentials made it possible to reconstruct models of reality that would be comprehensible to humanity. Reductionism came to be accepted as a fundamental approach in studying the unknown.

Responding to an Industrialized Society: Individualism and the Individualistic

Industrialization became the fundamental model for organizing production within society. In the nineteenth century, the factory system was continuously refined. Standardization of parts and processes made it possible for the assembly line to produce products efficiently. The discipline of engineering made standardization possible. The logical positivistic philosophy of science provided the reductionistic assumptions of engineering and in turn engineering demonstrated to everyone's satisfaction that reductionism had huge benefits in making production more efficient. Reducing reality to its essence makes it possible to rebuild reality efficiently in more useful forms. Reductionism and conformity then became the watchwords of industrialization. Henry Ford once noted (probably tongue in cheek), "People can have the Model T in any colour - so long as it's black."[24]

Bureaucratization at both the industrial and governmental levels was seen as being necessary to organize and control the large scientific, technological, and political apparatus that was evolving. For example, now that trains (and later automobiles and planes) were a significant method of transportation, they had to run on time. This turned out to be a larger social challenge than just putting a few trains on iron tracks. If trains were to meet people's needs, then they had to be organized and controlled so that they were where they were supposed to be when the schedule called for it and, more critically, not at the same place at the same time.

Schedules, blueprints, and design became the hallmark of an orderly society. Society had to be efficiently administered, and people were the minimum units of society. It was the role of engineers and administrators to organize those 'units' into productive, coherent wholes who could perform as needed. Efficiency and productivity became the supreme values. Productive 'units' like engineers and conductors were not free to 'stop and smell the roses' when they chose to. The efficiency of the productive enterprise could not be compromised by individual whim.

Liberal societies actually began to run into a paradox here; in one sense they were becoming more decentralized as people were increasingly freed to build their lives as they saw fit. On the other hand, the goals of a materialistic society demanded conformity to the discipline and controls of industrial standardization. People had to conform for the greater good of the productive enterprise. The consumer demanded responsibility from the producer, and the consumer earned the right to consume by being a good producer. Both individuals and societies had to struggle with this balance.

It should come as no surprise then that schools would become an important part of that debate. People believed the type of schooling young people received played a significant role in the kind of citizens they would become. That immediately became tied up with what kind of society was needed in the future.

How should schools respond to a democratic, bureaucratic, technological, industrial society? The Twentieth century has witnessed the development of a culture war over what constitutes effective education. The roots of this culture war reach back into earlier centuries, and each side has its champions. We will briefly describe the view points of some of these champions, and then study the response of Western society to them. The debate between the sides seems to contain several themes. The first is the nature of society, focusing on the relationship between individuals and society. The second theme is a discussion of the nature of students, and what constitutes effective teaching and learning. A third theme - which is not much discussed - is the organizational structure of schools and the effect of that on learning. A fourth theme is a discussion of the methodologies (processes) used to teach children. Of course these themes are not mutually exclusive. They do tend to overlap and reinforce each other.

Returning to an historical analysis for a moment, we see that following hard on the heels of the Enlightenment was the Romantic Movement. The debate between the Romantics and the Classicistsis partly centred on the relative merits of emotionalism and realism as a way of responding to reality. The Romantics believed that all things 'natural' were to be prized and elevated. To the Romantics, an emphasis on reason and its works - science and technology - created a dangerous artificial world. Romantics saw industrialization and its reductionistic, standardizing engineering ethic as a direct threat to all that was natural and good in the world. Mary Shelley, a sophisticated Luddite, wrote her novel *Frankenstein* as a warning about the dangers of hubris inherent in scientific engineering.[25] Romantics questioned the assumptions of scientific materialism. Would the material comforts promised by industrialization actually improve the standard of living of ordinary people? Many had serious doubts, because they felt the loss of personal relationships within nature and communities would not be offset by the material benefits stemming from industrial production.

Realists vilified Romantics as being out of touch with reality. In simple terms, the core reality is that life is hard. Human nature is deeply flawed. Nature is powerful and dangerous. The standard of living without scientific technology is abysmally low. Societies need to marshal all their intellectual resources to protect humanity from reality.

Of course, the dialogue flowed back and forth. Romantics believed that the emphasis on scientism was making the world more dangerous, not less. Nations were becoming more powerful through improvements in military technology. Urbanization was divorcing people from the environment and each other. Realists simply pointed to improvements in standards of living as evidence of success. People were no longer so hungry, they had better clothing and housing, and they no longer had to worry so much about disease. All of this was made possible by scientific realism.

This dialogue would permeate discussion about the nature of society and then how schools should respond to a vision of society. One thing both groups were somewhat agreed upon was that there should be a close relationship between a vision for society and a vision for schools. There were many thinkers who wrote copiously about this issue. In essence, the debate seemed to come down to whether one should take an organic view of society or an atomistic view. Inherent to that debate is the question of whether societal membership is based on individualism or on being individualistic. The difference between the two is not simply semantic.

The notion of individualism sees the individual as being an integral part of an organic society. Both Locke and Rousseau saw the relationship of the individual to society in this way. Locke argued that even in a state of nature, through their reason individuals saw the necessity of cooperating toward the end of creating a better life. Rousseau posited the notion that whenever people came together in a group, a group dynamic occurred which expressed the general will of the group. Members of groups accept the development of that will as providing direction and meaning for that group. From this perspective, society was viewed as organic.

A contrary perspective - the individualistic - conceives society as being atomistic. In this view individuals behave as separate self-contained societal units who do not easily meld into a unified and coherent whole. Given the individualistic behavior of people within Western societies, an atomistic conception of society seems more reasonable than an organic conception. Thomas Hobbes and probably Machiavelli described the individualistic, atomistic behaviour among people in society and predicted the need for some kind of strong external discipline which would pressure people to sublimate their individualistic needs in favour of the larger society.

Durkheim and Weber, two thinkers at the turn of the Twentieth century, did much to explicate individualism and the individualistic as a means of understanding the operation of modern societies. Durkheim was an organic theorist who believed society itself was an entity that guided people toward their own best interests. Durkheim used the concept of dance as a metaphor to describe the operation of society.[26] He suggested the dance has an inherent form that shapes and directs the behaviour of its participants. Durkheim believed society acts on its members in the same way a dance does on its participants. Both society and the dance provide the structure, concepts, and discipline necessary for successful participation. Once the notion of dance has been established, people are then able to modify and create new dances. In Durkheim's view, the dance comes first and the individual is able to consider variations on the basic dance structure afterwards. Durkheim argues a similar logic applies to the relationships between individuals and society. Without a pre-existing society, it would not be possible for individuals to modify or create any type of society. Durkheim did not believe humans constructed society. Rather, people are born into society and are constructed by it. Only after we are created by society can we even begin to think about modifying or creating society.

Durkheim, Rousseau and Kant believed morals have a solid substance. Morals are real in the sense that they have a rational base general to all human beings. Morality comes out of the general will of society.[27] It is part of the criterial structure of society, just as the rhythm and steps of the dance are part of the criterial structure of the dance. Are you in step or not? Can one remain in step and not obey the rhythm of the dance? It is difficult to imagine such an eventuality. In the same sense people must remain morally in step if they wish to remain active participants within society.

The problem with this line of logic is that many people seem to be willing to remain morally out of step with society. In *Thus Spake Zarathustra* (1883), Nietzche describes a scene in which Zarathrusta, while walking in a forest, encounters a mystic praying to God with enthusiastic belief. Zarathrusta decides not to interrupt the mystic's joyful encounter with God, but muses disbelievingly how it could happen that a mystic has not heard that God is dead.[28] For many nineteenth century thinkers, the notion of a universal morality broadly accepted within society was dead. Weber sat firmly in the 'morality is dead' camp. In Weber's opinion, there are no general values. All values are irrational in the sense that people chose them for arbitrary and illogical reasons. This position takes us straight back to Hobbes. Society can only have a moral and ethical coherence when there is some outside force which imposes that coherence upon society.

Weber argued that all states are founded on political violence and political legitimacy. A truly successful government depended upon force and belief systems as a justification for sovereignty. Weber recognized that the use of force is much more successful when it is supported by belief systems accepted by the people being ruled. Religious beliefs were useful because they have the power to threaten people with bad futures if they do not conform to the legitimacy of state sovereignty.[29] Other institutions and organizations within society might have significant influence on people, but under the sovereignty of the state they would lack the power to use force to control behaviour. According to Weber, only the state had such a right.

He admitted that the use of force by the state to control people tended to remain an unusual tactic. The consequences of relying on force as a control mechanism were so negative that its use really became a lose-lose proposition for both the state and its citizens. That being so, the state had to turn to other means to achieve its ends. Weber argued that governments of modern societies can effectively justify their authority with only a specific type of rational rule, known as legality. Using the principle of legality, governments are able to justify their demand for conformity to rules by convincing people that rules are formally correct and have been imposed by acceptable procedures.

Weber extended his argument by noting that in modern societies this rational/legal authority is also closely associated with bureaucracies. Weber defined bureaucracies as hierarchical organizations oriented by a set of rules. Weber saw bureaucracy as an essential, technical part of modern society. It is the professional way of obtaining certain ends within large societies, and cannot be dispensed with unless we are prepared to dispense with those ends. Weber also recognized the dangers of bureaucracies when he noted that uncontrolled bureaucratic domination of society was a great threat to society.[30]

Weber looked to the principles of democracy as a means of controlling the power of bureaucracies. He believed that democracy's great contribution to the organization of society was its capacity to provide leaders who could encourage people to rise above a rule-bound society. He argued democracy is almost unavoidable in modern society because the achievement of change within society requires effective leadership. Given that force is so destructive to societal relationships, effective leaders need some other means of persuading citizens to accept change. Charisma is that means. Weber defined charisma as the "absolutely personal devotion and personal confidence in revelation, heroism, or other qualities of personal leadership".[31] Charisma is essential to effective decision making within modern societies.

It may be possible to link Durkheim and Weber even though they begin with sharply contrasting assumptions about the nature of society. Frank Pearce argues that Weber's concept of charisma is more useful if it is integrated with Durkheim's understanding of society.[32] Durkheim understood charisma using the Polynesian concept of 'mana'. Mana is an impersonal spiritual force which confers good fortune or magical powers upon people. Durkheim saw society as having a similar power to confer charisma on people occupying certain roles. They role of kingship endows its holders with a force of character they otherwise might not have. Kings without thrones might be ordinary people. Durkheim saw charisma (mana) as a real phenomenon and a real social relation with the power to deify people who personify its principal aspirations. Charisma can take various forms, and it may or may not be stage managed. What is important about charisma is its ability to help individuals experience themselves as part of a larger national collectivity.

Schools are communities and the social dynamics of those communities parallel the descriptions of both Durkheim and Weber. Schools have the capacity to become organic wholes as described by Durkheim. Some schools achieve that distinction. Schools can also be as atomistic and individualistic as anything described by Hobbes or Weber. Some schools achieve that. The difference is the style and purpose of educational leadership.

An important aspect of charisma is the message that it offers people. If the message resonates with people then the charismatic qualities of those delivering the message are enhanced. Rather than shooting the messengers, we praise them. We saw an example of that with the Wesleys earlier in this discussion. The individualistic educational paradigm accepted in the eighteenth and nineteenth centuries made the Weberian assumption that some outside force was necessary to maintain order in atomistic classrooms. Coercion remained the default position for school leaders. There was something charismatic about strength, devotion to duty, responsibility, order, certainty, and predictability. It may be that the military model of social organization seemed so attractive because of its purported strength, order and promise of security in the wider society. Few in power could resist the utility they perceived in various forms of coercion, particularly when it came to dealing with unruly adolescents.

Much of this rings true in the context of the world of the adolescent and the world of the classroom. It is commonplace to point out the reality of peer pressure in the lives of adolescents. It is also interesting is to analyze adolescent society using the perspectives of Durkheim and Weber. Adolescents are both created by society and create society. The process is similar to Durkheim's analogy of the dance. Adolescents are defined by their society, while at the same time they continuously redefine it. Adolescent vocabulary is perpetually in a state of flux. Words come and go. Music pre-exists the young adolescent who adopts it, modifies it and passes it on. Costumes come and go. Despite this seemingly individualistic approach to society, teenagers very much accept individualism as defined by Durkheim. Their acceptance of peer pressure allows them very little latitude in questioning the sub-culture they find themselves in. Rejection by that sub-culture is extremely traumatic and is a powerful force for conformity.

Adolescent culture controls them powerfully, despite their denial of it. North American adolescents would reject out of hand any suggestion that they wear school uniforms. Yet, if one looks around any average classroom, students are remarkably homogeneous in their dress. Jeans and t-shirts are usually the common denominator. So much so that it appears as if a dress code were in effect. In reality there is, even though adolescents would deny it (if you want to test this hypothesis, go shopping for school clothes with an adolescent). Certain aspects of reality are simply not perceived. This pertains to other groups of people besides adolescents. It seems likely that the power of society to dictate behaviour is most powerful at the unconscious assumption level. Society becomes more individualistic as people in society become more self-aware.

Moving to Weberian theory, similar observations can be made about the power of charisma in adolescent lives. Adulation, hero worship, the behaviour of 'groupies' are all examples of responses to charismatic leaders which both Durkheim and Weber predict in their theories of social behaviour. Sports stars, rock stars and movie stars are idolized; people who are - apart from a particular skill or talent - fairly ordinary human beings. Adolescents become so invested in a vision of their heroes that their behaviour has the potential to become fanatical. These phenomena can have a powerful effect on adolescents beyond the narrow confines of the adolescent sub-culture. Military establishments have been aware of these phenomena for centuries. Young men respond well to charisma, which makes them good inductees for military training programs.[33]

The important question is what effect might the phenomena of charisma have for education? Coaches of athletic teams have exploited charisma for years. Why do charismatic phenomena appear to have much less effect in the classroom? A related question facing fundamental societal institutions such as education is the effect an individualistic mindset has on relations within those institutions. The individualistic mindset presupposes the necessity of a critical, analytical approach toward relations.

Everything in an individualistic society has to be made problematic. Problematizing is based on the suspicion that people in institutions are inherently untrustworthy and need to be watched and critiqued, or their performance will slip in serious ways. This approach applies not only to education but to the criminal justice system, religion, commerce, politics, etc. The problem, of course, is there is always some justification for suspicion. The downside of problematizing is the loss of the underlying charisma. It is much more difficult for schools and other institutions to function when they face a deeply held suspicion by their clientele. In the case of schools, the classroom stops working on the basis of individualism and becomes individualistic. Power relations then change from consent to coercion with a concomitant change in the way education is governed.

In modern societies, power relationships need to be monitored. As noted above, Weber argued that the provision of significant societal goals such as education requires the services of a bureaucracy. Without a bureaucracy the necessary logistics cannot be put in place. Weber was also highly aware of the dangers of powerful, self-serving bureaucracies. He argued that the strongest protection against such bureaucracies was democracy. People must have the right to demand and enforce accountability and change from bureaucracies.

School systems have become large bureaucratic institutions and they offer a unique problem in terms of democracy and accountability. The prevailing paradigm has become much more individualistic. There is a powerful sense of loss because individualism has been steadily replaced by an individualistic ethos. The loss appears on many fronts. There is the loss inherent in the feeling of having to fight to be included in society. There is the loss from developing a sense of cynicism about the purposes and means of getting an education. Learning for the love of it is replaced by working to get 'the piece of paper' recognized by society. Many institutions, schools in particular, strive to return to individualism by devoting time and effort to developing morale. Despite the efforts at morale building, individualistic power relationships continually trump individualism. Paradigmatic beliefs continue to demand that educational relationships between institution and client be made safe and certain. It is simply seen as being too risky not to reduce learning to its essentials and bureaucratize the whole enterprise.

Educational issues devolve down to rigour and predictability. The conservative is convinced a hard nosed approach to accountability (through continuous evaluation of teachers and students against a predefined set of standards) will ensure effective education. It is the responsibility of schools to be top down dispensers of information. Students need to be held responsible for learning through rigourous testing procedures. Given the reality of human nature, students will not learn otherwise. At the end of their school careers, students, parents, and society will be grateful for the support they received from the firm direction of educational institutions.

For nineteen century romantics and their progressive descendents, the conservative argument quite seriously misses the fundamental point of education. Romantics do not see the purpose of life as being answerable to the requirements of society, at least not in totality. Gaining an education and making a living are means to an end, not the end itself. At the end of every day, people must have the right to look at their lives and feel they have found some meaning, and hopefully some joy in that meaning. Student years are a significant part of life, and students have the right to look at their school days with anticipation rather than apprehension.

The problem with this dichotomy is that it is a false one. The choice is not between free participation and rigorous discipline. The real question is how to educate in a way that encourages self-discipline and voluntary participation while leaving students with an internal sense of satisfaction and achievement. As societies in the Nineteenth century evolved from authoritarian societies to various forms of democracies, educational issues were recast in terms of citizenship.

Democracies are founded on the assumptions of self-government. Self-government demands responsibility from its citizens. Liberal democracies further demand citizens be creative self-starters who are able to manage and direct their personal affairs and the economic affairs of the community without direction and guidance from some type of elite. Such an approach to social management depends upon fostering creativity and self-discipline among average citizens.[34] The assumption was that schools have a major responsibility in fostering the necessary social independence required by liberal democracies. The debate through the Twentieth century would centre on how to best accomplish those objectives. John

Dewey founded the progressive movement to provide a response to the needs of 'progressive society'.

Progressivism

John Dewey published his pedagogic creed in 1897.[35] Dewey was adamant that 'true' education can only occur when children respond to real social situations. Children learn best when they are allowed to actively participate in the formation of their own social consciousness. Developing social consciousness is a process in which the individual gradually learns to share in humanity's intellectual and moral resources. It is only by interacting with real social situations that children are stimulated to relate their personal intellectual powers to the intellectual and moral resources humanity has assembled. Dewey argues this critical relationship must be fostered by allowing that "the child's psychology made up of instincts and powers [to] furnish the material and starting point for all education."[36] Without this as a starting point, a child's education becomes haphazard and will lack intellectual growth.

Still, children cannot truly comprehend their mental powers until they understand the function and purpose of those powers. It is through the pursuit of real social relationships that children come to appreciate their mental powers. Psychological and social relationships are organically related in a kind of partnership that educates children about their mental powers. Focusing on mental powers without applying them to actual social relationships will make those powers seem barren and formal. Emphasizing a social definition of education without engaging the child's powers makes education seem a forced and external process. Such an education lacks purpose in the minds of children. A relationship between the psychological and the social has to exist, because humans are social creatures and societies are organic unions of individuals.

Education must be a real social process, not an artificial process divorced from the reality of society. Education has to be a process of living itself and not some kind of preparation for future living: "school must represent life - life as real and vital to the child as that which is carried on in the home, in the neighborhood, or on the playground."[37] Dewey charged present (circa early Twentieth century) education with ignoring the 'fundamental principle of the school as a form of community life.' Schools, Dewey believes, concentrate on dispensing information, lessons, and the formation of habits as something important to the distant future of the child's life. Such lessons become mere preparation for a distant unrealistic life, not something that is part of the child's life experiences and not something that can be truly educative.

Dewey points out that educating for the future is problematic, because it is not possible to know the nature of civilization twenty years into the future. What can be done is to help the child take 'command of himself'. Children should be trained in the full use of all their capacities so that they can decide for themselves how to respond effectively to the novel future conditions they will encounter. This kind of judgment can only be learned when the social reality of the community is successfully combined with the psychological reality of the child.

The subject matter of education should be driven by the social life of the child.[38] It is that which gives unconscious unity to the efforts of the child. Schools err when they introduce children to special studies such as reading, writing, geography, etc before they are ready to relate them to their lives. The true centre of correlation between the child and knowledge is the child's own social activities, not science, literature, history or geography. The way to make the children conscious of their social heritage is by enabling them to recreate the fundamental activities which make civilization what it is.

Dewey argues there is no succession of studies in an ideal school curriculum which makes one subject more important than other subjects.[39] Since all subjects reflect some aspect of life, all can play a role in the education of children and all must be subservient to the social roles of the child's life. Science is only of value to the child when it provides the child with the "ability to interpret and control the experience already had."[40] Dewey sees other subjects playing similar roles in the lives of children depending upon the nature of the subject. Education must be subservient to the development of the child's powers and interests.

Educational methods, to be successful, depend upon responding to "the law implicit within the child's own nature."[41] Methodology must recognize that "[the] active side precedes the passive." in child development. Dewey goes on to argue that "Consciousness is essentially motor or impulsive; that conscious states tend to project themselves into action."[42] Therefore, Dewey says, neglecting child development causes much wasted time in classrooms, because the child is thrown into a passive, receptive, absorbing attitude resulting in friction and waste. He defined reason as primarily the law of orderly or effective action. Dewey charged that teaching reason and judgment without a firm social basis for the ideas being taught end up being externally imposed and meaningless. Teaching without meaning is fallacious. Children must be allowed to select and arrange actual, meaningful activities which have a firm social basis in the child's life. Only then will real teaching have been achieved, according to Dewey.

Progressive education grew out of Dewey's philosophy of education. As Dewey saw it a progressive education is one which promoted an education that was experiential and that those experiences derived more from the student than from the teacher. Dewey envisioned a student-driven, student-centered approach to education. Dewey viewed education "as a continuing reconstruction of experience; that the process and the goal of education are one and the same thing."[43] Over the course of the last four centuries, there has been an ongoing struggle between those who saw schools as being individualistic institutions or were based on individualism. Dewey was in the individualism camp. He was highly concerned with balancng individualism and collectivism, however precariously.[44]

For Dewey that balance had to begin in the classroom by respecting the interests of children. In 1895 he attacked the Herbartian notions that children had 'no interests' and that it was the role of teachers to make children interested in subject matter. Dewey argued that such an approach was unacceptable. He believed the teacher's role was to search out and take advantage of children's interests as a vehicle to teach new ideas.[45] Dewey's ideas traveled widely, and were soon accepted in Canadian schools.

Progressivism was not entirely an education centred philosophy. Progressives were ultimately concerned with progress in all of society, not just in education. Progressives believed education was a part (possibly a leading part, depending on whom you talked to) of the social changes aimed at improving democracy. Dewey firmly believed that the enlightenment of students with the best ideas of society would ultimately improve society. In Dewey's mind, true enlightenment came by understanding society in real terms. As pointed out above, Dewey believed that any real understanding (learning) could only come through actively involving youth in society. Such involvement had to be democratic in the sense that students were involved in meaningful decision making. Such involvement would not only better educate young people, but it would also result in improvements to society. For Dewey, an improving society is one that is becoming more democratic.

The catch in all of this involved a definition of progress. Dewey's definition was based on the belief that all citizens - regardless of their vocation or their status in the community - had an important role to play in the creation of better societies. Logically such a belief had to include children as well, both because of their humanity and because they would be the future leaders of society. Dewey believed the nature and the kind of participation children play in their society determines the nature of their future role as citizens in their communities. The classroom is an important place (but not the only place) where children can be encouraged to practice democratic participation in a society. Such participation would only be valid democratically if students were allowed to make real decisions about their classroom society. Also, if learning as well as decision making is to be real, student decision making must involve decision making about their educational interests. Dewey believed this was the only way of producing an increasingly democratic society.

Unfortunately for the thrust of Dewey's approach, a variety of interpretations for progressivism evolved. Some scholars suggest there were four distinct branches of 'educational progressivism' . There were child centred progressives, measurement and efficiency progressives, social and cultural progressives, and intellectual progressives. Soon it became difficult to know exactly what was meant by the term progressive or what a "progressive" school was. Teachers and parents grew tired of interminable debates about the fine distinctions between the competing progressive viewpoints.

By the 1920s the efficiency definition of progressivism began to make its weight felt. In the Los Angeles of 1922, Franklin Bobbit stated that "education is primarily of interest to adulthood, not to childhood. We simply utilize childhood as the time of preparing for the fifty years of adulthood."[46] Bobbit was representative of an increasingly conservative element that would continue to redefine 'progressivism' over the next three decades. The educational debate was shifting its focus from liberal education of the kind espoused by Dewey to a much more utilitarian view of education.

During the middle half of the twentieth century, a major issue in educational debates was determining an acceptable definition of the notion of utility. Under utilitarian progressive education, the educational focus would shift from the needs of the child to the needs of society. Utilitarian education would emphasize practical training to prepare students for their place in society rather than educating them for personhood. The major issue that had to be resolved was the best approach to putting utilitarian education into practice. Initially, 'life adjustment' was suggested as the guiding philosophy for public education. The Life Adjustment program of the National Education Association (USA) advocated the provision of vocational schools to train 20 per cent of youth to prepare them for various skilled occupations. Another 20 per cent of the youth population would be prepared for college and the remaining 60 per cent would receive 'life adjustment' training. Such training would consist of guidance and training in citizenship, home and family life, use of leisure, health, tools of learning, work experience and occupational adjustment.

Response to the Life Adjustment approach was extremely negative. It was not so much that utilitarianism was bad, but that it was the wrong kind of utilitarianism. Conservatives charged 'life-adjustment' as being anti-intellectual. Conservatives assumed there were certain 'essential' pieces of knowledge students must learn before the fundamentals of civilization could be passed on to the next generation. Out of this belief, a philosophy of education known as Essentialism developed. Essentialism was a conserving philosophy which rejected the progressive view that society could be reformed and improved. Essentialists believe schools should transmit those values and intellectual knowledge which have stood the test of time. Education should model and pass on traditional values such as respect for authority, perseverance, fidelity to duty, consideration for others, and practicality.

Students need to be specifically taught the basics or essentials of academic knowledge and character development. Any definition of utility that did not include these essentials was doomed to failure. Essentialism quickly won the debate about the direction schooling should take. An academic based education was considered to be the proper preparation of young people for informed and involved citizenship, and for productive work. Conservatives were agreed that 'progressive' education had actually become 'regressive' because it denied intellect and individual capability. Arthur Bestor wrote a scathing attack on what he saw as a betrayal of the right of students to receive a liberal arts education.[47] The one thing both sides did agree on was utility: it was clearly the role of schools to produce a student product which would result in a progressive society.

What was missing from the Essentialist approach was Dewey's emphasis on the interests of students as the driving force in determining the purpose of education. Students were again regarded as receptors of curricula that was considered significant to and of benefit to the larger society. Paradigmatically, there would be no contest between essentialism and Dewey's interpretation of progressivism. The majority accepted the belief that protection and transmission of the intellectual heritage would best further the needs of society. The idea that the best interests of students were being served in this way was also accepted. Dewey's argument that children should be consulted was seen as inconsequential in the face of the 'larger' issues as defined by the Essentialist paradigm.

Essentialism

Essentialism was not new, of course. It had been the dominant paradigm of education since the eighteenth century. It was this paradigm that Dewey challenged with his notions of progressivism. By the 1950s, with the advent of the Cold War and Sputnik, education was trumpeted as a critically important vehicle for maintaining the future security of nations. International society was a competitive and dangerous place. Only those nations which remained on the cutting edge of science and technology would survive. Education was too important to be left in the hands of students, or even schools for that matter.

Essentialists developed a number of criteria for defining good schooling.[48] First and foremost schooling should be rigorous. The curriculum should consist of the most essential academic skills and knowledge. Such a curriculum would consist of traditional disciplines such as math, natural sciences, history, a foreign language and literature. Even when students study creative and performance related subjects such as music and art, the emphasis tended to focus on mastering a body of information and the basic techniques of the discipline. Knowledge was broken down into subjects and levels of understanding, and students could only advance from one grade to the next by demonstrating their facility with the required material.

Student decision making and choice were rejected by essentialists because students were not mature enough to handle the responsibility of those decisions. Classrooms should be oriented around the teacher who would serve as an intellectual and moral role model for the students. It was the role of teachers and administrators (reflecting the needs of society) to determine what students should learn. Student interests had to be secondary to the requirements of the academic curriculum. Student interests were also secondary to the need to develop discipline within students. Education requires mental discipline: study is hard; concentration is hard; order is hard. Students can only learn to be orderly and self-disciplined in a disciplined, orderly classroom. Essentialists believe students must learn self-discipline by persevering at something, even when they are uninterested in it. Students are not always aware of their future needs, so they must be guided to learn those things they would otherwise not learn.

Essentialism and Utilitarian Instrumental Progressivism

The modern high school system has grown out of a fusion of essentialism and utilitarian, instrumental progressivism. Instrumental progressives such as James B Conant recognized that students came to the schools with a variety of abilities, backgrounds and interests. In his book *The American High School Today: A First Report to Interested Citizens*, Conant argued that students needed to be tested and interviewed before they could be placed in the school system.[49] Such data would allow administrators to place students in learning situations more suitable to their abilities and interests. This approach to students would drive the creation of large, comprehensive high schools. Such large high schools could provide the resources for ability testing, ability grouping and the differentiated curricula and staff which could serve the needs of a differentiated clientele.

The curricula of these high schools were essentialist in nature emphasizing rigor, traditional learning, and discipline. Both instrumental progressives and essentialists were in firm agreement that the purpose of schools was to prepare people for the social, economic and political needs of society. Schools were to serve utilitarian purposes, and were only secondarily for the development of individual persons.

A number of serious ramifications for education have accompanied this paradigm. One major ramification has been the growth of educational bureaucracies. Bureaucracies are based on sets of standards; they are hierarchical, which is to say within the hierarchy each person has a role with a defined set of expectations; each role is connected to other roles in a chain of accountability; there is an impersonal, routinized structure of roles based on clearly defined rules giving role holders certain defined and legitimate authority within the bureaucracy; and relations between the various offices involve a considerable degree of formality aimed at maintaining a suitable social distance between occupants of the different roles. All of these standards are intended to maintain harmony and produce a stable set of mutual expectations within the organization.

Both instrumental progressivists and essentialists saw bureaucracies and education as useful utilitarian tools for the management of society. Together they could produce citizens who would be useful to the needs of society. Instrumental progressivism, essentialism, and the bureaucratic approach to managing societies together created such a powerful paradigm there was no need to debate the need for the creation of large bureaucratic institutions. Paradigmatically, there were many good reasons for bureaucratizing education. One example of an educational bureaucracy - the large comprehensive high school - was clearly seen as social progress.

At the same time another force, technology, had grown to maturity in twentieth century society. Technology may be defined as "the deliberate, rationalized, and standardized application of organized knowledge for the purpose of attaining some predetermined end."[50] Institutions - whether the army, the churches, the schools, etc - are all searching for the best way to accomplish their purposes. Once an approach has been developed, it is turned into a standardized procedure. The expectation is that all will conform to the established technological processes. Paradigmatically, it would seem too unreasonable and arbitrary to do anything else.

Bureau Technocracy

It was not long before the processes of bureaucracy and technocracy synthesized into something that come to be known as bureau technocracy. Social management could be accomplished best when a hierarchical, pyramidal, depersonalized model of human organization (bureaucracy) was linked to a standardized, rationalized means (technology) with the overall aim of achieving control, flexibility, and efficiency in reaching some commercial or social objective.[51] Bureau technocracy has become a paradigm which defines the 'commonsense' approach to dealing with the realities facing society. Bureau technocracy finds its roots in the industrialization and urbanization of society. Both industrialization and urbanization demand predictability and conformity if they are to accomplish their goals. People who live and work in urbanized and industrialized societies find themselves in cultural environments demanding standardization and reductionism. Engineering and economics converge because parts in machines and roles in social systems must be interchangeable and conform to the needs of the larger systems.

In a bureau technocratic society, systems are needed to make production predictable, reliable, and measurable. In industry, the approach is to standardize parts assemble using assembly lines, and to reduce work to measurable units of production. At the end of any period of production, the plant and the workers could look at hard figures which provide an unequivocal comparison of the production between today and yesterday or this month and the same month last year. Figures do not lie.

Bureaucratic standards of rigour and accountability demanded a similar approach in the schooling enterprise. A school's product would be the information its clients managed to absorb in a given period of time. The learning process would consist of reducing information to manageable pieces which could be efficiently absorbed. The assembly line would be the system of grades and classrooms established to impart this information in an orderly manner. Memorization was the quantifiable demonstration of the information learned.

The textbook became the foundation for this system. For many teachers and classrooms, the table of contents of a prescribed textbook became the course syllabus. Teachers were held accountable for covering the course (textbook). Primarily 'covering the course' means being sure students can recite significant portions of that information in a formal testing procedure. The essentialist assumption is that the text book will contain information that is significant and acceptable to the larger society. Textbook knowledge is official knowledge that is widely accepted as being above criticism. Other sources of knowledge are suspect and risky.

Textbooks homogenize information and student learning. Textbooks are prepared by businesses who wish to publish for as large a market as possible in order to gain economies of scale. The requirements of large markets dictate to consumers in small markets. It also gives the writers and publishers of textbooks the power to dictate what should be learned and what can be dismissed as irrelevant. The Essentialist doctrine of learning enforces the power of textbook in the classroom. If students wish to gain credit for the course taken, they must conform to the dictates of the prescribed text.

In a bureau technocratic world, information is power. Whose truth has the right to be considered reality? In an essentialist world certain types of knowledge are worth more than other types of knowledge. Tradition provides the imprimatur which stamps authority on certain pieces of information and rejects other pieces. Such an assumption demands conformity from students based on another assumption that the knowledge of immature students must be considered second rate to other sources of knowledge.

Bureau technocratic social systems promise social and economic reward in return for conformity. High schools and their students are caught up in that great trade-off. The role of the school in the larger system is to produce people who can function effectively in a bureau technocratic social system. Schools socialize students to accept both bureaucratic and technological mind sets. Students and their parents find it difficult to resist subject choices they believe give the student a social and economic advantage after the student leaves high school. The justification for attending school is quite clearly based on future societal rewards.

We return for a moment to the comments of Weber. He noted that modern societies depend upon bureaucracies to further the goals of society. They were, in his estimation, an essential, technical part of modern society. However, he was also deeply concerned about their potential for uncontrolled power. He believed bureaucracies had to maintain some form of charisma which would legitimize their power. Without some form of ameliorating charisma, bureaucracies would be seen as increasingly autocratic and out of touch with the needs and aspirations of its clients.

The problem for education is that it has more than one client group, each of which has different needs and aspirations. An important group is the opinion shapers of society. They are the intelligentsia represented by - among others - universities, media, and business. These individuals tend to be concerned about the capacity of high school graduates to either proceed successfully through post-secondary education or become successful employees. Given their goals for education, many support the essentialist paradigm of education. The second large group of clients is parents. They, understandably, desire successful lives for their students. Parents find it hard to resist the notion that a good education (usually academic) followed by a good job is the basic criteria for success. Finally, students - the clientele most directly affected by schools - need to be considered. Of all the groups mentioned here, students may be the most deeply divided in their attitudes toward schools. On the one hand, some long for a meaningful education, but are frustrated by the essentialist system of education. Others no longer care about education and only want to get a certificate of standing while expending as little effort and time as possible. Also, there are those who believe they have successfully adapted to the essentialist system of education, and would resist changing an educational system which they believe has given them success.

This takes us back to Weber and his problem with bureaucracies attempting to govern without charisma. The central problem for the charisma of high schools lies in their dependence on extrinsic reward. A bureau technocratic education based on utility, postponement of gratification, conformity, the prospect of graduating from one bureau technocracy to another, all for some future material reward is not one that rewards learners well. It does not reinforce a strong internal reason (need) for learning.[52] Essentialist education is based to a large degree on extrinsic reward. Students are asked to study information they find inherently uninteresting for a reward some time in the future. Students find it difficult to find a meaningful connection between their schooling and their present and future lives. This is as Dewey predicted. Even adults find it difficult to see much of a relationship between their lives and the schooling they received.

The important issues buried under the utilitarian assumptions about the purpose of education are questions about self-motivation, self-discipline, self-starting, independent thinking, etc. All of these characteristics - so esteemed by liberal societies - are dependent upon whether students learn to make intrinsic attributions toward their studies and their lives. If the student is studying in response to outside environmental forces, then one would speak of an extrinsic attribution being adopted by the student. Or, if the student is studying because of some internal motivation, then the student is making an intrinsic attribution.[53] Dewey, commenting on effective education, noted: "Without insight into the psychological structure and activities of the individual, the educative process will ... result in friction, or disintegration, or arrest of the child nature."[54] The question for schools is how to reward students; or in Weber's terms, how can school bureaucracies display their charisma?

Research on causal attribution shows that extrinsic reward has a detrimental effect on intrinsic motivation.[55] Researchers have concluded that extrinsic rewards undercut intrinsic motivation. Other research shows that rewarding behaviours related to low initial interest can result in an increase of the behaviour sought. Unfortunately, such behavioural change appears to last only last a few weeks.[56] This body of research underscores the difficult choices schools face.

Bureau technocratic school systems tend to opt for short term motivation, partly because their Essentialist assumptions do not allow much latitude in selecting material for study by students. The information is always the important thing. At the same time, schools must demonstrate student progress in the short run. Successfully demonstrating that students can pass the mid term examinations a month away becomes the focusing issue for schools and parents. The result from the student perspective is to learn for extrinsic reasons. 'Getting the mark' is all that matters. Learning for its own sake is incidental and mostly irrelevant.

Attribution research shows that individuals who have successfully interacted with some part of reality receive a personal sense of competence and mastery. These individuals are positively motivated for the long term. Exploration and curiosity are powerful intrinsic motivators because they leave people with a sense of achievement and mastery of the environment.[57] Based on those feelings of success, they are much more likely to make internal attributions and continue the behaviour without external pressure.[58]

Reaction to Bureau Technocratic Education

Despite the power of the bureau technocratic paradigm, people in the 1980s began to question the performance of their bureaucratic school systems. Neo-romantics charged schools with ignoring the nature of children by creating a school climate which crushed the basic nature of students and drove them away from learning. Conservatives complained that schools were not accomplishing the essentialist goals of rigour and discipline, and that these failures left the basics untaught. Soon both camps were producing action plans designed to save the school, each according to their respective philosophies. *A Nation at Risk* outlined a conservative plan for reforming education, which was countered by a variety of commentaries rejecting the conclusions of *A Nation at Risk* as being right wing propaganda.[59] During the eighties and nineties, a wide variety of suggestions made to modify the school systems were made, and many systems responded with changes. Despite all of the changes adopted by school systems, high school classrooms have changed little. Essentialism still forms the basic assumptions of day to day teaching.[60]

Another observation about these 'culture wars' is that both sides believe the other side is winning the war much to the detriment of students and the future of society. Conservative critics see the dark hand of progressivism everywhere: in curriculum, in teaching methodologies, in promotion policies, etc. Progressives rail about boring, stultifying, bureaucratic schools which regularly fail to respond to the needs of students. Both sides can trot out reams of 'evidence' to support their claims of school failure. The major problem in this debate is the propensity to generalize about what is happening in the classroom.

Despite the emphasis on philosophy, whether it be Essentialist or Progressive, what really happens in a classroom depends upon the thinking of the teacher. Yero notes:

> *Teachers' personal beliefs and values provide the unconscious foundation for their behaviour. Their metaphors shape their practice. The ways in which teachers perceive the world - create their mental models of "reality" are highly individualistic. Therefore, no two classrooms are, or can be the same.*[61]

This is an area where both sides find they have to recognize that good teachers can be found in both approaches. In this case, good teaching can simply be defined as that teaching which causes a personal sense of competence and mastery among students. What is less clear are the teaching routes to be taken in achieving this goal.

Let us move back to the mythical grade nine class we observed at the beginning of this chapter. There are thousands of these classrooms across North America and their equivalents in Europe, Asia, etc. One reality for students is that if they moved from a classroom in an average 'traditional' school to a classroom in an average 'progressive' school, they probably would not observe much difference between the classrooms. The average school is composed of a series of classrooms, each filled with 20 to 30 students, all facing a teacher who dispenses information in one way or another. Eisner notes:

> *Most school rooms are designed as cubicles along corridors and have a kind of antiseptic quality to them. They tend to be repetitive and monotonous in the same way that some hospitals and factories are. They speak of efficiency more than they do of comfort . . . . Most of the furniture is designed for easy maintenance, is uncomfortable, and is visually sterile . . . . The point here is not so much to chastise school architects but to point out that the buildings that we build do at least two things: they express the values we cherish, and, once built, they reinforce those values. Schools are educational churches, and our gods, judging from the altars we build, are economy and efficiency. Hardly a nod is given to the spirit.*[62]

What has changed in the last 150 years despite the efforts of a large variety of educational thinkers? Little, and the reasons for the lack of change are factors like bureau technocracy, academic disciplines, the power of universities, vocational purposes for schooling, a lack of spending on education, etc.

Those from the Essentialist paradigm assume that students need to be changed, not schools. Given their assumptions, Essentialists find it difficult to conclude that an unrewarding and unfulfilling essentialist curriculum, school organization and culture are the problems. Rather, the problem is with students who will not or cannot adapt and conform to the school system. What is remarkable about this perception problem is that every adult has a fund of horror stories they can recount about their negative encounters with school systems. Occasionally they love to regale each other with outrageous experiences they encountered in schools. The feeling seems to be education is a rite of passage, like hazing, which everyone should be subjected to. The prevailing essentialist paradigm is maintained when people conclude that 'tough' schooling has made one a 'man', or a woman as the case may be.

I can hear the rejoinders to this from many liberal, well meaning people who are saying school systems have made many adaptations and accommodations to the needs of students. They would continue their argument by claiming schools are very concerned about young people and do many things to make them feel welcomed and significant in the system. This is somewhat true, but the classroom represents a very large problem in this argument. Classrooms in their design and function have changed very little particularly in middle years and secondary schools. Primary classrooms have led the way in creating a basic design change, but little of that has filtered past grade seven where the 'serious' learning is supposed to begin. Actually many classrooms after grade four have not received the benefit of the primary grade's revolution. The basic organization and intent of classrooms has changed little over the years.

Motivation is the Challenge for Schools

This chapter has described a 500 year tension about the proper education of the young (actually, the tension is much older, as Socrates' death illustrates). This short history illustrates an ongoing ambivalence toward the younger generation. Can the younger generation be trusted to make good educational choices? As we have seen, there are powerful and strongly held points of view on both sides of the issue. Throughout this history all sorts of paradigmatic rationalizations were created and expounded upon, but inexorably two things happened: The younger generation succeeded the older generation, and the younger generation did not quite 'get' what the older generation wanted them to 'get'.

If one takes 25 years to represent an average generational span, there are approximately twenty new generations between the twenty-first century and where we picked up the story of educational development in the Renaissance. It is reasonable to argue that each succeeding generation learned some of their heritage well, and some of it not so well (it is also reasonable to believe that some heritage was deliberately discarded). Because of inadequate transmission of information between generations, and because new knowledge was developed by new generations using new assumptions and perceptions, we have change; and with change, progress is possible.

The two long-term paradigms we have examined are basically split over the issue of motivation. Are young people prepared to do the hard work necessary for satisfactory learning? In succinct terms, hard work depends upon motivation. If one assumes there is a body of knowledge everyone has to learn regardless of interest, then one also has to accept there will always be a significant lack of motivation among segments of learners and a concomitant need for coercive discipline to enforce such learning. On the other hand, if one assumes young people have a need to grow physically, emotionally, and intellectually, then there is something they will want to learn to help them achieve their own growth goals. Those young grade nine students we visited at the beginning of this chapter will eventually have their way, because time is on their side. The issue for societal education is whether it can have any long term influence on what young people learn?

If adults really wish to connect with young people because they believe they have something to offer them, then the challenge is to create engaging and meaningful learning activities. Schools need to become charismatic, not as an occasional exception, but as a general rule. It is possible to create these kinds of classrooms, and the purpose of this book is to show how this can be done with principles and activities. Many teachers and administrators argue it is not their job to entertain students. While teachers do not need to become standup comics, they do need to pay serious attention to motivation. Without motivation, the quantity and quality of learning is very limited. Teachers need to find ways of developing the kind of motivation seen in other areas of the lives of adolescents. True motivation to learn comes from within the individual. It follows, then, that the purpose of education is not about passing on culture or even developing the intellect of individuals, it is about helping people discover a personal motivation to learn. The sources of motivation are significance and meaning. If we believe something is important and we really need to understand it, we will be motivated to learn it.

The great ideas of the culture should be taught to students; the real question is how to teach them successfully. These ideas contain important tools students can use to improve their lives. They quite correctly belong in the high school curriculum because over time, people have found them to be helpful responses to reality. But until students see some application to their lives, they cannot appreciate their significance. Students must recognize, however dimly, the potential of these ideas before they can they can appreciate their significance as great ideas. Without a personal understanding, they are left with a lack of motivation and memorization as their primary learning tool.

END NOTES

1. Plato. *The Last Days of Socrates.* ed. by Hugh Tredennick Penguin. 1995. Apology 21a, and Apology 38a.

2. Raymond Nickerson, in "Why teach thinking", *Teaching Thinking Skills.* ed. Joan Boykoff Baron and Robert J. Sternberg. New York: W. H. Freeman and Company. p. 31, who references J. I. Goodlad, *A place called school: Prospects for the future.* New York: McGraw-Hill. 1983, and Brown and Saks (1984) p.572, both economists who comment: "there is no obvious argument for maximizing the reasoning skills of the population".

3. Raymond S. Nickerson, p. 32.

4. These statements will be discussed and supported in greater detail in succeeding chapters.

5. This is an important statistic that needs to be researched. My research indicates that there is not much documentation on this issue.

6. *Time Magazine.* Asian Edition. April 9, 2002. The lead article states: "East Asian countries knew how to produce winning students. But stressed and uninspired kids are dropping out and the region is rethinking its educational systems."

7. Many of these specialized programs provide programs that employ independent, self-study strategies, which work at developing self-esteem.

8. The term paradigm is being used here in the sense of a set of ideas, beliefs, and values which guide the behaviour of people in an institution. Before a set of ideas, beliefs, and values can be considered a paradigm, they must be arranged in a pattern that is broad and coherent enough to provide a logical and justifiable set of assumptions for what is being done by the institution. In education, there has been a welter of approaches suggested and partially implemented over the past centuries. It is easy to get lost in the detail. The notion of paradigm is used here to suggest that the different approaches fall into one of two categories: education should help students accumulate information, or it should help them construct knowledge. This is a basic divide in education.

9. The term majority as used here may not always reflect a majority in the numerical sense, although that is often the case. Majority may also connote those groups of people within society who are accepted as having the right to form opinions for others.

10. Thomas S. Kuhn. *The Structure of Scientific Revolutions.* Chicago: University Of Chicago Press, 1968. Chapter Ten.

11. Stephen Jay Gould. *The Mismeasure of Man.* New York: W. W. Norton & Company. 1981. p. 28.

12. John Locke. *Second Treatise on Civil Government.* 1690. (http://www.constitution.org/jl/2ndtreat.htm, Text Version).

13. John Locke. "Book One: Neither Principles Nor Ideas are Inate". *An Essay Concerning Human Understanding.* 1690

14. Thomas Hobbes. *Leviathan I 13*

15. John P. McKay, Bennett D. Hill, and John Buckler. *A History of Western Society Vol. II.* Boston: Houghton Mifflin Company. 1987. p. 645.

16. Quoted by B. W. Lorence. "Parents and Children in Eighteenth-Century Europe". *History of Childhood Quarterly 2.* Summer, 1974. pp. 1-2.

17. P.J. Greven. (ed.) *Child-Rearing Concepts, 1928-186* Historical Sources Illinois. 1973. pp. 46-7.

18. H. Matthews. *Methodism and the Education of the People 1791-1851* London. 1949. p. 20.

19. J.J. Rousseau. *Emile* tr. B. Foxley. London. 1963. p.56.

20. Ibid p. 57.

21. About Postmodernism: A Postmodern Essay (http://www.freewaybr.com/pomoessay.htm).

22. Gould. p. 28.
23. Gould. p. 29.

24. Henry Ford, from *Michael Moncur's Cynical Quotations.*

25. Luddite: a person who is opposed to the introduction of new working methods, especially new machines.

26. E. Durkheim. *The Elementary Forms of Religious Life.* 1912. (tr. English 1915.)

27. E. Durkheim. *Montesquieu and Rousseau. Forerunners of Sociology.* 1960. Containing translations of Durkheim 1892 on Montesquieu and Durkheim 1918 on Rousseau's Social Contract.

28. F.W. Nietzsche. *Thus Spake Zarathustra.* Part One. 1883.

29. Max. Weber. *Politics as a Vocation.* 1919. ed. Gerth & Mills. 1948. pp 77-128.

30. M. Weber. "The Theory of Social and Economic Organisation". trans. Talcott Parsons. *Wirtschaft und Gesellschaft* Vol 1.1. 1947.

31. M. Weber. "The Evolution of The Capitalistic Spirit". *General Economic History.* Chapter 30.

32. Frank Pearce. *The Radical Durkheim.* Canadian Scholars Press: 2ed. February 2001. pp.31-38. 1989.

33. Gwyn Dyer. "Anybody's Son Will Do". *War.*
National Film Board of Canada. 1985.

34. The term 'social' is taken to mean the activities in which people meet and spend time interacting with other people. A related term is 'society', defined as a large group of people who live together in an organized way, making decisions about how to do things and sharing the work that needs to be done. All the people in a country, or in several similar countries, can be referred to as a society.

35. John Dewey. "My Pedagogic Creed". *The School Journal*.
Vol. LIV, No. 3 January 16, 1897. pp. 77-80.

36. Dewey pp. 77-80.
37. Dewey p.78.
38. Dewey p.79.

39. Dewey p.79.

40. Dewey p. 5.

41. Dewey p. 6.

42. Dewey p. 6.

43. Dewey p. 6.

44. Daniel Schugurensky. *History of Education: Selected Moments of the 20th Century* Department of Adult Education. Community Development and Counselling Psychology. OISE/UT.

45. Spencer J. Maxcy. *John Dewey and American Education: in History of American Thought: Exploring the Diversity of American Intellectual History.*
Bristol England: Thoemmes Press.

46. Franklin Bobbitt. "Curriculum Re-Examination in Los Angeles." *High School Research Bulletin of the Los Angeles City Schools.* Vol. II, No. 9. February 5, 1923. p. 1; *see also* Franklin Bobbitt, "Continuation of Curriculum Work," *High School Research Bulletin of the Los Angeles City Schools,* Vol II, No. 13. April 9, 1923. pp. 1-4.

47. Theodore R. Sizer and Molly Schen. *Educational Wastelands: The Retreat from Learning in our Public Schools.* 2ed. Urbana: University of Illinois Press. p. 1. 1985.

48. J. Wesley Null. *A Disciplined Progressive Educator: The Life and Career of William Chandler Bagle.* New York: Peter Land Publishing. Chapter 4. 2003.

49. James B Conant. *The American High School Today: A First Report to Interested Citizens* New York: McGraw-Hill. 1959.

50. Charles A. Tesconi and Van Cleve Morris. *The Anti-man Culture: Bureautechnocracy and the Schools*. Urbana: University of Illinois Press. p. 161. 1972.

51. Tesconi and Morris pp. XI and XII.

52. Hal R. Arkes and John P. Garske. *Psychological Theories of Motivation.*
Belmont CA. Brooks/Cole Publishing Company. pp. 333-335. 1982.

53. Arkes and Garske. p. 334.

54. Dewey. P. 77.

55. Arkes and Garske. p. 335.

56. Arkes and Garske. p. 336.

57. Arkes and Garske. p. 338.

58. Arkes and Garske. p. 334.

59. National Commission on Excellence in Education. *A Nation at Risk: The Imperative for Educational Reform, A Report to the Nation and the Secretary of Education.* United States Department of Education. April, 1983.

60. An extensive search of the literature elicited very little research on the incidence of different philosophies being practiced in classrooms. What information was found indicated that there is little conscious concern or reference to educational philosophy in determining teaching and evaluation strategies.

-Kenneth R. Conklin. "Theory and Practice as Viewed From the Classroom," *EDUCATIONAL FORUM XXLIV*. 3 March, 1980. pp. 272-274.

-Helen McKenzie. *Education in Canada: Current Issues* (Government of Canada: Political and Social Affairs Division. May 1994.

61. Judith Lloyd Yero. *Teaching in Mind: How Teacher Thinking Shapes Education.* Hamilton, MT: MindFlight Publishing. 2002.

62. E. Eisner. *The Educational Imagination: On the Design and Evaluation of School Programs.* 3ed. New York: Macmillan College Publishing. 1994.

Chapter Two: The Characteristics of an Educated Person

It is important that students bring a certain ragamuffin barefoot irreverence to their studies; they are not here to worship what is known, but to question it.

Jacob Bronowski, *The Ascent of Man* (1975)

Table of Contents

THE GOAL OF EDUCATION

A memorable moment in every parent's life is the morning of the first day of school. Their daughter is full of excitement as she prepares for the next great adventure of her life. She will proudly tell you she's five. Her parents are full of nervous expectation: all their hopes and dreams focus on their child. When the little girl comes home at the end of the first day, everyone is concerned to find out 'how it went'. This event is so important to parents, because it is based on the belief - an act of faith - that education is critical to the future wellbeing of their children. The question that needs to be asked is: what is it about education that makes it so important? What will this little girl gain from spending 12 years of her life in the public educational system?

Canadians have an operational definition of education. They believe people should learn to be self-sufficient and be able to contribute to society. Education should develop within students the capacity to support themselves and to contribute to society. Education is seen as an investment in the next generation, and by extension an investment in the future of society. Canadians assume those who have had their dignity respected and their wellbeing cared for by society will be willing and able to contribute to society in the future.

Canadians have strong opinions about education. While most Canadians may not have given much thought to a definition of education, they will have opinions about what it means to be educated. Canadians believe educated people should be able to use language well; they should understand and use numbers easily; they should know Canada's geography and past history; and, they should know and appreciate the contributions from great literature, science, history, music, religion, the arts, and technology. Other criteria are more subtle, but in spite of that, they are critical to peoples' judgments about education.

CONFLICTING ASSUMPTIONS

This is where the controversy begins. Because people start from different assumptions, they find themselves in deep disagreement about what it means to be educated. Some Canadians believe the fundamental goal of education is learning knowledge. They argue that it is not possible for students to do any thinking until they comprehend a basic amount of knowledge. Others believe learning to think is the basic goal of education. This position holds that students must be taught the basic processes of thinking before they will be able to comprehend their studies and be able to think about them. Because both camps accept the other's objective as being a worthy goal of education, much of the disagreement involves emphasis and setting priorities for education. There are many worthy goals for education and not enough class time to achieve all of them. Priorities have to be established, and choices made.

Accumulating Information as a Goal of Education

One point of view holds that education should be about learning information. An educated person is an informed person. To some extent this approach is valid. However, a problem arises when one considers the enormous amount of information available to be learned in relation to the amount of time available for learning. This problem inevitably moves the debate to questions about what information should be selected for students to learn. Again, there are disagreements and competing points of view about the purpose of education.

Literacy as an educational goal

Many believe literacy and numeracy should be the basic goal of education. They judge people on their ability to use language and numbers. Do they speak and write well? Can they do basic mathematical operations accurately? Since the ability to communicate with others is critical to any successful interaction among people, it is not surprising people consider literacy to be a very significant criterion.

However, achieving fluent literacy is a complex process. Functional literacy depends upon the ability to think abstractly using concepts, principles, processes, and symbols. Solving problems and communicating ideas are obvious examples of complex intellectual processes, but there are others. Other systems of symbols include musical notation, symbolism in the visual arts, literature, and religion, computer programs, maps and blueprints, etc. Modern cultures expect people to be literate in the sense of being able to decipher a variety of different symbol systems. Most people are dismayed when they see a graduate from an educational institution displaying some kind of illiterate behaviour.

It is important to note that literacy means more than being able to decipher something. It means being able to think using a particular set of symbols as tools to gain and extend meaning. In referring to someone studying history at a university, the British use the term "reading history". Reading in this context does not mean only learning to read historic material. Students are expected to have learned a range of historiographic skills they can use to evaluate historical events. Only when these skills have been accomplished would someone be considered literate in history.

These are very high standards of literacy. Students are not going to achieve those standards in every endeavour, but they can learn to apply the abilities learned from one endeavour to others. People do not need to be experts about everything to make valid judgments about issues affecting themselves and their society. One does not have to be expert in medical technology to make judgments about one's medical treatment. But people do need to know how to solicit advice and evaluate that advice. This is the logic behind providing students with a liberal education.[7]

Thinking as an Educational Goal

Another, somewhat less popular criterion for educated behaviour is the ability to think clearly and logically. Accepted rhetoric among Canadians holds that education should teach people to think. It is here that assumptions, priorities, and emphases begin to conflict. Conflicting assumptions can be seen in the discussion of literacy above. Are discussions of literacy about the goal of learning information or are they about the goal of learning to think? Of course, they are about both; but in popular discourse and practice, there is an assumption that literacy is about learning information.

This confusion is not just an issue of semantics, because confusion over goals in the classroom creates a larger problem: a problem of confounding the educational goal of providing information to students with the educational goal of thinking. So much time and effort is spent on imparting information that little time remains for the processes of comprehending, applying and disseminating the information being taught. At what point does the literacy goal of teaching students to think and apply information in their day-to-day lives become important in the classroom? The people who espouse information as a goal tend to become very defensive when they believe a significant amount of class time is being spent on activities related to thinking rather than accumulating information. At the same time, they become very upset when students appear to be illiterate in some way. It seems clear that a balance has to be found between the goals of knowledge and thinking.

EDUCATIONAL CROSS-PURPOSES: ASSIMILATING INFORMATION VERSUS LEARNING TO THINK

Assimilating Information

Those with Essentialist views of learning emphasize assimilating information and efficient learning. These goals interfere with the goal of learning to think. The first goal of assimilating information requires students to prove that they have know large blocks of information related to a subject before they are considered able to do any thinking about it. Essentialist reasoning posits that student thinking is flawed unless they know a great deal about a subject. In effect, this line of thinking denies students the right to think about many issues. It is a profoundly undemocratic view of education.

The reality is that we can never know everything there is to know about a subject. Well-educated people readily admit that there is much they do not know. Despite that, we are forced to base most decisions on inadequate knowledge. The reality of working with inadequate knowledge can be seen in something as simple as predicting the weather. The weather person may say there is a 60 percent chance of rain. Such a prediction is tantamount to incomplete information. In planning for everyday activities, we have to consider how to react to many contingencies whose predictability is highly uncertain. People learn to live their lives on this basis.

EFFICIENT LEARNING

The second view holds that learning can be made more efficient by preselecting certain sets of information for students, which if taught, would make learning faster and more comprehensive. This is reductionism applied to education.

Learning efficiency is a question that needs to be addressed in terms of achieving educated behaviour. Is it more efficient to teach blocks of content that have been reduced to their essentials, or is it better to allow students time to explore the realms of thinking so they have an opportunity to construct patterns of thought in their own minds? This line of thought leads to another fundamental divide in assumptions: is memorizing significant pieces of information about a topic more or less efficient than spending time defining and thinking about a problem or situation with the goal of finding a useful pattern of ideas?[2]

Understanding the Thinking Process

In order to understand the learning process involved in creating patterns of thinking, one needs to consider the fundamentals of the thinking process. At the most basic level, the process of thinking involves creativity and criticism. When one is thinking, one imagines alternatives, and then evaluates their usefulness. The rotation between imagination and evaluation occurs quickly and unconsciously as individuals create and consider various alternatives available to them.

The process of creating and considering different alternatives requires the ability to synthesize and analyze. Just as creativity and evaluation work together, synthesis and analysis support each other. Creativity needs the analytical ability to dissect the parts and relationships of a situation or idea in order to examine them. Creativity also needs the ability to synthesize new patterns of relationships between the parts of a situation or an idea. A thinker flips between analysis and synthesis as she/he imagines and organizes various patterns of ideas.

Closely related to the creative process of synthesizing new ideas is the ability to think critically about a situation or idea. Analysis is the ability to define the parts of a whole and their interrelationships. Synthesis is the ability to select the significant parts and relationships from all those possible and arrange them into a pattern (model) that usefully describes some aspect of reality. Criticism is the process of evaluating whether or not the parts and relationships selected for a creative description (model) bear a true relationship to reality. Some evaluative questions that can be asked are: Is the model an accurate representation of reality? Are its predictions accurate? Does it work? Is it aesthetically pleasing?

Discipline and Learning

Many people, particularly those closely involved in schooling, have practical problems with applying the goal of educating for thinking to the classroom. Education for thinking can appear to be in conflict with other educational goals such as order, discipline, and good manners. Teaching students to think independently can look chaotic, time-consuming, and close to being out of control as students grapple with independent and creative thought processes: maybe for the first time. No one can force another person to think, it is a voluntary process. That means students must be given a role in setting the learning agenda in the classroom. If they are not, they will lack the motivation to think. Thought processes must occur in the student's mind before they are learned. They cannot be memorized for application at some future date. They will only be available in the future (i.e. learned) if the student actively and meaningfully uses them in the present.

The methodology necessary to teach independent thinking does clash with Essentialist views of effective teaching. So methodologically, we have a problem in which two fundamental goals of education - learning information and learning to think - contradict each other.

RESOLVING THE CONFLICT BETWEEN INFORMATION AND THINKING

What is efficiency in learning?

The answer to that question depends upon the criteria used to judge efficient learning. If the criterion is assimilating information primarily through memorization, then the Essentialist approach to teaching is efficient. If the criterion is learning to think, then the Essentialist view of efficient learning turns out to be very inefficient, because students do not learn to think with this approach. If the criterion is good citizenship in a democracy, then logically speaking it would seem more efficient for educators to spend their time teaching students to think effectively. Effective citizenship in a democracy requires the ability to make judgments about courses of action. Such thought processes are thinking processes, not memorization processes.

Efficiency in Learning: Memorization vs. Applying Knowledge by Thinking

The traditional classroom emphasis on information is extremely problematic for the teaching of thinking, because it attempts to supplant student thinking with someone else's thinking. No one can teach someone to think by thinking for him or her, just as one cannot learn to skate by watching others skate. Learning to skate requires the active participation of a learner who is willing to endure the process of learning. While it is true that people do learn by copying others and by being coached, people must still take an active role in the process themselves before they will be able to master it.

Yet memorization is widely preferred to thinking as a means of learning. Memorization seems neat and tidy, and therefore attractive. The use of memorization appears to provide more control and accountability in the classroom setting. Its results appear to be more accurately quantifiable. Despite these dubious advantages, memorization has other serious ramifications for the classroom. It sends mixed messages to students about thinking and learning. The distinction between thinking and memorization is being confused. Picking up ideas, memorizing them, and then passing them along to someone on an exam or a paper is not thinking in the sense of creatively constructing choices and critically evaluating those choices. For example, we call the use of crib sheets during examinations cheating, but accept the use of memorized crib sheets. But, are the situations really any different? We have long considered the use of someone else's ideas in a paper to be plagiarism. Yet, repeating the teacher's or textbook's ideas on an exam is seen as good scholarship.

Teaching Democratic Behaviour: Passive Learning versus Active Learning

Thinking is a frail flower that is easily discouraged and intimidated. Creative thinking is a risky process because there are many more silly misses than there are creative hits. Just as the skater has to endure the pain of falling in learning to skate, the creative thinker has to endure the pain of error in learning to think. If learning to think is to occur in schools, classrooms must incorporate the values of intellectual freedom and provide some emotional safety for students as they experiment with thinking. Students must have the right to question. They must also have the right to search for emotional significance and meaning from the information they are studying. Finally, they must have the right to communicate their ideas.

This does not mean that the more traditional values of the classroom are unimportant. Students also need to learn the values of meeting expectations, being accountable, respecting the rights of others, and of supporting the legitimate social order of a society, including the classroom society. Before students will feel free to think, they must believe they are in a classroom situation, which encourages and supports their thinking.

Paradoxically, order can make people feel free. One only has to think about smoothly flowing traffic on a highway to understand that logic. A definition of good manners is making those around you comfortable. A classroom should help the people in it feel comfortable and free. Achieving the correct balance between freedom and accountability, guidance and control, questioning and expectation, communication and social order is difficult for schools, which is perhaps why they have not been able to achieve it consistently.

OTHER CRITERIA DETERMINING EDUCATED BEHAVIOUR

So far, we have been considering popular criteria for evaluating success in education. There are a number of other, less well known criteria, that people tend to agree - after some reflection on the determinants of quality education - are significant.

Intellectual Ethics

An educated person is one who is willing to listen to other points of view and give them a fair hearing. Intellectually honest people expect to search for the truth and are prepared to use honest procedures in that search. That includes being open to new ideas and being impartial in their evaluation. When presenting or receiving information, people expect an honest presentation of those ideas. If they have a bias, they admit it and let people know there are other points of view. In this era of spin doctoring information, propaganda, and advertising, intellectual honesty does not occur as much as people would like. Some of the bitterness expressed against the political process and the media stems from people feeling lied to. Nevertheless, people still believe in intellectual honesty and believe that intellectually dishonest people, by definition, are not well educated.

Managing information

In the modern world of information explosion, educated people have to know how to find and manage information efficiently. Every year, approximately 60 000 new books are published in the North American market. Just keeping up with newly published books would mean reading 164 books a day: an impossible task, so skills in managing information are necessary.

Typically, people believe these skills involve knowing how to find significant pieces of information that meet a need. In reality, it involves much more than knowing how to use a card catalogue, the internet, etc. Educated people know how to summarize information accurately and extract meaning from their summaries using generalizations and inferences. Plagiarism is a problem in schools (and universities). We typically assume that students are lazy. While there may be some truth to the laziness assumption, it is also that true many students lack the ability to summarize ideas, and to generalize and infer more ideas from their summaries. If students do not have these skills, they are unable to construct and communicate meaning from their research. Unprepared students have little alternative but to copy and present someone else's work as their own.

Managing information means knowing how to communicate to one's self and others a message about the significance of the selected information. As someone once said: I don't know what I think about something until I have had an opportunity to write it down. In this sense, communication is creatively and critically thinking about something so that communication is worthwhile.

Social skills

People lose their jobs in the workplace because of incompetence less often than they lose their jobs because they cannot interact effectively with others. This is a statement about the priority placed on social interaction. We prize social skills more than we prize intelligence and competence, even if we are not always prepared to admit it. We are beginning to understand that social intelligence plays as significant role in what an educated person can achieve within society as does technical knowledge and cognitive intelligence.

As the organizations of society become more complex, the ability to work cooperatively in groups becomes a critical ability. The ability to work cooperatively subsumes many skills and attitudes such as teamwork, communication, empathy, humour, trustworthiness, problem solving, and so on. This situation is a paradox because the more secure a person is in their individuality, the less likely they will feel they have to be defensive about it. Openness and sharing are the way to achieving individuality, and the truly educated person understands this paradox.

EDUCATION IS A COMPLEX PROCESS REQUIRING COMPLEX CONCLUSIONS

So far, we have examined some of the basic assumptions Canadians bring to any discussion of education. As we have seen, some of the assumptions are contradictory and - at the least - require the establishment of priorities. Canadians periodically become very agitated about what they perceive to be the inadequacies of their educational system. Over the past decade and a half, international comparisons - often with Japan - have been in vogue. Studies trumpet major shortcomings in education, and offer quick solutions to the perceived problems: if children are not learning to read, phonics should be taught exclusively; if teachers are not teaching and children are not learning, governments should institute a program of compulsory examinations which make everyone accountable. These are examples where criticism focuses on one central assumption, arguing that an emphasis on this assumption would make all well in education.

This introduction has tried to demonstrate the inadequacy of using a narrow approach in evaluating the teaching-learning process. Like other institutions in the human enterprise, the institution of education is complex and multifaceted. Education is a human activity in which real people create their humanity. Education cannot be reduced to a formula any more than can the arts, science, the law, or religion. All of these institutions are a human response to the complexity of the human condition.

Occasionally a group will spend time and energy in creating a more comprehensive critique and plan for education that attempts to balance and order assumptions. One such organization who has created a comprehensive plan for education in Canada is the Conference Board of Canada.

A VISION FOR CANADIAN EDUCATION

Over the past two decades, educational critics have criticized schools for not preparing children adequately for the world of work. Some of that criticism has been of the 'back to the basics' variety, which holds there was an educational golden era where children performed much better than they do now. People with this point of view believe restoring a traditional educational system would result in better educated children. The 'back to the basics' critiques of education seem to assume that Canada has remained a rural, traditional society, and education should be preparing young people for that kind of world. Other groups, such as the Conference Board of Canada, call for schooling to produce people who can function effectively in a workplace where the demands on employees are changing rapidly. Successful adaptation to those changes requires that children learn a different set of knowledge, abilities, and attitudes than they learned in the past.

The Conference Board of Canada in 1983 developed a paper on the role of education within Canadian society entitled *Matching Education to the Needs of Society: A Vision Statement.*[3] The Conference Board conducted a consultation with representatives of business, education, government, labour, and youth and social services and from that developed a vision statement. The Board referred to their vision statement as "an emerging consensus" about the future directions education should take in Canada.

Two Fundamental Considerations for Education

According to the Conference Board, there are two fundamental considerations in education. Are children coming to school willing and ready to learn, and are teachers teaching children the skills and attitudes they need in their future lives? The Conference Board believe there are three factors determining childrens' success, both in school and later in life. Children must come to school ready to learn. Children must be helped to maintain a willingness to learn by communities who accept responsibility for nurturing childrens' capacity to learn. And finally, schools must teach these generic skills which enable students to perform successfully in work, academe, and in their personal lives.

Skills for Successful Learning

The Conference Board paper goes on to define these generic skills in more detail. The Board argues that Canadian workers, if they are to be employable, must have three clusters of skills necessary to "get, keep and progress on a job":

- the first cluster lists the academic skills and knowledge which provide the necessary knowledge foundation for work;
- the second cluster lists those personal management skills, attitudes and behaviours which enable a person to do their work successfully;
- the third cluster lists the teamwork skills needed to prepare young people to work in teams.

The Academic Cluster of Skills

The academic cluster has three basic sets of abilities. The goal of the first set is to teach future employees how to "understand and speak the languages in which business is conducted". They must be able to learn by listening; they must be able to read, comprehend, and use written materials; and they must be able to write effectively. Secondly, young people must learn how to think. They must know how to think critically, act logically in evaluating situations, solve problems, and make decisions. Students must learn to use mathematics as a tool to solve problems and be able to apply the results. Students must also learn to use technology, instruments, tools, and information systems effectively. Finally, they must learn sets of specialized knowledge, and related skills from the various fields of knowledge. All teaching must be done in ways that foster students' desire to continue learning after their formal educational careers are over.

The Personal Management Cluster of Skills

The Conference Board continues by saying that the modern workplace needs people who exhibit positive attitudes and behaviours. The personal management cluster involves developing qualities such as self-esteem and confidence. Employees need to be honest, and to have both integrity and personal ethics. They also need to have a positive attitude toward learning, personal growth, and the initiative, energy, and persistence to accomplish their goals. They need to be able to set goals, plan and manage their time and resources, and to be accountable for their actions in achieving goals. Workers need to have a positive attitude toward change. They need to recognize and respect the diversity of people, and to be creative in accomplishing their assignments.

The Teamwork Cluster of Skills

The workplace requires cooperative values, hence the need for a teamwork cluster. The worker needs to be able to understand the organization's goals and be able to work within the culture of the group. Workers need the skills and attitudes that will allow them to plan and make decisions with others in ways that respect the opinions of others. They need to be able to work as part of a team, and to be able to lead a team when appropriate.

THE CONFERENCE BOARD'S DEFINITION OF BEING

The Conference Board has added an important overlay to the definition of what it means to be educated. They believe motivation and attitude determines an individual's level of educational achievement. An educated person is one who wants to be educated and has the attitudes and skills to do something about it. Educated people are those who constantly search for opportunities to extend their knowledge and skills. From this perspective, being educated is an ongoing process of learning, rather than achievement of a certain educational standing. The paradox inherent in this view of education is that an educated person is an independent learner who learns cooperatively. This paradox recognizes that while learning is driven by the motivation and skills of the individual, it cannot be achieved in isolation. Learning is a social activity that occurs as the result of the give and take of ideas between people. It also recognizes that learning in modern society is an ongoing process.

Implications of the Conference Board's Vision for Education

The vision of the Conference Board is a demanding agenda for everyone, and particularly for the schools. It not only calls for a full academic load, it also calls for the addition of a broad range of abilities and attitudes to the curriculum. If teaching is to motivate the desire for learning required by the Conference Board's vision, it must be done in a way that is relevant and stimulating. Schools, if they are to respond to that vision, will have to change considerably. The Conference Board's justifiable call for life long learning will force change much more than its academic and skills agenda. If the schools are to do this successfully, they will have to pay much more attention to motivational issues than they have in the past.

One wonders how deeply the Conference Board considered the implications of their call for life long learning, particularly from the standpoint of priorities and emphasis. If there has to be a trade between academic success, skills training and lifelong learning, which will suffer? In considering the Conference Board's vision, it is important to keep one reality in mind. Over the course of twelve years of schooling, children receive 12 000 hours of instruction, or 1 000 hours per year.[4] Creating visions are useful exercises, but they need to be tempered with reality.

The Essentialist approach to education is going to have difficulty achieving the vision of the Conference Board. It has a limited emphasis on skill development. It has not paid much attention to individual values and attitudinal issues related to personal motivation. It is doubtful that Essentialism will stimulate a desire for life long learning among students, because it does not actively recognize and satisfy the students' need for personal relevance.

While the Conference Board's vision may be problematic in several ways, it is pointing in the correct direction. The Conference Board wants people who are motivated to learn, who have the skills to accomplish learning, and who are willing to learn for the rest of their lives. This approach is constructive more for personal wellbeing than for economic success. One of this paper's assumptions is that education is good in and of itself. Education should be personally empowering, and to the extent that the Conference Board's vision helps schools work toward the goal of student empowerment, it is a good vision.

A REVISED PURPOSE FOR EDUCATION

Imparting knowledge was the prime consideration in Essentialist education. Such an assumption is obsolete. Stimulating a desire to learn is now the prime consideration in teaching. The fundamental issue in selecting learning objectives is their capacity to encourage a personal desire for learning in students. When planning learning activities, teachers must begin by considering relevance and motivation. That usually means beginning with a value related issue, moving to skills, and only at the last arriving at knowledge. The important thing to note here is that learning objectives are 'stacked' in a relationship so that one set of objectives carries the student logically to the next set of objectives. Students must clearly perceive some significant, relevant reason for examining an issue; they, then, must wish to do something about it and, therefore, need to learn/develop/practice abilities related to dealing with the issue. Then, as part of doing something about the issue, they are more likely to decide learning more information about the issue is important and necessary.

Not every topic traditionally found in curricula will provide this kind of motivation. Therefore, people in educational systems need to review curricular topics to determine which are motivationally useful and which are not. Traditional subject groupings and approaches will be at risk from this approach. Students may well learn science and mathematics in the context of environmental issues, if that is where students' interests lay.

If educators are going to teach abilities such as teamwork and problem solving, they must provide models students can use to pattern their learning styles and lives. Modeling is a powerful teaching tool. People learn by watching and copying the behaviour of those who know how to perform an activity well. We can all think of people we have used as models. Children will work very hard to duplicate those things an admired teacher does in the classroom.

It is interesting in this context to consider the attitude and behaviour of admired teachers. Most teachers who are admired model respect for human dignity, encouragement and cooperation, relevance in learning, independent thinking, creativity, etc. If schools believe the vision of the Conference Board is the correct one for society, then it seems logical to apply it in the schools as a working model. In that way, children can see the model in action and use it as a template from which to learn. Otherwise, students are not going to learn the abilities or adopt the attitudes laid out in the vision of the Conference Board, nor are they going to become life long learners.

The Conference Board places traditional academics as one of three important goals for education, rather than as the only goal of education. And, when one examines the range of skills the Conference Board defines in the academic cluster, it is clear that learning to think and communicate are, at least, as important as the assimilation of knowledge.

The important thing to recognize in all of this is that learning abilities, learning to live and work cooperatively, learning information and - above all - learning to love learning are not necessarily in conflict with each other, and are certainly not exclusive from each other. The issue is not to emphasize one to the exclusion of the others; rather the issue is how to present the package in ways that seem relevant and meaningful to the learner so that she or he wants to accomplish all of them.

Motivation for Learning

People want to learn, and they learn best whey they feel respected and feel they are a significant part of the learning process. It is important to ask questions about the difference between successful and unsuccessful learning. If one spends time with preschoolers, it is easy to see the zest with which they approach learning. If one spends time with students in later years, it is not unusual to encounter anger and cynicism toward formal education. Something significant has happened in the intervening years. Educators need to recognize the change and be prepared to respond to it.

Many people have come to love learning despite having to learn under very difficult circumstances. One can speculate about why some chose to continue to learn and others do not. Some things seem clear about those who like to learn. They obviously find learning rewarding in some way. What is rewarding may vary significantly from person to person, but all receive some sense of accomplishment from the learning process. Other possible rewards from learning may be discovering beauty, discovering patterns, expressing creativity, discovering spirituality, or seeking power. By learning, the learner somehow feels able to exert an influence on reality that is inherently satisfying.

How much scope have educational systems allowed in their educational processes for this kind of learning? The honest answer is not much. This has occurred because school cultures based on Essentialist assumptions have always believed they know what young people should learn. They are also convinced that young people are not equipped to make decisions about learning. This point of view has been widely accepted in society, and educators see themselves as an arm of society empowered to impose learning on young people. This power tends to be dressed up in rhetoric about serving the needs of children, the need to place limits on student behaviour for their wellbeing, the importance of teaching the work ethic and self-discipline. If these are the only assumptions about learning, then there is not much room for the learner to exert any influence on the learning process.

Unfortunately, many students have adopted a number of strategies to cope with an Essentialist based education culture. For many, the major coping strategy is passivity: "tell me the rules, tell me what to think, tell me where to go and I will do it; just give me an A, and please don't humiliate me". This is a form of learned helplessness. These are survival strategies, and when adopted, they make it very difficult for students to become independent learners. Another strategy is rebellion: becoming the class clown, disrupting classes, feigning supercilious cynicism; searching for ways of getting as much as possible for as little as possible, finding other pursuits to focus on: sports, sex, drugs, cosmetics, TV: there are many possibilities here. At least rebellion offers the possibility of life long learning, because the rebel, misdirected as he or she might be, is attempting to retain control of her or his life. The sad thing is all the wasted time spent achieving little in schools.

PURPOSEFUL LEANING

Paradigms have power because they focus and direct our attention. Our attitudes toward student motivation and responsibility are as firmly fixed as the attitudes toward the shape of the earth five centuries ago. Unfortunately, students are also affected by the prevailing educational paradigms, so they fall into line and act out the expected irresponsible behaviour. The conclusion of this chapter is that the Essentialist paradigm needs to be challenged if there is to be any kind of progress in education. In order to challenge the notion that students are uninterested in learning, we need to strip away accepted paradigms and take a hard second look at students. Let us begin by assuming for the moment students do want to learn, even though many of them appear to be quite uninterested in learning. We now have a contradiction to unpack. In order to do so, we need to consider those factors which govern motivation for learning.

People learn for a purpose. Information serving a need of some kind is more likely to be considered useful and retained. Nothing pleases students as much as the 'ah haa' experience. Not even the jaded, cynical student with an attitude of 'teach me, I dare you' is immune to a genuine, personal 'ah haa'. Unfortunately, a great deal of education students receive mystifies rather then clarifies. Ask your students to explain why one should invert and multiply when dividing fractions, and likely you will get a blank look or a disinterested shrug. In fact, many teachers tell their students not to worry about the explanation, just memorize it. Classrooms are filled with young people attempting to learn information that is personally meaningless and purposeless. There is a direct relationship between student disinterest in learning and the lack of meaning in the information they are learning.

We seldom question the assumption that the provision of information is the primary purpose of education. Nor do we question a related assumption that more information is a solution to the schools' or society's problems. We need to pause and carefully reconsider our emphasis on information. How does a certain piece of information contribute to the learning process? If we assume true learning comes from finding personal meaning instead of using the information assumption, how might the fundamentals of learning in schools change? Further, if we asked students - in a meaningful way - what they would consider to be meaningful learning, what might students recommend be taught, and how would that change student attitudes toward learning?

Students come to us with a deep need to understand the world they live in. Like the rest of us, they fervently hope such an understanding will give them some control and predictability in their lives. They really would like help in achieving a better understanding of their personal reality. They need a better understanding of who they are. They also need to understand the social realities in which they find themselves. Both can be large and sometimes hurtful mysteries. When we truly succeed in helping them gain a significant understanding of some kind, students are grateful and motivated to learn more. When we do not succeed, students simply lose interest in what we have to offer.

Education is about Epistemology

We understand reality as sets of patterns. Rightly or wrongly, we assume that reality is patterned, and we further assume that by understanding the patterns of reality we can predict and possibly affect reality in some way. We understand culture and society in the same way.[5] Both operate as patterns which can be understood and predicted. Students need to understand how we comprehend reality by creating models of it in our minds. We attempt to match the patterns in our mental models with the patterns we perceive in reality. Sometimes we get a good match, sometimes there are significant gaps.

A hypothesis is simply the belief in the appearance of an acceptable match between a mental model and some aspect of reality. Once we decide a personal mental model does fit reality as we perceive it, we feel we can make some predictions about the behaviour of reality. Once students can do that they have become empiricists, because empiricism is the process of testing a mental model against reality to see whether it is a match and does in fact make successful predictions about reality. A hypothesis, when it successfully passes our empirical tests, becomes a theory. So, a theory is just a conclusion that a particular model truly duplicates aspects of reality.

Patterned Thinking

If you watch children at play, you can see them go through this process. I remember watching a baby dunking her crackers in milk and then holding the dripping mass up above her head only to redunk them. The baby was outraged when her mother made her stop.

She was curious and was testing the mixture of cracker and milk to see how it would react in different situations. In the process the baby was creating mental models. This is what play is about, and if they are allowed to, children will continue to go through this process for a lifetime.

We need to help our young people understand this fundamental process of learning. It also happens to be fundamental to Western epistemology.[6] We need to practice epistemological processes in ways that are concrete and real for students. If we mystify epistemology with jargon - such as epistemology, hypotheses, empiricism, scientific method, and theory - without helping students understand that they do much of this quite naturally, we do them a disservice.

We need to encourage adolescents to step back from their thought processes and examine how they actually use those thought processes in day to day activities such as play, work, social life, etc.[7] The issue is not so much that we have to instill thought processes. Rather, we need to help students discover their personal capacity for this type of thinking, and appreciate its possibilities. When this happens, students are in a much better position to understand cultural tools such as the scientific method. It is not a waste of time to spend a lot of time in the classroom reflecting on the thinking process. It is a waste of time to attempt to teach thought concepts without firmly grounding them in the reality of students' lives.

Reconciling Mental Models with Reality

At the most fundamental level, critical thinking is making the distinction between the patterns in a mental model and the patterns in reality. It is crucial that students come to understand the distinction between the mental models created by humans and reality itself. This is a complex issue which can rapidly become quite abstract and difficult, particularly in relation to cultural reality. Unless careful work is done in the classroom, students will come away from their schooling believing the mental models they were taught are, in fact, reality.[8]

In teaching this distinction, there are a number of problems to be considered. One difficulty is that many children come from family backgrounds where hypothetical thinking either does not happen or is discouraged. These children need play experiences to stimulate and practice hypothetical thinking. As children mature into adolescence, they need to participate in many kinds of thought provoking conversations.

It is important for teachers to model thinking. It is critical that students be given opportunities to practice thinking with each other. When students begin to mature into abstract (formal) thought, they should spend time reflecting on their personal thought processes (metacognition). Metacognition is important to gaining mastery of thought processes, because mastery means understanding how to perform a thought process, and how it can be applied to situations encountered in day to day life.[9] Without metacognition, students will have a truncated appreciation of the power of their thought processes.

It is very easy to confuse mental models with actual reality. This is a common mistake at the abstract level of thought. It is relatively easy to understand the difference between one's mental model of a cup and an actual cup. It is quite a bit more difficult to differentiate between one's mental model of culture and the actual reality of culture. Both are abstract. Consider this epistemological problem: is the organization of a school system a mental model or is it an abstract reality? At some point a school system began as a mental model which was later developed into reality. A school system exists and functions, so it is real. Some of it is concrete (teachers, administrators, buildings, etc.) while the rest of it - the rules, regulations, expectations, procedures, etc - are both abstract and real. But, when we discuss the abstract aspects of a school system, we can easily slip into discussing only our mental models and believe we are discussing the actual system. This is the great problem in prejudice and racism. The mental model or stereotype becomes the reality. For racists, their mental model of humanity is reality and they refuse to accept any other possibility. In the same way, strong believers (fanatics) of a particular ideology may come to believe that their mental (ideological) model is reality, and that nothing else is acceptable or possible.

Unless care is taken, students will have great difficulty making this distinction and slip into similar ways of thinking. The thinking of small children is very egocentric. Children make no distinction between their thinking and reality. As children mature, they learn to see distinctions at the concrete level more quickly then they do at the abstract level. Helping young people with abstract thinking is critical, because so many important controversies are abstract. Confusing distinctions between model and reality compounds misunderstanding. Confusion is added to misunderstanding, and propagandists thrive on this kind of confusion.

In human affairs we tend to create models of models. Is culture a model of reality or reality itself? It is both, of course. The school system example which we spoke of above began as a mental model, was turned into reality and since then - in all probability - would have been reformed several times according to different mental models.

This process illustrates a basic question to be faced in teaching social studies. For example, diagrams of government structures on the chalkboard may be portrayed as a description of political reality of some kind. The history book, which is a model of history, becomes the reality of history. All too often in these classroom examples the model is turned into reality. Parenthetically, we should realize that this is not just a social studies problem; all subjects need to come to grips with this situation. Because students find it so difficult to learn these abstract models, teachers will tell you that there is no time or inclination left to move from the model to reality. Students most often handle this problem by memorizing the 'stuff' and then forgetting it.

FUNDAMENTAL TEACHING PRINCIPLES

There are two fundamental principles for teaching inherent in this situation. One is that teachers should never teach mental models deductively, and secondly, they should always help their students appreciate the difference between the mental model and reality. When teachers begin to teach with a textbook, it is almost impossible not to begin with the mental model. This is an abstract and difficult way for students to learn. Many students cope by memorizing the model. More importantly, students' ability to be active critical and creative thinkers of a model they are given deductively has been seriously limited. If all students receive is a model of reality, they have nothing to check it against. In such a situation, students have little option but to memorize it as truth.

However, if teachers approach teaching inductively many things fall into place for students. For example, let us assume this is an economics class, and the objective is to teach the law of supply and demand. Supply and demand curves are highly abstract models of reality which are intended to explain how price is established in a market economy. Students should always have opportunities to decide for themselves the validity of the models they are studying. It is important to start with the students' reality by giving them the opportunity to examine and question price fluctuations based on their own experience. This is more likely to make it make it a real issue for students. Students could discuss price fluctuations and begin to work out those factors which affect price. By starting with the students' reality, the teacher is providing a situation where students can practice creative thinking as they try to devise a model which adequately describes the patterns they see.

Students could brainstorm a list of commodities (consumer and producer) and then begin to look for any patterns in price fluctuations they can find. The patterns they come up with can then be arranged into tentative pricing models which would be subject to both critical and creative thinking. Then, once the students have created a model which satisfies them in a preliminary way, they can recompare it with reality. They might look at a historical situation to determine whether their model has made accurate predictions.

Models Are the Basis for Critical and Creative Thinking

When students have both a model and a grasp of reality, they have a firm basis for doing critical thinking. Students may believe they have created a good model about the behaviour of prices in various situations. Is it really? What are the parts of the model? Do these parts correspond accurately with reality? Does the model account for fluctuations in price? Does it apply to every situation? What are the exceptions? How are these exceptions to be explained? All of these are analytical questions. Other types of questions become possible: What can one predict (infer) from this model? Are the predictions reliable (evaluation)? How might the model be changed (creative thinking), and will those changes make the model better (critical thinking)? Understanding and applying the entire thinking process described here is a large, large step towards becoming an independent learner able to cope with new learning situations as they arise.

Once students have done some serious thinking about supply and demand and possibly feel they have reached the end of their expertise, someone might say: "maybe someone has written something about this problem? Maybe we should do some research for ideas which would help us with our model?" Students are now in a position to compare their models with the models of economists. They have enough background to allow them to begin the process of critically and creatively evaluating their models and other models they can find against reality as they understand it. This is the point at which studying different models of reality will begin to expand and broaden the students' grasp of reality.

Every thing described above is valid and useful, but the significant principle for students to appreciate is the understanding that ideas found in print are only models of reality created in someone else's mind. Once they understand this reality, they can better understand they have the capacity and the right to critically and creatively evaluate whatever they read or hear.

THE ROLE OF TEACHING

What has been described so far is not an attempt to suggest that there is little role for the teacher, and that students can easily learn by themselves. This is simply not the case. Before students can become effective thinkers, they have to master some very sophisticated ideas and processes. It is the responsibility of the teacher to help three things happen. First, students need to conceptualize a set of necessary ideas (concepts) which they can use to comprehend reality. Second, they have to learn a set of intellectual skills which will enable them to think critically and creatively. And finally, they have to learn to use values as criteria against which to evaluate their responses to the moral and ethical situations they will face. None of these abilities come to students without a great deal of careful teaching on the part of teachers and school systems.

Moving from an Information Paradigm to a Construction of Knowledge Paradigm

Change is a difficult process for most institutions, and education is no exception. Presently, there are two fundamental paradigms struggling for influence in the high schools. One might be labelled the information (Essentialist) paradigm, and the second the construction of knowledge paradigm. The differences between the two paradigms - despite the labels - are not so much about whether or not information and thinking should be included in each paradigm. Both groups believe that information and thought are important components of education. The differences have more to do with how students should learn than what they should learn. According to proponents of the information paradigm, teaching should help students accumulate and store information for use at some point in the future. Learning a body of information is the priority. The construction of knowledge point of view believes that teaching should encourage students to think about and create information, which will help them to independently understand reality. Learning to think has priority over accumulating information.

Traditionally, secondary education has been much influenced by the information (Essentialist) paradigm.[10] Providing students with information is fundamental to a good education. Any evasion of the duty to teach information is just pretence at education. A related assumption of this paradigm is that the most efficient way of providing young people with information is to tell it to them. At the heart of the Essentialist education paradigm is the belief that teachers should directly teach information to young people. Teaching and lecturing are considered to be the same thing. From the standpoint of the traditional education paradigm, the assumption that teaching is lecturing is such an obvious relationship that it is not much discussed.

A second belief underpinning the Essentialist paradigm is that learning should be efficient and not waste time. Teaching can be made more efficient by organizing and predigesting information before it is presented to the learner. The learner should not have to waste time finding and determining the meaning of something. Students should concentrate on learning and remembering information. It is pointless to allow students time to reinvent the wheel when so much good work on wheels has already been done. Students' objectives should be to get up to speed on wheel building as quickly as possible, so that they become capable of making a contribution in the future. Since there is so much information students need to know, it is important the processes of information dissemination be made as efficient as possible.[11]

Essentialists believe people who lack knowledge cannot make good decisions about what they need to know.[12] They need the guidance of a teacher. If students were capable of making those kinds of decisions, they would not need to be in schools. Students have to accept that they must learn information for which they presently cannot see a need. They have to trust that they will eventually understand the need for certain pieces of information. Allowing students the right to make decisions about what they learn is usually an inefficient waste of student time. Even worse, it can be a fraud, because students will mistakenly learn things which are either unnecessary or wrong. Schools have a duty to protect students from these kinds of errors.

Supporters of the construction of knowledge paradigm - which is also competing for influence in the high schools - believe knowledge is constructed by individuals as they learn. They believe people can comprehend reality only after they build some kind of duplicate of it in their minds. This process of constructing reality is the process of learning. Thus, the basic assumption behind the construction of knowledge paradigm is that students must be actively involved in some aspect of reality before they can construct its meaning in their minds. Memorization is considered a limited form of learning because it forces students to replace the construction of meaning with memorization. Memorization short circuits knowledge construction. Unless the process of intellectual construction occurs, there can be no meaning for the individual. The conclusion of this paradigm is that everyone spends their lives busily reinventing the wheel so they can better understand it.

The fundamental assumption underlying the construction of knowledge paradigm is that people learn by doing. Therefore, the classroom should provide many activities where children can actively engage reality in their learning processes. A second related assumption is that children best learn by proceeding from the known and the concrete to the unknown and the abstract. Given these assumptions, it is believed that children do learn best by reinventing the wheel. Once they have been allowed to do the basic concrete thinking, then, if they are old enough, they will be in a better position to do higher level abstract thinking.

Based on these assumptions, active, participatory activities such as play, discussions, role playing, experimentation, etc. are considered to be more useful teaching methodologies than lecture methodologies. These teaching techniques are believed to help students construct personal knowledge through the active engagement of reality. The belief is students learn more and remember better when they are active rather than passive. It is assumed people learn through the use of all the senses, not just through seeing and hearing. If all these assumptions are the case, then the classroom should be filled with activities and situations requiring students to make active choices as they respond to the classroom reality.

THOUGHT IS THE FUNDAMENTAL PURPOSE OF EDUCATION

The conflict between the two paradigms raises two significant issues, which need to be carefully considered. The first issue is do we want students to learn information, or do we want them to learn to think? Both paradigms would agree that students should be able to think about information they understand. One cannot think in an information vacuum, nor can one think without having learned an array of thinking skills. So the issue dividing the two paradigms is not information versus thinking, but the appropriate balance between the two. The fact is that both are necessary, but thinking must take precedence over information accumulation.

The second issue dividing the paradigms is significant because it involves the question of what constitutes learning: does learning occur only after one has committed to memory pieces of information, or is learning the result of systematically thinking about information? If the fundamental learning objective is to teach quantities of information which students will memorize, then the use of a teacher centred lecture approach may be the most efficient approach to take in the classroom. If the fundamental learning objective is to select certain significant pieces of reality and help students learn to think about them, then the teaching methodologies used need to show students how to do that. If the educational objectives have changed from the accumulation of information to critically and creatively thinking about information, then it is reasonable to assume that teaching methodologies will have to change as well. What is not reasonable is to assume students will learn to think without help and guidance.

Teaching students to think about information is a complex and difficult.[13] The provision of effective help and guidance in developing thinking skills requires hard work, creativity, and good judgment on the part of the teacher. The teacher must be more professional, not less. To be effective, teachers must have defined a very clear set of objectives for each activity they plan to use, and work hard to actualize those objectives in the classroom. Teachers must know the subject areas being taught well enough so that they can ground abstract principles into concrete reality for their students. They must have a fund of information, anecdotes, situations, etc. at their finger tips which they can use to make abstractions real. They must know thinking skills well enough so that they can constantly organize and model them for students. They must creatively devise activities related to the information being taught which allow students to actively practice those thinking skills.

JUSTIFYING EDUCATIONAL CHANGE

From the perspective of traditional information paradigm (Essentialism), educational change has received a bad name because the 'new' teaching techniques are seen to be unproductive. Traditionalists consider student centred teaching techniques a waste of time, because students are allowed to pool their ignorance and pretend they are learning something of significance. Traditionalists charge that teachers and students dislike the lecture as a teaching method because it is hard work.[14] Traditional critics of educational change believe it has pandered to student individuality while not teaching them much. In many classes, students seem to be spinning their wheels, accomplishing little.

There is enough reality to these charges to make them believable and worthy of serious consideration. The fact is that the teacher is and must remain the educational leader of the classroom. Very little learning will happen within the classroom without careful preparation and guidance by the teacher. Schools are still necessary, and students need their support if they are to learn.

If we truly believe in thinking, despite the difficulties listed above, we have little choice about finding alternative teaching methodologies to the teacher-centered, lecture varieties we have relied upon in the past.[15] Students will not learn to think unless they actually think. This fundamental reality has to be accepted. When the teacher controls the thinking, then the students merely copy the teacher's thinking, and the class has reverted to memorization.

MOTIVATION DETERMINES WHAT CAN BE LEARNED

Two issues follow: the first is motivation. The student - and no one else - ultimately decides whether he or she will think (construct reality) or simply memorize. Before students will feel free to perform the thought processes rather than depend on the teacher, they must be given permission and encouragement to do so. The second issue is whether students have been helped to develop a set of thinking skills to draw upon. Students cannot think unless they have learned the pre-requisite skills to guide their thinking. It is doubtful that students will learn these in a classroom where the teacher does the thinking and the students do the listening. Thinking skills, like other skills, are only mastered through practice. The classroom needs to be restructured so students are doing the thinking.

If students are to feel free to think, teachers must have the skills to do their job as facilitators rather than as authority figures. Those skills involve being able to motivate students to stay on task without appearing to be a heavy handed taskmaster. They involve being able to model thinking skills so that students can see them being applied. The work load increases when teachers go down this pedagogical road. Many teachers who teach this way will tell you they would find it easy to go back to the 'good old days' where they could walk into the class, do a lecture, assign some questions, and watch the students answer them.

TEACHER SUPPORT

Teachers need help. Everything described so far is only part of the reality of a teacher's day. There are many demands on a teacher's time and energy. One of those demands is the teacher's extra-curricular responsibilities. These can be quite demanding. If a high school fields a basket ball team, creates a jazz band, stages an operetta, or takes part in a debating tournament, etc. the performance expectations are very high. The performance had better be good. Being good takes time and energy.

Other demands are the various bureaucratic and professional expectations placed on a teacher. Teachers are expected to be leaders in the school, and to work to make their schools better learning environments. When all that is done at the end of the workday, the teacher is expected to evaluate the many student writing research assignments. Students rightfully expect the teacher will have carefully and thoughtfully evaluated their work. If a high school teacher teaches four classes of say 25 students per class, the teacher is responsible for evaluating 100 students. Devoting only ten minutes to reading and evaluating each student's work (which is minimal) amounts to four hours of marking per class assignment and almost 17 hours for all four classes. In addition teachers need to do the necessary reading and research to stay current in their subject areas as well as creating, designing, and producing new teaching activities for their courses. After all of that is completed, teachers should find time and energy to be good parents, spouses, and community members as well.

Teachers do not find curriculum guides very helpful. They tend to be based on unfamiliar pedagogical principles. They typically contain a thin outline of the information content to be taught and long lists of skills and values to be developed. What is usually missing from the curriculum is any practical discussion and illustration of how all this is to be done within the classroom. There appears to be a great reluctance among the officials of education ministries to prepare developmental materials for classrooms. A large part of that reluctance has to do with money. It is expensive to keep a staff of educational consultants available to do development work. Governmental decision makers justify the lack of classroom activity based curricula on the basis that teachers are the professionals and capable and responsible for developing classroom activities. A common comment: if departments of education accept responsibility for producing educational materials, teachers will be encouraged to stop doing producing materials for their classrooms.

Tyranny of the Textbook

The non-activity approach to curriculum development might have worked with the information paradigm. Under this paradigm, curriculum development involved updating and revising course information. Text book publishers would get the revised curriculum and write text books to provide information support for teachers. Teachers would then use the tables of contents as a course outline on which to base their lectures, note taking assignments, examinations, and any other assignments they might decide to do. The text book was the key document in translating curriculum documents into classroom reality.

In large measure, we have not changed our thinking much when it comes to curriculum development. In curriculum design and implementation, what we have done is apply the assumptions of a construction of knowledge paradigm without discarding the assumptions of the information approach. Teachers and students are falling between the cracks of these two paradigms. It is just wrong to assume that teachers will successfully make the transition from the information paradigm to the construction of knowledge paradigm without help. There are too many problems to be solved with too few resources to provide solutions.

Problems in Responding to a Paradigm Change

Many middle school and high school teachers are aware of the shift in paradigms, but only in the uneasy sense that some kind of change is in the air. When they are confronted with a construction of knowledge based curriculum, they are at a loss to know how to respond. The construction of knowledge paradigm requires a fundamental shift from focusing on memorizing information to focusing on students actively thinking about information. To accomplish this shift, teachers have to learn to present information in different ways. They have to motivate and discipline differently. Their assignments have to be different, and their evaluation procedures have to change. It is not helpful to go to a teacher and say that you have to change everything you do, but we are not going to support you in doing it. Half measures do not work well in this situation.

Making changes in a piecemeal fashion do not accomplish the shift from the information paradigm to the construction of knowledge paradigm. For example, if teachers try to present information in some kind of discussion group format without changing their motivational and evaluation procedures, students are unlikely to respond positively. The teacher reaction: "See, I knew this was not going to work."

It is not surprising teachers are reluctant to spend time researching and reflecting on educational theory. It is also not surprising teachers resent curriculum change. New curricula usually mean teachers have to do a lot of work and take a lot of risks with very little support. It seems to them they have much more to lose then they have to gain.

Teachers respond with the 'pocket veto'. They simply put new curricula in their pockets, close their classroom doors and ignore it as much as possible. Some teachers ignore new curriculum by learning to be good at parroting the current curriculum party line. In meetings and discussions they leave the impression that all is new and changing in their classrooms. The reality can be quite different. If one looks at the day to day objectives and methodologies they employ, it is difficult to see how anything new is happening. Other teachers erect a philosophical rationale to justify resistance to change. They can provide a whole set of ideas explaining why the status quo is superior to the proposed curriculum change. All of this makes them feel very professional without having to do anything.

Educational thinkers and leaders need to appreciate that many teachers have not received any professional upgrading for many years. The average age of teachers in Canada is somewhere in the 40s. Most of these teachers will have been teaching for twenty years, and are a long way from any teacher training.[16] Many of them are uncertain and threatened by changing educational objectives and methodologies. Unfortunately, there is little systematic, ongoing inservice to help teachers learn to apply new procedures in their classrooms. One-shot afternoon inservices do not change teaching behaviour. Changing teaching behaviour requires long, consistent training, supported by classroom observation and feedback. If these things are not done, teachers easily slip back into their former teaching habits.

Developing a Construction of Learning Methodology

Even if inservice were consistently done, there is still a fundamental problem in educational change. There is a gap between educational theory and educational practice. The cause of the gap is the small amount of time and effort invested in creating, testing, and producing educational activities.[17] This is particularly true at the high school level where writing and distributing a new text book is considered to be educational development. What passes for the creation of educational methodology at the institutional level tends to involve buying teaching materials (text books, audio visual materials, etc.) produced by book publishers. This approach may have worked under the information paradigm, but it leaves a lot to be desired under the construction of knowledge paradigm. We now see a plethora of web sites and web searches, but are these, at bottom, information based or construction of knowledge based? They can be both, and which one they are depends upon how the teacher approaches their use.

Compare this to other institutions in society. Consider the situation in medicine. Like the teacher, the doctor is the core contact professional for the client. The doctor is supported by fundamental research, technical research, the pharmaceutical industry, teaching hospitals, general hospitals with an array of professional support, laboratory systems etc. In medicine there is no doubt about the importance of developing new treatment techniques. If a new technique seems helpful, then the pressure is for doctors to use it. But before the technique is used, careful research and training has to be done to make sure it does work.

It is difficult to see a comparable set of supports for teachers. Little work is being done in systematically turning research into tested practice for the high school classroom. There is no pharmaceutical equivalent in education doing research in establishing new educational techniques and determining the range within which they work. Most of this is left for teachers to work out flying by the seat of their pants at the end of a long work day. Many teachers skip the challenge.

The fundamental purpose of this book is to make practical, classroom useable connections between learning theory and effective teaching. Despite what many believe, there is a close relationship between educational theory and effective teaching. It is learning theory which defines suitable teaching objectives and it is those teaching objectives which determine how we teach, and whether our teaching has been successful or not. We now know quite a lot about how people learn. Learning theory clearly suggests some basic principles for an effective pedagogy. Effective teaching is using those teaching techniques which constructively achieve reasonable educational objectives as determined by learning theory.

INDEPENDENT LEARNING IS THE GOAL OF EDUCATION

Schools should create independent learners. Students who have completed twelve years of education should be able to learn by themselves. Both conservative and progressive critics of education question whether independence is actually being achieved. The problem is that a focus on learning a surfeit of information seriously interferes with the processes of individual learning and thinking. Schools find themselves in a difficult position on this issue, because individuals and groups believe there are critical gaps in what students know which must be filled. This worry leads them to put pressure on the state to add more information to the curriculum. Schools are faced with teaching more information, while little traditional material is withdrawn from the curriculum.

Given the information explosion, despite whatever schools do or do not do about the provision of information to students, students will continue to miss out on large amounts of important information. The situation will continue to worsen. We will have to accept that reality. Mystified and unmotivated students are missing out on important pieces of information anyway. Society needs lifelong learners who are able, by themselves, to examine a novel situation and learn from it. With that ability in place, students can redress future deficiencies in their education.[18] But before students can become independent learners, they must know how to learn, which means they must learn how to go about understanding reality. The real issue for education is epistemology: the process of knowing and understanding reality. It is not memorization.

DEVELOPING A PERSONAL MOTIVATION TO LEARN

Schools have to accept that lifelong learning means the development of a personal motivation to learn. Personal motivation is dependent upon fostering a feeling of self-worth and dignity, which at the heart is a belief in one's personal worthiness and one's right and ability to exert control over reality. Neither of these beliefs is to be found in dependency and learned helplessness. Self-worth and dignity cannot be forced. It must be developed, and it can only be developed in conditions where the learner has the freedom to choose to do those things that are meaningful and relevant to him or herself. Lifelong learning, if it is an honestly accepted objective, will be truly subversive to the existing educational system.

End Notes

1. Essentialist education has traditionally taken the view that attaining a high level of literacy in one area teaches the student to appreciate thought processes in other areas.

2. Issues of memory are discussed in much more detail in the chapter on working memory. Suffice it to say here that research on memorization indicates students retain very little of what they memorized over the long term.

3. Conference Board of Canada. *Matching Education to the Needs of Society: A Vision Statement.* 1993.

4. If one assumes 200 days per school year and five hours of instruction per day for four years of high school education, students will receive a total of 4,000 hours of instruction. Again, assuming students take the traditional eight courses (English, mathematics, social studies, science, health, physical education, art, and music in one way or another) over the course of their school careers, they will receive an average of 500 hours of instruction per course. If they take two more courses (extra language, computer science, home economics, and various vocational courses) - and many do - students will then get an average of 400 hours of instruction per course. By way of comparison, it is estimated that attaining fluency in a foreign language can take up to 5000 hours of instruction.

5. I am aware that this can be a major philosophical issue. For example, Post Modernists would probably argue that the claim to some underlying pattern to reality is not defensible. That may be so philosophically, but few people base their lives on a post-modernist world view. People, including high school students, assume there is some kind of pattern to reality which can be perceived and relied upon (predictability). They accept the possibility they might misunderstand reality, but they usually do not infer from their misunderstandings there is no pattern to reality.

6. It is an important process in other cultures as well. We especially esteem an empirical approach to reality in the West. Yet schools are reluctant to allow young people to practice empiricism on their own. It becomes even stranger when one considers that the rote empiricism practiced in schools, which expects people to duplicate and come up with pre-established answers, is not really empiricism at all. Empiricism is about falsifying the "correct" answers, not duplicating them. The baby who was busily dunking her crackers is right, the schools are wrong.

7. As they enter high school, most adolescents are becoming formal thinkers. Formal thinking is thought about thought, which can also be a definition of epistemology. Research indicates young people by their early teens have developed the innate capacity to do formal thinking. Other research indicates the successful expression of the capacity to think formally depends upon whether young people have received cultural experiences which provide them with models and experience in formal thinking. This is the critical issue for determining whether adolescents will become formal thinkers. Formal thought appears to be something that does not happens automatically.

8. This is not to suggest students be taught to reify the abstract into the concrete. Rather it is the other direction:, being able to see the abstract in the concrete.

9. Metacognition is simply another term for thought about thought (just as formal thinking and epistemology are). Metacognition is our ability to evaluate our own personal thought processes. They usually involve questions like "how am I doing", "will this work", "maybe I should do . . . ", etc. The ability to metacognate is prerequisite to successful formal thought.

10. The middle schools and high schools are still very much affected by the Essentialist point of view on the primacy of information. The primary schools much less so. Early childhood has recognized that children learn best when they are in a position to construct their learning.

11. For a detailed discussion of this approach, see the seminal book on pedagogy by Ralph Tyler. This little book has exerted a profound influence on modern high school pedagogy. Ralph W. Tyler. *Basic Principles of Curriculum and Instruction.* Chicago: The University of Chicago Press. 1949.

12. Larry J. Shaw. *Teacher Education 954: Humanistic and Social Aspects of Teaching* (SDSU http://edweb.edu/LShaw/f95syll/philos/phessent.html)

13. Unfortunately, it is easy to do badly. Many teachers have their students do discussions, role plays, etc, with little clear idea of what is to be accomplished. It is an easy way to spend a Friday afternoon without running into the heavy motivation/discipline problems required to get something constructive accomplished. These techniques make it easy for the teacher to mistakenly believe that something significant is being accomplished.

14. Bill Bennett, Secretary of Education

15. It should be noted here that lectures (particularly the Socratic approach) are highly effective when judiciously used. Teachers need to learn to use a wide variety of methodologies and be prepared to use them as needed. Teachers need to consider their fund of methodologies as a kit of tools, each of which has an appropriate and significant use, and not to be confused.

16. Most of the teacher training they did receive will have been done in the early 1970s, mostly under an information paradigm.

17. It is actually difficult to define a term that captures everything that would involved in this process. At the classroom application level, activity covers all of the concepts, skills, and values objectives, the general information objectives as well as the activities and behaviours students would actually do in learning as well as some evaluation procedures. An activity, if it is to be useful to teachers, needs to cover all of these bases and be soundly based on educational and epistemological theory.

18. In today's crowded high school time tables, students who are highly motivated to learn are forced to make difficult choices about what they will study. "Should I take calculus or history?" can be a choice forced on the student. This is why independent learning - defined as learning how to learn - is the critical objective for high school education. With the best intent in the world, students will find that there will be gaps in their background. The gap most difficult to repair is the inability to learn by oneself.

CHAPTER THREE: CHANGING SOCIETIES, CHANGING CHILDREN

TABLE OF CONTENTS

The A.C. Nielsen Company reports that children watch on average 1,680 minutes of television per week. Based on this figure - using a simple, straight-line calculation - by the time they graduate from high school, they could have watched something on the order of 26,000 hours of television. During the same period they would have received approximately 13,000 hours of schooling.[1]

Statistics such as these represent a generalization. Not all students watch this much television, nor do they reflect the hours young people spent on video games of all kinds.[2] Video games have become a multibillion-dollar industry in which youngsters spend a lot of time and money. Over the course of a school career, students will be exposed to many more hours of television and video gaming than hours of schooling. Many people believe this imbalance is having a major impact on young people, but so far it has been difficult to define its effect very clearly.[3] This whole notion is very controversial. The media deny any cause and effect, and challenge their critics to prove a causal relationship. Those who work with young people on a daily basis over the course of a couple of decades are not nearly as sure as the media.[4]

Teachers believe children have changed significantly over the past two decades. They point to the increase in class discipline problems; the lack of readiness to learn; the lack of support from parents and the community; the rise in the number of single parent families; as well as large numbers of latch-key children whose parents work long hours away from the home. Other factors include life in large anonymous cities without the support of an extended family; increased emotional, physical, and sexual abuse; family stresses resulting from being unemployed and living on a limited income; and all the other pressures of living in a competitive, materialistic society. These problems exist in many classrooms.[5] Despite all these problems, there are also many parents, parents' groups, and community groups who actively support the schools. Many children come to schools with serious problems, but at the same time many are well prepared and supported. Therefore, this line of reasoning provides conflicting evidence about the causes of student change.

There is, however, another line of reasoning to consider because it affects both groups of children mentioned above, albeit in different ways. Marshall McLuhan pioneered this reasoning when he demonstrated that the technology of mass media affects people beyond the information that they receive.[6] It is beyond the scope of this discussion to pursue McLuhan's reasoning, except to say that he provided a theoretical basis for analysing the effect of the media on people's behaviour.

THE IMPACT OF THE MEDIA ON LEARNING

Television and video games are major factors when examining the impact of the media. In our use of television, we have been performing a giant experiment on children with no more than a hazy idea of the consequences. Many children have grown up with a steady diet of television, usually several hours a day. Postman wrote in The Disappearance of Childhood "The lives of our children are shaped by what they will see and hear in the media. Children are the living messages we send to a time we will not see."[7] For many small children, television is the babysitter. This has allowed television to influence children from a very early age, and by extension, to influence the future.

An experiment was done on babies to discover whether they attended to television as it played in front of them. In the experiment, the babies had to use a soother to keep the television image focused. The babies worked very hard on their focusing task, indicating they cared about receiving a clear image. We know that early learning exerts a profound influence on the development of children. Early learning provides the basic assumptions children live with for the rest of their lives. They unlearn those assumptions only with great difficulty.

What are children learning from television that affects their approach to schooling? In thinking about this issue, it is necessary to review the role the media plays in the lives of people, and its role in the organization of society.

THE ROLE OF MEDIA IN HISTORICAL CHANGE

Changes in communications technology affect the way people communicate and the way they think. There are several historical examples, which demonstrate this process. A very early example of changing media is the Iliad and the Odyssey. Scholars point out that the poetry of Homer is from a preliterate society. It was developed to tell stories face to face in small groups. These stories were passed orally from generation to generation and were not written down. Only after the development of writing was Homer's poetry put to paper. Transcribing the Iliad and the Odyssey to the written page did not change it from being oral literature because of its oral origins. Literature conceived for the written page is different, because the development of writing changed the way people express themselves, and presumably the way they think. The advent of written language created a different social order with different interrelationships among people.[8] The issue for schools is to consider the effect of the electronic revolution on students presently enrolled. Historic events suggest that significant changes in media have an effect on the thinking and organization of society.

The printing press initiated a similar process of social change. One effect of printing was to freeze the written language so that it soon reflected the conventions of an older spoken language. Spoken language (accent & vocabulary) continued to evolve, but written language did not, leaving us with many anachronistic spellings (right for *rite*, cough for *coff*, etc.). On the political level, it is generally agreed that printing and distributing thousands of books - such as the Bible - had affected traditional power structures such as the Catholic Church and feudal kingdoms.[9] A few years after the invention of the printing press, the annual publication of books in Europe went from the order of ten books per year to tens of thousands of books per year. Within decades, the availability of books in Europe increased markedly. The electronic revolution in the late twentieth century was not the first communications revolution. The communications revolution generated by the printing press during the Renaissance was as profound in its way as was anything occurring in the twentieth century.

As people began to read and think about the ideas in the powerful books being published, they began to question the status quo in many feudal institutions. Of course, feudal institutions were threatened and defensive, and did as much as they could to prevent people from thinking for themselves. Ultimately, it was to no avail: the genie was out of the bottle. Change was inevitable, and religious, economic, and political institutions had to respond to it.

Our children are adapting to an electronic revolution in communications. They might be referred to as the nintendo generation. For example, there is evidence that the hand-eye coordination of these children related to using video games is superior to their parents because of the hours of early practice on electronic games. Test this statement by competing with some of these children to see how well you can compare. Learning is going on in the video arcades. When the military needed people who could guide missiles by using a small target on a television screen, this early training was a significant advantage. The Gulf War indicated how much modern electronic warfare resembled our electronic games, or vice versa.

THE IMPACT OF THE MEDIA ON STUDENT ABILITIES

On the more practical classroom level, the electronic revolution is changing the abilities of students. There is good evidence to suggest that the brain is quite malleable in early life. As it grows, it responds to the demands made upon it by laying down patterns within it that allow certain behaviours to proceed expeditiously. It appears that after a certain age, the brain stops doing that and it becomes increasingly difficult to learn new patterns as efficiently as a young child does.

Michael Jordan is a superb athlete and does things in basketball few other people can emulate. When he attempted to become a baseball player, he could not learn to play baseball at the level of his basketball game. The hypothesis is that Jordan had not spent time in his early life developing the hand-eye coordination necessary to hit a three-inch ball moving at 150 kilometres (93 miles) per hour with a baseball bat.[10] Rather, Jordan had spent his childhood developing the ability to shoot a basketball through a hoop from a variety of improbable positions. Even with a couple of years of practice in the minor leagues, Jordan was never able to become a major league baseball player.

ATTENTION SPAN

We hear a lot about sound bytes and short attention spans. People worry that students may be developing shorter attention spans. This is actually a cultural phenomenon. More people than students have developed short attention spans. In the nineteenth century, it was common for people to listen to three-hour speeches. Even for 'print people', a three-hour speech would be unacceptable now. Many people dislike movies to last longer than 120 minutes. Attention spans have declined. Whether that is a bad thing or not is debatable. Surely, orators can make the main points of a three-hour speech in a half hour without sacrificing too much meaning.

In addition to cultural changes, other factors affect student attention spans. These factors range from physical problems to events in the personal lives of students. Research with babies and young children show they have longer attention spans when they are interested in the subject.[11] A lack of motivation may determine the attention spans of students. If students are interested and committed to what they are learning, attention span is more likely to be adequate to the task. One can check this assertion by watching young people while they are engaged in something that interests them. The first issue for schools is to be aware of what is happening to people as communications technology changes. Then classrooms need to reflect at least some of the new realities in media technology.

PRINTED PAGES, COMPUTER SCREENS, AND LITERACY

Learning in early life is significant to later performance. I am a book person who grew up during the 1940s and 50s. This was pretty much a pre-television era and certainly pre-computer. In my forties, I had to learn to write and think using a computer. After a lifetime of experience in reading and writing prose, I found I did not detect mistakes on the computer screen. I would be amazed to see the number of obvious mistakes in plain view when I examined a paper copy of my work. It took a lot of practice to become comfortable with a computer screen, yet even now I prefer the printed page.

Modern children may be going through the reverse of this process. Children learn to read and write well when they live in an environment that prizes books and reading. Being read to and encouraged to look at, discuss, and enjoy books are the significant variables in becoming a successful reader. This is not happening in many childrens' lives. They spend their time watching television. Many of them then may go on to use computer screens as the primary way of getting information. Yet when they attend school, the printed page becomes supreme. The justification for this is that children must learn to be literate.

The achievement of literacy is not the issue. The issue is how to achieve literacy. Is there something inherently superior in learning literacy from a piece of paper? Alternatively, are we as 'print people' allowing our biases to get in the way of effective pedagogy? It is now possible - via the internet - to read daily newspapers over the computer. Vast amounts of information are available on compact discs. The process of switching the storage of information from paper to electronics is likely to continue. Are the schools responding to this challenge in the same way the Church and other institutions responded to the print revolution in the sixteenth century?

Schools are still committed to the printed page and its display of information. Since most teachers are essentially print people, this is hardly surprising. Teachers are more comfortable with print and uncertain about how to respond to the way computers present information. This means many children have to deal with a medium with which they are less comfortable. Print people believe students have to learn to use the printed page, and to some degree that is true, because both electronic and print media will be used for some time to come. It is also true students will need to be able to communicate using language in both media. A sentence is a sentence regardless of the medium. In fact, it is arguable that electronic media demands more clarity and precision, since people do not have the opportunity of rereading a sentence several times as they do on the printed page. Growth in the use of e-mail may well restore letter writing as an important means of communication. The issue is not whether students should learn to communicate, but rather how they learn to communicate.

The Effect of Media on Perception

There are other effects of the electronic communications revolution. Studies have shown that people who watch a steady diet of television tend to gain a skewed view of reality. Old people who are chronic television viewers tend to be much more paranoid about the level of crime in society. Young people are also much affected by what they see on the mass media. At the time of writing this, there is a news report of the brutal murder of a young girl by 'friends' who were emulating the behaviour of other young people they see and hear about on television, on movies, and on 'gangsta' cds and videos.[13]

People in media institutions protest that most young people can distinguish between reality and the fiction portrayed on the media. They argue that the media does not cause young people to behave in antisocial ways. In their view, other factors are responsible. While other factors do have a bearing on the behaviour of young people (and many are listed above), the fact remains that the media does affect young people profoundly. It is interesting how the media on the one hand proclaims that its programming has no effect on people, and on the other hand persuades advertisers to spend billions of dollars on advertising campaigns whose purpose is to affect the behaviour of its viewers. Either media has an effect or it does not. Advertisers obviously believe in its effect enough to invest a lot of money on it.

Nevertheless, it is not just a question of softheaded young people misled by a slick, crafty media, although some of that may be true. Modern young people are no more softheaded than any other generation, and are perfectly capable of making personal judgments about reality. What the media does is give people permission to think and behave in ways which might not have seemed possible before. Reality follows art. Just as people in the sixteenth century believed what they were reading, people in the twenty-first believe what they are watching. What beliefs is the television audience assimilating, and how are these beliefs affecting behaviour?

MYTHS CREATE MEANING AND PURPOSE

It would be hard to over state the significance of social acceptance for young people. The telephone is a lifeline to social acceptance: "Why doesn't it ring - maybe they don't like me any more - what is everybody doing?" Sometimes the phone just stops ringing and its silence is deafening. Nothing can be more critical because acceptance and rejection are at stake here. There are more deaths than physical death, and for young people marginalization is social death. Rejection happens, and it can be sudden and unequivocal: "You are not acceptable - go away!"

As they grow, young people face a barrage of challenges related to their personal identity, their place in the social structure, and the meaning and purpose of their lives. They have to resolve many issues related to conflict, rivalry, and place in the social pecking order. These issues demand quick decisions from them. They turn to the mythical structures of their society for guidance and permission. Myths tell them - in ways their parents and schools cannot - what is acceptable and what is not acceptable.

While teaching a grade ten social studies class, I had been trying to help students become more aware of how their basic assumptions affect the way they perceive reality. We had spent time observing and discussing a variety of situations in which peoples' perceptions were affected by surrounding circumstances. We had also examined several historical eras in which perception had shifted. As well, the students had studied the psychology of perception, and related it to the examples above. The students had an extensive background in perception before they were involved in the following exercise.

I had my sixteen-year-old daughter record a series of television commercials on video tape. I asked the class to view and analyze them. The intent was to increase student awareness of advertising techniques to help them become critical viewers of television. We viewed and discussed a variety of commercials. Initially, the process generated quite a lot of animated discussion. Finally, we analyzed a well-done lawn mower commercial in detail. The students were quite perceptive about the advertising techniques used and needed little coaching in defining them. They quickly picked out the techniques and analyzed the reasons for their use.

As a final exercise, I thought I would have the class re-examine a Coke commercial I had shown earlier. It was one of a series in which Coke had used famous rock singers to sing "Coke songs". Some of the songs had actually done very well on the pop charts. This commercial contained one of those. When the commercial came on, the class, as they had done the first time they watched it, began to sway in time to the music and then began to sing along. "Fine", I thought, "now we will be able to examine something they obviously enjoy, and I know they have the conceptual tools to do it." I began the process of encouraging them to probe and analyze the Coke commercial. They would not do it. The more I pushed, the more resistant and angrier they became. As far as they were concerned, I was an "old guy" who just wanted to criticize their culture and way of life, and they were not going to play my game. They refused to accept what they considered my frivolous analysis of something they believed to be significant and moving. They could do the critical analysis; that was not the problem. Their problem was the reduction of significant parts of their culture to sociological babble. They were right to resist.

Myths Are the Source of Our Fundamental Beliefs

The issue here is to determine the role the media plays in the lives of students. On the rational, cognitive level, students can be critical of what they view, but on the emotional, subjective level, they may choose not to be critical or they are unable to be critical. We must remember that emotions provide meaning and emphasis in our lives.[14] Reason and cognition are tools which can perform certain critical thinking jobs for us if we choose to use them. My students could adamantly choose not to use their reasoning tools on the Coke commercial. It is at this attitudinal level people are given permission to think and behave in certain ways by the significant myth builders in their lives. Whether they like it or not, the media are significant myth builders. Ultimately, they will have to be accountable for the myths they impose upon society.[15]

There is evidence that television helped to spread the anti-Communist revolution in Eastern European countries. Romanians, when they discovered they were to be denied the political changes they were seeing on television, were outraged and stimulated to revolt against the communist regime.[16] Other examples, such as the role of television in the Vietnam war and the Gulf War are instructive. During the Vietnam war, television reporters were relatively free to report the events of the war as they found them. In the Gulf War, the military actively circumscribed the ability of television to report events freely. The level of criticism by the media on the conduct of the Vietnam war was quite different from that of the Gulf War.[17] Among the public, the resultant attitude to these wars was also quite different.

We should not be surprised then that young people have been profoundly affected by the thousands of hours of television they have watched. What we may not clearly understand are the ways in which this influence is manifested. A very significant way is on the level of myth. We uncritically accept many stories, explanations, and descriptions of significant aspects of reality. These are myths. Santa Claus is a myth told to us as children. Many times, these stories and explanations come from sources we trust, and are things we want to believe. Because they sound plausible, we base our lives on the assumptions contained in the stories and explanations. Adults continue to propagate the myth of Santa Claus with their children because adults enjoy it. In the propagation process, it is not uncommon for people (and societies) to adapt and twist the myth to suit their personal needs. No shopping mall would be complete at Christmas without a Santa Claus accompanied by a photographer.

Over time, myths change and adapt to suit new conditions. Many changes and additions have been made to the celebration of Christmas. For many people, Christmas is more than a myth: it is a sacred, holy reality. However, that has not prevented people from adding myths to the Christmas celebration. There is little evidence to suggest that Christ was born on December 25. What was happening, around December 25 was a major Roman festival celebrating the return of the sun. Early Christians just hooked the celebration of the birth of Christ to that festival, and it stuck. Much of our approach to Christmas comes from the Victorian era. They built many of the myths defining our view of Christmas. It was we in the

Twentieth century who developed myths like Rudolph the Red Nosed Reindeer and the Three Chipmunks. From the vantage point of 2000 years of history, Rudolph seems like a fairly recent addition to the array of Christmas myths. From the vantage point of a young child, Rudolph has always been there. This is the process of myth building.

The Modern Media is a Source of Myths

Television is a major source of modern myths. In the world of television, life consists of 25 to 50 minute dramas where problems are resolved neatly, dramatically, and romantically. They teach an expectation or myth about the way social reality ought to work. Young people learn a view of social reality from the media. Adolescents are particularly prone to adopting assumptions from the myths they see. They have a powerful need to find ideas and beliefs that make sense of the reality in which they find themselves. They borrow ideas from those aspects of the culture they find meaningful and trustworthy in order to create a personal knowledge base they can depend upon.

Adolescents must define identities that are separate and distinct from those of their parents. Without that, they cannot become their own person. This is a critical process necessary for growing into independent, mature adults. For a time, adolescents need to be critical and rejecting of the values and institutions of their parents. Everything from the older generation is 'tainted' and suspect. This mindset makes them prey to the manipulative propaganda of interests who appear to be 'new', 'with it', 'modern' or whatever the current 'in thing' is

The Conflict between Belief and Scepticism

A profound problem is the conflict arising from the need to suspend disbelief in order to enter into the world created by artists on stage, movies, books, etc. This problem is central to what students will really learn in the classroom. Can one become enthralled with something and still retain one's ability to be critical of it? It is a significant problem, because if students find something so meaningful they are motivated to make it a focus of their lives, can they retain some objectivity about it? All of us willingly set aside our critical faculties and pretend we are part of another world for a time. At some point we have to leave that imaginary world and rejoin the 'real' world, where we critique and analyze reality in order to decide what it means for us. How do we draw this balance in the classroom?

In the realm of myth, the transformation of one's mindset from suspension of disbelief to scepticism is a difficult one to make. An anthropologist recalls how he was watching a group of Aboriginal Peoples performing a religious ceremony.

Their body language was tentative and embarrassed as they kept checking to see what the audience thought of their performance. He could tell that the performers had become full of doubt about the validity of their myths. They were embarrassed and sceptical about what they were doing. Gone was the joy in surrendering to a belief system that explained everything beautifully. How can people preserve their precious mythical assumptions if everything has to be subject to doubt and criticism? My students were facing this problem when I asked them to analyze the Coke commercial.

A few years back a tragedy was exposed in an orphanage for boys in Newfoundland. Over a long period, their caregivers had sexually abused their young charges. People across Canada were outraged. The caregivers, who are innocent until proven guilty under the assumptions of our criminal justice system, were to be tried by judge and jury. Before the case could come to court, the Canadian Broadcasting Corporation prepared a docudrama of the event and was ready to run it on the national network. Mixing the two formats, documentary and drama, caused a controversy about whether the docudrama would jeopardize the defendants' right to a fair trial. Could people, after suspending disbelief while watching the docudramatization, objectively evaluate the guilt or innocence of the caregivers? It was a serious enough concern the that courts enjoined the CBC from broadcasting the docudrama before the trial.

This is a conflict between the fundamental beliefs of Canadian society: our myths in other words. We want to protect children from exploitation. We want people to have a fair trial. We believe we have the right to know what really happened at the emotional level as well as the factual level. How can these conflicting issues be resolved? It was a struggle for Canadian society. This is exactly the kind of problem young people have to resolve if they are to be educated beyond the merely factual level.

OUR EMOTIONS ARE GUIDES TO SIGNIFICANCE

We cannot make decisions about the significance of reality without recourse to our emotions. "Just the facts Ma'am" is not good enough. We need to have the complete context: factual, emotional, philosophical, ethical, etc before we can decide what we believe about a situation. The problem is that once we take an emotional position on something we are tempted to reject any other point of view about it. We keep what fits and discard the rest. This is why those who argue for objectivity reject the emotional in favour of the factual. The problem with this approach is that the emotional is also factual. It is a fact that emotions play a role in everything we do. Ignoring them does not bring us closer to the truth.

In the classroom, ignoring emotions gets one farther from the truth, in the sense that students stop searching for truth. Without emotions, the search seems pointless. Helping students search for truth becomes a dilemma, because too much emotion will also halt the search for truth. Students make up their minds prematurely and refuse to look any further. This is a defensive position by those who feel vulnerable about their beliefs. There is another level of understanding where the defensiveness begins to dissipate as feelings of vulnerability lessen.

Discovering Meaning

John Updike has said that for him, as a child, the Saturday afternoon movie was a religious experience. Sitting in the quiet and dark of the theatre, he confronted all the questions of meaning and purpose, truth and dishonesty, beauty and ugliness, honour and dishonour, morality and immorality. The classroom needs to deal with these realities. I remember occasions in a grade eleven history classroom, when - as part of a study of the causes and effects of World War I - we watched an old grainy print of *All Quiet on the Western Front.* I learned not to turn the lights on too rapidly at the end of the film. For a moment, students needed the privacy of a dark room to compose themselves and prepare their public faces.

For many students this old film was a powerful, moving experience, which would likely only happen in a classroom situation. Classrooms can and should provide opportunities for epiphanies. This kind of experience is about more than objective facts, although facts are obviously important. An epiphany is a synthesis of experiences, emotions, beliefs, beauty, self-sacrifice, dignity, etc. that strikes the individual in an overwhelming, convicting way. An epiphany leaves individuals with an insight that appears to be truth. It is only after the experience that individuals can unpack and evaluate for themselves why an epiphany must be true.

Students need opportunities to evaluate meaningful experiences so that they may create rationales with which they can feel secure. Such processes allow them to decide what they believe, and why they believe it. The establishment of a fundamental principle or value will have been achieved in the student's belief system. In further discussion or debate, the student will feel better able to defend the value position(s) they have taken. Then they do not feel so much under attack. Students can now discuss how the principle can be applied to different situations rather than whether the principle is true or untrue. Modern media presents many opportunities to initiate this kind of process.

UNDERSTANDING THE DIFFERENCE BETWEEN MYTH AND REALITY

For many people (and not just young people) the media mythologizes those they see. One can cite example after example at random beginning with Frank Sinatra, moving to Elvis, the Beatles, Madonna, Princess Di and so on. In the minds of students, the characters and the stars playing the characters form a media mythology larger than life. They are not people with real lives and real problems. This is not true, of course. They are all too human, and are subject to the same follies as the rest of us.

The culture of the media is a human culture as much as any other segment of culture is human. Students need to understand that. They need to know that aspects of movie making can be as mundane and boring as classroom activities. Someone once noted an important ability for a member of the Royal Family is to have an infinite capacity not to go to the bathroom. Day after day of being on parade can take its toll. Students need help in putting the media into perspective without feeling their culture has been attacked. It is not so much what students think about the stars that is important, but what they think about themselves. It is the role of education to help students believe they are personally worthwhile, and can be as creative and live as exciting lives as media stars. It is student acceptance of the myth of personal inferiority and subservience that needs to be attacked, not the students or their culture.

CONSIDERATIONS IN USING MODERN TECHNOLOGY IN THE CLASSROOM

Students must have direct personal experience in using modern technology before they will be able to comprehend the implications of its use. As that comprehension grows, they will gain a better understanding of the power of media in creating and propagating myths. They will begin to realize that the myths they see in the media are human creations, and more importantly, they can create and understand them as well as anyone. In this way, students can gain some perspective about modern culture without feeling attacked. It will allow them to step back from it and evaluate for themselves what they are going to accept and what they are going to reject.

Students need to feel that their culture is valid and worthy of serious discussion. The establishment of a basic level of trust about cultural expression will help students feel less defensive about their way of expressing themselves. Classrooms need to give up their fixation with 'good' literature, and instead focus on helping young people determine meaning in their culture. If that means the Soaps, then so be it. If we believe the Soaps are immature claptrap, ignoring them or railing at them will do no more good than my attempt to analyze the Coke commercial. Students need to meet the Soaps on their own terms.

One approach would be to have a class watch enough of a Soap series to understand the characterization and plot so that the students can discuss (in groups) and make predictions about the future course of events in their Soap. Soaps move so slowly that students would easily have time to consider the plot, write a prediction and present their alternatives to the class.

What is important here is encouraging students to be active rather than passive participants. They can do this by looking at characters and the situations and projecting a course of action. At some point in the process, students will discover a capacity, in their terms, to be critical of the characters and the plots. They then will learn to discuss the assumptions of the characters, their flaws, the reality of the situation, and make some personal judgments about the Soaps. But, without this process, our rants against the Soaps will make little difference to students truly committed to them.

Movies are no longer new technology, but they are treated as such by the schools. Movies as literature are still considered secondary to other forms of literature. This is the case, partly because they are seen as 'frivolous' and partly because they are not print. The bias that information in print is more serious than information in video continues. Hence the belief that Shakespearian plays should be presented to students as a print medium. The assumption behind this approach is that Shakespeare in print is more serious and profound than as a play on the movie screen. Is Shakespeare about profundity or entertainment? When one watches *Much Ado About Nothing* on stage or in movie format, it really seems to be much ado about nothing: on about the same intellectual level as a Bill Murray screwball comedy. If Shakespeare were alive today, he would fit into Hollywood very well. It is not so strange then that Shakespeare's work can be presented remarkably well by movie technology. Shakespeare was an impresario who knew he had to entertain if he wanted to attract an audience. Shakespeare would probably like a fair chance to work his magic in the classroom.

If you are studying Shakespeare, have the students in groups discuss how they are going to portray a scene, plan it and rehearse it. Have the students film their scenes and then share their efforts with the rest of the class. Fortunately, simple video equipment is relatively inexpensive and readily available. For example, get some videocameras and start making movies with the students. It would now be possible to have a serious critical discussion about how a particular Shakespearian work should be portrayed. At the end of the exercise, hold an Academy Awards ceremony - filmed of course - so the students can see themselves on television receiving their hard-earned awards.

Often we watch movies with our minds in neutral. The unreality often has as much to do with what is not portrayed about characters and the way in which they are not held accountable for their behaviour. The characters and the situations in movies and television can be made more realistic. Pick some incidents from a video and discuss the events not portrayed on the screen. What are the mundane parts to the screen lives of the characters they watch: what do they eat, where do they buy their ammunition, how did they deal with the insurance companies and the police after a high speed chase, what was James Bond's childhood like, did he go to Sunday School, how often does he call his mom, and so on? Have the students write and share their speculations about an interview with an insurance adjuster after a high-speed chase, or pick one of the minor characters who were killed and write a scenario of how someone would explain to the family why their father is dead.

Students also need to look at the lives of the stars themselves. What does Madonna do for a hobby? What is life like on the road for a rock star: how do they get their clothes washed? How does it feel to be on stage in front of 100 000 people? Does the lack of privacy matter? Students need to understand that there is a context to the human condition that no one can escape. It would have been almost impossible to believe n the 1940s, but Frank Sinatra did get old and die. So will Madonna, and she will have to deal with that reality. So will the students.

The problem is schools impose a university ethos of literary criticism on students. The belief seems to be that Shakespeare must be justified as serious literature rather than as delightful entertainment. Students will not readily accept the myth of literary criticism any more than they would accept my critique of their beloved Coke commercial. We need to pay attention to that conflict and search out ways that will allow them to enjoy and still be critical of what they are hearing and learning in the media.

There are some examples of how this might be done. If the electronic media continues to grow and will eventually be the dominant method of transmitting information - which seems likely - then students will need to know how to use that medium effectively. Should students be concentrating on writing essays, stories, and so forth in print, or should they be learning to do documentaries, plays, etc on video tape? Learning to make a documentary or a drama or a comedy is to learn a set of communication techniques. It is through learning these techniques that students learn to be critical about what they hear and see on television. It is a similar argument to that used for the need to learn to write well. By actually writing one learns to be a more critical and appreciative consumer of other writing. Just as one becomes a good writer by reading the work of others, one can become a better producer of television and movie material by watching the productions of others.

A similar argument can be made for learning to be critical viewers of the prevailing societal myths. Students need to understand that media create and impose myths. Good drama does that. People go into the theatre and willingly suspend disbelief. Students need to understand how the creators of movies are able to further the process of suspending disbelief. Students can learn to do that early in their careers. There are drama teachers who successfully help their students take a drama production from the initial brainstorming phase, through script writing, mounting the production, and performing it before an audience. High school students are quite capable of all these skills. This process could be repeated with any of the media. In fact, television studios could be made available to high schools so that students would have an opportunity to learn and use that media. It is only as students witness the power of good television editing to substantially change the meaning of a text will they really began to understand the propaganda power of television.[18]

The fundamental issue for education is to create classrooms which are active rather than passive. Active classrooms, if they are to be successful, must work with where students are, not where the schools would like them to be. That means recognizing students come to the classroom with a culture and with learning needs they want satisfied. By doing this, the so-called problem of declining attention spans may turn out to be a chimera caused by the failure of the schools to adapt to new realities.

You may recall that we began this discussion with an attempt to define an educated person as a way of determining the vision and mission for education. We examined an example of a vision for education outlined by the Conference Board of Canada. The Conference Board correctly noted that students have to become life long learners to meet the demands of modern culture. It was noted that lifelong learning presupposes a high degree of motivation for and commitment to learning. If schools are unwilling to adapt to the changing realities of communications technology, then they are not going to be successful at instilling lifelong learning.

A variety of educational techniques can be used to implement he vision many in society have for learning. So far we have only explored these possibilities anecdotally as examples of the need for change and of the possibilities for successful lifelong learning. In the next chapters, we will discuss in detail that is more specific some of the things schools can do to make education a meaningful experience for students.

END NOTES

1. A.C. Nielsen and Company.
(http://www.csun.edu/science/health/docs/tv&health.html#tv_stats)

2. A. C. Nielsen and Company. *Personal Communication.* 1992.
(http://www.ed.gov/pubs/OR/ConsumerGuides/tv.html)

3. Thompson, F.T. & Austin, W.P. *Television viewing and academic achievement revisited.* Education. 2003. pp. 124, 194-203.

Razel, M. *The complex model of television viewing and educational achievement.* Journal of Educational Research. 94. 2001. pp. 371-379.

4. Clark, C.S. *TV Violence.* CQ Rrsearcher 3. 12, Mar 26 1993. pp. 167-187.
Funk, J.B. Reevaluating the Impact of Video Games. Clinical Pediatrics 32.
2 Feb 1993. pp. 86-90. PS 521 243.

5. Cotton, K. *Instructional Reinforcement.* Close-Up No. 3. Portland, OR: Northwest Regional Educational Laboratory. 1988.

Craig, W., Peters, R. and Konarski, R. *Bullying and Victimization Among Canadian School Children.* The Working Paper Series for the Applied Research Branch, Human Resources Development Canada. Hull, Qc: October, 1998.

Craig, W. and Harel, Y. (2004). "Bullying, Physical Fighting and Victimization" (pp. 133-144) in Currie et al (Eds.) *Young People's Health in Context: Health Behaviour in School-Aged Children (HBSC)* Study, International Report from the 2001/2002 Survey. World Health Organization.

6. In her paper, Megan Mullen comments that McLuhan "wishes to argue, rather, that as humans bring new media technologies into our lives, the ways we adapt those technologies to our needs help shape future practices and needs. Indeed, existing technologies do call for future technologies - but without the uses determined by humans, surely not by the technologies themselves, there would be no development whatsoever. McLuhan also makes the strong assertion that 'The *content* of any medium is always another medium . . . [but] the *message* of any medium or technology is the change of scale or pace or pattern it introduces into human affairs.' "

Megan Mullen, "Coming to Terms with the Future He Foresaw: Marshall McLuhan's Understanding Media", Technology and Culture: The Journal for the Society for the History of Technology Volume 47 Number 2. April 2006. She references Marshall McLuhan *Understanding Media: the Extensions of Man* (New York, 1964) pp.23-24.

7. N. Postman. *Amusing ourselves to death.* New York: Viking Penguin. 1985
N. Postman. *The Disappearance of Childhood.* New York: Delacorte Press. 1982

8. McLuhan argued the Renaissance represents a shift from a primarily oral/aural way of perceiving the world to a primarily visual or literate one. He says language that is centred on the spoken word is aural, impermanent, rhythmic, subjective, inaccurate, resonant, time centred, participatory, and communal. The written word, by contrast, is visual, permanent, fixed, ordered, objective, abstract, space centred, detached, timeless, and individualistic. Therefore, the thinking of literate humans tends to be logical, visual, linear, fluid and anti literal.

McLuhan believed the impact of modern, electronic media is to "re-emphasize the rich totality of human experience." People in a "phonocentric" society favour oral culture over a literate one.

Postman also recognized this phenomenon, but sees it more negatively. Both Postman and McLuhan believed it was no accident that the Age of Reason was co-existent with the growth of a print culture, but it was Postman who argued television has a negative effect on culture as a whole, because it destroys the ability for logical thought, which was fostered by a print culture.

9. Ruth Finnegan. *Communication and Technology* in Open University Course D101: *Making Sense of Society,* Unit 8, Block 3, Communication. 1978.

10. Steve Wulf, 'More Air Goes Out of Baseball." *Time Magazine*, March 20, 1995.

11. Joe L. Frost. *Revisiting Early Childhood Education.* New York: Holt, Rinehart and Winston Inc. 1973). pp 200-201.

12. *Toronto Globe and Mail.* Nov. 27, 1987

13. We had looked at the psychology of perception and then had studied such historical eras as the Renaissance, the Reformation, French Revolution, Industrial revolution, etc. We had looked at all of these using the concept of paradigm and its relationship to shifting perception.

14. Daniel Goleman. *Emotional Intelligence* New York: Bantam Books. p.53. Golemsn recounts the story of a young man who - because of neural surgery had lost contact with the emotional centres of his brain. His cognitive abilities remained unimpaired, but he could attach no emotional significance or value to the different possibilities he faced. As a result he could not make good decisions.

15. It is important to remember the dramatic concept of suspension of disbelief in this context. Every night, people go to movies, and for a couple of hours they suspend their disbelief. The question here is when this suspension stops. There have been some studies showing peoples' driving to be more aggressive and risk taking after watching a movie portraying that kind of driving. To what extent are people being given permission to practice certain kinds of behaviour by the media?

16. The dictatorial government of Burma (CSPD) has erected many different barriers to the media, because they do not want the people of Burma to know what is happening in the outside world. Even knowing about democracy is considered to be subversive, let alone watching it nightly on CNN.

17. The Disney Corporation has amassed a fortune making, using, and propagating myths. One need only spend a small amount of time in any of the various Disney Worlds to see this.

18. CBC has produced an excellent documentary series for the schools in which they show how sophisticated technology is used to completely change the meaning of video footage without the viewer being aware of it.

Chapter Four: Life Long Learning

Education is what remains when we have forgotten all that we have been taught.

George Savile

Table of Contents

The Concept of Working Memory

A working memory can recall information to consciousness for one reason or another. It may be only a memory that more information is available somewhere on a topic. It may be useful information about how to do things or where to find things. It may be information that reminds us how we felt in certain situations, or reminders we have stored to warn us about certain situations. It is the information we rely on when we consider how to approach a situation. Other information not meeting these tests tends to be lost (not voluntarily retrievable) somewhere in the brain. It is remarkable how the name of a person to whom we have just been introduced does not meet the test of becoming part of a working memory. Placing and keeping information in a working memory is a problem for all of us.

The concept of working memory has important implications for determining what learning is and whether it has occurred. Traditionally, the purpose of education was to give students a broad array of knowledge so their minds would have a fund of information to use as needed in their future lives. It was hoped that they would remember and appreciate phrases like "Out, damned spot! Out, I say!" when they encounter them at some point in the future. The problem with the traditional approach is that students forget most of the information they were taught. Much of traditional teaching is a waste of student and teacher time because students remember so little of the information they are taught. The concept of working memory suggests that school systems should carefully reconsider what they teach and how they teach it.

What Do We Mean by Learning?

A teacher says, "I taught that three times, and the students still do not know it." Is teaching without learning an oxymoron? Perhaps nothing was taught in the first place? The problem of learning from the standpoint of working memory becomes quite complex. Traditionally, the process of committing material to memory, reciting it, and successfully practicing the material in some way was considered learning. With this type of learning in place, at some point in the future students would be reminded of the material they had learned, and would be able to recall and use it in some way. Sometimes that works, many times it does not. Studies show that students forget as much as 90 percent of the information they learn in this way.

In the last chapter the notion of life long learning was being touted as the more useful definition of learning. It seems likely that life long learning related to any subject requires taught material finding its way into the working memory somehow. In Chapter Nine, we will discuss the concept of 'gist' as the primary vehicle for that process. Suffice it to say here that some material makes it into working memories, seemingly permanently, as the gist of an idea. As we shall see in Chapter Nine, this is a significantly different process than memorization.

As a means of determining whether the information taught has become part of the working memory - and thus capable of becoming a life long learning, working memory - could be tested as a means of evaluating teaching methodologies. After a period of time has elapsed (say one year), students could be tested in a variety of ways to determine the ratios of remembered material to forgotten material. The teaching methodologies used in teaching information to students would bea significant variable that could be analysed. Does the teaching methodology used play a significant role in determining whether information becomes part of a working memory or whether it is forgotten? Once one establishes a ratio of remembered material to forgotten material among students, do certain teaching methodologies make a significant difference in the ratio?

One could also test for differences in information taught. What effect does the type of information have on the ratio? Once that had been established satisfactorily, then questions could be asked about why certain methodologies and information perform better than other methodologies and information.

As we shall see in a moment, the other problem is how we associate peripheral, often emotional memories with learning certain kinds of information. Many students remember history as unending boredom. What is stored in their working memories is a personal warning to never ever put yourself in the position of having to do anything with history if you can avoid it.

Finally, we need to consider whether information found in the working memory is a valid indicator of learning. Can one argue that the only material students have truly learned is the material they can recall and use from their working memories? A good case can be made for that point of view. In terms of educational productivity, it is information found in one's working memory which is useful and productive. For example, it is the mathematical information found in working memory that defines one's understanding of mathematics, and determines whether one can apply it to current problems in life. The competence of a doctor in an emergency ward is defined by her/his working memory, not by the memory that a needed procedure was studied sometime in the past and can be found in a certain textbook. A much more stringent definition of learning is the ability to recall and apply information from working memory to a specific situation as needed.

Implications for the Development of a Working Memory

At this point, we should consider some other types of learning and their relationship to life long learning. The behaviourists see learning as responses to stimuli, which become more and more habitual as those responses are reinforced. Many basic assumptions and values are learned because they have been strongly reinforced by our emotions. These assumptions and emotions in turn govern how we see and respond to reality. They are learned at the unconscious level, and even though they are not conscious, they are part of working memory because they have the capacity to affect our conscious thought processes. We have developed feelings, needs, and intuitions influencing our responses to various situations. This level of learning happens regularly, and is highly significant in our behaviour.

Another type of learning, known as cognitive learning, enables people to evaluate and make conscious choices about their personal behaviour. It is a process of comprehending and storing concepts, skills, and values in one's working memory which can be consciously applied to reality as needed. One reality it must be applied to is those unconscious assumptions supported by emotions, which so powerfully affect our thinking and behaviour. Sophisticated thinking requires the capacity to reflect on one's personal thought processes. Critically evaluating our thought processes and the assumptions they are based on is metacognition. It represents a juncture between unconscious and conscious thinking.

Learning is a process that ultimately results in the storage of information considered significant in the working memory. Emotions play a large role in determining what is significant. When they reinforce a stimulus powerfully, that stimulus is much more likely to be included in the working memory. The development of a working memory is dependent upon information being used many times, continually reinforced in behaviourist terms. Emotions play a role in that they can reward people for using and reusing certain pieces of information. Because of the reward factor individuals enjoy using and reusing information over and over. The clearest example is of children at play with new ideas. This is why play is such a powerful learning tool. This process can work in a negative sense as well. An individual avoids stress and pain by using certain pieces of information. Individuals get great satisfaction in being able to manage their lives in ways which minimize pain and increase satisfaction. Sometimes this may be a useful process in the sense of learning effective social skills. Other times, this may be very detrimental when strategies of procrastination or drug use are developed and employed. All of these processes have the capacity to become significant parts of personal working memories.

Cognition plays an important role in organizing ideas into chains where one idea links to another. Metaphorically speaking, the mind creates a kind of card catalogue of ideas or concepts linked together into a pattern, so that remembering one idea stimulates the memory of another idea. Whole patterns of ideas leap into being - so to speak - triggering certain ideas in the mind. Because of this process, one's personal working memory can also be somewhat stereotypical. Once one knows and understands a person well, it is often easy to predict accurately likely responses under different situations.

THE PURPOSE OF EDUCATION

If we assume the purpose of education is to provide students with useful and relevant information they can use for the rest of their lives, the concept of working memory raises a number of issues for consideration. The purpose of education should help students develop working memories in ways which encourage them to participate in life long learning. Students typically ask why they have to study a particular piece of information. If they found the information relevant in some way it is unlikely they would be asking this question. Many times teachers struggle to come up with a more adequate answer than saying "your culture has determined this is really important information which you must know, so be-patient and you will understand why when you get older" or "you are really going to need to know this when you go to university." Despite the ubiquity of these answers in the classroom, they really are not very useful in motivating a desire for life long learning.

Buried in this exchange is a fundamental issue for education. Whose purpose should be served by the education enterprise: cultural preservation or student need? As was noted in Chapter One, cultural preservation has always been considered a primary purpose of education. Such a focus obscures issues raised by concepts like working memory, which as we will see has to focus on student need.

Cultural preservationists assume the exposure of young people to information ensures they will learn the material. They also assume exposing students to information will stimulate them to want to learn more; and if it has not, the fault lies with the student. The problem is not entirely with traditional information (Shakespeare can be highly entertaining). It has much more to do with the purpose, attitudes and style of the presenters, who believe the information they are presenting is so significant that young people will obediently learn the information because it is good for them.

There are some serious problems with any approach, which ignores student need. Young people now - more than ever - have access to a variety of information. They can make choices about what they learn. Schools have to compete with all the other sources of information in the media market place. Schools no longer have the luxury of putting a young person's questions off with a patronizing comment about understanding the significance of a piece of information after the student matures. Much of the information presented in this way simply will not gain access to the working memory, except as a memory of a bad experience with learning. It is those bad memories we are so careless about. They are devastating to life long learning because they establish the basic unconscious assumptions about learning that last a lifetime.

Another problem with the cultural preservationist approach is that many students often do not master the information well enough to make it part of their working memories. First year instructors of mathematics complain about students in their math classes who do not know the basic algebraic concepts they were taught in secondary school, probably only the year before. The concepts are not only gone from the students' working memories, they are gone from their recognition memories. It is as if the students had never been exposed to the concepts. Everyone is frustrated: the student who may fail mathematics 100, the university instructor who is reteaching elementary concepts, and the secondary school math teacher whose reputation as a teacher is on the line.

The Relationship of the Learning Process to the Purpose of Education

What has gone wrong? Rather than play the blame game, it is more productive to ask some questions about the learning process and attempt to relate that to the larger purposes of schooling. Actually, this is not entirely an either/or question in the sense of either relevance or cultural preservation. There are important ideas in our culture that need to be preserved, and should be able to compete in the media market. What does need to happen is to change the presentation of information, so that students can see a reason for retaining it in their working memories.

The traditional argument is to say that students need to study subjects such as chemistry systematically so they can use them in their future lives (typical parental and student reasoning justifies taking courses like chemistry on the basis that students may need chemistry at some point in their post-secondary training). The reality for most of us is we will never know enough chemistry to be able to do any meaningful work with it. Unless we are prepared to do the necessary work to become a chemist, we will have to rely on knowledgeable, well-trained chemists to provide us with that kind of information. So, what is the ultimate utility of learning chemistry for most people? Is it enough to say that it prepared them for the college of medicine at some university? What about the other students who do not go on to science oriented careers?

Does learning a few concepts of chemistry and gaining some experience with laboratory skills teach enough about the scientific values inherent in chemistry to warrant the time a student spends learning chemistry? Depending on how it is taught, it can be a very useful subject. The real test is the information that makes it into the working memory and the usefulness of that information to the future lives of students. Subjects like chemistry can be taught in ways that add significant pieces of information to an individual's life. For example, what role do chemicals play in the environment, and how do they affect our health? What role does chemistry play in good nutrition? It is possible to teach chemistry in a way that adds useful information as well as a basic knowledge of chemistry to a student's working memory.

THE POWER OF PERSONAL WORKING MEMORIES

Students come to school with working memories filled with information they have been gathering and retaining since birth. That information describes and defines reality for them. People learn many models of reality, which they use to understand the world they live in. All of these models make up their personal culture, and is the basis for their worldview .

Language would be a good example of how personal working memories affect worldview and learning. An obviously significant part of peoples' working memories would be the language (dialect) they learned in early childhood. In effect, they have developed a personal model of language with a vocabulary and a set of grammatical rules, which tells them what is proper in language expression. Their personal models of language might be different in important ways from the Standard English dialect.

It is important to remember that these models also include attitudes about the significance of ideas like language for their lives. They may have decided long ago that reading and writing is irrelevant, or that they are not competent to do those things. All of these attitudes and information affect their responses when they are taught a grammar that runs counter to their personal model of grammar. Students tend to reject a new grammar. They are much more comfortable with their personal working models. It is important to remember that this process occurs in areas other than language. Driver training is a significant example. It can also apply to subjects like history where students come with nationalistic, ethnocentric, possibly racist views about relationships among people in the past and present.

FACTORS AFFECTING THE DEVELOPMENT OF A WORKING MEMORY

What is critical to understand here is that people accept new information into their working memories based on how well it fits with what is already there.

Existing information in the working memory has priority over new information. New information running counter to well accepted and established information (which is there because it has proven useful to the individual in a variety of ways) is likely to be discounted and ignored (forgotten). New Information is much more likely to be retained when it can build on the existing information in an individual's working memory.

Working memories are developed through an interactive process of receiving information and then applying it to a variety of situations. The most critical stage in developing a working memory comes when the learner considers what has been learned in the application process. It is this point - when the working memory broadens and deepens with new information - that may become part of the learner's permanent repertoire of useful information.

There are many examples of this process at work. Theoretical pedagogy is often taught to beginning teachers. It is a testament to the power of early experiences that when many young teachers begin to teach, they teach the way they were taught rather than attempting to apply the teaching models they learned in their education classes. Some other kinds of learning must occur before unfamiliar teaching methodologies are available in usable form as a working memory. It is through the actual experiences of teaching and being coached by a mentor in a classroom that young teachers begin to develop a pedagogical working memory beyond that of their personal experiences of teaching as pupils.

What is it about early learning that is so powerful? One simple answer is that it got into the working memory first. Early learning receives 'squatter's rights' in the working memory. More seriously, a number of factors determine what is and is not retained. First and foremost, we copy the behaviour of those who model complex behaviour for us. We watch what others do, and if their model appears to work - and we decide we are capable of that behaviour - then we adopt the model. A powerful teaching tool is the process of visualization. If the learner is encouraged to visualize him or herself performing some action positively and constructively, the learner is likely to learn and retain that behaviour. Much of this is done with very little conscious, analytical thought. These processes are a significant part of childrens' play. In play, children experiment with and adopt complex behaviour as their own. The model of behaviour they adopt becomes the 'right' one, the 'only' one, and anything else will come to seem 'foreign' and 'unusual' deserving rejection. A new idea that is in conflict with an existing model has an uphill battle in being accepted.

Secondly, information being learned has to be meaningful and useful. If it is, it will likely be reused repeatedly. We know that the more something is reviewed, the more it will be retained. Material learned in an active hands on process is more likely to be retained in the working memory. People learn by doing things. Learning is an active process of refining and practicing new ideas in order to discover what works. It is an adult version of what children do as they play. This idea is contained in the concept of recreation. To understand this idea, think of the word as re-creation. People when they play are re-creating reality in their minds. An example might be people playing/learning with/about their new computer. Re-creation is interesting and enjoyable: that is what the word has come to stand for in the culture.

Thirdly, what we place in our working memory has significant emotional context. We learn well those things that are important to us emotionally. If boredom is the dominant emotional context in learning, this does not bode well for its future in the learner's working memory. On the other hand, if a piece of information seems very significant for the individual's personal wellbeing and has been interesting and exciting, it is highly likely the information will be retained.

All of these factors have the power to act as mental screens. Certain kinds of information make it through the screens and others are disallowed. When my son was around eleven years of age, he had the bad luck of living through the escalation of the Cold War during Ronald Reagan's presidency. We finally had to make sure he did not watch the news because all the 'sabre rattling' going on upset him so badly. Because he had no way of putting the information in perspective, he would become terrified at the prospect of World War III breaking out during the night. For a long time his working model of international relations consisted of powerful men who were prepared to hurt people in order to get their way. It is not a completely inaccurate perspective, just a limited one. The problem for my son was that no other perspective on international relations could get through his emotional screens.

Creating Complex Working Memories

It is a multifaceted process to learn and assimilate large complex bodies of information into one's working memory. It requires the development of complex thinking abilities. Concepts have to be learned which have the power to create meaningful thought patterns. Skills have to be learned which can organize information usefully. In addition, criteria (values) have to be learned which serve as the basis for evaluating information and skills. Concepts, skills, and values have to be generalized in the working memory so that an individual is able to deal constructively with the many different situations of day to day life.

When these abilities have been accomplished, then the learner is in a position to evaluate alternative pieces of information consciously and decide what is worthy of retention. However, until this level of thinking has been achieved, thinking will remain an automatic, unconscious process. When students are able to evaluate information, they have taken a giant step toward life long learning.

Eventually my son learned to do this very well, but that is a story for another section later in the book.

It requires commitment and dedication on the part of students, teachers, and communities to create this kind of learning. Students have to be prepared to take an active role in the process of comprehending information. Comprehension involves understanding concepts and knowing which abilities are needed; practicing the processes by applying their understandings and abilities to novel situations until they are sure they clearly understand the information. This is what children do when they play; so under the right conditions, children are motivated to do this kind of learning. Unfortunately, during their formal education, many students lose their desire to learn somewhere along the way. What is more hopeful is that some students lose motivation to learn in their formal education, but retain it for certain learning in their personal lives, away from formal education. What this suggests is that many students still want to learn, they just want to do it in some other way.

Principles of Learning

Teachers and educational institutions - if they are interested in the kind of education called for by the Conference Board discussed in Chapter One, and if they are interested in life long learning - will have to make some adjustments in the way learning is conducted in schools. Many of my suggestions will be discussed in detail later in this book, so suffice it to say here that there are some pedagogical principles that need to be applied:

Start with the Student

Learning must start with where the student is. An event in my son's education illustrates the significance of this principle. He was taking part in a simulation game exploring the causes of World War I. The students in his grade eleven class were divided into roles representing the great powers and the few small powers that happened to play a key role in the events leading to the war. The object of the simulation was to help students understand the consequences of different behaviours in international power politics. They were given roles, which had built into them assumptions accepted by the great powers of that era. The students then had to respond to some of the critical historical events that led to World War 1. Initially, they decided that it was possible to ignore some of the inherent conflicts between the nations, and to simply create an alliance that united everyone. At the family dinner on the day the class had accomplished this alliance, my son announced proudly that they had solved the problems of international relations; he went on to say that it was really too bad that adults wouldn't let young people run the affairs of government, because it was obvious they could do so much better.

When we make decisions, we rely on the information in our working memories to guide us. That is what these young people were doing. The information in their working memories seemed perfectly adequate to them, so they could see little need to search out different information. As noted above, students tend to allow into their working memories pieces of information supporting what is already there, and reject the uncomfortable, inconsistent stuff. We approach and evaluate experiences based on the existing information in our working memories (Can we do anything else?). If a new experience seems significant and fits with existing information, we may decide to add that information to our working memories. Piaget defined this process as assimilation. It is an important part of the learning process.

My son and his classmates were unconsciously using assimilation. However, they quickly found their situation was more complex than they had anticipated. Despite their agreement to set up a grand alliance, there were still many issues to be resolved in the simulation. As they struggled with the issues, they ran into trouble. The framework of international relations they had established for themselves was not adequate to resolve their disagreements. This became apparent at the dinner table a couple of nights later, when I enquired about the progress of the simulation. My son responded angrily: "You would not believe how stubborn some people can be! They just will not listen to reason!" He went on to explain how they were frustrated by problems they could not solve, try as they might. The grand alliance they had created was breaking up.

Circumstances were forcing cognitive dissonance upon them. New information ignored earlier in the learning process needed to be considered. They now had to question the assumptions they had accepted in their working memories. All of this could only occur when the students had learned enough to understand there were problems with their model of international relations. The students could now understand the significance of certain information. They also realized that they must deal with it in some way, despite the fact that it was contradictory and in conflict with what they previously understood to be true. This is the point at which the students began to realize that their model of understanding was inadequate, and that they needed to revise it.

This is where my son was at in our second dinner conversation. He was not enjoying the frustration, but he was beginning to learn something new about the way reality worked in international affairs. So back he went to his simulation, somewhat wiser and more sophisticated about international relations. The students began the difficult process of revising their working models, searching for a way to resolve their differences. They had to give up 'winner take all' bargaining and replace it with 'interest' based bargaining. They had to learn how to find some common ground of interest on which they could erect a compromise all could live with. They had discovered ignoring important differences does not assure long-term peace and security. Now they would learn true negotiation is a difficult process of searching for creative ways of reconciling and bridging differences in order to reach some greater goal, in this case international peace and security.

At some point in the evolution of our understanding, we reach a stage where we find we have to significantly modify the models in our working memories because they no longer fit reality as we now understand it. This is the process of cognitive dissonance at work. The new model will be different from the one that was there earlier. Some people refer to this as a 'raising of consciousness' to a level where personal change becomes possible. The learner becomes willing to use new information to make significant changes to their models of knowledge. Piaget refers to it as the process of accommodating new information.

At the end of the simulation, my son had to write an essay about the processes of international relations. One evening, as we were discussing the history of events leading to World War I and possible conclusions about international relations, he made the comment: "this stuff sure is complicated". He no longer had a naive understanding of the complexities of international relations, and was now much more able to grow in his understanding of them. It was not so much the specifics of what he had learned in this situation, it was the knowledge that we all start out with incomplete information, and that as we learn we have to be prepared to change the way we think about reality. He had established a much stronger basis for life long learning about some important aspects of reality.

This is not to say that a breakthrough in the consciousness of one aspect of reality automatically means a breakthrough in other parts of reality. We have many sets of assumptions (prejudices) that block growth in understanding, and that need to be broken down. It is likely that the attitudes learned from the cognitive dissonance of one situation will predispose us to examine the cognitive dissonance in another situation. It is in this way that we grow intellectually.

Role of Communities

Students live within many communities, each buried within the other. The two communities we are most concerned with are the school community and the classroom community within it. Nevertheless, we should never underestimate the significance of other communities to students.

Community here represents the totality of communities impinging on a student's life. A rough outline of those communities would begin with the family, but as the child gets older, the cultures of other communities become important.

The child's friends and their parents are major sources of additional culture. Quickly, peer communities become highly significant in a student's life. Other sources of values and attitudes are the media, advertising, and work. Athletic communities provide values and attitudes for young people. Student community culture has powerful values and attitudes, and these are used to select, reject, and grade people for membership. The pressure to conform becomes very powerful.

Community members collectively create the culture of the community. as community members, students help create the cultures in which they live. In fact, adolescence is that time in young people's lives when they begin to insist on adult treatment by the community of which they are a part. The school culture and its classroom cultures are as rich and complex as any other sub-culture in a pluralistic society. The teacher is only one member of the classroom culture, and must always carefully consider the other factors affecting the classroom culture.

The Power of Culture

Culture creates the climate of significance that signals to students those things that they should incorporate into their working memories. Modelling is a critical way in which this is done. Children pick models from their environment to emulate. The models with the most influence on working memory will be those children admire. If learning is modelled positively and constructively, their attitudes will be much influenced by that experience.

All communities - including the classroom community - have sub-cultures that govern the behaviour of its members. A culture establishes the set of ideas, beliefs, and values members of the culture believe they have to work with. Modern, pluralistic cultures are very complex with a great variety of sub-cultures. Most teenagers behave as if the sub-culture they belong to defines the totality of culture available to them. They voluntarily allow the values of a sub-culture to categorize them into a set of behaviours, and they allow those values to screen out ideas, beliefs, and values from other parts of the culture. In other words, they are accultured by the communities they join.

Clothes people choose to wear are a manifestation of the acculturation process. This process applies to all groups of people, not just adolescents, but let us begin with them. Nothing signifies the differences between parents and their teenagers as much as disputes over dress and appearance. "You are not going out in that!" followed by "Dad, you're so quaint" is a common exchange in families with adolescents. Parents can be just as caught up in the dress culture as their children. Am I suitably dressed for work, for the social occasion, for the golf course? The issue underlying all this is personal acceptability. Values screen behaviour with an absolute, rigid power. Clothes are important because they signal who we want to be by proclaiming the sub-culture we claim. So, we subscribe fervently to the values of the sub-culture. The dark suit a senior executive wears is as significant to him as the grungy blue jeans complete with holes is to the teenager.

Sociologists refer to face-to-face behaviour as a description of acceptable behaviour within a group. There have been many books, plays, etc written about the emotional turbulence involved in moving out of one sub-culture into another. Each sub-culture has its set of rules about acceptable, 'in' behaviour. People like Miss Manners make a good living issuing dictums about the "do's and don'ts" of living within the middle class sub-culture. Many people take great delight in commenting on and correcting the speech patterns of others. All of this confirms one's place in the sub-culture. It is a difficult process filled with the pain of rejection.

Inherent in these models are assumptions about learning. Children can learn they are competent and significant. They can learn information is useful. They could also conclude learning is a positive experience. Communities play a critical role in fostering academic success. The children of those communities who put a very high premium on academic success did much better on standardized tests than did those children from communities that plainly showed they placed little significance on learning.

Adolescent Goals

Nevertheless, what do adolescents want that is so unworthy of the larger culture? What parents and teachers fear are alcohol, drugs, sex, fast cars, non-conforming behaviour, and a reluctance to take their studies seriously (in no particular order of importance). For a sixteen year-old male, the driver's license and a car often are clear signals of adulthood. For sixteen year-old girls, it may be a boyfriend. These are rites of passage in a culture that has few of them. Adolescents demand the right to be taken seriously, and to take their place among other adults.

Adolescents want to adopt the 'sophisticated' adult behaviour they see modelled in the culture: they want power, they want relief from boredom, and they want meaningful (in their terms) learning. Classrooms have to create a culture that is prepared to respond to adolescent issues honestly. For adolescents these issues have primacy and issues related to school subjects are secondary in their lives. A classroom culture has to find a way to enable subjects like mathematics to make a meaningful contribution to adolescent life.

People are easily deceived by appearances. Parents in particular can be misled by the behaviour of their adolescent children. Parents both overreact and under react to adolescent behaviour. As a teacher, I would sometimes casually encounter the parents of a student in a shopping centre or on the street. During the course of conversation which typically involved school one way or another, I might mention how their son or daughter had made an excellent contribution to a class discussion and possibly had demonstrated leadership in some way. I was often surprised to see the parents exchange quick looks of incredulity as if to say: "who is he talking about?"; "It can't be that childish person we left at home because s/he won't get up until noon or later."

Children obviously have to enter the family as infants, and they and their parents establish a set of mutual expectations (values) governing their relationship. These become habitual, and change slowly. It is not just children who are habitual. Parents often find it very difficult to change their responses toward their children. The school and the classroom are different cultures, and children quickly learn to respond to them. If the classroom culture demands adult behaviour, the student will voluntarily and quickly conform. They are more likely to conform voluntarily when the classroom runs on democratic principles, and students have played a significant role in establishing the norms of the classroom community. They may save their childish behaviour for the family, but that is another issue. It is important to note that the reverse process can happen. Students may be behaving immaturely in one sub-culture or another and the parents could be the last to know that their child is in serious trouble.

Power of the Classroom Community

If properly used, the classroom community has the power to ameliorate some of the community effects listed above. Classrooms are communities with cultures that have the power to govern the amount and kind of learning allowed within its purview. A primary responsibility of those in charge of classrooms is to establish effective learning cultures. An effective learning culture is based on those principles of learning (discussed above) that facilitate learning. The most effective learning environment is a democratic classroom. Studies have been done which support this assertion. Classrooms can fall either into authoritarianism or into anarchy. Both are counterproductive to learning, because both are inimical to self-discipline. Authoritarianism denies students the opportunity to practice self-discipline, and anarchy provides no models of it to copy. Democracy, with its emphasis on freedom and accountability, offers students models of self-discipline and the opportunity to practice them.

Democratic classroom culture has the capacity to instil constructive, mature behaviour in students without coercion. In practice, this means allowing students to play a significant role in the decision making of the classroom community. Such decisions might include establishing a human rights code, which govern how all members of the community - including the teacher - will treat each other. Other decisions students can be part of are what and how they learn, the evaluation procedures used, classroom projects, etc. This is not a call for 'anything goes' in the classroom. Rather, it is to call for letting students know they have choices to make, and they will have to accept responsibility for the consequences of those choices. If you choose to treat others badly, expect some bad treatment in return. If you choose to learn nothing, then expect the consequences of ignorance.

Democratic Citizenship

Students need experience in three things: they need to learn how to make good decisions; they must realize that self-discipline is involved in successfully putting a decision into practice; and, they must understand and accept their moral responsibility for the consequences of decisions made. This is what life long learning is really about. Democratic classrooms teach this process by providing models of decision making, responsibility, and moral accountability for students. Democratic classrooms create opportunities where students can observe both the teacher and other students practicing various kinds of behaviour related to decision-making and self-discipline.

A difficult concept for citizens of a democracy to learn is their ultimate responsibility for the collective decisions made by their community. Typically, after a bad decision is made, people blame others for making the decision. Nevertheless, despite the complaining, everyone has to live with its consequences. What is difficult for people to accept is that before a decision is made, they must discipline themselves to understand a decision and its consequences before it is made. Otherwise, it is too late for them to play a creative and responsible role in the decision making process. They must be creative because they have to imagine the consequences of a decision in the future. They must be responsible because they will have to determine the effects of a decision on others and decide whether those effects are morally acceptable. This is a large burden, which is not to be taken lightly.

The same problem applies to the classroom. It is all too easy for students to blame others for the consequences of their personal decisions. I failed that exam, not because I didn't study, but because the teacher was mean and unfair. It is more likely that acceptance of personal responsibility and self-discipline will occur when students are allowed to help define the questions for the exam. At least they would know why the questions were set, even if they disagreed with them. All the reasons and logic for making citizens part of the decision making process in society also apply to classrooms. There can be no moral growth unless the citizens of a classroom community are allowed to play an active role, and to accept responsibility for that role. Again, this should be seen as critical life long learning.

The Trap of Imperialism

Returning for a moment to the parental fears of sex, drugs, fast cars, and a lack of study, we should understand that these fears can easily lead us into a trap. We want to protect our children, and we want them to be successful. They seem so frail and prone to error. So why not make sure they are given strict guidance so there can be no doubt about what they learn? Why not make sure they are allowed to take silly, unacceptable risks? Freedom, even if it is dressed up in high-sounding language about democracy, is just too risky for young people. They are not ready for it. The problem with this approach is that schools become trapped into power struggles with student culture they cannot win. There was a time when long hair was anathema in high schools. Now the debate over hairstyle seems irrelevant. It would be more productive for schools to learn to work with student culture.

The trap is very similar to what imperial nations discovered after World War II. The people of India, Asia, Africa, and South America were no longer content to be treated as 'our little brown brothers'. They recognized their treatment for what it was: demeaning, paternalistic, patronizing behaviour, which was mostly self-serving on the part of imperialists. Schools are great colonizers. They believe they have a duty to act as imperial powers forcing young people to conform. In fact, schools could learn a great deal from development theory: that it is necessary to work with cultures rather than attempting to colonize them.

Coercion - even when it is all dressed up in soft, velvety rationalizations about caring for young people - is coercion. The trap for schools and classrooms which adopt coercive strategies is that they become the enemy, and lose all moral authority in the eyes of their students. The teacher, the principal, the school become the enemy and disobedience and disregard is justifiable. Most often, disobedience takes the form of passive resistance, which is seen as both necessary and justifiable. School decision makers have to decide whether they want student contributions to the classroom culture to be an ally or an enemy.

Adolescents, because they are in the process of self-definition, easily fall into the trap of making the school the enemy. They perceive quickly, - and in many cases correctly - the imperial designs of the school system. Adolescents know intuitively that the road of colonization is not the road of individual, personal growth, and the brave ones resist it with all their resources. Where schools and their classrooms do have meaningful power is in the decision of whether they are or are not going to make peace with student culture.

Developing a Coefficient of Learning

We have seen that information does not gain easy access to personal working memories. It has to earn the right so to speak. This is a critical issue for schools because they want access to students' working memories. Schools in the past assume when students memorize information, it will somehow gain access to the working memory. With a little research, one could work out a ratio of the amount of information 'retained' in the working memory divided by the amount of information learned over a standard period of time. That would establish a coefficient of learning, which could be used to compare the efficacy of different pedagogical approaches.

There are some problems to be worked out in this approach:

- one would have to do this for different types of knowledge, such as pure information, knowledge of skills and abilities, understanding of a variety of intellectual processes;
- while it is important to measure the amount of knowledge retained in the working memory, it would be very informative to measure the ability retained in the working memory to apply the information to novel situations;
- one would need to establish a baseline measure of the existing knowledge in students' working memories so that one could infer what it is that schools have actually taught.
- it would be useful to conduct this type of research as a longitudinal study to determine what is retained of the classroom experience into adulthood; and,
- research then could be done to examine the effect over time of different pedagogical styles such as rote learning, Socratic teaching methods, discussion groups, research and writing in groups and individually, etc.

Based on this approach, one can begin to see that much of what schools attempt to do is very inefficient. More to the point, it could help schools discover what they do well. They might be surprised about what makes it into the working memory and why that occurs. However, it is not just schools that face this problem. It is an issue for all the educational processes of society. The issue for life long learning is to understand this process because it is critical to understanding why some people continue to learn and others do not.

THE ROLE OF EMOTION IN LEARNING

Emotions play a significant role in determining whether something is retained by a student's working memory? This is where the role of emotion becomes so significant in an individual's motivation. The student decides whether a piece of information is worth retaining for one reason or another, and often with little conscious thought. Perhaps it is interesting, and is something the student ponders at odd moments. Alternatively, perhaps it is useful, and the student uses it regularly to solve problems. Perhaps it fits with and supports something the student already knows or believes.

Whatever the case may be, it is the student who finds a reason for maintaining the idea in his/her working memory. Consider a piece of information the student either does not understand, or can see no relevance or use for it. It is conceivable that at initial contact with the information, the student may be neutral about the need to commit it to his or her working memory. Now consider the situation in which the student encounters the information. If the situation were threatening and frightening, fear and anger will be associated with the information. Given these conditions, students are unlikely to allow that information into their working memories in any constructive way.

I used to tell my students that the best way to study was to think about the information in their courses as they lived their day-to-day lives. For example, I suggested they could review their lessons in their minds while riding the bus to school. The more they did that, I went on, the easier it would be for them to retain the material they were learning. The students were very clear about how ridiculous they considered this idea. They had no intention whatsoever of spending any portion of their free time thinking about something that they disliked so much. As long as this level of motivation attains, there can be little life long learning.

Yet these same students, when placed in a situation that motivated them to think about information that they have considered meaningful, will continue to discuss related issues outside the classroom. Teachers of other classes have told me that students who have left a simulation game will continue to discuss the issues in the next classes. The interesting quality of this situation is that the students are not consciously saying to each other: "we ought to discuss this stuff." Rather, they are doing it because they have to do it. The ideas are so significant and compelling that they need to discuss them. This is motivation at work. Much of it has an emotional overtone in terms of meaning and significance. This information will be more likely to be retained in the working memories of students.

Fear is another critical factor determining whether or not information should gain access to a working memory. We now know that panic pretty much shuts down the working memory, because in frightening situations the working memory is preoccupied with the source of the fear, not with learning something about it. Schools are not supposed to be fearful, but many classrooms can be inherently fearful places: when the material being taught is incomprehensible; when the pace at which material is taught is too fast; when students are worried about having to respond publicly and be humiliated; when they know they have to compete and be compared with others; when they know they will publicly fail; when they know public failure will limit their access to education and jobs in later life; and when they know they are being judged as 'good' or 'bad' students. If some or all of these conditions pertain to learning, students will be fearful, and they will do whatever they think is necessary to protect them from that fear. Most often what they do is memorize, because they believe this is the least risky way of dealing with a fearful situation. What they are unlikely to do is to voluntarily ponder the material so that they can get it into their working memories. To the extent they reject their working memories, they are rejecting life long learning.

Some Concluding Ideas

It is important to remember the purpose of education is not to learn information per se, but to learn to use information in meaningful ways. People do not need to be walking encyclopaedias. Information is available everywhere. We are drowning in it. The real issue for education is to teach those significant pieces of information students need to form judgments about their behaviour within society. No one can be an expert on everything all of the time. This being the case, the issue becomes learning how to learn. Being able to formulate questions, learning where to direct those questions, learning to interpret and organize information in the answers received, and learning to use information in making decisions. It is more important for students to know how to organize and manage information than it is to accumulate it in their memories.

Learning must be much more active than the old model of information accumulation if it is to succeed at becoming life long learning. Students will need to have an active approach to learning modelled for them in the schools. By acting as a model for active learning, schools can have their greatest impact on students. Classrooms need to change in order to accomplish the goal of life long learning. They need to become beehives of activity, full of personal motivation, providing a sense of purpose and accomplishment for their inhabitants. Students should look back on their education as a time when they gained a real sense of their personal significance in the world of learning. Based on that significance, they will come to believe they can play an important role in society.

END NOTES

1. We also store material in our minds that we seem unable to retrieve voluntarily. We need some kind of reminder that certain information is in our memories, which we have 'forgotten' . . . this part of the memory might be labelled the recognition memory.

2. There is evidence that information we have forgotten is not lost, but is stored out of reach of the conscious (working) memory. Wilder Penfield, the Canadian neurosurgeon, demonstrated this when he would stimulate the surface of the brain with a mild electrical current during an operation. The patients would report that they could clearly remember scenes and situations that had happened to them years before, and which they had completely 'forgotten'.

3. William Shakespeare. *Macbeth.* 5. 1.

4. Marshall J. Farr. *The Long-Term Retention of Knowledge and Skills A Cognitive and Instructional Perspective.* New York: Springer-Verlag. 1987. pp. 97-100.

5. G. B. Semb and J. A. Ellis. "Knowledge taught in school: what is remembered?" *Review of Educational Research.* 1994. Vol. 64:253-286. p. 16.

M. A. Conway, G Cohen, and N. Stanhope. "On the very long memory of knowledge through formal education: twelve years of cognitve psychology". *Journal of Experimental Psychology*: General, Vol. 120, pp.269-279.

6. C. J. Brainerd and L. L. Gordon, "Developoment of Verbatim and Gist Memory for Numbers, Developmental Psychology, 1994, Vol. 30, No. 2, p.175.

7. The ability to do metacognition is developmental, and partly learned. Students who are given practice in doing "thought about thought" learn to do it earlier and better than those who are not given such practice (Piaget, Arlin etc.)

8. Metacognition is thought about thought. It is the ability to reflect on one's assumptions and thought processes and to consider whether there might be other approaches that could be taken. It is the capacity to stand outside yourself and evaluate your thinking.

9. Universities have had a profound effect on what is considered important information for students to learn. Teachers have tended to adopt the university model of teaching as the valid model. One example of this in practice is the adoption of literary criticism as the approach to be taken in studying pieces of literature, as opposed to teaching for enjoyment. The issue being begged by the focus on literary criticism is whether students will ever again look at pieces of literature they studied under its aegis, and whether it will be stored in their working memories in any kind of usable form.

10. The attitude is that theoretical, academic information is more significant than prosaic information about living life. The paradox here involves studying the work of poets through critical literary theory at the expense of a focus on their message about the lives of people. This is really a holdover from classical civilization's attitudes, where the elite learned only theory. Ordinary people learned about practical things, and it was left to aristocrats to focus on aesthetics.

11. Presentation is another holdover from the past when there were simply not enough books to allow every student to have one. Lecturing to many students was a way around that problem. That is not a problem today, but old traditions die hard.

12. Many students take courses which they have very little interest in based on this rationalization. Often they give up courses they are more interested in to take these courses. Everyone loses in this exchange, but most especially the student. In the end, it might be more efficient to take a course later when there is clear need for it.

13. A worldview is the totality of ideas, beliefs, and values about reality held by an individual. These are the basic assumptions an individual turns to when trying to understand and make decisions about a valid response to reality. People in society also collectively subscribe to aspects of a dominant worldview. Usually, it is from this dominant societal worldview that individuals choose assumptions for their personal worldview.

14. Merlin C. Wittrock. "The Learning by Discovery Hypothesis" *Learning by Discovery: A Critical Appraisal.* ed. Lee S. Shulman and Evan R. Keislar. Chicago: Rand McNally and Co.; 1966. pp.33-75

15. Albert Bandura. *Principles of Behaviour Modification.* New York: Holt. 1969.

16. R. W. White, "Motivation Reconsidered: The Concept of Competence." Psychological Review, Vol. 66 (1959) pp. 297-333.

17. Lynn D. Selemon et al. "Prefrontal Cortex". Prefrontal cortex and working memory. *American Journal of Psychiatry*. 152, 1995.

18. Concepts, skills, and values will be discussed in greater detail in succeeding chapters.

19. Cognitive dissonance is the process of reconciling new and contradictory pieces of information that do not fit with existing information in our working memories. Cognitive dissonance makes us uncomfortable and for that reason, we like to handle cognitive dissonance by ignoring the material that causes the discomfort.

20. Barry J. Wadsworth. *Piaget's Theory of Cognitive Development*. New York: David McKay Company, Inc. 1971. p.10.

21. Interest based bargaining assumes that despite powerful conflicts of interests between groups, there are also areas of common interest which can be used to find enough common ground on which to base a resolution of the conflict.

22. Barry J. Wadsworth. *Piaget's Theory of Cognitive Development*. New York: David McKay Company, Inc. 1971. p.15.

23. Wadsworth. p. 15.

24. This is where the notion of heuristics affects the process of understanding. A heuristic is a fundamental question that, when posed, launches the questioner along a new line of thought. It is often defined as a rule of thumb that neatly summarizes and explains a situation in meaningful and utilitarian terms.

25. Hal R. Arkes and John P. Garske. Psychological Theories of Motivation, Second Edition. Monterey: Brooks/Cole Publishing Company 1982. pp.351-353.

26. Edgar Z. Friedenberg. *The Vanishing Adolescent*. Boston: Beacon Press. 1964. Preface.

The applicable concept here is the question of creating meaningful institutions within society. The traditional high school is largely a model of a factory. This model is usually defended based on the need to reproduce society: students need to learn the values and attitudes which allow them to function (conform) in other societal institutions, that it is the most efficient (cheapest) model of schooling, and - of course - tradition (if it was good enough for me, then it's good enough for them).

27. Richard A. Schmuck and Patricia A. Schmuck. *Group Processes in the Classroom.* Dubuque: Brown Company Publishers. 1983. p.63.

28. R. W. White and R. Lippit. *Autocracy and Democracy.* New York: Harper & Brothers. 1960. As quoted in Schmuck and Schmuck p. 109.

29. One afternoon, while teaching a Grade 12 psychology class, I noticed a young man drawing some caricatures on a scrap of notebook paper. By the time I spotted him, he had done several that were all somewhat similar: they were phalluses mounted between two large dragster wheels, and the wheels were spinning powerfully, creating a large amount of smoke. They were very well done ,indicating some natural talent. He hid them from me when he saw me watching him. He was quiet, defensive, and not what the school would consider a good student. He dropped out, and I lost track of him until I encountered him late one evening on a large busy street in our city. It was a street where young people cruised back and forth all night. The young man was alone, and pulled up beside me. He did not wave, and stayed there, refusing to allow me to change lanes and not so subtly harassing me. One could create many hypotheses about this behaviour, but one thing seems clear: he is interested in power. I suspect he feels both powerless and a sense of desperation. How many people like him pass through the schools without making any meaningful contact that could give them a sense of validity?

30. Daniel Goleman. *Emotional Intelligence.* New York: Bantam Books. 1995. Chapter 2. pp.13-29. In this chapter, Goleman cites the work of JosephLeDoux on emotional memory systems of the brain.

31. We know that the human mind is very good at perceiving relationships and patterns, and we know that it is poor at storing information. Yet in the schools we persist at emphasizing data storage to the detriment of looking for patterns. Students will be happier - and schools more successful - when the emphasis changes to pattern development. More on this later in the book.

CHAPTER FIVE: UNDERSTANDING REALITY

There is nothing so practical as a good theory.

Kurt Lewin

TABLE OF CONTENTS

TWO EDUCATION PARADIGMS

Current educational thinking is struggling with two paradigms of learning. The traditional paradigm might be characterized as the information paradigm. Followers of the information paradigm believe that the basic purpose of education is to provide students with information. The role of educators is to select significant pieces of information and to present those pieces of information to students in the most streamlined and efficient way possible. The students' role is to absorb and store all this information. By concentrating and streamlining information, students can learn the basics about a wide variety of subjects. With a broad background of basic information, students are prepared to select and train for what they wish to focus on in their post-secondary education.

On the surface, the information paradigm appears to be a logical and reasonable approach to learning, and has dominated secondary education for generations. However, the approach of the information paradigm ignores three critical questions. Do people learn best by storing large quantities of learning information in their minds? Even though we often choose to ignore it, we know that people are not good at storing large quantities of information. They forget it rather rapidly. Secondly, does storing information have anything to do with the creation of knowledge? We also know that we learn best by creating knowledge within our minds. Knowledge is created through an active engagement with reality. The learner learns by creating personal models of reality and empirically testing them for their accuracy. Finally, do we learn abstract information well? We know knowledge is not easily constructed by applying abstract, theoretical approaches to reality. Most knowledge is created by applying the concrete to the abstract.

Because of these concerns about the information paradigm, another paradigm of learning is steadily gaining favour among educational thinkers. This paradigm might be labelled the construction of knowledge paradigm, because learning is a process of constructing knowledge by the learner rather than a process of memorizing existing knowledge. Successful learning is an active process, not a passive one.

Patterns and Reality

The need to store large amounts of data in one's mind is a relatively recent phenomenon. For most of human history, the storage of information was of much less importance than the ability to recognize and understand patterns. Consider the life of a Stone Age hunter on the plains. Survival depended upon being able to recognize and respond to patterns in nature. If the hunter did not quickly perceive the anomaly - the dangerous element within the background pattern - the hunter would die. If the hunter did not understand and plan for the behaviour patterns of his game, he and his family would starve. Women had to know the patterns of vegetation so that they could forage for food successfully. Each season had its pattern and the lives of hunter-gatherers were carefully matched to the demands of the season.

The human mind demands explanation, because unpredictability is very dangerous. Out on the grasslands, the grass and the bush are the background patterns; the lion is the significant variable. For people living among lions, survival depends upon the earliest possible perception of that variable. When people face a situation that demands their reaction, they do not have to time to remember and consider all the random pieces of information that might have occurred in the past and might be occurring now. What people must do is learn certain patterns and their variations so that they can quickly recognize them and react suitably. The randomness of a situation can be understood and made predictable by learning its patterns. In the same sense, people driving on a dark, rainy night depend upon rapid perception of patterns for survival. It is the reaction to patterns and their shifts, not memory that is critical here. The human mind was developed for this kind of thinking. It is good at it. These minds sit in our classrooms everyday.

Even as people developed a more settled way of life and took up agriculture, the patterns of nature remained critical to their wellbeing. One can find many statements in Shakespeare such as the following: "These late eclipses in the sun and moon portend no good to us."[1] These are not just clichés. People believed that the patterns of stars and planets controlled the patterns of their lives.[2] It is likely that the builders of Stonehenge believed there was an important relationship between the cosmos and human fate. We know little about Stonehenge, and even less about its builders, but we do know that it quite accurately predicts the motions of the sun, other stars, and the moon throughout the year. It is a gigantic calendar, erected with great effort to predict the behaviour of the cosmos. The specific cultural reasons for its existence must remain conjecture, but we know that planting at the correct time of the year is critical to a successful crop. Plant too early and you will suffer frost damage, plant too late and you will also suffer frost damage. Timing is only one of the many variables farmers have to consider. The builders of Stonehenge understood the universe was patterned and repetitive, and they knew those patterns held significance for their lives.

We do not learn by accumulating and memorizing all the variations in reality The human mind does not perform well as an encyclopaedia. We learn by searching out patterns and then storing those patterns in our minds for future reference. The mind is good at recognizing patterns and perceiving variations in those patterns. For those of us who are interested in teaching and learning, there are two important concepts here: patterns and wellbeing. These concepts determine how people learn and why they learn. They go to the heart of education.

Patterns and Meaning

We do not accumulate and store random pieces of information well, unless those random pieces of information can be seen in the context of a pattern. If they do not have a context to give them significance, they are likely to be forgotten as inconsequential. For hunter-gathers, the flitting of a small bird in a bush is a piece of information in the same way that the movement of a lion is a piece of information. However, it is doubtful that much attention will be paid to the small bird unless it is the time of year when food is in the nest. We do not naturally clutter our minds with random pieces of information, but we can and do willingly store patterns of information for future use when they are significant to our wellbeing.

This suggests that there is a significant relationship between meaning and remembering. Without meaning, there is not much remembering. In fact, remembering is not really the issue at all for people. Much more significant are issues such as meaning, explanation and predictability. We remember that which explains and predicts the events in our lives. We create a context for those events that we hope will give meaning to the reality in which we find ourselves. A context is simply a pattern of ideas that explains our relationship to reality. When we have that context, we have a way of judging the significance of the pieces of information coming from the barrage of information we receive every moment of our lives. Then we can decide whether or not to remember the information, and where to store it for future use if we do.

Patterns and Predictability

After centuries of studying the stars, the Ancient Peoples developed complex models of the cosmos that allowed them to perceive anomalies within them. Occasionally a light would inexplicably come out of nowhere and just as suddenly disappear. Who knew why? At other times, the sun would lose its light in the middle of the day and then regain it. Again, who knew why? The ancients knew these were anomalies, and assumed they were significant in some way. Their approach was to explain the natural patterns they observed and use that explanation to make predictions. While their explanations were mystical rather than secular-empirical, they never the less were attempts of deal with reality as they understood it. The world is filled with monuments illustrating the amount of effort the Ancients were prepared to expend to put their explanations into effect. Stonehenge is possibly the most famous example.

The Thai peoples have a myth that explains thunder and lightning by saying that a beautiful young goddess uses a crystal ball to tease a huge giant with an axe.

The goddess knows the giant wants the crystal ball so she turns it in the light to make it sparkle and gleam like lightning. The giant throws his axe at her in an effort to get the ball. Of course, he misses and the axe falls with a loud crash. The giant throws his axe repeatedly until the goddess tires of the game. When she stops teasing the giant, the thunder and lightning are over. This is a way of understanding and remembering reality in the same way we do when we say, "all good boys deserve fun" - a, g, b, d, f - in an effort to learn and remember musical notation. We still create explanations of reality, but we have moved from myth to science and label our well-accepted explanations scientific theories. We (humans throughout history) play these intellectual games because we are good at them.[3] It gives us satisfaction and security.

Epistemology: the Science of Knowing

At this point in the discussion, we should consider the ways in which we discover knowledge, how we learn, and how we store those things that we have learned. All of these processes are part of epistemology, which in summary is simply how we know things. I would like to digress for a moment here and briefly discuss the role of theorizing in our thought processes. There are people who pride themselves on being 'practical'. They derisively dismiss theorizing as something done by 'egg heads' who have nothing better to do than spend their time developing theories that have little to do with the real world. It is important to note that we all create theories which are - in effect - our personal road maps of reality. We use these road maps cum theories to guide us through reality. We constantly test their guidance against reality as we currently perceive it. That means we make small adjustments to our theories as necessary so that they continue to correspond to reality. We then announce proudly to the world that we understand reality; we know what is going on. Therefore, we all have theories of reality.

Epistemology itself is a system (theory) of ideas made up of patterns and processes. It is based on the assumption that patterns are critical to our understanding and appreciation of reality. We understand reality by understanding its patterns. Patterns provide the context in which an individual piece of information can have meaning and reality. But more than that, reality is made up of many pieces of information (facts)[4] that operate in patterns, some of which may be static as in a puzzle, but are more usually in motion and operating as a system or a process. Usually, when we try to stop the process or system to study it, the system will fail.

The reality we live in is like a dynamic kaleidoscope of patterns, some of which are static and others that constantly shift and change. Our minds love that reality, because that is what they were created to deal with. A baby lying in her crib looks up with interest at the mobile hanging over her. Her instinct is to reach out and touch it. It moves. Her curiosity is piqued. She touches it again and it moves again. She intuitively decides this is something of real interest that will need to be played with (worked at) until its patterns are well understood and predictable. She is doing epistemology. Patterns of epistemology are as comprehensible to adolescents as the patterns of computer systems, and have the potential to be as interesting.

The Basic Processes of Epistemology

At the most fundamental level, we all want to make sense of reality. Creativity and critical evaluation are two basic approaches we use in this process. Creativity allows us to imagine new relationships within reality, thereby providing for new possibilities of meaning. Critical thinking allows us to decide whether the meanings we imagine have any worth. Both are important to the process of knowing. More about these ideas later.

We are bombarded with information every moment of our lives, and we filter most of it out as being irrelevant and not worth our attention. The information that we do attend to we classify into conceptual categories. We use these conceptual categories in two ways: first, as storage places and retrieval systems; and second, as elements in the thought patterns we create as we think.

If I say the word skating to you, and if you allow it, it will release a set of related ideas, beliefs and attitudes you have stored about skating. Your mind has also stored many other related concepts that can be retrieved by hearing the word skating. If I say blade and sharpening, you can probably search your memory and retrieve definitions of these ideas that do not involve knives because the conceptual context is different. If I say skating is very good exercise, you might be able to offer ideas which adds some kind of meaningful expansion to my opinion. In forming your opinion about skating, you will arrange concepts into a thought pattern that has your personal stamp of meaning on it. I have some Thai friends who would not be able to do that very well because they have an extremely limited set of skating concepts for obvious reasons. However, if I said Sepak Takraw (a Thai form of volleyball in which the feet and head are used) they would have much to say and you might have very little to say again for obvious reasons. The formation of concepts is critical to our thought processes. Without them, it is extremely difficult to do any kind of sophisticated thinking.[5]

In organizing concepts into thought patterns, we also make assumptions about reality. Despite all the information we receive at any point in time, there are many unknowns and imponderables to the reality we face. We are forced to create thought patterns with insufficient information. Therefore, we make assumptions about the way reality works. We may believe that honesty is the best policy, so whenever we have to think about the best way to handle our personal relationships, we turn to the concept of honesty as a good assumption from which to work. Because honesty is also a values concept, it can have a major effect on the way we construct our thought patterns as we think about our day-to-day lives. Values concepts act as criteria determining the significance and organization of the other concepts with which we have to think.[6]

Epistemological Creativity

One of the great abilities of humans is to imagine and create patterns that did not exist in the past. At this point, let us take a moment to consider the basics of how we create and understand parts of reality. A good example is music. We create music from the sounds available to us. Some sounds are noise others are music. An epistemological issue is how to distinguish music from noise? For most people this is a silly question; obviously, the sounds of traffic are noise and the sounds played by a band are music. However, what is the difference between music and noise? Some would argue that much of modern music is merely noise. Others would suggest the same for 'elevator music'.

If I sit at a piano and randomly hit the same key repeatedly without any discernable beat, I would justifiably be accused of making noise. Therefore, music is more than just playing a bunch of musical notes. Yet, Mozart can begin a clarinet concerto with a note that seems to be held for an eternity and whose musicality is sublime.[7] The difference is the musical patterning that Mozart can do and the musical patterning that I cannot do. Music is a pattern in which each individual note contributes to a whole that is much more than the sum of each individual part. People respond to those patterns intuitively. I do not have to be a trained musician to hear the beauty in the musical patterns (although training does deepen the appreciation).

Epistemology is the study of the ways we discover and create order out of the seemingly random. The composer creates musical order out of chaos. Music is patterned, but it is also creatively random. There is a fine balance between order and chaos. Too much order means boredom and repetition. Too little order creates meaninglessness. Both are frustrating to the listener. While listening to a Beethoven symphony, one can hear sounds come in from nowhere, disappear and later reappear in a different context. Jazz musicians do this all the time. However, they only appear to be random sounds, because in reality they are part of an overall pattern. Creativity is not being random. Creativity is the process of finding something that is unique, and it adds something to an existing system that is just right. When you listen to the discordances of a Beethoven symphony, you want to say: Yes! That is so right, and so unboring!

Composers who are attempting to be at the cutting edge of musical patterns may find that they have created patterns which are too random, and therefore unmusical for many listeners. Many audiences rejected Beethoven's music as being unmusical when it was first played.[8] Today Beethoven is no longer seen as the cutting edge of musical patterning. Our understanding and appreciation of musical patterns has moved on.

Another aspect of creativity can be found in the fusion or synthesis of patterns. Sometimes people come along who are able to take two distinct patterns and see a way of fusing them into a new and different pattern. For example, this occurred in the music world after World War II in the United States. Aspects of rockabilly and bluegrass music were fused with aspects of Black music, gospel and jazz, and a different musical pattern was born: rock and roll. Over the past 40 years, the patterns of rock and roll music itself evolved into somewhat different musical patterns. If you listen to the conversation of adolescents, you can hear them debating the merits of each pattern. Their parents, still listening to rock patterns 20 years old, will seem outmoded to their children.

The Epistemology of Critical Thinking

Critical thinking involves making a clear distinction between the models of reality in our minds and external reality. They are not the same thing, even though we work hard at reducing the difference between the two. *Figure 5.1* is a picture of a windmill. Even though it unmistakably looks like a windmill, we would never mistake it for a windmill. Obviously, an image of a windmill can never be a windmill.

Fig.5.1

Neither should we confuse the models of reality stored in our minds with external reality. Comprehending and understanding reality is a two-step process. One-step in the process is perceiving the 'out there': what is reality? The other step is creating an internal reality, which is our understanding of that reality. Therefore, 'seeking truth' is attempting as honestly as possible to match external reality with our internal reality.

It is very easy to confuse the two. We are confusing realities whenever we assume the reality we carry around in our minds is the same as external reality. Much in our minds appears to us as reality. In a crisis, we often do the same thing repeatedly in a panic. Rather than thinking about reality, we keep repeating a mental pattern, refusing to pay attention to what external reality is trying to show us. We often approach change in the same way. We refuse to believe our model of reality needs to adapt to changing realities. This is what people believe when they assume their ideology is the only possible model of reality. That is the way of the fanatic.[9] If students are to be critical thinkers, they are going to have to be keenly aware of the division between actual and mental realities.

The Epistemology of Understanding

Have you ever noticed how many things you do automatically? Evening after evening, you drive home from work on automatic pilot over your usual route, your mind occupied with other things. You stop at stop signs and wait for lights without giving them much thought. Then, one evening you encounter an intersection with a stop sign where there was none before. Suddenly, your routine is disrupted. Your wife/husband shouts: "You just went through a stop sign!" Your first thought is: "What stop sign? I didn't see a stop sign?" You probably did not, and will not until you modify the street map in your mind. We create models or maps of reality in our minds to help us handle it efficiently. You can test this assertion by comparing how well you can travel around a strange city in comparison with your home city. The difference in your ability to get around depends upon the mental map you have of each city.

The point of all this is that we comprehend reality only after we have constructed a model of it in our minds. When we talk about understanding something, what we mean to say is that we believe we have constructed a model or accurate representation of it in our minds. With a personal model of reality, we can anticipate its patterns and develop the necessary behaviours to deal with them. Consider again the problem of being lost in a strange city. The problem is your inability to predict the streets you will encounter when proceeding in certain directions. Unless you get help, you will have to rely on chance to find your way - probably a time consuming process. In your home city, because of your mental map, you can easily predict the best route to follow.

Maps and diagrams are models of reality. They can be on paper or in your mind. Both types are useful and both have limitations. Consider Christmas Eve. You have a box filled with the pieces of a complex toy, which has to be assembled before dawn. Somebody's faith in Christmas hangs on your performance. You pick up the instructions, (a verbal model) which begin by saying "attach part 3-2 to part 4-5 being careful not to . . . " Then you see a diagram and say to yourself: "Thank goodness!" For most people, diagrams or pictures are better models to work from than verbal models. We seem to have a difficult time transferring verbal models into reality.[10]

Of course, maps and diagrams are not the only models we use to comprehend reality. There are many different kinds of models: fiction can be models of human relationships (as are plays, movies, etc.); when they plan to make something, craftspeople often make small replicas of it to serve as a model; blue prints are another approach to modelling; by creating pictures and sculptures, artists are creating models of reality that make comments about what they see; mathematicians create mathematical models to describe reality; and more recently, computer models have been created which provide very complex descriptions of reality.[11]

We use these models in a variety of ways. Stories have been used for centuries as a way of understanding and evaluating the consequences of certain kinds of behaviour. After we go to a movie with friends, the discussion over coffee may revolve around whether the movie is an accurate representation of reality. Even the far out Godzilla movies involve this process, because people like to imagine what things would be like 'if *such and such* happened'? Movies are models that allow people to do that. In a limited sense, this resembles what scientists do. Scientists are constantly making models and testing them to see if they accurately reflect the reality that they have observed.

Reality is complex and difficult to understand.[12] It comes at us in a vast variety of ways. Our senses are constantly bombarded with stimuli. Somehow, we have to pick and choose our way through the mass of stimuli we receive, deciding which are significant and which can be safely ignored. We often get reality wrong, because our models are incomplete and do not take into account certain significant pieces of reality, or because they contain incorrect assumptions about reality. With our models, we try to systematize reality so that it is more predictable. That way we hope that life will be safer and less embarrassing for us.

The Epistemology of Learning

It is difficult to be an adolescent, because the adolescent model of adult reality is still incomplete and untested. Grade ten students are often very frustrated people who are easy to dislike because of their anger. Age sixteen (approximately) is a difficult time of life for young people. They are moving into the early stages of adulthood, and their expectations often exceed their abilities. They need time to develop mental models that will allow them to achieve those expectations.[13]

Being able to drive an automobile independently is a major rite of passage. The problem is that the mental models of adolescents do not contain sophisticated driving skills and especially not the knowledge that allows them to anticipate events and their consequences. They need time to develop the mental models of experienced drivers. Driving is only one obvious example; there are many more situations where young people have to go through the embarrassment of learning from their mistakes as they perfect their mental models. What is important is that they be given an opportunity to make mistakes in ways that are neither dangerous nor completely humiliating.

Young people come to school experienced in playing games. They have been playing and discussing the playing of games for years, so they have much expertise in the theory and practice of games. Let us consider the kinds of thinking required by games. Starting at the complex level, bridge and chess can demand a lifetime of study and special aptitudes to be successful. Other games can be less complex strategy wise, but still require high levels of thinking. The 'simple' child's game "I Spy with My Little Eye" requires the player to categorize information: is it bigger than a breadbox? If it is, the inference is instantly made that all things smaller than a breadbox can be eliminated from consideration. Other categorizing questions follow: is it brown, living, near, hanging, etc? Questions are asked until the possibilities are narrowed down so that a hypothesis is possible: is it . . . ? This little game is filled with hypothetical and analytical thinking. In playing this game, the players are recreating a piece of reality in their minds. It is not so different from scientific processes used to search for meaning.

In this context, it is useful to think of the word recreation as a hyphenated word: re-creation. When we play, we re-create reality. Watch small children as they play, they are re-creating reality. Adolescents do it as well when they are given the opportunity. Piaget understood this when he commented: "children will not truly understand a concept until they have had an opportunity to re-invent it for themselves."

Knowledge is a mental construct. Babies learn by constructing patterns of reality in their minds. We enjoy the delightful misunderstandings that occur when small children describe their view of reality. At a certain point in a child's life, everything that has four legs and fur is a doggy. Therefore, cats and rabbits for a short time may all be doggies. Small children construct and reconstruct reality amazingly quickly. By the time they have reached school age, many patterns have been developed and set. If certain patterns have not been created - or if some are destructive - they are difficult to modify. The mental constructs laid down in early childhood are fundamental guides for their lives and last a lifetime. Obviously, not all the work is completed in early childhood; we continue to construct patterns of reality in our minds throughout our lives. We depend on patterns to understand surrounding reality as we encounter it.

The models we create in our minds to explain external reality need to grow and change, because reality is complex and changing. Sometimes we get the models right and they serve us very well. Sometimes we discover that we too are using "doggy" to explain everything. Sometimes external reality changes and our models become incomplete. Typing becomes keyboarding, and writing becomes word processing. We adapt the patterns in our minds to the new realities and continue with our lives. Many times, we grouse about the changes because we are comfortable with the old patterns, but external reality doesn't care. The rest of the world is metric and Canadians will just have to accept that. If we want to understand reality, if we want knowledge, then we have to get on with the business of constructing new models of reality.

Epistemology and the High Schools

A few years ago, I was beginning a new school year with a grade nine class. The young people in the class were typical grade nine students. They were enthusiastic, shy, and very excited about beginning high school. In their minds, graduating to high school represented moving into adulthood, and they were ready for the challenge. They earnestly hoped this change would translate into significant and relevant learning that suited their new maturity.

After class one afternoon, a grade nine girl stopped in for a chat. We began to discuss some activities we would be doing during the semester. She became very animated about some of the ideas for the class and blurted out: "Can we learn some 'neat' stuff?" Of course, I was instantly attentive: "what kind of 'neat' stuff do you have in mind?" I asked her. As to be expected, she was not sure; in fact, my question was somewhat irrelevant, because one definition of 'neat' in her mind were all the delicious historical mysteries she knew nothing about. Her hope was that I would be able to open a window on the past that would allow her to enjoy some interesting social experiments and dazzling accomplishments from the past. She did not want the trite, commonplace ideas that had been boiled over until they were common knowledge; she wanted mystery and romance. But more than that, she was a bright, well-read girl who wanted fresh ideas at the cutting edge of knowledge.

These are the students teachers have to work with in the high schools. These people can be leaders in the classroom establishing cultural norms about the learning we all say we want. How are these people to be treated? My grade nine student is a complete human being despite her youth, immaturity, and academic inexperience. There are great gaps in her knowledge and understanding of the world. It is not at all possible to consider her mature intellectually. Still, this could be a description of most of us. Despite my age, a lifetime of experience, and a graduate degree, I know there are great gaps in my knowledge and understanding of the world. It is not possible to consider me complete either, but I still expect to be treated with dignity and respect. I expect to have some say in what I learn, even though I may not know as much as someone who is more learned. I will determine the things that are 'good' for me. I consider myself a complete, mature human being in spite of my limitations. My grade nine student feels this way, and so she should.

We can never know everything there is to know about reality. We research, we think, we plan, we systematically put our plans into effect, and still they do not turn out as we would like. Remember the rueful jokes: "I made a mistake once four or five years back"; or comments about the need for erasers on pencils. These days we joke about the need for the delete button on computers. Maybe the best illustration of our problems in comprehending modern reality is the humour concerning adults needing a fourteen year-old to explain the operation of their new computer (or TV, VCR, cell phone etc.).

The fact is that my young grade nine student was bright, well read, and had a range of experiences that I had not had. She had much in her mind that could help her learn what she needed to learn. And that is what I discovered as we worked together over the course of the semester. She was able to question and reject ideas in her search for truth. She soon learned I would not always have 'neat' knowledge for her; but that was okay, because sometimes I did, and she enjoyed those moments greatly.[16]

'Neat' Knowledge

What makes knowledge 'neat'? In answering that question, I would like to remain with grade nines. My student was filled with romantic curiosity. She had the sense that back in antiquity there were strange and interesting cultures that were a mystery to her. She felt a need to fill her knowledge gaps. Curiosity is wonderful because it drives us to explore and expand our horizons. For lucky 60 year-olds, curiosity is still there and drives them to take up activities like scuba diving.[17] But 'neat' knowledge is more than that. It is those discoveries, those insights that provide us with a better understanding of reality. There is nothing like a good "ah haa!" experience to make your day.

I remember another group of grade nine students who were working on time lines. We had created a large time line that essentially went around the room in order to create a scale big enough to allow us to examine major historical events from the Cretaceous to the present. (Previous to this time line we had gone out onto the street and made a time line of the major events of the universe that stretched for a couple of blocks). As we began to place historical events on the time lines, students began to discover 'neat' knowledge. Now, 'neat' was coming to represent insight rather than artefacts. One of their first discoveries was that approximately 60 million years separated the first humans from the last dinosaurs. One young man was surprised to discover that whatever movie he had been watching was so historically inaccurate. Another insight that "blew them away" was the discovery that the pyramids were as far away in time from the Romans as we are. With these insights, the students began to conceptualize time into meaningful patterns. They found that 'neat'.

Understanding is the Process of Creating Patterns of Meaning

Students were gradually gaining insights about historiography. They could see that history was not random. It had patterns they could comprehend, and from which they could learn. Part of the above exercise was to pick the most significant events they could think of and place them on their time line. Before they could do this, they had to decide what criteria they would use in determining whether an event was significant and then apply the criteria to the suggested events. For example, should the first moon landing be considered more or less significant than the Beatles' music revolution? They enjoyed themselves as they placed events on their time line, debated historical criteria, and searched out and discussed relationships between historical events, and soon forgot that they were researching and interpreting historical data. The insights began to pile up as they plumbed the historical data they were accumulating.

The students were creating their own historical patterns by interpreting and evaluating historical facts and then placing them into a historical context. This concrete experience touched the students' emotions because it was meaningful and interesting. The process of creating real history made the effort of creating a mental model to make it possible seem worthwhile. This pedagogical approach created a situation where students could see the need for a mental model of history. But more than that it, it showed them the possibility of building historical models for themselves. With their self-created personal models, the students had developed a set of criteria or context, which they could use in interpreting historical facts as they find them. As they develop and use their personal historical model/context, it would form part of the mental patterns they would carry in their heads for a lifetime.

Mental Models Are the Route into the Working Memory

It is important to emphasize the significance of this process, not just for history, but for all subjects. The creation of mental models is critical to the development of a personal working memory about any subject. At any point in the future, these students - particularly if they do little additional history - will have to rely on something to help them interpret and evaluate historical information. The historical models they create in their minds are the models of history they will turn to in the future. Without a mental model, they are unable to place the new pieces of historical information they encounter into some kind of historical context. A pattern of historiographic concepts - coalesced into a model - creates a place to park discrete historical facts.[18] Otherwise, each historical fact is just a random piece of information the student has to remember in and of itself. Most students can remember only a very small proportion of those solitary pieces of historical information.

Creating Meaning by Using Models

Without some kind of model, historical reality appears random and chaotic. Every historical datum looks unique and distinct. The facts come out of nowhere and disappear into nowhere. When there is no overriding pattern to be discerned, then history becomes a long list of names and dates to be memorized whether the teacher intends that to be the case or not. The only connecting reality for the students is that these events and dates appear on the same piece of paper copied from the same history text.

More importantly, how is the student to interpret and evaluate these historical facts? How does the student decide whether a certain piece of information is more or less important than some other pieces? Without a model to provide some kind of criteria for evaluation, it is not possible.[19] A criterion is a piece of information used as a benchmark to compare other pieces of information. A common criterion is measurement. If I say something is 30 cm. long, (12 inches for those of you who use the other model of measurement) you get a mental picture of my meaning. We use certain basic concepts and values as criteria to evaluate other ideas we contact. These criteria are part of the mental models we create as we learn. Critical thinking can only happen when the student has developed a model of reality to use as a basis for comparison. If the expectation is that young people learn to think critically and independently, then these young people must be helped to develop personal models of reality they can use as a basis for evaluation.

The Role of Mental Models in Life

Models are necessary to any thinking about reality because they create a context for thinking. When students go looking for information with a mental model, they have some sense of where information might be and what to do with it when they find it. Models create classification systems for information. Information organized into classification systems is easier to locate and remember. Classification systems allow thinkers to place facts in categories for comparison with other facts. It is through a process of comparing that interpretation becomes possible. When students can interpret information, they can decide whether it is or is not significant. Classification systems provide criteria by which a thinker can make judgments about the utility of pieces of information.[20] By creating personal thought models, students create working memories they can draw upon all of their lives.

The Problem of Plagiarism

Plagiarism is a problem in schools. When people think about the causes of plagiarism, the usual explanation is laziness. In some cases that may be true. There is another equally significant explanation. If students are assigned to research and to write an essay on some topic, they will encounter serious problems if they cannot comprehend the information they are researching. If students read paragraphs of information in an encyclopaedia without the support of personal mental models, students can do little with that information. They will not be able to summarize the information because they cannot decide what is important and what is not. The material cannot be interpreted because there is no context on which to base judgments. The student will not be able to make inferences because they have no basis from which to ask questions. In the absence of any mental model to guide their thinking, they copy down what to them are essentially meaningless ideas to, they hope, satisfy the teacher. Many plagiarizing students are so unaware of context; they do not understand that the writing style of the plagiarized material is easily distinguished from their writing style.

Even for the 'lazy' plagiarizers, the concept of mental models is important. Many students find writing essays extremely difficult and laborious. They may have worked very hard in the past and achieved very little success, because their approach to essay writing was so clumsy. They have given up. They have no idea of what is expected, and they are certain they will fail despite the work they do. For them, cheating seems like the simplest way out of a very difficult situation. Maybe these students could be taught a better way.

Teaching the Truth

Teachers worry about students getting the wrong idea about something.[21] Inherent in this worry is the notion that there is a correct model of reality to be taught. Teachers assume it is incumbent on them to make sure that students learn correct interpretations. Teachers who emphasize teaching information worry about giving students freedom to create models because they are sure students will get them wrong. Actually, many of the so-called 'accurate' models taught to students in the past have eventually come to be shown that they have inadequacies. In my education, I was taught that milk was the perfect food. Now milk as a food is being criticized on several fronts. Swimming after eating caused cramps. Now we are told eating has no cramping effect. History continues to be rethought. Is Louis Riel a hero or a villain? Was aerial bombardment of Nazi Germany the correct strategy? Truth and education would be better served if the teacher and students were to embark upon a search for truth, rather than a search for a certainty to be memorized.

If the choice is no model or an inadequate model, the student is better off with an inadequate model. If a student does not have a mental model, the student will have extreme difficulty doing any interpretation and evaluation of reality. With an inadequate model, the student may go through a thought process and come up with a poor conclusion, but at least there was a thought process, and there was a conclusion. It is likely that the student will discover flaws in his/her personal mental model and will make improvements to the model as they do more interpretation and evaluation of reality.

Models Are Motivational Tools

Maybe surprisingly, models are also motivational tools. The opportunity to create historical patterns or a model for themselves made the process of learning history more interesting for the grade nine students. They were playing the historical game themselves, recreating history in effect. People like to do that. That is why they like playing games. They enjoy re-creating patterns of some sort. For you Solitaire lovers, all you are doing is classifying cards into an established pattern out of a random assemblage of cards. Solitaire creates a pre-established model, which provides you with a pattern to follow, and a set of rules (criteria) about how to interpret each card as it comes up.

All of this has to do with locus of control. People like the challenge of confronting the chaos of reality, understanding a pattern and imposing order on the chaos in some way. People get a sense of satisfaction from demonstrating their ability to order reality.[22] Young people are fascinated by this process because they intuitively know that this is the route to personal competence, and they are determined to walk down that route.

Working Memory and Mental Models

In discussing the concept of working memory earlier, we noted it was the student who determined whether something was worth retaining. Now we are going a little further, and saying that in building a working memory, the student is actually constructing patterns of meaning. By the time students are approximately 14 - 15 years of age, they have already constructed patterns of meaning. Both the student and the teacher need to understand and accept that reality.

The patterns of meaning students hold in their minds screen reality for them. Those patterns provide criteria, which they use to judge new information. Everything the student learns will go through those screens of knowledge. Their models guide their response to events in their lives. Counsellors have to deal with student mental patterns everyday. A student may be making serious errors in judgment and behaviour. Despite counselling, the student continues to miss the obvious conclusions about acceptable behaviour, and continues to be sent to the principal's office for discipline. Many students do not understand why this has happened, and they won't know until they find the insights that allow them to understand the model of reality they are working from. Only then will they be in a position to change their destructive patterns of behaviour into something more constructive.[23]

A teacher has to deal with examples of the power of personal models in the classroom as well. I remember a young man who was a grade twelve student in my class. He was a gentle, soft-spoken person who was cooperative and pleasant in class. He had a bit of a philosophical bent and enjoyed discussing issues beyond the class work we were working on. At a certain point in the course work, we had to deal with some issues of racism. I was surprised to discover he was a racist. No matter, I thought, he is a reasonable person and together we can work toward a more constructive viewpoint on human differences. Not so. As I attempted to discuss some of these issues with him, he became more and more defensive of his racist views. It became clear that by continuing the discussion I would only reinforce his racist views. I could not find a way of breaking through the mental model in his mind.

The Power Game: Whose Mental Models Should Dominate?

In the classroom, whose patterns and models of reality should have primacy? The intellectual models of young people are often quite immature. As representative of a society, the teacher - whose interest is expressed by the curriculum - is charged with teaching young people to use more sophisticated models. Young people may be unwilling or unready to accommodate a more sophisticated model. They have some other model(s) they would rather work (play) at developing. Whose point of view should prevail?

It is here power confrontations occur. Young peoples' models are discounted in favour of the more sophisticated societal models the teacher is teaching. The problem is that young people can only build on the models currently existing in their minds. If the new patterns of reality are to be meaningful, they have to be made to fit with the students' existing models of reality. That is all they have to work with. If they are forced to accept models that they are not ready for, their recourse is memorization. If they are allowed to work with their personal models with the intent of helping them develop more sophisticated models, then higher forms of learning become possible.

Piaget developed the concepts of assimilation and accommodation to explain the processes of learning that go on in peoples' minds as they learn. As has been noted, everyone from the very earliest age works from an existing model of reality. When people encounter a new reality in the form of a fact, idea, concept, etc., their first response is to add it to the existing models in their minds. Piaget defined assimilation as the process of adding information to an existing mental model without changing the fundamentals of the model.[24] Assimilation is the process of making external reality fit a mental model.

At certain points in peoples' lives, assimilation reaches the end of its usefulness, because the new information is just too contradictory to fit into the old model. The individual becomes intuitively aware their personal mental model no longer corresponds very well with the patterns of external reality. People often attempt to live with a lack of correspondence, but over time their personal models begin to have less and less coherence. It becomes difficult to square one part of one's mental pattern with another part. Something seems contradictory. Still, the individual resists changing the model; partly out of inertia, partly out of fear, partly out of a need for social acceptance. But at some point, it may no longer be possible to ignore certain pieces of information. Reluctantly, the individual begins the process of developing a new model, which will 'accommodate' the contradictory information. Sometimes this process comes as a delightful surprise - the "ah haa" of insight; sometimes it is a painful, agonizing experience stemming from a personal tragedy. Because schools are reluctant to wait for this to happen in students' lives, accommodation occurs more often in their personal lives than in the classroom.

Literature abounds with many examples of the accommodation process. Another term often used for accommodation is the raising of consciousness. Authors like these stories because they describe interesting and dramatic personal conversions. Mark Twain's novel *The Adventures of Huckleberry Finn* is a good example. Much of the book describes Huck's introspection as he wrestles with his personal mental model of American society. For much of the story, Huck simply assimilates information while feeling increasingly guilty about his friendship with his Black friend Jim. Huck's problem is that he simply cannot square his racist mental model with the reality he sees in Jim. Huck clings to the old racist model despite that, because he is afraid of being ostracized. As his mental model becomes more and more logically incoherent, Huck becomes increasingly fearful and resistant to changing it. He thinks of himself as a bad person who is going to go hell, a fate he believes he richly deserves because he cannot see reality as he ought to.[25] Finally, he and Jim get in trouble with the law, and Huck is faced with the reality of losing Jim altogether to slavery. Huck has to accommodate a new mental model that is not racist: "All right, then, I'll go to hell . . . " Huck is going to stand by Jim despite the cost.[26] Huck's intellectual growth is not yet mature enough for him to tell society: your racist model is wrong and my non-racist one is correct. At this point, all Huck can do with his model is state that he is prepared to make a huge sacrifice for Jim.

A final example: Erich Maria Remargue's novel *All Quiet on the Western Front* illustrates a growing awareness of the futility of war in the mind of a young German soldier.[27] It was not helpful to the young German soldier's mental model of patriotism and hatred of the enemy to discover that the enemy were also young soldiers who were likeable and had families. After sharing a Christmas dinner with them, he found it hard to coherently assimilate their reality into the model of hate he had been taught. It was even harder for him to share a bomb crater with a young French soldier and listen to him slowly die from the bayonet he had thrust into the French soldier's body. There is a scene where the young soldier challenges the mental model of his former history teacher, who is full of patriotic zeal and nationalism but devoid of the reality of the horrors of war. The young soldier's mental model has developed farther than that of Huck Finn's. The young soldier knows his model is superior to his history teacher's, and is not going to give ground at all on the futility of war.

DEMOCRACY REQUIRES PLURALISM OF THOUGHT

Sadly, racism and war are still realities in our society. As such, these and others like them are issues for the classroom.[28] This is why the issue of whose reality should dominate in the classroom is an important philosophical question. We are back to the issues Socrates raised when he criticized the injustice and corruption he found in society.[29] The students in our classrooms, like Huck and the young soldier, will have developed mental models in an attempt to deal with reality as they find it.

It really is fortunate that young people do not get their mental models quite right. If they were able to create mental models that conformed perfectly to the prevailing reality of society, it would be difficult to achieve change. Every young person creates a new version of reality, and in the interaction of all those new versions; pressure for change grows within the larger societal model of reality. This is not to argue that every mental model a young person comes up with should be accepted carte blanche. It is to argue that both young people and teachers should think in a climate of openness where they can examine ideas and learn from each other. Maybe something can be learned from Huck and the young German soldier about racism and war. But only if the young people in the classroom are free to do what Huck and the young soldier were doing.

This is one of the problems with the transmission of culture as being the primary objective of education. No mental model is perfect, including the models of the larger society. Historical longevity, traditional acceptance, and societal rationalizations are not sufficient to guarantee that a societal model has truth, morality, or beauty. Aspects of the model may have, but other aspects need to be questioned, and every generation has the right and responsibility to do just that. If each generation had not done so in the past, then we would have been without Joan of Arc, Copernicus, Thomas More, Galileo, Luther, Cromwell, Newton, Voltaire, Jefferson, George Sands, Dickens, Darwin, Madame Curie, Gandhi, King, and the thousands of young protestors who played a role in ending America's involvement in the Vietnam war (many of those must be women). All of these people share one commonality: they could not make the existing societal models square with the reality they could see from the standpoint of their mental models.

Should a sixteen-year-old have the temerity to place her or himself among this pantheon of the great? Absolutely! All of the 'great' begin their lives as children who had to struggle with much as they attempted to make sense of reality. Martin Luther tells of long struggles with his faith, his personal relationships, and his overwhelming guilt. It must have taken great courage to nail the 95 theses that argued that the model of the Catholic Church was wrong on the church doors at Wittenberg. Einstein did not begin as a scientist in the formal, occupational sense. He was a customs clerk who "messed around" with some ideas in his spare time. In fact, he had been rejected for further study, partly because he had been considered a hopeless student who could not cope with the German school system. With the benefit of hindsight, we know that all of these people are critical historical figures, but we need to remember that they began as young children and students.

What about the future? Who in our schools will make the great contributions? As important as that is, we also need to think about students who are going to make all of those small, unsung contributions that make a civilization great. How is the school system contributing to that? We hear much from students about learning being dreary and meaningless. It does not have to be that way. Learning should be dramatic and exciting, challenging the full range of student emotions and intellect. High schools really need to ask themselves how they can make this happen.

THE INTELLECTUAL NEEDS OF ADOLESCENTS

Recall the grade nine students who had fun creating their own historical time lines. They were having fun because they were being allowed to use their intellectual abilities on their own terms. An analogy can be found in athletics. Consider some kids age 10 and 11 who are being forced to compete in basketball with well-coached, college athletes. For a little while, the kids would enjoy it, but after a bit they would realize they were out of their league. It would not take long for the kids to become discouraged and bored. If that were all they ever got from basketball, they would likely abandon the sport. Compare that to the excitement of a pick-up basketball game among kids of the same age and ability who are constructively competing with each other. This is pure recreation (re-creation) as the kids attempt to emulate their basketball heroes. Over the years, as they grow and mature, some will learn to play at the college level. Others will continue to enjoy a Saturday afternoon pick up game with their buddies.

The grade nine-history students were re-creating history in the same way the basketball kids were re-creating basketball. Granted, these grade-nines were not doing history at the Ph. D. level, but the basketball kids are not either. Many of the basketball kids will join leagues where they learn the skills and tactics needed to play competitive basketball. This compares to the formal classroom experience in history. The problem for most kids taking history is that they seldom get a fun-filled 'pick up' experience in history. As a result, their experiences with history tend to be dominated by a 'this will be good for you someday' variety of instruction. It is little wonder young people do not feel intellectually stimulated by the classroom. Evidence is accumulating that overly organized and competitive leagues damage young peoples' motivation to participate at the competitive level. The seasons are too long, and the competition is too intensive, so kids lose interest.[30] We must always remember that there must be a personal pay off for someone to work voluntarily at an activity. A person ultimately must be internally motivated if they are to expend energy voluntarily on thinking or physical activities.

We have bought into a myth that young people do not want to exercise their minds. If a constructive intellectual climate suitable to adolescents can be created in the classroom, young people would be more eager to think. If the classroom climate continues to be more like a basketball game between college players and 12 year-olds then the exercise will be a failure. Students will quickly get the point that their thinking is not good enough. Then they will mentally shrug their shoulders, memorize the 'pearls of wisdom' from their teacher, and take their A's for being docile students.

But it can be different. Because of a recreational experience with time lines, grade nines were able to create historical patterns of reality in their minds. Some had fun and some gained insights, which allowed them to create new mental patterns in their minds. Those patterns are now their patterns, which they can use to form a mental model of history. Once they have accomplished that, they will be able to retain a larger proportion of any historical information they contact in their working memories.

Besides romance, curiosity and insight are among the characteristics that are important to students (another significant issue is power, but more about that later). Insight is the more significant process, because that is what satisfies curiosity while ironically creating more curiosity. Students know they need to find insights that will allow them to create more adequate mental models.[31] The student decides whether something is an insight, because it is the student who constructs the mental models. Only the student knows where the gaps are in his or her mental models. The young grade-nine girl knew she had gaps and was eager to fill them. She was eagerly ready for some things I could offer, and other ideas fell by the wayside. Insights can only occur when the student is ready for them.

This is the source of commitment, which is another motivator to learn. Students are prepared to learn when they make a personal commitment first to themselves, and then to their ability to deal with the reality within which they find themselves. When an individual decides that I am significant, that I am worthwhile, and that I wish to be myself, then that individual can make a commitment to meaningful learning. In his book *Personal Knowledge*, Karl Polanyi states that science is personal, committed knowledge. He believes all knowing involves taking risks, is uncertain, and only comes as the result of a deep commitment to a disciplined search for truth. It is not, he argues, objective information that just happens to be lying "out there". Emotions such as passion have a place in the search for truth because passion drives the commitment to know.[32]

Whose Ego Is Being Massaged?

Like most social institutions, schools are hierarchical. There is a hierarchy of need that is entirely natural and useful. If someone has knowledge that I do not have and need, then I will likely be content to learn from that person. Adolescents clearly understand that relationship. They resent attempts by teachers to be buddies, particularly if the attempt is a cover for not having anything substantial to offer intellectually. There is also a hierarchy of dominance where power is being held for the pleasure of dominating others.[33] A wise friend observed that if you wish to understand where the power lies in any relationship, watch to see whose ego is being massaged.[34] It is in the exchanges between teacher and students that determine whether it is a democratic or an authoritarian classroom. For adolescents (as for all humans), a big issue is power and control. If adolescents are going to feel free and motivated to learn to think, they must feel part of a democratic culture that respects and values student contribution.

In a democracy, freedom is not license. Democratic freedom means being free to make choices, with the understanding that you are accountable for the choices you make. In any classroom, there is a fine line between authoritarianism and anarchy. Authoritarianism may take the form of being dictatorial, but it often takes the form of being patronizing. Adolescents are being patronized when they are spoon fed and made dependent on an all knowing, all wise school system; a system which is neither. The opposite mistake is to assume too much for adolescents, and abandon them to their own devices. When teachers withdraw from their natural leadership position as a better-educated, more mature adult, students are cast adrift. Most sink intellectually in this condition. Students are being treated with dignity when they are given help without feeling patronized or abandoned. They are patronized when they are not held accountable, and they are abandoned when they are not helped.

SCHOOLS NEED TO TEACH EPISTEMOLOGY

Unfortunately, we do not spend enough time helping students understand epistemological processes. It seems fair to say that Western culture considers time spent thinking about epistemology wasted because it interferes with real learning. The attitude seems to be "Let's get on with the important issues of learning facts, rather than spinning our wheels with things like epistemology".

And yet, in most of the endeavours of human activity that we consider important, we are prepared to devote a great deal of attention to the theory and techniques of whatever is being learned. Starting with a possibly less significant example such as athletics, we see that effective coaches spend much time teaching both the theory and techniques of the game. "Think about what you're doing; that was not a smart play" and "Let's do it over until you get it right" are standard comments on the practice field. The athlete is learning effective patterns of play (strategy) and good techniques (skills). Strategy and technique are discussed and practiced until they become second nature for the athlete. Both of these have to be melded into a whole within the athlete's mind before she/he has mastered the sport. Turning to more vocational examples, we can see the same principle applied in trades such as mechanics, carpentry, etc. Vocational students are expected to learn both theory and practice. In medicine and other professions, people need both before they are considered capable practitioners.

When it comes to secondary education, we seem to be reluctant to teach the theory of knowledge (epistemology) and the techniques of acquiring information. If students were encouraged to understand how knowledge is created and how knowledge structures are used to organize information, they would be better able to organize information in their own minds. Students need to understand why those patterns are important and how they can be useful to the learner. They need opportunities to practice creating knowledge by using knowledge patterns as models. This would give them the opportunities to develop the techniques inherent in the thought patterns they are studying, so that they can assimilate them into their own minds.[35] Finally, they need time to reflect on how they are doing with the patterns of reality they are working on.[36] They need to ask questions of their thinking: what is this all about; how will it help me with what I want to do; how well am I doing in using these techniques; and where can I make improvements?

The approach is not so different from what is done in other forms of endeavour. We do this to some degree with specific subjects in the high school curriculum, but we do very little of it with the theory of knowledge. If the assumption underlying the purpose of education is to produce independent learners, then we need to help young people understand and use the theory of knowledge. It is as much a game and a process as basketball. Students will become independent learners when they have mastered the game of epistemology well enough to play it by themselves It is important that we teach students the theory of epistemology and its processes.[37]

The problem stems from a confusion of objectives. Most teachers in high schools are subject specialists. Teachers consider themselves history teachers, chemistry teachers, algebra teachers, etc. Starting from that assumption, it is easy to believe the information inherent to a subject are the most significant things to teach. Therefore, it is the historic events rather than the notion that patterning those events according to a set of criteria that are important. When a teacher's students are struggling to learn more history information than there is class time available to teach them, the teacher will find it difficult to believe valuable time should be taken to teach the theory of knowledge at levels adolescents can handle. This line of logic is the result of a confusion of educational objectives.

The Construction of Knowledge Paradigm

This takes us to a consideration of the fundamental objectives of education from the perspective of the construction of knowledge paradigm. If we believe in fostering independent learning, there are some fundamental thought processes students need to master and turn to as automatically as they presently turn to memorization. Teachers also need to know them, and model them systematically in their teaching. Teachers must also make sure that students use them in a wide range of interesting and meaningful applications so that students have the opportunity to master them through practice. Students should always know what processes they are working with, and should be encouraged to think about how they are applying the process and the results they are getting. It is not enough to be critical thinkers about information; they must also learn to be critical about the thought processes they are learning.

Fundamental Thought Patterns

So far, we have been discussing the need for teaching basic thought patterns of epistemology from a general perspective. It is time to begin looking at specific thought patterns young people need to understand and practice. As a beginning, we should consider inductive and deductive thinking as two fundamental thought patterns students must learn to practice automatically.

Inductive thinking attempts to make sense of information as reality provides it. *Figure 5.2* below outlines a pattern of inductive thinking. An example of the way we carry out inductive thinking on an automatic and simplified level is the way that we approach the weather. On a winter morning, we might look out the window and see sundogs around the sun, snow blowing across the street, and people covering their faces against the wind. We may see many other things, but for our momentary purpose we select certain observations to use as a summary of significant information about the weather. From this summary, a generalization that it is cold and windy seems obvious. You might observe to your spouse that the wind chill today must be at least 2000, and people have to be very careful about frostbite. In your thinking, you have turned your generalizations into the concepts of wind-chill and frostbite. These concepts and with other related concepts such as "car plugged in", "winter wear", "travel", "safety", etc. can then be classified into a pattern of thought. You might express these concepts in comments like "we had better make sure the car is plugged in, and get out the heavy coats." Then you might extend your thinking by saying: "We should also consider postponing our trip out of town, because travel on the highways could be dangerous." In the second sentence, you have moved to the hypothetical, inferential stage in your thinking. Cancelling travel is the hypothesis, and worry about safety is the inference. Both the hypothesis and the inference are contingent on how the reality of weather evolves. You will continue to evaluate the weather. If it gets worse, then the hypothesis and the inferences will be confirmed, and you will cancel your trip.

You will notice several thinking skills outlined in the inductive thinking pattern (*Fig. 5.2*).[38] Students must be able to practice these skills before they can successfully do inductive thinking. At a minimum, students must be able to summarize significant aspects of reality, make generalizations from their summaries, conceptualize those generalizations, organize (classify) those concepts into patterns of ideas they can use to make predictions (inferences) about reality or decide how to approach reality (hypotheses). Students must become familiar enough with these skills to be able to do them automatically.

We turn now to the deductive reasoning pattern (*Fig. 5.3*).[39] We often use deductive thinking when we are uncertain about the validity of our personal conclusions. Our uncertainty may stem from a lack of information, or it may be the result of a lack of understanding. Whatever the reason, we assume that other ideas with which we have come into contact are better than our own. We elevate these ideas to the status of assumptions, principles or values. Given a set of uncertain circumstances, we prefer to rely on these trusted assumptions/principles rather than the conclusions we might have arrived at using inductive reasoning.

Returning to the weather for an illustration of deductive thinking, let us assume the weather conditions of our earlier example remain marginal. You really must make a business trip requiring a four-hour drive to another city. In summary the temperature is low, the winds are high, and there is a 40 percent prediction by the weather office of heavy snowfall accompanied by rising winds in approximately three hours. Now conditions for a trip on the highway are barely acceptable. What should you do?

Despite a careful summary of the information you have, you still find it inadequate. You do not have a clear picture of what the weather might do during the course of your trip. So you turn to your assumptions and principles for help in making a decision. Your first assumption might be a variation on Murphy's Law: the weather will get worse the farther you travel from your city. You might also have established a personal principle that no business trip is worth the risks of winter travel. Your assumptions and principles are now acting as criteria against which you evaluate statistics such as a 40 percent probability of snow and high winds. The criteria you have selected place much more weight on the probability that the snowfall will happen. At this point you might express to your spouse the following pattern of ideas: "I think I will phone my people to tell them the meeting will have to be postponed until the weather clears. I will watch the weather and go when it seems reasonable to drive on the highway." A decision has been made, and is expressed as a hypothesis that is contingent on the future reality of the weather. If the weather changes, the hypothesis will change.

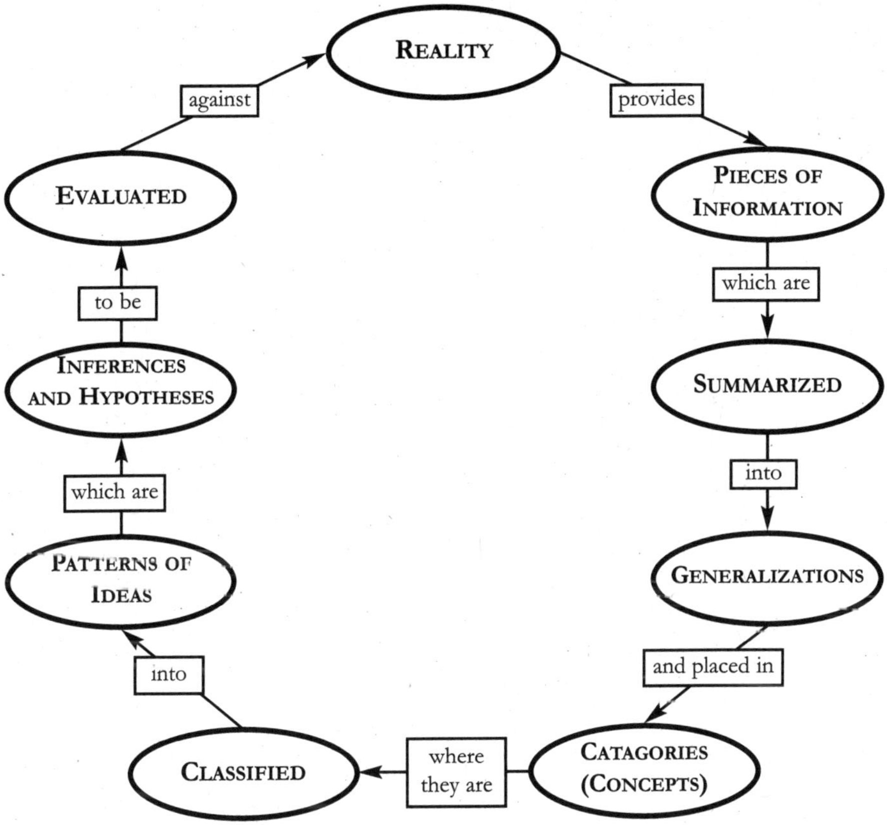

Fig. 5.2. Inductive Thought Cycle

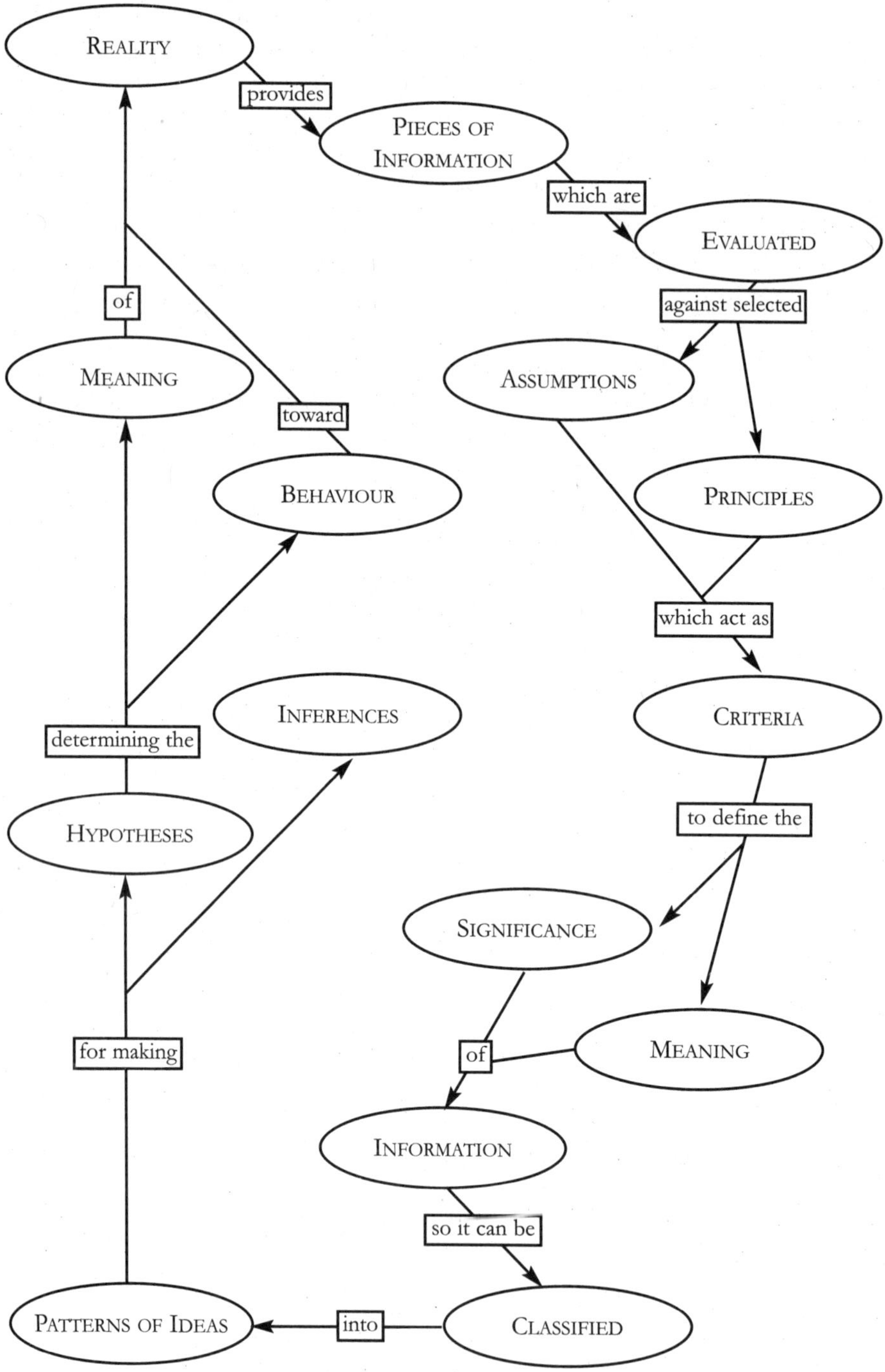

Fig. 5.3. Deductive Thought Cycle

In the deductive thought pattern, there are skills similar to those in the inductive thinking pattern and some new ones. Students will need to understand the concepts of assumption, principle and criterion. They need to understand how we use these concepts as a standard for evaluating the significance of information available to us.[40] Some pieces of information will be given more significance, and will affect the way we organize the patterns of ideas in our minds. We will tend to downplay the less important ideas.

In the inductive pattern, the thinker is more prepared to allow the information to determine how it should be organized. If the generalizations are valid and their categorization into concepts accurate, then there is the possibility of organizing information into thought patterns which have some objectivity. Of course, objectivity is a concept which students will have to assimilate at some point in their intellectual development. Deductive thought patterns operate from the premise that certain assumptions or principles are as important as reality itself. Therefore, the meaning of information will have to be judged against those beliefs the thinker holds to be important. This makes the thought processes of the thinker somewhat subjective. This is not to argue information is unimportant in deductive thinking, it just means information is evaluated from more than one perspective.

In practical day-to-day thinking, in our personal lives or in some academic pursuit, we do both inductive and deductive thinking. In fact, we shift back and forth between the two without giving the shift much thought. Returning to our weather example, we look outside in an effort to assess the weather. This is inductive thinking, because we accept information from reality, which we assess without too many preconceived assumptions. When we get to the decision making process, we generally become more deductive in our approach to thinking about reality. For example, you and your teenage daughter have both looked at the weather and deduced quite different conclusions from it. Her principles and assumptions might be based on style and social acceptance, and yours might be based on health and comfort. You think she should dress one way, and she thinks she should dress another. It is not that she does not appreciate the reality of winter, she is just prepared to accept more discomfort than you would to look pretty.

Thinkers use both systems of thought interchangeably. People feel uncomfortable making decisions without a clear understanding of reality. But, when they believe they have reality conceptualized well enough to comprehend it, they turn to a fund of assumptions and principles they have assimilated from their culture to search out criteria to use in evaluating it. They are intuitively asking questions like what does this mean, how will it affect me, what is the best response to make in this situation? It is at this point that reality has to compete with principle for significance. Non-dogmatic thinkers will readily flip back and forth between induction and deduction. Dogmatic thinkers are more likely to plump for a set of assumptions and impose those on reality.

Some students are capable of the kind of thinking outlined above. Many will intuitively do it with issues in their personal lives. In the context of their personal lives, they find nothing mysterious about this kind of thinking. In the context of academic thought, in research, and in writing, they will have problems in handling deductive and inductive thinking. It is very risky to assume that students will transfer inductive and deductive thinking from their personal lives to their academic studies without preparation and encouragement. They need practice using both types of thinking so they can begin to comprehend the process in their own minds, which entails building a personal model of thinking they can use as a personal tool of learning and decision-making.

If students are to build a personal model that works for them, they require the opportunity to work with these thought patterns on a regular basis in their studies. Students need to study these patterns on at least two levels. They need to understand the global patterns as being described here. For many students it helps to have a diagram (such as those in figures *5.2* and *5.3*) which gives them an overview of what is being learned. It is much better to develop these flow charts inductively in a general class discussion then to drop them on students. They need to know, conceptually, what inductive and deductive thinking are and when and why they are used as intellectual tools. But, they also need to understand the thinking skills buried within each thought pattern. As they work with the skills within the thought patterns, they should think about what they are doing and why they are doing it. All of this takes time and patience to develop.

Learning to understand and apply these thought patterns is a complex and demanding process. It is critical that students be given an opportunity to work through these thought patterns with familiar information.[41] They must understand the information with which they are working that they can concentrate on the thought patterns. If this does not happen, students will rely on memorization; either because they do not understand what they are doing, or because they lack the motivation to care about learning the thought patterns. Either way, students will not achieve mastery of the thought patterns.

Goals of Education

Inductive and deductive thought patterns are an important first step, but only a first step in becoming an independent thinker. A related form of thinking students must learn to do is the 'if this, then this' syllogistic form of thinking. Both inductive and deductive thinking can get one to the first 'if'. Returning to our weather example, one can arrive at the conclusion the weather is likely to become a blizzard either inductively or deductively. The high probability of a blizzard then becomes the major premise upon which further thinking is based. The minor premises then can be that visibility on the highway will be extremely reduced, the possibility of becoming stuck in the snow, and/or sliding into are much more likely. Both the major and minor premises suggest the conclusion that driving in blizzard conditions is very hazardous.

These basic thought patterns then lead to a series of related thought patterns that students can use both to organize and direct events in their personal lives, and by so doing become independent academic thinkers. It is always difficult to define a set of critical thought patterns students should know. There are so many, and people have different points of view on this issue. But, here are suggestions for a basic tool kit of thought patterns everyone should know: the process of making models; the process of presenting a reasoned argument; the process of decision making; the process of resolving different points of view; the process of conflict resolution; and the process of moral decision making. All of these thought processes are interrelated, and share skills and thought approaches. Skills such as summarizing, generalizing, hypothesizing is found in all of them. Thought patterns such as inductive and deductive thinking are found in all. The need to do syllogistic reasoning is required in all.

These thought patterns should be the primary objectives for teaching. This does not mean that information will not be learned, but it does mean that information must always be learned in the context of thinking. Information is a means, not an end in itself. Paradoxically, when information becomes a significant means in a student's thinking, the information achieves much more significance and is much more likely to be retained.

The Fundamental Mission of Secondary Schools

There is a story told about the Cunard Shipping Company. Supposedly, after World War II, senior management met to discuss the future direction the company should take. At that meeting some executives argued that Cunard should become involved in the airline business. Their reasoning was that air transportation would come to dominate the transatlantic market in the future. Other executives resisted, arguing that Cunard was a steamship company and should not get involved with airplanes. They won the day, and Cunard missed out on one of the great growth industries of the Twentieth Century. What some Cunard executives failed to realize was that they were not a steamship company; they were a people transportation company. They had overlooked the fundamental mission of the company.

The mission of schools must be to give students the knowledge, skills, and attitudes that will enable them to become independent learners.[42] At the end of twelve years of schooling and on the verge of some kind of post-secondary education, students must be able to manage their own learning. The overriding objective for our teaching should be to help young people learn to learn independently. As important as chemistry, algebra, history, or English might be, their importance must be subsumed by the objective of achieving independent learning. The information explosion is creating the same kind of changes that people in the transportation industry faced after World War II. We can either allow our students to drown in a sea of information, or we can teach them the knowledge and skills to manage it more effectively.

We have many disoriented students in our classrooms, because they have not developed a personal model of knowledge that explains what knowledge is and how you acquire it. Without a personal theory of knowledge, students are unprepared to make the fundamental choices they need to make. Their disorientation manifests itself in many ways.

One obvious manifestation shows up when you ask high school students at the end of grade twelve what they want to do with their lives. It is usual to get a vague shrug of the shoulders. They do not know. They are vague because they are overwhelmed by the choices available. They struggle with information overload, which could be defined as having too much information available with too little knowledge to understand it. It would be very helpful if students could develop mental models which gave them some understanding of how the subjects they are studying related to career choices, and thereby could help their lives: even if only in making career choices. Students need to get an "ah haa!" experience from their studies that tells them this is what they could be.[43] It is then that they begin to visualize a model of their future. They begin to see themselves successfully becoming something that is meaningful and worth working for.

A personal model of knowledge should give students a set of skills and attitudes that will allow them to define and cope with different aspects of reality independently. It should provide students with an understanding of problem solving and decision skills. It should include the administrative skills necessary to create and implement plans that would actually do something about the problems or decisions students face. The theory should include an evaluation component in which students learn to examine critically whether the plans they create actually do what the plans were intended to do.

People disagree. Well meaning people honestly disagree. Life is full of controversy and conflict and students need to understand the processes involved in their resolution. A personal model of knowledge should extend the skills and attitudes of students' so they can deal more effectively with others. They should understand how to go about finding creative solutions to difficult interpersonal relationships. Learning to deal effectively with people and groups is a worthy objective for students.

Students must come to understand that decisions have consequences for themselves and others. They must also understand that they have responsibility for those consequences. Because the consequences of a decision may not always be clear, people turn to moral and ethical codes for guidance. So in essencc, responsible behaviour requires that students learn how to practice ethical decision making. They need to have opportunities to think about and practice the concepts and skills of ethics. With this background, they will be in a better position to develop an ethical code they can rely for guidance.[44]

But more than all of this, in the process of learning to be effective people, students could also discover a great deal about themselves. They could learn to visualize a positive model of their personal lives. They should be encouraged to maintain the capacity of imagining themselves performing various roles in the future. This kind of modelling would serve as a basis for use in making constructive decisions about what they want to do and where they want to go in their lives. This capacity needs to be constructive, rather than the negative kind of self-putdown head talk that is so prevalent these days. Students need to be encouraged to learn to think: "I can see myself doing this". They also have to learn to say: "No, I can't see myself doing that" and mean it in a personally constructive way. When rejecting a personal alternative, a student should reject it in terms such as: "I can do something else much better, so I would be better off doing that" (what is unnecessary and is so prevalent is the self destructive guilt associated with an unrealistic ambition of being successful at everything). Then the students would be in a position to ask important questions about their future lives: who am I, who do I want to be, and what kinds of things do I want to learn and need to learn in order to achieve my personal model of life? With a personal life model in place then, they would begin to understand why they are learning certain ideas and how those ideas fit into some overall big picture that might be significant to their lives. Schools need to encourage and help students develop a personal theory of knowledge that will let them take charge of their lives.

END NOTES

1. William Shakespeare. *Hamlet.* Act One, Scene 1.

2. Judging by the interest in Astrology, many people still believe there is a relationship between the cosmos and human behaviour.

3. The intellectual devices described here are also heuristics, rules of thumb, used by people to understand complex reality quickly and frugally. The role of heuristics in thought is explained in some detail in Chapters *Eight, Nine,* and *Ten.*

4. There are many labels for the fundamental parts of reality, depending upon which system of reality is being referred to. In terms of looking at patterns of information (information systems), terms such as facts and ideas are used. In chemistry, terms like elements, atoms, etc are used. You can imagine many others. For purposes of simplicity, I am going to generalize all of these by referring to pieces of information.

5. For a more detailed discussion of concepts see *Chapter Six.*

6. For a more detailed discussion of the role of values see *Chapter Eleven.*

7. Wolfgang Amadeus Mozart. *Clarinet Concerto in A Major, K581, II Larghetto.*

8. Jeremy Yudkin. *Understanding Classical Music:* 3ed. Prentice Hall:
Upper Saddle River. 2002. p. 200.

9. Richard W. Paul. "Dialogical Thinking: Critical Thought Essential to the Acquisition of Rational Knowledge and Passions". *Teaching Thinking Skills.* Ed. Joan Boykof Baron and Robert J. Sternberg. New York: W. H. Freeman and Company. p.134.

10. If you would like to test this hypothesis at a social gathering some evening, bring a small tent and ask some volunteers to set up the tent blindfolded while following the instructions of a leader who can only tell them what to do. Most volunteers find this to be a difficult task.

11. Boeing Aircraft Corporation has designed a computer simulation system that models every part of a plane being designed. All aspects of the parts are interrelated, so the computer can predict how changes made in one part of the plane's design will affect other parts of the plane.

12. There has been interesting research done on people who, for one reason or another, were blind from birth and had their vision restored later in life. The assumption was that these people would be able to see, and would quickly adopt vision as another wonderful tool in their lives. Unfortunately, their brains lacked vision models, and because of that, these people could not comprehend what they were seeing.

Another similar example is to compare the changing ways a small child draws figures as the child matures. The early figures will have no arms, later the arms are drawn on as an after thought and then the figures become more sophisticated as the child's model of people becomes more sophisticated.

13. Part of the problem here are the competing models of reality in an individual's mind. Adolescents, particularly young males, pick up other models of driving, which make certain *machismo* assumptions about driving. These models are in competition with the models of safe driving presented by driver trainers. Unfortunately, the machismo model becomes dominant in too many cases.

14. Jean Piaget. "Intelligence organizes the world by organizing itself." *La construction du réel chez l'enfant.* Neuchâtel: Delachaux et Niestlé. 1937. p. 311.

15. This grade nine girl is not exceptionally different from average grade nine students. Young people want to learn, and many grade nine students come to high school hoping it represents a fresh start where they can find a way to be successful. They do not come to school intending to be failures. It would be a great mistake to assume that most high school students have to be forced to learn.

16. What was ironic was that sometimes things I thought were boring and trite, she found neat. The reverse was sometimes true as well.

17. As I write this, I am living in the home of a 92-year-old woman who learned to use the Internet a couple of years ago, and avidly watches for news on the space program.

18. The role of concepts as mini-models of reality will be discussed in detail in *Chapter Five.*

19. See *Chapter Eleven* for an in depth discussion of the role of criteria in evaluation.

20. The role of criteria will be discussed in detail in *Chapter Eleven.*

21. Society and teachers worry about the problem of being sure that students understand the difference between ideas that can be considered relative and those that must be considered absolutes. Ultimately, students have to decide for themselves what they consider relative and absolute. This is not to say that students do not need help in thinking about and making decisions concerning these issues. They do. *Chapter Seven* will discuss this issue in much more detail.

22. J. B. Rotter and D. J. Hochreich. *Personality.* Glenview. III: Scott, Foresman. 1975. As quoted by Hal R. Arkes and John P. Garske. *Psychological Theories of Motivation.* 2ed Monterey: Brooks/Cole Publishing Company. 1982. pp199-200.

23. Arkes and Garske. pp. 351-353.

24. Atherton, J S. *Learning and Teaching: Piaget's developmental theory.* 2005. [On-line] UK: Available: http://www.learningandteaching.info/learning/piaget.htm .

25. Mark Twain. *The Adventures of Huckeberry Finn.* London: Collector's Library, 2004. pp. 256-259.

26. Twain. p. 259.

27. Erich Maria Remarque. *All Quiet on the Western Front.* New York. 2003.

28. It is interesting to note in this context that *All Quiet on the Western Front* was banned because authorities felt it was dangerously subversive to patriotic values.

29. Plato. *The Last Days of Socrates.* ed. Hugh Tredennick. Penguin. 1995. Apology 21a. Apology 38a.

30. It should be noted that this problem also exists in organized sport as well. The issue seems to revolve around the question of whether young people learn a sport best playing pick up games or whether they should be in leagues undergoing intensive coaching and competition. Organizations such as the Ontario Hockey Association have become concerned enough to do research on the issue.

31. For those students who have had their curiosity destroyed by fear, punishment, and a very negative self-concept, the best thing is to be part of an active, vital classroom culture, which models another approach to life for them. It can be very helpful to their development.

32. Polanyi M. *Personal Knowledge.* Chicago: University of Chicago Press. 1958. This quotation and others like it (Einstein, Kierkegaard, etc) can be found in Rogers Freedom to Learn p. 278...

33. One should not become a Pollyanna about adolescents. Some, if given the opportunity, love to dominate - and in some cases, to bully - others. If they have grown up in a very authoritarian school system where it is acceptable to dominate others, they will have assimilated those values. In the short run, when a school is changing to a democratic model of instruction, many of these students will attempt to dominate their teachers and the class. They will, for a time, perceive democratic teachers as being weak.

34. Errol Young. Personal communication.

35. Teachers fear that this will come at the cost of not learning important ideas from the subject matter being taught. The irony is that this approach will help the student learn the subject matter better. For an illustration of this approach in actual units and lessons, see *Chapter Eight.*

36. Many coaches and teachers teach their students the process of visualization. This involves visualizing yourself going through the process of doing a patterned behaviour. In your imagination, you watch yourself doing the activity repeatedly until you are satisfied with the performance you gave. This can be applied to many different kinds of reality. It is a powerful learning process.

37. Whether the term epistemology is used or not is much less relevant than whether its concepts and techniques are taught in a way that allows students to appreciate and master the thought patterns involved in epistemology. Mastery has less to do with labels such as epistemology than understanding the patterns. What is important, though, is that whatever label is used, students should be aware they are learning a specific approach to learning. So in that sense, it needs a label of some kind so that students can categorize and give it significance in their own minds.

38. This is a highly simplified model of inductive thinking intended to be illustrative rather than a completely definitive description.

39. These thought processes will be discussed in detail in Chapter *Six, and Seven.*

40. See *Chapter Eleven* for a complete discussion.

41. This is why I chose a mundane example - the weather - as the illustrative example for the discussion of inductive and deductive thought patterns earlier in the chapter.

42. Independent learning does not mean learning by oneself. It means being able to assess the things one needs to know, and then being able to find sources of information that will help one learn those things. Independent learners know how to formulate and ask questions, and they have the social skills that encourage others to answer them.

43. A less obvious manifestation is the trouble that many first year students have in coping with post-secondary learning. Many simply cannot organize a systematic, disciplined learning plan and carry it out.

44. See *Chapter Eleven* for a detailed explanation of this process.

Chapter Six: The Role of Concepts in Thinking

Children will not truly understand a concept until they have had an opportunity to re-invent it for themselves.

Jean Piaget

Table of Contents

Preamble to Part Two of *So Much More for the Mind*

So far, the book has discussed secondary education from a somewhat theoretical and global perspective. It has argued for a shift from information based teaching to thought-based teaching. Inherent in that shift is a shift in the role of the student in the teaching-learning process. Students must be allowed to be active participants in the learning process. That requires the recognition of their needs, accumulated experiences, and interests. It also requires imagination and creativity to create those conditions, which stimulate thought. In order to understand what this must look like in classroom practice, we need to shift our focus from theory to the reality of the classroom. In the next six chapters, 'the rubber hits the road' so to speak.

Reality is always more complex and messy than theoretical models, and the classroom is no different. Motivating and teaching people to think is a more complicated and uncertain process than teaching them to memorize. Sometimes the approaches to helping students understand the thinking related to a topic appear convoluted and indirect. This occurs because teachers need to create conditions where students will think in spite of their cynicism or their disinterest. Those conditions often do not reflect the order of the traditional classroom. That is not to say there cannot be accountability and discipline, but it is to say that the look and feel of the classroom may be different. To understand how this works out in classroom reality, it is important that we take a hard look inside the 'black box' of the classroom. It is here that theory translates into reality.

The remaining chapters examine strategies that have proven to be effective in the classroom. There are many such strategies 'out there', but they have not been collected and organized into a coherent approach to teaching thought. They will work, but only if the teacher takes the time to understand and learn to implement them in the classroom. The next six chapters are intended to provide teachers, administrators, teacher trainers, and parents with a template that will guide them in making the transitions from information to thought. Change is always difficult and controversial. The ideas here are intended to help people visualize and prepare for a new approach to educating young people.

Introduction

We live in our minds and use them constantly, but we pay little attention to them. Thoughts just seem to happen or not happen, as the case may be. In a flash our minds sort, classify, interpret and we are barely conscious of it happening. When thought works well, ideas appear in an intuitive flash. When it does not work, nothing much appears at all. We literally draw a blank. It is paradoxical that conscious human thought is so unconscious. For most people, thinking is a mystery they can live with. They are much more concerned with the content of their thought then the processes of thinking.

Educators do not have that luxury. The systematic teaching of thinking requires an understanding of thought. Teaching is about creating those conditions that make it possible for students to think. Students learn to think more readily when they understand the thinking process.[1] Therefore, an important objective for classroom teaching is to clarify the rules and processes of thinking for students. While students are capable of many thought processes, they are like people who are self-taught at other activities (sports, music, art, etc.). Teaching, coaching, and mentoring releases the latent potential in the individual.

Clarification requires a careful consideration of what happens when we think. The question of what constitutes thinking subsumes both why we think (purpose) and how we think (approach). Mostly, we think in an attempt to understand and respond to reality. Based on this assumption, thought can be defined as the creation of meaning out of reality. Thought is the process of constructing meaning and then checking to see if it corresponds to reality in some way. We end up with two realities. There is the factual reality we began with and the reality we have created out of our imagination. In some cases we agree that reality created by the imagination does not have to exactly correspond to factual reality. In other cases, we expect an exact correspondence between factual reality and imaginative reality.

The first step in demystifying thinking is to make a distinction between thought and reality. Thought is related to reality, but it is not reality. Reality is what we think about, but it is not thought. If we assume that thought is the process of constructing meaning of some kind, we can then claim there are two distinct fundamentals to thinking. The fundamental pieces of reality are facts, and the fundamental pieces of thought are concepts.

The information paradigm tends to assume that facts are the fundamentals of thought. Therein lays the mystification of thought. A fact by itself lacks meaning. It just is. A fact can only have meaning when it is provided with a context. It is the interpretation created by thought which provides the context. The most basic context that can be provided for a fact is to decide that it belongs in one concept rather than another.

Concepts are the fundamental categories of thought. Concepts may be ordered or classified into patterns of concepts, which in turn provide larger contexts or interpretations for the thinker. When a thinker has the necessary concepts, the context creation process occurs very quickly, and for all intents and purposes unconsciously.

Adolescents are making the transition from concrete thought to abstract thought. A concrete thinker is one who has a limited ability to make the interpretations that create meaning. For the concrete thinker certain conceptual categories about thought are missing. Without those concepts the concrete thinker is unable to imagine methods of systematically creating contexts for the facts at her or his disposal. So the concrete thinker draws a blank. Certain conceptual possibilities simply do not exist for the concrete thinker. Concrete thinkers are forced to accept limited interpretations of reality, because they are unable to attach a richer, broader meaning to it. On the other hand, abstract thinking is the process of creating a mental reality consisting of interpretations, explanations, or conclusions about the nature of reality. But we must remember that meaning is not reality itself; it is a model of reality which may or may not accurately reflect reality.

To become liberated from the tyranny of concrete thinking, young people have to learn the rules, procedures, and processes that abstract thinkers follow as they construct meaning from reality. Game playing is a good example. In actuality, games are a process of abstract thinking where people interpret the reality of the game to their advantage. We know adolescents comprehend the strategy of a game; we know they plan their approach to the game strategy; we know they can anticipate the strategy of other players in the game; we know they can and do evaluate their personal performance as they play the game; and finally, we know they make adjustments as needed both during and after the game. Young people do learn to play games very well. It follows then that they can also learn the rules of abstract thinking.

The kind of sophisticated thinking described above is known as metacognition. Metacognition is the ability to stand apart from oneself and examine one's personal thought processes. It is as if one is watching the performance of someone else. The thinker is acting as a somewhat detached spectator who is evaluating the performance of someone else. Metacognition allows one to consider a variety of possible approaches, and thoughtfully and purposefully choose an approach which appears most likely to achieve the thinker's purpose. Metacognition is a critical part of being an independent thinker, because it allows the thinker to become self-evaluative. At the end of the educative process it is the student who should be able to say "Hey, I understand this and I can do it: no problem!" This chapter will attempt to describe the fundamental processes of cognition.

Motivation is the other critical part of becoming an independent thinker. Students need to be able visualize themselves successfully doing independent thinking. One of the reasons adolescents are successful at metacognition in games is because they have learned to visualize themselves as successful players. From this perspective, metacognition is not a threat to the student's self esteem. It can be seen as a constructive process where the individual is improving his or her capacity to play the game.

Students, who believe they are academically incompetent, visualize failure. With a perspective of failure, metacognition becomes negative self talk which destroys self esteem. Negative self talk creates a destructive cycle where the student feels less and less competent to think for him or herself. Psychologically healthy students resist playing this game. If an objective of the education enterprise is to create successful independent thinkers, then educators have to provide exercises where students learn to visualize themselves successfully doing the processes of thinking. The next chapters will describe ways in which this can be done.

Concepts Are Critical for Comprehension

Your computer won't work. No problem, you think as you turn to your manual for advice.

The following example is the kind of advice you would get from my computer manual:

> AUTOEXEC.BAT. A special **batch file** created during installation of **PC DOS** and stored in the **root directory**. **AUTOEXE.BAT** contains a series of commands that **PC DOS** carries out sequentially immediately after executing the commands in the **CONFIG.SYS file. AUTOEXEC.BAT** can contain any commands you want to carry out when you start your **system**. This **file** can contain commands that define the **port** to which your printer is connected, **clear your screen** of **start up messages** or start your favourite **application program**, for example.[2]
>
> (Bolds are mine.)

Unfortunately for many of us, the information in computer manuals provide tends to be opaque. Jokes abound about the mistakes people make while learning to use computers. There is a story regarding a gentleman who believed his computer wanted him to close his office door, because it told him to close the door - meaning the door for the disc drive - before it would work. He would get up regularly and close the door before continuing to work with his computer. The problems and frustrations people have with technology have led to the publication of a series of books entitled *DOS for Dummies*, *The Internet for Dummies,* etc. These books are aimed at all of us who would find it difficult to understand the 13 bolded words in the quotation above.

For those of you who are well trained in computers, the information in the quotation would seem completely basic. For the untrained, it is mystifying. The purpose of the *Dummies* series is to do is make jargon/concepts more meaningful to people who have limited conceptual backgrounds in certain areas. Judging by sales, these books have done very well. Obviously, there are many people who believe they need to learn new concepts before they can manage the intricacies of modern life.

Concepts are categories that we create to organize the complexities of reality into patterns of meaning. Reality comes at us in many different ways, and in an unbending barrage of information. Each piece of information or fact is discrete, separate, and meaningless until we can fit it into a pattern that has meaning. In order to create patterns of meaning, we first create categories, and then organize or classify those categories into patterns or systems. Let us consider this process with a few mundane examples.

Suppose we were in a room with many pieces of furniture, and I said: "Bring me a chair please." You would look around the room and select an object that had four legs, supporting a horizontal platform and a vertical back and say: "Is this what you want?" I might look at it, and after brief consideration say: "No, I really need a stool rather than a chair." "Is there one here?" You would then look around for an object which has three or four legs more closely spaced, and which has longer or shorter legs than the chair. It would have a smaller horizontal platform, and may or may not have a vertical back. Of course, you would not laboriously go through the check list of characteristics I just described, at least not consciously. Yet you quickly distinguish the chair category of objects from the stool category.

You can distinguish chairs from stools, because in your mind you have established a pattern of characteristics determining which objects fit the concept of chair, and which fit the concept of stool. These characteristics are known as the critical attributes of a concept, and it is they that define and separate one concept or category from another. When I asked for a chair, you did not bring me a desk, even though a desk category shares some attributes of the chair category. Desks have other attributes which distinguish them from chairs and stools.

As a test for yourself, decide whether you would place a student desk in the category of chair, or in the category of desk. Perhaps it needs to have its own category. On what basis do you make that determination? A student desk is a combination of chair and desk. A regular office desk has a separate chair. Certain attributes are critical to the definition of a concept. If an object or idea lacks the attributes for a certain conceptual category, then it cannot be made to fit that conceptual category. A desk has space on which to write, a chair does not. You can think of other examples. Trucks have certain critical attributes which make them different from cars, for example.

A Definition of Concept

Before we move on, we should think about the concept of concept itself. I am not trying to create double talk here. I am simply suggesting that the idea of concept is also a concept. Concepts have four parts:

- attributes: these are the defining characteristics that generally determine whether certain objects/ideas can be admitted to a conceptual category;
- critical attributes: certain attributes are critical determinants of whether a certain object/idea can be said to be part of a conceptual category;
- generalization: the generalization provides an overall sense of the meaning and purpose of all the attributes in the concept/category;
- label: the name applied to a concept/category of ideas. It acts as shorthand, relieving us of the burden of having to list the attributes and the generalization whenever we wish to use the concept. It is important to remember that the label is not the concept/category, any more than the name of a person is the person.

If one thinks about the examples we have been using, it is possible to see how this works in practice. Chairs, stools, and desks all share certain attributes that make them look similar in some ways. They also have certain critical attributes that make it impossible to lump them all together in the same concept/category. With a little thought, each of us could come up with a generalization that would summarize and differentiate each concept. Finally, we store all of that information under a label which allows us easy access to the information.

Creating Patterns of Reality

Concepts make it possible to create patterns of ideas within our minds. These patterns determine our responses to reality. Without a pattern of concepts we cannot respond in a thoughtful reasoned way. Returning to the quotation from the computer manual, we can see this process in action. Compare your understanding of the conceptual examples we have discussed so far to your comprehension of the concepts of *autoexec.bat* and *config.sys* file. Those with computer training and experience have stored the set of attributes that define these concepts as patterns. They can refer to these patterns and respond constructively to them. For those with little computer training, these terms do not relate to any stored patterns in their minds. There are no attributes, critical or otherwise, they can turn to for help in defining the information they receive about computers. Autoexec.bat only dredges up confusion and uncertainty.

Abstract Concepts

So far, we have been discussing concrete concepts. With concrete concepts, the critical attributes make the distinctions between concepts quite straight forward. However, many concepts are abstract. The critical attributes can be less clear and some distinctions fuzzy. People disagree among themselves about definitions. How is love different from friendship? It is generally accepted there is a difference, but making a precise distinction can be difficult. There are many such concepts and most of us live our lives without pinning them down very precisely.

Young people face this problem all the time. Often the information they are taught in high schools contains concepts that are fuzzy and poorly defined. Consider the following paragraph:

> The seventeenth century which witnessed the development of **absolute monarchy**, saw the appearance of the **constitutional state**. While France and later Prussia, Russia, and Austria solved the question of **sovereignty** with the **absolutist state**, England and Holland evolved toward the **constitutional state**. What is **constitutionalism?** Is it identical to **democracy?** Constitutionalism is the limitation of **government** by **law**. Constitutionalism also implies a balance between the **authority** and **power** of the government on one hand and the **rights** and **liberties** of the **subjects** on the other. The **balance** is often very delicate.[3]

The fifteen bolded words are abstract concepts which students need to understand before they can understand the ideas being expressed in the above quotation. For many students, this quotation will be no more meaningful than the one quoted from the computer manual earlier. If the concepts within a learning experience are not clarified for students, they will not understand much of it. Without a conceptual base, students have no option but to memorize any information they are responsible for learning. Without concepts, students are unable to construct meaningful patterns or models in their minds. The net result is memorizing information for an exam and then forgetting it.

The standard approach to this problem by the information paradigm would be to define all the bolded words and assume that this will clarify the reading for the students. Usually it does not. Before this reading can be understood, a hierarchy of concepts must be understood as a pattern of thought. Students must accommodate these concepts in their minds as a self-constructed pattern of meaning. While each student will create somewhat different patterns of personal meaning, all students will need to begin with experiences that relate meaningfully to their lives.

Using Concepts to Interpret Reality

Given this reality, teachers need to ask themselves what fundamental human condition is being described in the reading on the seventeenth century. Students need to reflect on a pattern of concepts within their lives that could give meaning to this reading. Most students will not have much direct, personal experience with absolute monarchs, constitutional states, sovereignty, constitutionalism, etc. to draw upon. Even their understanding of the concepts of government, rights, and liberty will be limited. Without these concepts, they cannot form the patterns of meaning necessary for interpretation and analysis.

At the same time, students do have some ideas about power relationships within groups. Without having thought about it very much, they know that people have to live together, that some people have more power than others, that power can be used unjustly, and that groups attempt - however imperfectly - to control the abuse of power. Students have some sense of the abuse of power, of rights, justice, and the need for a social contract that tries to maintain justice within a group. Watch children at around age 10 play. Their conversation about the rules of games and the proper etiquette in playing will revolve around the concepts we are discussing. This is the level at which a teacher needs to begin. By discussing the basic issues of how to interact with others, abstract concepts like social contract can be made concrete. We need to understand that a broad pattern of concepts underlie a child's cry: "That's not fair!!!"

It is here that abstract concepts begin to resonate with student emotions, giving the concepts personal meaning and significance. It is these emotions which will help students understand why people in the French Revolution were prepared to risk their lives for the abstract concepts of liberty, fraternity, and equality. Students need opportunities to connect the concepts already in their minds with the more abstract academic concepts they confront in their studies. It is through the interplay of students' personal conceptions and academic concepts that student understanding of concepts are broadened and deepened.

Teachers need to select a set of concepts students can use to interpret the aspects of reality they are studying. If students were studying the quotation above with a view to understand the French Revolution, then the concepts selected needs to build toward ideas like society, power, justice, and social contract. From fundamental concepts like these students build patterns of concepts or models of reality in their minds about societies and social change. The process of concept attainment is building mental models of concepts and then creating patterns of them in order to create meaning. It is only after this process has been completed that students are ready to apply the mental models they have created to eighteenth century European history as described in the reading. It is much easier for students to accomplish this by beginning with concrete ideas from their personal reality before turning to the abstract ideas of European history.

When considering what concepts need to be taught to prepare students for material such as the above quote, teachers need to carefully consider the familiar concepts as well as the unfamiliar. Obviously concepts like constitutionality and absolutism will have to be carefully developed so that students can create the various patterns or models of governance adopted by different societies within their minds. However, teachers should remember that familiar concepts such as power can be traps for the unwary. Sometimes familiar concepts need as much or more careful teaching as unfamiliar concepts.

Understanding Concepts

Power is a good example of a familiar concept that needs careful teaching. In history and the social sciences, the concept of power is a fundamental category of human relationships. Power, its use, and its limitations also happens to be a concept we use regularly in our lives.[4] Most of us, including students, are pretty certain we know what power is. We use the concept of power without giving very much thought to what we mean by it. This can cause difficulties for students, because they may end up with a confused grasp of the reality of power and its relationships to other concepts such as constitutionality or democracy. Without a clear understanding of its reality and the role it plays in social relationships, students will have difficulty in making history meaningful.

Power illustrates the organization of abstract concepts. Power has one difference in its organization. Power is a label for two related sets of critical attributes and generalizations. This in itself can be confusing, unless the conceptualizations of power are clearly defined.

One conceptualization of power	Another conceptualization of power
Power is a situation where certain people have control over some or all of the following attributes (sources) of power: - resources: controlling wealth allows one to buy the services of others; - organization: control of an organization allows one to control and direct its services; - numbers of people: having the support of large numbers of people allows one to direct their energies; - information: certain information enables one to control others. The generalization underlying this conceptualization would be: "If someone has some combination of the sources of power, then she/he has the power to make other people do what she/he wishes them to do." The label for this package of ideas is: Power.	Power is based on the willingness of people to obey the wishes of another person or group: - charisma: people obey a certain person or groups because they respect their personal qualities; - authority: people obey certain people or groups because they have a legitimate right to demand obedience; - force: people obey certain people or groups because they are afraid of them. The generalization underlying this conceptualization is "people are willing to submit themselves to the control of others when there is a good reason for doing so." The label for this package is also: Power.

Fig. 6.1

An overall generalization of the two conceptualizations of power could be; "People have power when they control some or all of the following: wealth; loyalty of large numbers of people; an organization, and/or the information people receive. Wealth, loyalty, organization, and information can be used to control others by persuading them to like the people applying controls (charisma), or to accept the legitimacy of the controls, or to be afraid of the force that will be applied if they do not obey.

Power is an abstract concept. It is not concrete and static, as a chair is. Power is real, but it is ephemeral, hovering in the background of human relationships, controlling and directing the way people respond to each other. It is a 'now you see it, now you don't' kind of concept. Because of its abstract nature, people may have different conceptualizations (models) of power. They are often unaware their personal conceptual model is different from the conceptual model being used by someone else. This is not to suggest that one conceptual model is necessarily more correct than another, it simply suggests that a lack of clarification will lead to misunderstanding and disagreement.

UNDERSTANDING THE ROLE OF CONCEPTS IN THINKING

Before one begins to teach abstract concepts like power, students need to be made aware of the role of concepts in their thinking. They need to understand that concepts are the critical juncture between information and thinking. To begin, they need to understand the difference between concepts and facts. Consider again our simple example of chair. If I say bring me that chair, I am referring to a specific fact. Only a certain chair will do. But if I say bring me a chair; I am referring to the general category of chair, any one of which will do. If you are thinking that this is a very fine distinction, you are correct. It is a fine distinction. The important point about concepts is that they are the first small step a thinker takes in moving from specific facts to making interpretations and generalizations about those facts.

Thinking is the application of various thought processes to factual information or reality. For example, one might look at an object and ask what is this thing? The assumption underlying this question is that any thinking about the object is limited until some kind of interpretation and meaning can be assigned to the object. If it looks like . . . ; sounds like . . . ; smells like . . . ; then it must be a duck.[5] In other words, a comparison is being made between the characteristics of the object and the critical attributes of concepts stored in one's mind. This is the process of interpretation. When an interpretation has been made, then the object can be assigned to some conceptual category in the individual's mind. Now the door is open for more thinking about the object. However, if an interpretation cannot be made, then the object may be dismissed as meaningless, and attention focused elsewhere. The exception to this generalization occurs when the thinker senses that there is some very good reason to do the work developing the concept in his or her mind.

Concept Attainment

There are two considerations for teachers who want to help their students learn conceptually. The first is that students need to be engaged in concept attainment activities that allow them to conceptualize the information they are learning. The second consideration is that students need to be taught methods of using concepts as an aid to organizing and managing information so they can more easily draw conclusions from the reality that they have been studying.

The Learning Cycle

The learning cycle outlines an approach for introducing new concepts, skills, or values to students. It also demonstrates a way of moving from the assumptions of the information paradigm to those of the thinking paradigm. The fundamental intent of the learning cycle is to teach students to think independently by helping them relate the new ideas they are learning to their personal backgrounds

Figure 6.2 is a model learning cycle for concept attainment.

CONCEPT ATTAINMENT CYCLE

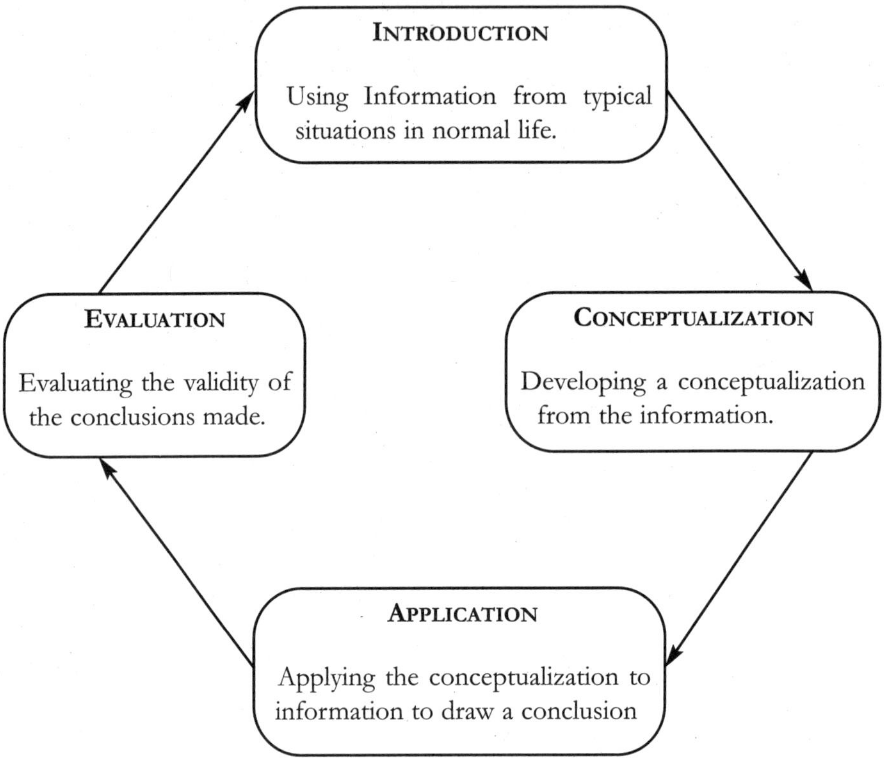

Fig. 6.2

The basic assumption of the learning cycle is that all learning must begin with student thought. Students learn new ideas best when they can relate ideas to information which is familiar to them. It is much more difficult to learn abstract ideas such as concepts if one is also dealing with unfamiliar information. Once students have firmly and clearly related a new idea to their personal background of information, they are in a position to build and extend their grasp of a concept by applying it to other information.

As can be seen from the diagram, there are four stages in this model. Stage one begins the concept attainment process by basing all learning on the student's background experiences. The teaching activities at this stage are aimed at helping students relate their current knowledge to some new concepts that will be useful for them to know. Once that has been accomplished, students may be ready to move to stage two, which is the conceptualization stage. It is here that they begin to conceptualize information into a concept. With a firmer conceptualization in place, students can move to stage three, the application stage. Here they can practice applying the concept to familiar information and later to unfamiliar information. At some point in stage three students will likely move to stage four or the evaluation stage by themselves. The change from stage three to four begins once they start asking questions about the validity of the conclusions they are making, and whether or not the concept they are using is sufficient for their purposes.

Usually there will be a natural flow from one stage to another. If stage one has been successful in helping students appreciate the significance of what they are learning, the movement in student thinking through the stages will be directed and controlled by the students themselves.

EFFECTIVE TEACHING OF THE LEARNING CYCLE

Stage One - Introduction

Instead of labelling the new concept and dictating a definition, teachers should provide students with a situation that encourages them to consider familiar information from the standpoint of the particular concept being studied. When this happens, students are likely to discover that they already know something about the concept. If the concept has not been labelled, students are much more likely to search their minds for their personal grasp of the concept. They are likely to find something that fits. What they find may not have the official conceptual label, but aspects of the concept may be in the students' minds. Even if it is not, students are in a position to start building a new conceptualization from concrete material with which they are familiar. This provides students with a much more secure base to think about new ideas.

This was the approach taken when the concept of power was discussed at the beginning of this chapter. Chairs are conceptual categories that students can easily understand. The concept of chair offers a simple way of helping students understand the idea of concept without having to struggle with learning a new concept as well. A concrete concept like 'chair' allows students to easily understand how chairs are an integral part of a pattern of concepts that make up the furnishing of a room. They can see how these concepts interrelate to form a meaningful pattern of reality.

The discovery by students that they already have some personal understanding of the notion of concept is a critical motivational step in deciding whether to consciously and deliberately use concepts as a tool in their thought processes. Without this motivation students are much more likely to memorize new concepts and then ignore them as being irrelevant to their lives. Ultimately, a memorized concept will be forgotten and lost to the student.

It is important to introduce abstract concepts using the background of students. An abstract concept such as power needs to be introduced in a way that allows students to see how they deal with the concept within their lives. Students need to see that the concept does play a significant role in their lives. The point of discussing games and the need for rules to cover disputes about play is to illustrate to students that they have been dealing with power relationships all of their lives. They are vitally concerned with issues of who makes the rules, who enforces them, and whether they have been applied equitably. These issues are discussed every day on the playground. At this stage, there is nothing new about power. All that is being done is nailing down an operational definition of the concept of power.

If students are given labels like power before they have gone through this introductory thought process, they may assume they do not know the concept. Then they will be tempted to skip the process of searching their minds for a personal understanding of the concept and simply memorize the new label. If the concept is genuinely new and after careful consideration of some familiar information the students come up dry, much has still been gained.

Stage Two - Conceptualisation

By now, the students have begun the process of gathering the critical attributes of the concept and relating them to their personal experiences. They are beginning the conceptualization stage, which will give them a conceptual understanding of the situation, and which will help them make the concept their concept. In the learning cycle, there will be a smooth flow from one stage to another. Once they have the critical attributes in their minds, they will be able to create a generalization of the concept which makes sense to them. Then, they will either give it a label themselves, or to accept the 'official' label the teacher provides. The important thing for students to understand is that the label is not the concept, anymore than their name is them.

In our discussion of chair and power, we reached the conceptualization stage. It is at this point that we defined the criteria or critical attributes which would admit an object or idea into a particular category. If the students are well prepared, this phase should go rather rapidly. When they get to the generalization part of the process, they will be able to say things like 'chairs are for sitting on' and 'power is the ability to make others do what you want them to do'. If students have really assimilated the concept, they often comment about how easy and obvious this exercise was. A high accolade a teacher can receive from students is the comment: "You mean that's all there is to this! These ideas are really simple."

It is important for teachers to understand that this does not necessarily mean that students have mastered the concept. It only means that they have a good preliminary understanding of the concept. Major concepts are complex and have a great deal of depth to them. Metaphorically, one could think of a concept as an ice berg where the ice above the water line represents the conscious understanding of a concept and the ice below the water line represents that which remains to be learned. A complex, abstract concept like love can require a life time of experience before one can claim a full understanding the concept.

Stage Three - Application

As students' comprehension of a concept matures and deepens, they will be able to accommodate new ideas about the concept into their personal conceptual structure. When students become comfortable with a new concept, they are ready to 'play' with the concept by applying it to a variety of contexts. They are now at the application stage.

The application stage is the point when students need to think about different situations using the concept(s) they are studying. It is helpful to students if the teacher judiciously introduces different material that students can use to think about with the new concept(s). With concrete objects such as chairs, the application process is relatively straight forward. (When do you use a stool and when do you use a chair?) With abstract concepts like power, more care needs to be taken. For example, the class could discuss power relationships within the school. Who has power within the school and how do they use it? It is still helpful in the early stages to keep the 'new' information as concrete and as familiar as possible. When students learn new information in this way (especially if the information is concrete), students are much more likely to discuss the information in depth and assimilate more of it.

Concepts Are Templates of Reality

It is in the application stage that the connection between conceptual categories and factual information is re-established. By their nature, concepts are organizers of information. They help people create models of reality within their minds. These mental models in effect become templates which make reality manageable.[6] A template can be a thin piece of wood or metal used as a pattern or mould. A cookie cutter is a template which can work in different kinds of media. Concepts act as intellectual templates, because they arrange sets of related facts into patterns that make reality comprehensible.

With a conceptual template or model in place, students have the ability to examine these relationships more systematically. This examination would not only apply to cases they are studying, but also to cases they have to deal with in their personal lives.

There are many situations in society that can be analyzed using power as a conceptual template. In the case of power, the concept describes a set of factors which affect relationships between people. Students can discuss the interpersonal relationships involved in various situations, and use them as a basis for making interpretations and for drawing inferences about the role of power in those relationships. In the process of doing this, they will be building personal mental models about power and society. They are now in a better position to understand and make predictions about the reality of power. This would be an inductive approach to understanding concepts.

On the next pages are some examples where the concept of power is used as a template to consider the reality of human relationships within society. In the first example there are five scenarios, each describing a conflict between people with different objectives. The people in the conflict have a certain amount of power they can marshal in an attempt to impose their point of view on another person. Students could be encouraged to identify with the points of view and attempt to determine what sources of power are available to each.

SITUATIONS In the situations below, decide for each person:	**THE SOURCES OF POWER** Power is a situation in which certain people have control over some or all of the attributes of power below:			
- What are the sources of power each person could reasonably use? - who will get their way?	**RESOURCES** Being able to use wealth to buy the services of others.	**ORGANIZATION** Being able to influence or direct people in organizations.	**NUMBERS OF PEOPLE** Being able to get the support of other people.	**INFORMATION** Being able to use skills and knowledge .
SITUATION ONE: A student and a teacher disagree about the mark an essay should be given.	In this situation, wealth passing hands could be considered bribery, and would be illegal.	The teacher has more of this power than the student because of the teacher's position.	The teacher would tend to get society's support; students would get student support.	The teacher has more knowledge at his/her disposal.
SITUATION TWO: The province of Alberta has passed a law which makes it illegal for young people to smoke in public.	The Government can afford to hire lawyers and police to enforce their decisions.	The Government has the legal right to pass laws. The students have constitutional rights which may apply.	The government has resources to seek and elicit public support. Students could work with the press, etc to gain public support.	Research on the effects of smoking on health supports the Government's position.
SITUATION THREE: Driver safety groups (D.S.G.) and young people disagree about whether the driving age should be increased to eighteen years.	D.S.G. would have more money for advertising than students.	D.S.G. could lobby on the basis of safety. Students could lobby on the basis of freedom.	Public opinion would be divided between: the safety and freedom arguments	D.S.G and students could debate the research on the driving records of young people.
SITUATION FOUR: At the next school dance, one group of students want to have more formal dance music. Other students want rock music.	Does one of groups have money and effort which it is willing to spend on advertising?	Does one of the groups have more influence with the S.R.C?	Does student public opinion favour one or over the other? Will some students change their opinion?	Does one group have a better understanding of how to affect public opinion?
SITUATION FIVE: Certain groups within society would like to censor the violence in movies because they believe it contributes to social violence. Movie companies disagree.	Movie companies are rich and can afford advertisers and lobbyists.	Politicians need money to get re-elected. Politicians like to support what the majority want.	Many people enjoy violent movies Others are worried about their effect.	Both sides will appeal to research to support their point of view.
What examples can you think of?				

Fig. 6.3

Scenario five presents a conflict between large movie corporations and citizens groups over the issue of the media's portrayal of violence. Students could be encouraged to speculate about how the movie companies and citizens' groups might use their sources of power to protect their interests. Some examples of what they might do follows:

	Movie Companies	Citizens' Groups
RESOURCES	- They might mount an expensive advertising campaign arguing that any controls imposed on them amount to censorship for everyone. - They could hire lobbyists to persuade politicians that censorship is a greater danger to society than violence in the media.	- Raise money to allow the leaders of citizens' groups to travel to capitals to persuade government leaders that something needs to be done about violence in the media.
ORGANIZATION	- They could use columnists and commentators from the newspapers and television stations they own to argue against censorship of the media. - They could put their lawyers to work finding legal ways of using injunctions to prevent citizens groups from interfering with media rights.	- They could talk to the editors of newspapers and magazines (media) in an attempt to influence their editorial policies on violence in the media. - They could contact political parties, church groups and other groups to persuade them to support the passage of laws against violence in the media.
NUMBERS OF PEOPLE	- Appeal for support from the many people who go to and enjoy violent movies.	- Appeal for support from the many people who are upset and worried about violence in the media.
INFORMATION	- Find and do research which shows that violence in the media does not lead to violence in society.	- They could find and do research which shows that violence in the media does affect the behaviour of people.

Fig. 6.4

A number of these examples can be used in discussion think about how power is applied in human relationships.

Power is more than just sources of power. It is also about making people do things they may not wish to do. The following scenarios are examples of applying power to others. The application of power often causes conflict and may hurt people. It is often accompanied by large doses of propaganda aimed at confusing people about their legitimate interests so that they can be more easily persuaded the power being applied to them is legitimate. Students need opportunities to consider the ethical application of power, and to consider how they can protect themselves from its unethical use. Conceptual templates allow them to cut through the propaganda and see what is actually happening in a situation. Without concepts to form their own models of reality, students will lack the ability to create credible alternative views of reality, and without those, they cannot be critical thinkers. All they would be left with is the point of view the propagandist wants them to accept.

Some examples of situations which call for the application of power are laid out in templates below. It would be helpful for students' conceptualization of power to discuss the implications involved in applying power. The first template involves a consideration of how power should be used. What are the consequences of the use of force as opposed to using a more charismatic approach? Students are often on the receiving end of power, so they will have had some experience with these issues. The second template involves analyzing the power sources people can draw upon in responding to the application of power. The third template examines the appropriate way of applying whatever power sources the students might make.

	The Application of Power The Types of Power and the Consequences of their Use Is choice A, B, or C the best way to enforce the decisions below?		
Decisions to be Enforced	**Charisma** People obey people or decisions because they believe in them.	**Authority** People obey people or decisions because they believe they have the right to make them.	**Force** People obey people or decisions because they are afraid of what will happen to them if they do not obey.
Governments should pass laws that make it illegal for young people to smoke under 18 years of age.	A. Governments should create an advertising campaign that shows smoking to be an ugly, uncool habit.	B. Governments should explain how cigarettes are an addictive and health destroying habit.	C. Governments should fine anyone caught smoking under the age of 18 years.
The majority of Canadians believe that Quebec must not be allowed to separate from Canada.	A. Canadians should work very hard at making the people of Quebec feel welcome in Canada.	B. The Government of Canada should use whatever legal authority it has to prevent Quebec from leaving.	C. The Government of Canada should use the Canadian armed forces to prevent Quebec from seceding.
The general public wants something done to discourage people from committing violent criminal acts.	A. Publicity should focus on the pain victims feel as the result of crime so that everyone is aware that crime has very serious consequences.	B. The government should establish programs to teach people that a law abiding life is more satisfying then a life of crime.	C. Governments must pass strict laws with harsh punishments and give the police the resources to find and arrest people who commit crimes.
International public opinion believes that rulers of nations who are dictators and use their power to kill thousands of people must be brought to justice.	A. The international community should offer investment money and advice to encourage and help countries find a better way of managing their affairs.	B. The UN should explain why human rights abuses are wrong and back that up with legal and economic sanctions as necessary.	C. The UN, supported by the international community, should be prepared to use military force to protect people against their dictators.

Fig. 6.5

IN THE SITUATIONS BELOW, DECIDE:	USING THE SOURCES OF POWER TO RESPOND EFFECTIVELY TO THE ABUSE OF POWER BY OTHERS			
- the sources of power available for use by each person - the best sources of power to use in the situation?	**RESOURCES** Being able to use wealth to buy the services of others.	**ORGANIZATION** Being able to influence or direct people in organizations.	**NUMBERS OF PEOPLE** Being able to get the support of other people.	**INFORMATION** Being able to use skills andknowledge.
1. A young female high school student is working at her first part time job and the manager makes a pass at her				
2. A young man's father is an alcoholic who regularly comes home drunk and beats him.				
3. A business is polluting the environment of the community in which you live and refuses to do anything about it.				
4. A minority ethnic group is being badly treated by the majority ethnic group within the country.				
5. US states have passed a number of laws aimed at controlling the behaviour of young people: - *Louisiana* - young people must address teachers as "Sir" or "Ma'am"; - *Utah* - teens may not drive between midnight and 5 a.m.; - *South Dakota* - children can now be fined if they are caught smoking; and, - *Indiana & Tennessee* - parents must approve all body piercing				

Fig. 6.6

Decisions to be Enforced by the Abused Person	The Application of PowerThe Types of Power and the Consequences of their Use Is choice A, B, or C the best way to enforce the decisions below?		
	Charisma People obey people or decisions because they respect them.	**Authority** People obey people or decisions because they believe they have the right to make them.	**Force** People obey people or decisions because they are afraid of what will happen to them if they do not obey.
1. The young female high school student decides to confront her supervisor. How should she do it?	Explain that she is a good employee and should be respected and left alone.	Explain that she will report him to his superiors and the police if she is not left alone in the future.	Explain that her boyfriend and his friends will beat him up after work if he tries anything again.
2. The son decides to confront his father. How should he do it?	Explain that he loves and respects his father and wishes the father would tell him what he has done wrong rather than beating him.	Explain that the next time a beating happens he will tell the police, social services, and the school principle about what has happened.	Explain that the next time he, the son, will fight back with whatever force is necessary to protect himself.
3. You are a member of an environmental group who want to stop the polluters. How should you do it?	Explain to the polluters that they also live in the community and that they and their children have to suffer the effects of the pollution.	Explain that you will go to the courts and get an injunction which will shut down their plants.	Explain that you will use sabotage against their plants to stop them from polluting.
4. What should the minority group do to protect themselves from the majority group?	They should explain to the majority that everyone loses when a society does not have human rights and a democracy.	Appeal to the UN and its international legal agencies to investigate and take action against the majority.	Form terrorist groups and sabotage the majority with bombs, etc.
5. What should young people in the following states do: - *Louisiana* - requires all young people to address teachers as "Sir" or "Ma'am"; - *Utah* - teens are not permitted to drive between midnight and 5 a.m.; - *South Dakota* - children can now be fined if they are caught smoking;	Create an organization of young people that will demonstrate to the majority of citizens that the majority of young people are law abiding, polite people who want to make good decisions about their lives.	Go to court and argue that these laws should be dismissed as unconstitutional, because they infringe on the basic rights of people.	Start a protest movement that will use civil disobedience so long as these laws remain in force.

Fig. 6.7

It is critical in the concept attainment process that concepts are fully discussed by students. In the case of power, it is particularly important students carefully consider the consequences of its use. Students must understand that power is often misused, and its misuse can affect both the users and receivers of power. By highlighting and defining the sources of power and discussing the ways in which power can be applied, the teacher makes it easier for students to comprehend and think about power relationships. Students are now able to create for themselves a more specific grasp of power relationships than the vague, intuitive understanding they may have had before. They now have a vocabulary to discuss and think about the relationships they see.

Suppose a young woman in your class has encountered sexual harassment in the workplace at her Saturday job. She is now in a better position to understand how a superior in the organization she is working for can use prestige and power to coerce young women into doing something they do not want to do. With this knowledge, she might feel more empowered to define and react to the power relationships she faces. She might also have a better understanding of how to use her personal power to react to this inappropriate use of power in an appropriate way.

Stage Four - Evaluation

Finally, students reach the evaluation stage in their thinking. Evaluation comes in many forms. Initially, it can be expressed in introspective questions by students: "What does this mean to me and my life?"; "How is this useful?" and "How does this change the way I understand things?" Much of this thinking will be somewhat unconscious. If students have been examining historical and/or current events material, their evaluative thinking will be critical of leaders and their policies. They may question the way certain historical figures have used power. They may question decisions made in the past. They will suggest there were other, better ways of using power. All of these indicate students are using the concept(s) they have learned as criteria to evaluate the behaviours and decisions of others.

The great and difficult leap is to introspect about personal behaviour. How do they use power when they have it? Does the end justify the means in their minds, or are they willing to accept some moral and ethical constraints on their personal use of power? Are they willing to accept new approaches for their lives or for the social policies of the society they live in? They may now be ready to apply a newly learned concept as a guide to the way they live their own lives.

The final step would be to begin to evaluate the validity of the concept itself. Good critical thinkers are able to question whether the concept itself is providing adequate criteria for evaluating reality. Is power the only -or even the best - approach to use when evaluating social situations? Another important evaluative leap for students to make is to ask whether the concept itself is an accurate reflection of reality. Is power a good perspective to use while considering social relationships? What are the consequences of using power as a way of understanding social relationships? These are the kinds of questions that students are now ready to consider.

Evaluation is a natural, logical outcome of the thought processes initiated by the learning cycle. Once students begin to truly conceptualize reality, they are able to understand and appreciate it. Then they cannot help but think about it. They will apply 'their' concepts to unfamiliar reality in an effort to understand it better. Along the way, they will ask evaluative questions about whether they agree with conclusions that have been developed in the class exercises. They will ask evaluative questions whether the teacher wants them to or not. It is an inevitable process.

Using the Learning Cycle to Teach a Concept

Power is an important but limited concept. There are many other important concepts students need to be familiar with if they are to understand historical issues. Let us suppose a class of high school students is embarked upon a study of the French Revolution. Of course, power plays an important role in the French Revolution, but there is another concept - social contract - which overrides the concept of power in significance. Students need to understand the notion of social contract if they are to have any conception of what is happening in a revolution.

Social contract is a significant concept because it establishes the ground rules for the way people within society interact with each other. It operates with all sizes of groups, cuts across socioeconomic classes and age groups, and can be found in all periods of history. It brings together social, cultural, political, and economic relationships. The concept of social contract can help students organize the behaviour of historical figures into patterns of behaviour that can be discussed and analysed. The concept of social contract needs to be taught, and the learning cycle is a good way of teaching it.

High school students, partly because they are going through an individualization process, tend to believe that they do not use social norms to govern their social behaviour. Many are frustrated with the socialization process and see it as a way of limiting their personal freedom by keeping them in a state of childhood. Based on these kinds of assumptions, adolescents believe they interact with each other without adopting the social norms they see adults following. Given all of this, adolescents will be predisposed to discount the concept of social contract as something that has little relevance to their lives unless they can be helped to see its relevance.

Introduction of the Concept in the Learning Cycle

It is critical to introduce the concept of social contract by using examples from the adolescent social milieu. At this point, it is not necessary to refer to or use the term social contract. It would be better if were not used until the conceptualization stage has been completed. As part of a class discussion, some or all of the following questions could be discussed:

- Does the adolescent society of which they are a part have rules about acceptable and unacceptable behaviour related to speech, behaviour, dress, school, parents, activities, etc?
- Do they have a set of beliefs and values which control their behaviour?
- What happens when these beliefs and values are disobeyed?

Out of the discussion, solicit a list of important rules about behaviour from the students and place them on the chalkboard. Now ask the students to consider what sanctions can be imposed for violating those rules.

- Ask students to consider privately how their personal behaviour is controlled and limited by these sanctions.
- Record those controls and sanctions that students agree are used in society to control behaviour beside each rule.

In this kind of a discussion, it is very helpful for the students if the conclusions they come to are recorded. With this aid, students do not have to remember more than they are capable of. This makes the discussion much less abstract and helps everyone follow the direction of the conversation. In effect, the teacher is acting as the secretary of the meeting by keeping minutes. Students should be aware that this is the primary function for recording ideas. As students become used to this model, they may wish to act as secretary themselves, thereby taking over more control of their discussion processes. By using this approach, the teacher is also modelling analytical thinking, which will be discussed in more detail later in the book.

Below is a template that could be used as a discussion guide; yet this template is both a discussion guide and a model of how to organize reality. If teachers use these templates consistently, students will come to expect and rely upon them. In the process, students will begin to assimilate these templates for use as part of their own lives. These templates do not stifle creativity. Research now indicates that they do just the opposite. A template provides the structure which people use as a springboard to creativity. Students are much more likely to come up with creative ideas when they have the intellectual support of a template.

A Suggested Template for Recording Ideas

BEHAVIOUR (Ways in which people in your group behave)	VALUES (The ideas people in your group have about the correct way of behaving)		SANCTIONS (The ways people in your group control the behaviour of others)
	ACCEPTABLE BEHAVIOUR?	UNACCEPTABLE BEHAVIOUR?	
- SPEECH			
- BEHAVIOUR			
- DRESS			
- PARENTS			
- ACTIVITIES			
- SCHOOL			
- OTHER SUGGESTIONS			

Fig. 6.8

Now move the class discussion to the question of the validity of these social controls. Ask them why they submit to these controls with their sanctions? Are the social controls recorded constructive and helpful? If so, why are they helpful? If they are not helpful, why do they continue to accept them?

A Suggested Recording Pattern for the Chalkboard

VALUES about acceptable behaviour for:	HELPFUL? Which of the values are helpful, and which are not?		ACCEPTANCE/REJECTION Why do you accept certain values and reject others?	
	HELPFUL	UNHELPFUL	ACCEPTED VALUES	REJECTED VALUES
SPEECH				
BEHAVIOUR				
DRESS				
PARENTS				
ACTIVITIES				
SCHOOL				
OTHER BEHAVIOURS				

Fig. 6.9

The discussion might also explore related concepts like manners. What is the role of manners in society? Does adolescent society have a code of manners, even though it may not exactly follow the adult code? How is it similar and different?

At this point, the discussion of governing conduct could be extended to other areas of life. For example, what is the social code governing the conduct of sports? Once students have explored this idea, have them make a list of areas (families, schools, traffic, business, military, politics, etc.) in society and consider how these areas are governed by codes of conduct. Where people are free and where are they constrained? What are the sanctions that enforce these codes of conduct? It would be useful at this point to discuss positive sanctions as well as negative sanctions. For example, is praise more powerful in controlling human behaviour than criticism?

Social Controls in Different Areas of Society

	Codes of Conduct		Sanctions	
Areas of Society	Acceptable Behaviour	Unacceptable Behaviour	Positive Sanctions	Negative Sanctions
Families				
Schools				
Traffic				
Business				
Military				
Business				
Military				
Politics				
Other areas				

Fig. 6.10

Conceptualization Stage in the Learning Cycle

At this point, the students should be ready for the notion that human affairs are governed by a central concept. Like other concepts, this concept has a set of attributes that form the basis for a generalization, and collectively the attributes and generalization are given a label. In outline form, it looks like the following:

- This notion of human relationships has the following attributes:
- It is an agreement between individuals within a group;
- It occurs within all groups;
- It consists of unspoken assumptions about the proper relationships between people;
- Among other things, these assumptions govern the rights and duties of each member in a group;
- The agreement is enforced by sanctions.
- These attributes may be summarized as a generalization:
- Groups create agreements to define the rights and duties of each membe,r which are enforced by sanctions.
- This set of ideas is labelled social contract.

The concept of social contract is fundamental to understanding how societies work in the present, and how they worked in the past. An understanding of social contract is necessary in order to understand what a revolution is and why they occur. That is why students need to learn some fundamental concepts before they can study an historical event like the French Revolution.

We will continue to discuss the relationship between the concept of social contract and historical events like the French Revolution in the application and evaluation phases of the learning cycle several pages on. In the meantime, it is necessary to discuss two important methods of developing an initial conceptualization with students.

Two Approaches to Developing a Conceptualization

There are two ways of helping students conceptualize a category of ideas. The inductive way is to give students examples of situations from social reality, and then ask them to generalize the critical attributes that constitute a social contract from the situations The deductive approach would be to give the students the critical attributes and have them look for examples in the social reality with which they are familiar. Both approaches are useful. In fact, both should be used. Once students have gained some familiarity with the concept of social contract, they will then apply the concept deductively to a variety of social situations as part of their analysis of the social situation. There will be more about that when we discuss the application phase of this process.

From the standpoint of helping students learn to become independent learners, the inductive approach should be used as much as possible. If a class of students have had the opportunity to consider many of the examples of social conduct during the introduction phase discussed above, they will already have many of the critical attributes of social contract in place in their minds. Conceptualization then becomes a process of identifying the critical attributes and arranging them into some kind of meaningful pattern (a generalization) and assigning that pattern a label, in this case 'social contract'. If students are well prepared by the introductory discussions on social reality, they will have little trouble making the leap. It is likely many of them will be thinking: "What's the big deal?"

The deductive approach is also useful. With this approach, the teacher would lay out the pattern of critical attributes that make up a concept and then ask the students to either find or think of examples from reality. For teachers who may not be completely familiar with a concept and feel the need to go slowly as they experiment with the concept in the classroom, the deductive approach is a good one.

The Deductive Approach to Conceptualization

Below is a conceptual pattern defined by the critical attributes of the concept. A teacher might place this template on the chalkboard, and consider with the students in a class discussion how various social groups create a social contract to guide them as they interact with each other.

What would be helpful in developing the independent thinking of students is to give students the structure of critical attributes of the concept social contract as laid out in the first column of the template below. Then in a class discussion apply the critical attributes of the concept to a variety of social groups students know. Three are listed as examples in the figure below. There are many others: athletic teams, the work place, church, clubs, etc. It is important to encourage the students through discussion to determine how the social contract is organized and applied for each social group discussed. The examples in the figure below should not be deemed to be the "correct" answer but should be seen as examples which illustrate possible ways a social contract can work within different social groups. (The possible student answers are in italics.)

A SOCIAL CONTRACT IS:			
an agreement . . .	to form a group of friends	to get married	to be part of a high school
. . . between members of a group . . .	*by a group of young people who live in the same neighbourhood and go to the same school*	*between two people*	*between:* *students; parents; teachers; society; taxpayers; employers*
. . . which awards rights . . .	for: *- friendship in the form of...* *- social activities such as....* *- support in times of trouble...*	for: *- love...* *- friendship...* *- sharing...* *- support...*	for: *- education...* *- friendship...* *- personal development...* *- athletics...* *- arts...*
. . . and imposes duties . . .	and requires: *- loyalty...* *- sharing...* *- caring...* *conformity...*	and requires: *- loyalty...* *- giving...* *- sharing...* *work...*	and reguires: *- work...* *- dedication...* *- obedience...*
. . . enforced by sanctions.	enforced by: *- rejection...* *- gossip...* *- ridicule...* *- low status...*	enforced by: *- rejection...* *- beliefs...* *- law...*	enforced by: *- rejection...* *- marks...* *- failure...* *- punishment...*

Fig. 6.11

After students have completed laying out the pattern of critical attributes found in a concept, and agreed upon a label for the concept, they need to make a generalization about the concept. A generalization is a kind of summary or definition that sums up the essentials of the concept. It is the gist (See *Chapter Eight* for a discussion of Gist) or meaning of the concept that we remember as we go through life. It is unlikely that we will be able to retain long lists of critical attributes of many different concepts. If we know the concept we can work up the lists of critical attributes as needed. For day to day thinking, we will rely more on the concept's generalization. In this case the generalization is quite straight forward and is already laid out for the students: a social contract is an agreement between members of a group which awards rights and imposes duties enforced by sanctions.

The Inductive Approach to Conceptualization

In the inductive approach, teachers should encourage students to look for common patterns within those social groups students know well. Have students give an example of a social group they belong to, and ask them to think about how that social group works. Discuss whether there are any rules that everyone obeys. Discuss why people obey these rules. Give students a template like the one below and use it to guide the students' discussion. Ask students to think of other groups they can use to compare with the first group. Look for the similarities and differences among the different groups. Do these similarities form some kind of pattern?

While working on these templates in class, encourage students to look under the surface of each group and begin to ask themselves what causes the pattern of group behaviour they see. Encourage students to brainstorm ideas that might be valid. They should feel free to add, reject, and modify their ideas as needed until they have a satisfactory pattern of ideas. The template below is an example of what this process might look like when the students have finished their discussions. The answers in italics are intended only to be illustrations and are *not* intended to be the "correct" answers students are expected to give.

TYPES OF GROUPS	REASONS FOR BELONGING TO A GROUP	WAYS OF CONTROLLING THE MEMBERS OF A GROUP	CHARACTERISTICS OF EACH GROUP
INFORMAL STUDENT SOCIAL GROUPS	- I like to be around people my own age that I can talk to and share things with. - It is so fun to hang out with friends and talk about boys/girls and things. - I like it when we can share clothes and the way we talk, - It is cool to be different from all those old guys	- I don't like being around Geeks, nerds, and wimps. - I like friends who stand up for each other. - I get so embarrassed when my parents make me wear something weird. - We want to do the things we like to do and not be bossed around.	Student social groups have the power to: - accept or reject members; - demand loyalty from its members; - demand conformity form its members; and, - decide what is important and unimportant.
SPORTS TEAMS	- I love to play hockey, soccer, etc. - I love to win when I play. - I like being on a team where everybody jokes around and helps each other. - It feels great to be good enough to play in a championship game.	- I work very hard at learning to play my position well so I don't screw up. - I don't like guys who won't help others on the team. - I really worry about being cut from the team	Sports teams have the power to provide their members with: - interesting activities - opportunities for success; - opportunities to share and work with others; - a sense of achievement; -to decide who gets to be on the team and who does not.
CLUBS	- I love to play bridge - This club gave me the opportunity to become a better bridge player. - I like to talk to people about how to play bridge. - I have made many friends in this club.	I would sure miss playing bridge. I could not have learned to be a good bridge player by myself. I would get lonely if I could not talk to other people about bridge. I don't know what else I would do if I did not have my bridge friends	The group has the power to provide their members with: - things to do that fit their interests; - a place to improve their abilities; - a place to share their interests with others, - a place to make friends and have a social life.
			continued . . .

HIGH SCHOOLS	- You need an education to get somewhere in life. - I want to get marks being successful - I want to go to university and become a …. - I like those classes that teach me interesting things. - I have made a lot friends at school.	- If you don't work hard, you'll fail your exams - You better pay attention to what your teachers tell you if you don't want to get in trouble. - I work harder at the classes I like. - I work harder for the teachers I like. - I try to do things that my friends will like.	High schools can help its students: - achieve their hopes and dreams; - become successful at the things they want to do; - satisfy their curiosity about the world; and, - find friends and establish social relationships.
JOBS	- I need to make money in order to support myself and my family. - I feel important when I am doing my job. - Being in charge of things and doing something new makes me feel good. - I like working with people when we can get something done. - I like to do a job that is interesting and means something	- I like earning a good pay cheque. - I would be really upset and hurt if I were fired. - I work hard to make sure things are done right. - I don't want to let people down. - I like it when I know people respect what I have done.	A job provides the opportunity to: - to make a living;. - do things that are worthwhile; - do things that others are not able to do; - work with others to accomplish something; and, - to feel part of something that makes life meaningful.

Fig. 6.12

When students have completed their thinking about groups, ask them to compare their conclusions about groups with the critical attributes of the concept of social contract. What are the similarities between the behaviour of groups as they see them and the predictions of the social contract concept? If there is an idea missing from the students' conclusions, let them know that they may still add the idea to their conclusions about the nature of the different groups provided it seems acceptable. Allow them to discuss the predictions of the concept of social contract as fully as they need to? A template like the following might help the students see the relationships more easily.

A Template for Comparing The Characteristic of Groups

Informal Student Groups	Sports Teams	High Schools	Common Attributes
Student social groups have the power to: - accept or reject members; - demand loyalty from its members; - demand conformity from its members; - decide what is important and unimportant.	Sports teams have the power to provide their members with: - interesting activities; - opportunities for success; - opportunities to share and work with others; - a sense of achievement; - decide who gets to be on the team and who does not.	High schools can help its students: - achieve their hopes and dreams; - become successful at the things they want to do; - satisfy their curiosity about the world; - find friends and establish social relationships.	- People want to belong to groups. - Groups give their members permission to do certain things. - Groups tell their members what they may do. - Groups punish their members for disobeying the group.

Fig. 6.13

Once students have completed this part, ask them to compare their conclusions with the critical attributes of the concept social contract using the following template. Once they have done that, have them think of other groups such as their families, jobs they know about, other clubs, Canadian society, other societies they know about and societies from the past. Do they fit the pattern laid out by the concept of social contract?

Their Conclusions about the Characteristics of Groups	Concept of Social Contract	How well do other groups fit with the concept of Social Contract?	How well do other groups fit with the concept of Social Contract?
- People want to belong to groups. - Groups tell their members what they can do. - Groups tell their members what they must do. - Groups punish their members for disobeying the group.	A social contract is: - an agreement: - between members of a group; - which awards rights and imposes duties; - which are enforced by sanctions.	Example #1	Example #2

Fig 6.14

THE APPLICATION STAGE IN THE LEARNING CYCLE

Concepts are intellectual tools which were invented to help us comprehend the world we live in. They are not an end in themselves. We learn concepts in order to understand other things. You will recall that the original intent behind teaching students to understand and use concepts such as social contract was to prepare them to understand historical events. The French Revolution would be an example.

Students will need some concrete experiences in using new concepts in a variety of situations. Concepts look somewhat different when they are applied to different situations. Students who only have a preliminary understanding of the concept based on a narrow set of examples are likely to become confused when they begin to apply it to different situations. Role play or Simulation gaming is a useful technique for helping students see concepts operating as a social process.

Personal Experience as Application

The French Revolution can be simulated very nicely. The class should be divided into the First, Second, and Third Estates proportionately to the actual population size of the estates in 1789. Allow students some time to study the various problems facing French society in 1789 from the point of view of their estate. Soon they will begin to understand that their estate has a definite point of view. When they are ready, have them role play the Estates General at the time it was called into session by Louis XVI. As the students debate and make decisions, they tend to make decisions similar to those the historical figures made between 1789 and 1795.

After the simulation game is over, it is important for students to review events in the simulation game they enacted as a prelude to understanding the social processes that occurred in France during the revolutionary years. The concept of social contract provides a good structure for that. The diagram below outlines a template that can be used to guide a discussion about the effect different interpretations of the social contract had on French society before and during the French Revolution simulation.

Social Contract	Social Contract Existing Prior to 1789	First Major Change	Second Major Change
A social contract is: - an agreement: - between members of a group; - which awards rights and - imposes duties; - are enforced by sanctions.	- Who made the agreement? - Who enforced the social contract? - Who had rights and who did not? - What duties did people have? - How were these duties enforced?	Who disagreed with the existing social contract? How was the old social contract broken? How did the rights, duties, and the way they were enforced change?	Who disagreed with the revised social contract? How was the revised social contract changed? How did the rights, duties, and the way they were enforced change?

Fig. 6.15

After students have had time to think about their behaviour and their decisions, they should have an opportunity to examine the events of the French Revolution. An excellent motivational tool to introduce students to the romance of the French Revolution is the movie based on Charles Dickens' novel *A Tale of Two Cities*. As the movie tells its story, the students will be able to identify with the classes and to appreciate the underlying struggle over changing society. After watching and discussing the movie, students will be in a good position to begin an independent historical study of the events of the French Revolution. Students now have a conceptual basis from which they can make meaningful interpretations. They also have two models of historical interpretation, from which to launch their research. They can compare the historical model developed in their simulation and the model developed by Charles Dickens with what they find in the histories they research. There will be variation and those variation will a stimulus to critical and independent thinking about the events of the French Revolution.

If students have been allowed to think their way through this process, they should have a good concept of social contract. They will be able to use the concept as tool to understand how people in other places and times organize their societies. There are many ways the concept can be used as a tool.

Research as Application

Concepts can be used as templates to guide and direct research. If students are encouraged to use the question stems 'who, what, when, where, why' in conjunction with the critical attributes of the concept, it would be quite simple for them to create a whole set of research questions. An example of such a template might look like *Figure 6.16*.

THE CONCEPT OF SOCIAL CONTRACT	RESEARCH QUESTIONS SUGGESTED BY THE CONCEPT:	INFORMATION DISCOVERED AND RECORDED:
A SOCIAL CONTRACT IS:	THE OLD REGIME WAS A SOCIAL CONTRACT BASED ON TRADITION:	1.
- an agreement:		
- between members of a group;	Who made the agreement?	2.
- which awards rights and	- What did it say?	2A
- imposes duties; and,	- Why was it made?	2B
- which are enforced by sanctions.	Who had rights and who did not?	3.
	- Why were rights divided as they were?	3A
	- Why did some people get more rights then others?	3B
	- Who determined how rights would be divided?	3C
	What duties did people have?	4.
	- Why were duties divided as they were?	4A
	- Why did some people have more duties then others?	4B
	- Who determined how duties would be divided?	4C
	- How were these duties enforced?	5.
	- Who were involved in these decisions?	5A
	- Who did the enforcing?	5B
	- Why did people originally accept these sanctions?	5C
	- Why were fewer and fewer people accepting them now (1789-95)?	5D

Fig. 6.16

Student research is greatly facilitated by setting up their research program along conceptual lines. By this time, students should have developed a mental model about the effect of social contract on the organization and behaviour of people within society. When students go to the library with a personal mental model and a related research program, they will have a much clearer set of research objectives.. When they read data from various sources, they will be able to put the information into some kind of personal context. With a personal and research context they are able to make interpretations much more readily. After they have gathered their research data they have a model to organize their information into a pattern which will be useful to them when they begin to write a paper.

Writing Essays as Application

The concept also provides students with a preliminary outline for their paper which is clearly tied to their research data. Students now have a research plan which gives them have a conceptual basis on which to make interpretations, a set of research questions to work from, a method of recording their data in an orderly fashion, and a preliminary outline for their paper. This is enough background for students to plan, research and write a simple expository paper. This approach can also be used to compare and contrast societies. For example why would two societies faced with similar conditions make different choices about their social contract? Why did London and Paris make such different choices? This is the question Dickens was wrestling with in *A Tale of Two Cities.*

Evaluation in the Learning Cycle

Evaluation is often something we are tempted to skip in the classroom. Time is always a pressing issue, and when a unit of study is done, teachers feel a strong need to move on so they can cover the course. Sometimes everyone is just tired of the topic and cannot think of a single useful thing that still needs to be said. Sometimes students are upset about what they have learned and are asking rebellious questions. This is likely to be the case if students have developed mental models that allow them to see reality in new ways.

Students should always be encouraged to ask the question "so what?" At this point in the learning cycle, they need to be encouraged to ask tough evaluative questions. In the example we have been using, students should be asking themselves whether all the information they have learned about the concept of social contract and its relationship to different societies has anything to do with their lives. Their thinking may have advanced enough that they are ready to question the Canadian social contract. Time should be set aside to encourage them to do that. These kinds of questions might be a logical outcome of some current events discussions:

Louis Pasteur once said: "Chance favours the prepared mind." Discovery is less the result of chance than it is result of a capacity developed enough to recognize something that was always there. The fact that students now have some intellectual tools in place allows them to think of more probing questions. Certain issues and problems become part of their awareness in a way that they had not been before. Students may now wonder why certain countries continually undergo violence and social disruption, while other countries solve their problems in more constructive ways. Conceptual models allow one to observe reality more clearly, and more importantly recognize the significance of what is seen. Students need to know that this is what is happening to them.

Students under the spell of new concepts are prone to fall prey to cynicism about the imperfect world they have just discovered. If one thinks of concepts as messengers bringing new perceptions and interpretations to the viewer, the viewer needs to be careful not to shoot the messenger simply because they do not like the message. Students have to be helped not to avoid these kinds of mistakes as they do their personal evaluations. They need to be helped to channel their thinking along constructive lines of thinking. Cynicism is a blaming evasion of personal responsibility. Students need to be challenged to accept personal responsibility for their lives by learning from the mistakes of the past and the present rather than by blaming. Then the issue becomes how can what has been learned to make constructive improvements in one's life and on that basis advocate improvements in the way public policy is conducted.

Students might be interested in comparing social contracts between societies: What are the basic assumptions of social contracts for the following societies?

- Their high school?
- Canada?
- Some other societies that happen to be in the news?

Students might be interested in examining the lives of some great reformers:

- Martin Luther King;
- What kind of a social contract was he and his followers faced with?
- What reforms to the social contract did King advocate?
- What ways and means did King use in forcing change to the existing social contract?
- Do similar problems exist in the students' high school and within Canadian society?
- What changes need to be made and how should people go about making the changes?
- Have students discuss contrasting approaches to changing existing social contracts:
- How does Osama Bin Laden (or some other similar current example) compare with Martin Luther King?
- Ends and means: does the way you change a social contract determine what the new social contract will look like?

This kind of personal advocacy requires that students do their intellectual homework. Another common mistake at this stage is to advocate simplistic solutions for complex problems. Students must be willing to admit, at least to themselves, that their mental models have the potential to be inadequate. They must be willing to challenge and revise their conceptual assumptions. They must also be willing to do the necessary research that will allow them to do complex thinking about complex problems. The classroom is a good place to gently but rigorously examine some of the complex issues facing humanity. Students need the opportunity to try out ideas in a forum where they can consider their utility without being beaten up too badly intellectually.

As students begin to use this process, they will also discover that they need more information. Concepts without information are not very useful. Neither is information without concepts. Information and concepts are truly partners. If students are going to be willing to do their intellectual homework on an ongoing basis, they need to develop research tools which can be readily used. If research remains a difficult, laborious process, few are going to do it. When anyone does research, it is the conceptual models they have developed that guide the research.

Some General Conclusions

Concepts have the potential to give students the necessary intellectual templates to support the research they want to do. Students can learn to develop research templates similar to the one used in the discussion above on the French Revolution. As discussed earlier, with its conceptual structure, this template can provide a research plan, a set of research questions to work from, a method of recording data in an orderly fashion, and a preliminary outline for their paper. When students learn to apply these four functions, research becomes less daunting; making it more likely they will do it.

Teachers' most powerful contribution to this process is through modelling so that students can see the evaluative process in action. Then they can copy the model all the while mentally visualizing themselves doing the process. Visualization is the key. When they are able to visualize themselves doing evaluation successfully, they will do it in their personal lives. Success is critical. When students introspect they need to feel that it is an important process and they are doing it successfully.

END NOTES

1. Barry Beyer. "Improving thinking skills: Defining the problem". *Phi Delta Kappan.* 1984 Vol. 65 No 7 pp.486-490.

2. Suzanne Wexel. *IBM PC DOS Microsoft Windows.* Indianapolis: Que College 1995. p.164.

3. John P. Mckay, Bennett D. Hill, and John Buckler. *A History of Western Society Volume II: From Absolutism to the Present.* Boston: Houghton Mifflin Company .1987. p. 524.

4. It should be noted that this is also inductive thinking.

5 Concepts are rubrics in the sense in the sense that they act as a heading, rule or guide to reality.

6. In *Chapter Eight*, the process of defining and evaluating criteria will be discussed in more detail.

Chapter Seven: Critical and Creative Thinking

To have that sense of one's intrinsic worth which constitutes self-respect is potentially to have everything."

- Joan Didion

Table of Contents

INTRODUCING CRITICAL AND CREATIVE THINKING SKILLS

Students need to master a wide variety of thinking skills. By the high school years, students have some thinking skills in place and will be using them in their personal lives. Other skills will remain to be mastered. High school education should focus on helping students recognize the skills they do have, and encouraging them to develop those skills they do not have. Since academic thought is mostly outside students' personal experience, students need training in applying both groups of skills to their academic pursuits. Such an approach accomplishes two important goals. One is motivation, and the other is positive self-worth. Critical and creative thinking reguires self-motivated individuals who want to accomplish something by thinking. Self-worth contributes to thinking because it can be risky, and individuals who are confident are more likely to think critically and creatively then those who are uncertain about their right to hold and express a point of view.

Respect for self-worth and motivation are critical considerations in the design of successful classroom practices related to thinking skills. Self-worth plays an important role in determining whether the skills students already know and practice in their personal lives will be used in the classroom. This is a critical concern when students are moving from an information based teaching situation to one that is thought based. Students from an information based background are likely to believe personal knowledge is irrelevant in the classroom. Information based approaches tend to ask students to think about situations far from their personal experience; hence it seldom occurs to them to use thinking skills they already know in the classroom.

While motivation is closely related to self-worth, it is also related to the need to think about something inherently interesting to the thinker. One can list a number of considerations here: relevance to the thinker's life; a problem needing to be solved; a mystery calling for an explanation. Whatever the activity is, to motivate, it has to provide a real reason (need) to think. That reason, necessarily, has to be from the thinker's perception, not from the teacher's.

The first chore for high school educators is to lay the groundwork for an ethic of thinking among students. Such an ethic needs to be established early as possible in high school careers. That way, the academic life of students will be richer as they learn to apply and augment their thinking skills for use throughout their academic lives. If the significant purpose of education is independent thinking and learning, then it follows that attaining those skills which make independent thinking and learning possible is a critical objective for the classroom.

Here is an example of an activity that works well with grade nine students. It does stimulate critical and creative thinking, and it does so at a level that allows grade nine people to think. The underlying purpose of this exercise is to prepare students to conceptualize a set of thinking skills, but the students are not going to be told that just yet. The exercise is to think about a simple mystery. Show the class, unannounced, a brown paper bag filled with a mystery substance of some sort. Hand the bag to a student who will gingerly take it with a somewhat puzzled expression. Meanwhile, other students quickly become curious. Take the bag from the first student and hand it to another student elsewhere in the class. Now all eyes are on the bag, and the level of unspoken questions are rising. Transfer the bag to a third student. By this time someone will have asked; "What is this?" Another; "What's this all about?" A third; "What's inside the bag?" Around the classroom students will begin to call out; "Let me see it!"

Everyone loves a mystery. We are all curious, and a bag filled with something unknown demands an explanation. We are also very tactile. Every student longs to hold the bag believing that touch will somehow magically explain the mystery. When you refuse an explanation for your behaviour, the students will regard you with amused frustration as they think to themselves; "What nonsense has the teacher come up with? Again!"

What skills do students need to know in order to perform independent thinking? Let us follow the progress of the brown paper bag exercise for a while to see if we can discover an answer. This lesson is going to provide a model of thinking, which guides the thinking of students as they attempt to solve "The Mystery of the Brown Paper Bag." But before we do that, we need to consider the concept of metacognition.

Metacognition: The Process of Understanding and Evaluating One's Thinking

Metacognition is the ability to stand back from oneself and ask whether the thinking one is doing has the potential to be successful. Before students can do this they have to master some thought operations. They need to have conceptualized a set of thinking skills from which they can select those that will support their thinking needs. They need to understand how thinking skills can be organized into a variety of different patterns suitable to the current thinking project. Then they can decide whether they have chosen a productive approach. They must learn that if one organizational pattern does not produce the desired results, another might. Creativity involves being able to imagine new and productive ways of organizing one's thinking.

Some metacognition for the teacher: So far in this chapter, we have been considering the organization of a thinking skills unit. The objectives for the unit are to help students conceptualize thinking skills, understand that thinking skills are used in patterns, realize that the organizational pattern may change from situation to situation, and realize that the test for any pattern of thinking skills is whether it produces acceptable results.

In previous chapters, we looked at a teaching heuristic called the learning cycle. You will recall that the learning cycle begins with a personal, concrete experience of some kind (the brown paper bag in this case). Then students are helped to conceptualize their learning (which is what we are about to do below). Then they are given opportunities to apply their learning to other situations as a way of extending and consolidating their conceptualizations. And finally, students should be given opportunities to critically evaluate what they have learned. This is the formal metacognition stage in the learning cycle.

In helping students move to the conceptualization stage of the learning cycle, it would be useful now to review with students what they have done so far. Tell students they are going to be 'flies on the classroom wall' watching their behaviour in the 'brown paper bag' exercise. In this debriefing exercise, it would be useful to diagram all the stages so students can follow the thought processes they used. Give students a template something like the one below, and use it as a guide for discussion. It would be most useful for students if the template were developed as the class discussed what had happened during the activity.

Student Behaviour: (What did you do?)	**Student Thinking:** (What were you thinking?)	**Thinking Skills** (What thinking skills were you using?)
1. We observed a brown paper bag.	We were wondering: "What is this all about?" "What's in the bag?"	We were asking questions about this mystery. DEFINING A PROBLEM.
2. We scrutinized, handled, squeezed, and smelled the brown bag.	How can we find out what is in the bag?	We were searching for as much information as we could find. GATHERING INFORMATION.
3. We thought about the information we had gathered.	We tried to figure out what was in the bag from the information we had gathered.	We made a list of ideas we were certain about. CATEGORIZING INFORMATION
4. We made as many suggestions for what might be in the bag as we could think of.	We were trying to imagine what contents would fit with what we knew about the bag.	We made a long list of every possibility we could think of. BRAINSTORMING
5. Now, we wondered how to decide which of our suggestions were correct.	We made a list of what we knew for certain about the contents of the bag.	So, we compared each possibility with the list we had made and threw out those that did not fit. CLASSIFYING INFORMATION
6. By now we were sharing hunches about what was in the bag.	We kept asking ourselves which one of the possibilities is the most likely one?	We kept thinking about what could be soft, smooth, light, and small enough to go into that bag. MAKING INFERENCES
7. Soon most of us were making up our minds about what was in the bag.	We were thinking that it has got to be a certain thing, because that's the best fit.	We were making up our minds. DEVELOPING AN HYPOTHESIS
8. We disagreed with each other about the contents of the bag.	We tried to convince each other why it had to be a certain thing	We really needed to explain to each other why it had to one thing and could not be another. ANALYSIS
9. But, when we began to listen to other people's ideas, we became less and less certain we were right.	We began to second guess ourselves.	We found ourselves going over all the stuff we had thought about to see we had missed something. EVALUATION
10. Finally, we decided there is only one thing really makes sense.	"Most of were quite certain this could be the only real possibility."	We finally made up our minds DRAWING A CONCLUSION
11. Now we were ready to check for certain what was in that bag.	"But, we still wondered whether we had found the correct answer."	We would never be satisfied until we had a chance to find out for sure what was in the bag. EVALUATION

Fig. 7.1

This activity should be seen as an introductory activity, the purpose of which is to help students understand they have used these skills many times in their lives. There are many examples of personal life experiences the students could discuss. Have them recall various decision making situations they were involved in. Ask them whether the thinking in this exercise varied much from the thought processes they used when deciding what they would like to do on a weekend evening for example? The template above could be used as a model to help students trace their thinking in a variety of decision making or problem solving situations.

NOMENCLATURE - CATEGORIZING THINKING

We have been and will continue to use a number of terms for the processes of thinking. Each term describes a somewhat different aspect of thinking. Traditionally, skills have been used as a term to label the various processes of thinking. As a view of thinking, the term 'skills' defines thinking too narrowly, because it assumes thinking is only behaviour. Such a view presupposes students learn thinking skills by watching others, copying them and practicing the behaviours they see. As students practice thinking, they become more adept at it. There is some validity to this view, but it misses other critical aspects of thinking.

Another term used to describe thinking abilities that reflects a more recent view of thinking. Its approach is somewhat similar to the term skills, and is often used in tandem with skills, as in 'skills and abilities'. Ability is a somewhat broader conception of thinking that describes capacity as well as behaviour. Ability refers to the mental power to do certain things. Ability is usually followed by an infinitive: as in the ability to analyse. Thinking viewed in this way assumes thought processes require knowledge as well as skills.

Before one has the ability to think, the thinker must be able to understand and arrange concepts in systematic patterned ways For example, In the brown bag exercise, the fundamental thinking skill of categorizing data required conceptual knowledge related to the composition of materials i.e. soft, smooth, light, etc. It is very difficult to categorize without being able to conceptualize. Categorization and classification are critical precursors to analysis, an important thought process.

The term thought process views thinking as a process. Thinking is not just applying one or two skills and abilities to a situation and coming away with a conclusion. Solving the mystery of the brown paper bag was a process in which a number of thinking skills and abilities were used in a sequence to arrive at a conclusion. No single skill or ability would have been able to provide an adequate answer. When thinking is viewed that way, it becomes obvious that thinking requires the ability to create heuristics.[1]

Skills are also concepts. Thinking skills (abilities or processes) are not usually thought of as concepts. But if we define concepts as categories of reality created to simplify and organize it into meaningful components, then it is clear that behavioural abilities such as thinking may also be categorized this way. For example, walking to work is conceptually different from running to work. In both cases one is moving toward a destination, but the approach being taken is obviously quite different. So it is with thinking. Summarizing and analysing conceptualize different aspects of thinking about information. A list of thinking skills is also a list of thought concepts defining different aspects of thinking.

Before students are capable of independent thinking, they must have a conceptual understanding of skills/abilities/thought processes depending upon the preferred terminology. When students understand thinking conceptually, they will gain the ability to determine which thought concept is the most appropriate for their needs. Most problem solving and decision making situations are complex ,and require the use of more than one approach. Students must know learn to select an appropriate set of thought concepts and organize them into a pattern (in other words create a heuristic) and apply them systematically to achieve a solution. Learning to think in this way constitutes the major learning task for students.

THE SCOPE OF THOUGHT CONCEPTS

Before we embark upon a detailed discussion of techniques to teach thought concepts effectively, it would be useful for us to consider what fundamental thought concepts students need to know. With the paper bag exercise, we have briefly listed some of those skills. Below is a relatively short list of thought concepts fundamental to critical and creative thinking. The list below is suggested as a basic minimum every student should know:

- COMPARING & CONTRASTING;
- SUMMARIZING;
- CATEGORIZING;
- GENERALIZING;
- CLASSIFYING;
- INFERRING;
- HYPOTHESIZING;
- ANALYSIS;
- SYNTHESIZING;
- EVALUATION.

These thought concepts were chosen because they represent fundamental, conceptual processes in thinking. There is little thinking that can be done that does not make use of these thought concepts in one way or another. This is why students already have some experience with them.

Thought concepts are analogous to the four basic operations in mathematics. They perform a role similar to the roles addition, multiplication, subtraction, or division play in thought about numbers. Adding or subtracting is among the most fundamental operations one can use to make numbers meaningful? Similarly there are fundamental operations which make information meaningful: it can be organized by placing it into categories; it can be systematized by placing it into a classification system; meaning can be ascribed to it by creating an inference; and so on. The purpose of these thought processes is to organize information so that more sophisticated thinking can be done about it. Just as multiplication allows one to perform mental operations on a set of number facts in order to discover new relationships, classifying information is a method of performing mental operations on facts in an attempt to discover new relationships among them.

Of course, mathematical thinking is more than the four basic operations. That is also the case with the ten thought concepts listed above. They are only a starting point. But they are vital, because if students do not construct these thought concepts in their minds, they will lack the intellectual tools to do sophisticated thinking.

This short list of ten thought concepts makes it possible for students to construct other thinking skills. More complex skills, many of which are rubrics, are simply combinations of the ten thought concepts. A seemingly simple skill such as writing a paragraph is really an amalgam of many fundamental thought concepts. A successful paragraph writer needs to know how to categorize and summarize information, classify it, draw inferences from it, create a hypothesis, do some analysis, write a conclusion, and possibly do some self-evaluation. Students who lack these skills resort to plagiarism. Paragraph writing should be considered a rubric rather than a skill. Later in this chapter we will discuss the role of rubrics in more detail.

Effective Teaching of Thought Concepts

Students need to have a purpose for thinking before they are willing to expend much effort on it. The need for purpose takes us back to the learning cycle discussed in chapter five. You will recall that the introduction of new concepts was more successful when it was grounded in the reality of students. This is also the case with thought concepts. Students must be given example after example of practical, grounded situations requiring thought so that selecting and applying thought concepts becomes second nature.

There are several requirements to be met before thought concepts can be successfully learned. The requirements are outlined in the learning cycle diagram below. This learning cycle has been adapted for teaching thought concepts. In general the pedagogical principles are similar to more traditional concept attainment exercises.

Thought concepts should be introduced using familiar material. The object of this exercise is to stimulate the student to perform thought processes inherent in the thought concept being studied. The exercise should do two things: it should give students a reason for thinking with the thought process and some structure and guidance in actually doing it. It is important to use familiar material so they do not have to learn new information at the same time as they learn a new thought concept.

Once students have some experience with a thought concept, they can use that experience to construct the thought concept within their minds. At this point, they are moving to the conceptualization stage in the learning cycle. By conceptualizing students are constructing an understanding of how its critical attributes make certain kinds of thinking possible. A good way to accomplish this is to use a class discussion to review (debrief) as was done in the introductory (Brown Bag) exercise.

After that, students need experiences where they learn to apply the thought concept in a variety of new circumstances. At this stage in the learning cycle they can be challenged to apply a thought concept to unfamiliar material.

As they do that they should have opportunities to self-evaluate their performance in using the skill (metacognition). They should also be prepared to ask themselves whether the conclusion they developed is suitable.

Figure 7.2 outlines this process:

SKILLS/ABILITIES CONCEPT ATTAINMENT CYCLE

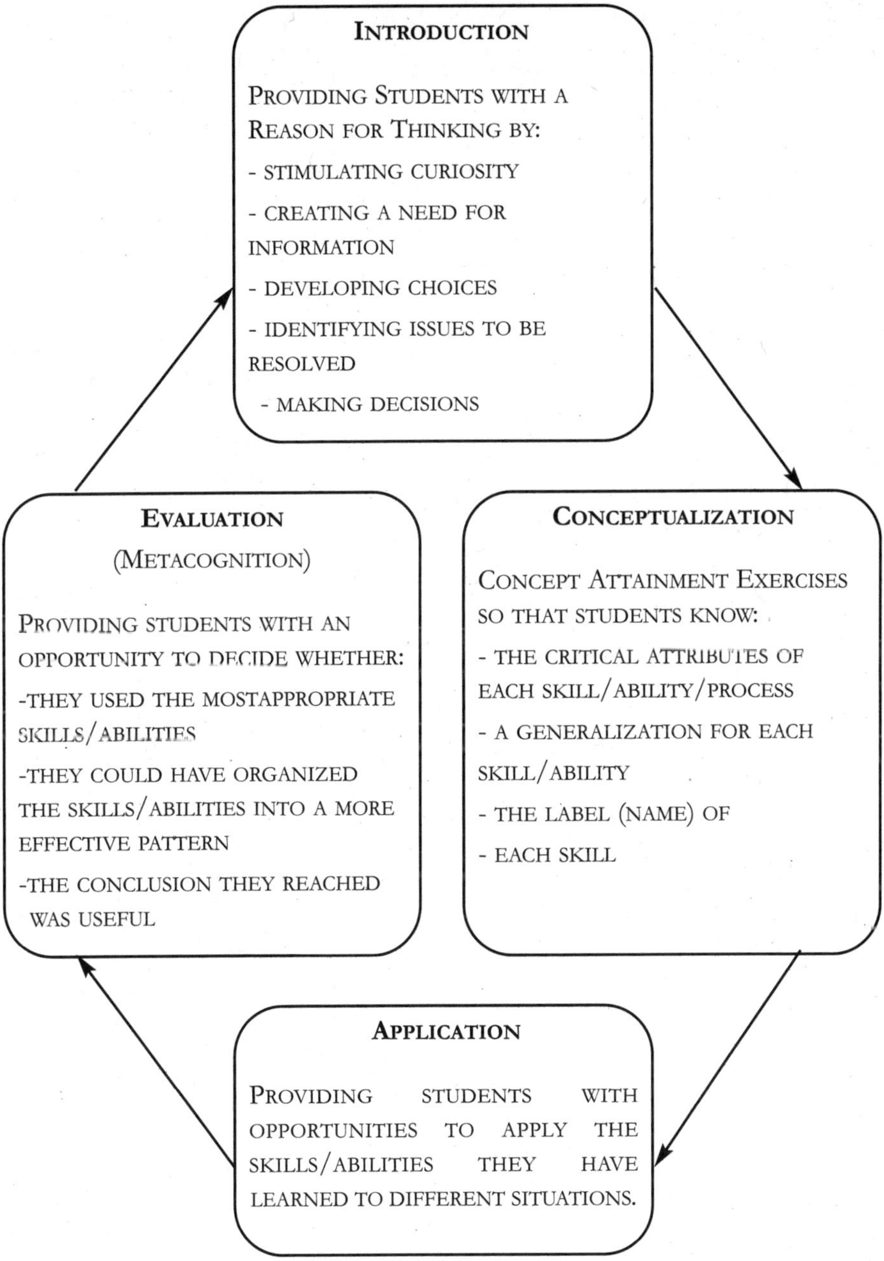

Fig. 7.2

Understanding Reality

To appreciate the significance of these thought concepts, we need to consider the basic organizational pattern of reality. Reality consists of a myriad of interrelated wholes or parts. A classroom is a whole which is part of a school which is part of the school system, etc., etc. Each whole in turn is a part of another whole. In past chapters, we have tended to label these wholes 'concepts'. A whole may be a concrete object, it may be a set of relationships, or it may be an idea about something. A classroom, for example, could be all three. Each whole also consists of parts which are also wholes and are interrelated with each other in some way.

Critical thinking consists of defining the parts of a whole and searching out relationships between them in an attempt to better understand the whole. Creative thinking is similar, except that the creative thinker attempts to understand a piece of reality by creating a hypothetical whole. The creative thinker, hypothetically, arranges parts into a novel pattern of relationships. The product is a model (It may also be referred to as a plan, a description, story, history, etc) of some aspect of reality. Critical thinking becomes involved at the evaluative stage when the creator (or someone else) questions how accurately the model reflects reality. The thinker may then "compare and contrast" the parts of the model with reality to determine the accuracy of correspondence between the model and reality.

A Conceptual Description of the Critical and Creative Thought Concepts

Comparing and contrasting is an important example on the list of fundamental thought concepts we discussed above. Comparing and contrasting is both a way of organizing information and a way of drawing inferences from it. Each thought concept represents a different approach to organizing and thinking about information. Comparing and contrasting is conceptually quite different from summarizing, even though both are organizers of information and thought processes.

Thought concepts, as do other concepts, have three parts; a name, a set of attributes, and a generalization. The attributes define the thought operations which each thought concept perform. The generalization is an overall description of the mental processes performed by each thought concept. As in all concepts, the entire thought pattern (critical attributes and generalization) is grouped under a label which serves as a communications shorthand. It is important to remember that the label is not the thought concept. The critical attributes and the generalization actually make up the concept.

THE ANALYTICAL SET OF THOUGHT CONCEPTS

Categorization$_2$

FROM A CRITICAL THINKING PERSPECTIVE:

- Label:

  Categorization is the label for the analytical thought process described below

- Attributes:

  Categorizing has the following critical attributes:

.- Purpose:

Identifying parts (wholes) of reality;	(What is this thing?)
Seperating the parts of a whole from other parts of a whole;	(What is this thing made of?)

THOUGHT PROCESSES:

- Definition: Defining the characteristics of each part	(What is this thing like?) (What does it feel, look, sound, like?)
- Criteria: Searching for a group(or concept) whose characteristics match those of the part	(What should I call things like this?) (Is this thingamajig a ....?)
- Grouping: Assigning a part to a specific group (concept);	(I think it must be a ....)

- Generalization:

  The critical attributes can be generalized as a thought process, which orders parts of reality (wholes) by placing them into groups (concepts) with which they share a set of similarities.

This is a laborious description for something that people do at lightning speed and mostly unconsciously. It is only when we encounter something truly novel that we become conscious of the categorization process outside of our own personal experience. Otherwise we look at something and instantly categorize it. We sometimes watch this process with gentle amusement as we see small children attempt to categorize some part of reality for the first time. A small child for a time may call everything with four legs and fur "doggy". So as he passes some sheep, the child may call out excitedly, "doggy, doggy!" It is remarkable how quickly children correct these mistakes as they categorize and recategorize their mental consrtucts.

Categorization From a Creative Thinking Perspective

Sometimes we find ourselves in situations where we do not have the categories or concepts we need for one reason or another. The concepts may be absent simply because of our ignorance, or it may be that the existing culture has lost the concept. In some cases culture has evolved so much that traditional concepts are inadequate. In all of these situations, if we are to have concepts, we will have to invent or reinvent them.

Many times people are faced with an unknown set of artefacts or ideas. There are many examples of this situation. This is usual in the lives of travellers, archaeologists, research scientists to name a few examples. The archaeologist finds an artefact and has no idea what it might be. This may be more usual in the lives of young people. They are constantly constructing (reinventing) concepts in their minds. They sometimes use their own labels for their reinvented concepts until society attempts to correct them. Adolescents strenuously resist giving up their labels, preferring to maintain an arcane language for use among themselves: witness language such as 'geek' and 'nerd'. The interesting thing is that some of these adolescent conceptual labels have found their way into the larger culture. They may still be categorized as slang, but they are universally used. One of the drivers of cultural evolution is the fact that each succeeding generation reinvents categories slightly differently than their parents did.

Historical change demands the invention of new concepts. Here creative thinkers have to first ask themselves what a particular situation calls for. The creative thinker would define the characteristics of the situation. Those characteristics become the criteria which any new concept (invention) must satisfy.[3] Then the creator has to actually invent a concept and test it against the preselected criteria. There are many historical situations where this has occurred. The industrial revolutions, space exploration, and the computer revolution are just a few examples. Thomas Edison and Henry Ford are two famous historical figures who significantly reconceptualized cultural reality.

History can be successfully taught from this perspective. At every point in an historical study, students should be encouraged to look at the historical situation and be challenged to conceptualize the choices facing the people of the day. They should ask themselves what concepts could have been used to deal with that historical reality. With some of that kind of experience, students would be more prepared to critically examine the current cultural situation with the intent of creatively considering what concepts need to be reinvented.

Creative Categorization is Concept Attainment

In cases that do not appear to have a conceptual category, the creative thinker has to define the characteristics of the unknown artefacts or ideas, or situation. In each case, similar characteristics are placed together in sets. Each set of characteristics become the attributes of the new concept. Next a generalization describing all the sets of characteristics is derived. Lastly, the sets of reorganized characteristics and the generalization are given a label. At this point all of this becomes a concept.

A couple of important things can be done with a new concept. Its validity can be tested by seeing if it can accurately predict the existence of more artefacts/ideas. If the concept is valid, then knowledge has been extended. It can also used as a fresh guide for searching out new patterns of behaviour and approaches to decision making which fit the attributes of the concept. Again knowledge is being extended.

Typically, categorization is the first stage in reflecting on some part of reality. Once we have accomplished categorization - or in other words, conceptualization - we may turn our attention to classification as a way of broadening and furthering our thinking on a subject.

Classification

From a Critical Thinking Perspective

- Label:

  Classification is the label for the analytical thought process described below.
- Attributes:

  Classification has the following critical attributes:
- Purpose:

To create a context for thinking about some part of reality;	(How should I look at this?) (What is the best way of looking at this?)
Searching for a context or system in which to locate a part of reality	(In what way should I think about this?) (Where does this belong?)

Thought Processes:

- Categorizing Identifying the characteristics of the parts being located in a system;	(What do these things do?) (What are these things like?)
- Alternatives: Searching for a system whose characteristics match those of the part;	(What is the best way of thinking about this?) (Where should I put this....?) (Maybe we should try it this way?)
- Criteria: Examination of system criteria to determine what may be admitted to groups and what may not;	(Let's look at it this way, shall we?) (Maybe it is this because....) (I think it fits best here.) (This is the most suitable place for it.)
- Grouping: Placing the part of reality within a context or system.	(It belongs to the ... system.) (We have to think about it this way.) (It has to go here.)

- Generalization:

  The critical attributes can be generalized as a thought process that orders parts of reality (wholes) by placing them into a context or system with which they share a set of similarities.

Classification is similar to categorization, in the sense that both thought concepts are used to place something in a larger context. Classification occurs after something has be categorized (or conceptualized) and then the question arises as to what context or contexts should the category fit. Classification is placing a piece of reality within a larger context than a concept. Suppose you come across a wallet on the side walk. The categorization part is obvious: it's a wallet. Now the more difficult part is the moral-legal context that has to be considered. How should you classify the wallet? Is it now your property, or should it be turned into the police?

We constantly go through these processes in our lives. Suppose you meet an acquaintance and she makes a comment about your work. Later as you think about it, you cannot decide how to react to the comment. Should you categorize it as being snide or was it a joke? You think about her past behaviour, and based on that context you decide what she intended. Your past relationship with her provides you with a context or classification system which you can use to categorize her comments. She wasn't serious, you think. She was only kidding.

There are similarities between the thought processes of categorization and classification. In every day language, categorization and classification tend to be used as synonyms. Both are thought to mean placing objects in groups. There is, however, an important distinction to be made between the two. Categorization is the process of creating the simplest most basic group in which to place a part of reality. Classification is the next higher stage of organizing information. It is the process of placing basic groups or concepts into a larger pattern or system of groups as a method of imparting more meaning to the groups.

Defining the Processes of Classification

The terms classification, patterns, systems, and models are being used somewhat interchangeably. They are closely related pieces in an intellectual puzzle. Classification is the process of placing selected parts of reality into a context or system or model in which there is a match of some kind between the characteristics of the parts and the characteristics of the context, system or model.

In order to understand the relationship of the process of classification to the terms context, system and model, we need to understand the role it plays in our attempt to comprehend reality. Classification systems stem from our assumption that there are underlying patterns within reality that would be helpful to us if we understood them, . But it is up to us to create the classification systems.

Therein lies the problem, because it is we who are imposing systems on reality. People can and do disagree over how various classification systems describe reality. Some systems are accepted, and others are quite controversial. The periodic table is largely unquestioned while evolution is constantly questioned. Regardless of how problematic classification systems can be, we go on creating them because we need them.

A created classification system is someone's model which tentatively describes the way some part of the world works. The term model is used, at least, initially because there may not be a broad agreement on whether the model is a true reflection of reality. Despite this, we create models because they are useful. What they do is organize a coherent pattern of relationships we can use to understand and locate artefacts and ideas within reality. The classification system or model provides information on which to base predictions (inferences) about the future behaviour of reality. If the predictions turn out to be accurate, then the model will increasingly be accepted.

Classification From a Creative Thinking Perspective

It is not at all unusual to encounter categories of reality which seemingly bear little relationship to each other. Currently, weather has been much discussed. Many people believe we are encountering unusual weather patterns. Weather does not appear to behave according to the predictions of traditional climatic systems. Along coffee row, one can hear people arguing that weather patterns have changed, and that weather persons do not know what they are doing. In other words, the coffee drinkers would say that existing climate models do not classify current weather systems accurately, and that we need to develop new ones..

When people encounter a series of ideas, events, and/or artefacts which seem to be related, they search for patterns and relationships. A whole industry grew up attempting to explain the assassination of President Kennedy. Many of the explanations were farfetched and heavily criticized. A similar has happened with 9/11. Despite that, models continued to be created, because people resist the notion of randomness and coincidence. They insist there has to be a 'reasonable' explanation for the events they see.

How does one create a useful classification system and avoid the foolishness? There is a fine line here, because creative models may initially look quite foolish: "That contraption will never fly Orville." Students need to understand classification as a thought concept so that they can avoid pitfalls in model building. The attributes of classifying can provide a thought pattern (rubric) to follow in creating a new classification system:

- First, they need to study carefully the characteristics of the parts of reality they wish to explain. At this level, it is really true that the devil is in the details. The small, overlooked characteristic can turn out to be quite critical.

- Second, the characteristics they select become the criteria they use to search for a classification system. In the event that they cannot find an existing model that is suitable, they will have to create one which meets the criteria they have established.

- Thirdly they will test their model classification system by attempting to place within it the parts of reality that they are concerned with. To a limited extent, students were working through this process with the brown bag exercise.

Two things can happen now:

- The model classification system can be revised if some parts do not appear to fit.

- Or, it is possible that new characteristics of the parts will be discovered, leading to further thought and revision of the model classification system.

Once these steps have been completed satisfactorily, the creative thinker may decide that he or she has a model that does help explain a segment of reality accurately. Of course, the next step is to communicate the model to the rest of the world and allow them to critically evaluate, which they will.

Summarizing

Summarizing is typically defined as an expression of the main points of a communication. The thought concept of summarizing also contains the thought concepts of categorizing and classifying. If one thinks of categorizing as the process of defining the main parts of a communication, and classifying as the process of re-expressing those parts in a succinct system, then one has defined the main processes of summarizing. Summarizing is simply an application of categorizing and classifying.

- Label:

  Summarizing is the label for the analytical thought process described below.[4]

- Attributes:

  The process of summarizing has the following critical attributes:

- Purpose:

To determine the main parts (ideas) of a communication	(Asking oneself: "What are the basic ideas here?")
- To communicate the essence of someone else's ideas to others;	(Preparing to tell someone: "This is what it's all about...")

Thought Processes:

- Overview: Gaining a general impression of a communication;	(What is this all about?)
- Categorizing: Dividing a communication into its basic parts;	(What are the basic parts (ideas) in this?)
- Comprehension: Conceptualizing the main parts (ideas) (actual and implied);	(What does each part (idea) really mean?)
- Classification: Organizing the main parts (ideas) into a meaningful pattern;	(How can I make sense of all this?)
- Communication: Restating each part (idea) in one's own words;	(How can I explain these ideas clearly and succinctly?)

- Generalization:

  the critical attributes can be generalized as a thought process in which the reader or listener defines the main ideas of a communication and restates them in a meaningful and succinct form.

Summarizing is a difficult skill for many students. Students' inability to summarize quickly and effectively is a major stumbling in doing the necessary research for other intellectual demands such as essay writing, speeches, etc. Summarizing is an important skill, because it is a precursor to many higher order thought processes. Most assignments require students to do a certain amount of research. Effective research involves locating quantities of information and reducing that quantity to a manageable amount.

There are different ways of summarizing information. When one thinks of summarizing, the typical format that comes to mind is the written form. There are other forms. Knowing how to classify information provides the student with many creative ways of reorganizing information so that it is meaningful and manageable. If students are comfortable with classification, they will be more likely to think of a way to organize information. If they do not understand classification and by extension summarizing, then plagiarism becomes their fall back position. When all fails, copy.

Comparing and Contrasting

The thought concept of comparing and contrasting is an application of categorizing, classifying and summarizing. Comparing and contrasting is the process of systematically comparing the parts of two wholes to determine their similarities and differences. To accomplish this, the thinker has to define and categorize the parts of the whole being considered. The thinker then has to create a classification system which summarizes the essentials of each whole, and arranges them in a way such that the parts may be compared and contrasted. Are the parts the same or different? Once this has been done, the thinker is in a position to draw some conclusion about the similarities and differences between the two wholes.

By way of illustration, ask your students to tell you what they think about school: what, in their opinion, is the best description they can make for schools? They will begin to search their minds for an analogy. It cannot be just any analogy; it will have to be a comparison that expresses their viewpoint about schools. Now, there are many analogies for schools students might come up with: communities, families, teams, businesses, to name just a few. It is doubtful they will refer to any of these. Comparing schools to prisons appeals to their biases. Suggest that this is a bias and not necessarily true, and they will strongly disagree. Here is an opportunity to help them think through a point of view. In order to do this, they need to learn the thought concept of comparing and contrasting:

- Label:

  Comparing and contrasting is the label for the analytical thought process described below.

- Attributes:

  The process of comparing and contrasting has the following critical attributes:

- Purpose:

To determine the similarities and differences between the main parts of two (or more) wholes.	*(Are these things the same?)*

THOUGHT PROCESSES:

- Categorizing: Dividing each whole being considered into its basic parts;	(What are the basic parts of these things?)
- Comprehension: Conceptualizing the main parts;	(What is each part all about?)
- Classification: Organizing the main parts of each whole into a pattern that accurately describes the whole.	(What does each part say about the whole?)
- Comparison: Examining the parts of each whole for similarities and differences.	(What is similar between these things?)

- Generalization:

  The critical attributes can be generalized as a thought process in which the thinker defines the main ideas of two or more wholes, organizes them into patterns which accurately portray each part and their relationship to the whole, and then compares the parts and the wholes for similarities and differences.

The thought process of comparing and contrasting is a good technique for resolving issues like the true nature of schools. Are they really the same as prisons? In our thinking we use analogies all the time as a method of understanding or explaining some part of reality. Some times the analogies are fair and accurate and as such do a good job of explaining reality. Other times an analogy is just an obscuring comparison of 'apples and oranges'. It is important that students learn to systematically think through their analogies by using thought processes like comparing and contrasting.

Place the term prison on the chalkboard and ask students to suggest the major parts (characteristics) of a prison. The students might come up with something like this:

PRISON
- Guards
- Cells
- Lack of freedom
- Work without pay
- Big building
- Warden
- Prisoners
- etc.

Now ask the students to do the same thing with schools. The students might come up with something like figure 7.3.

PRISON	**SCHOOLS**
- Guards	- Teachers
- Cells	- Classrooms
- Lack of freedom	- Lack of freedom
- Work without pay	- Work without pay
- Big building	- Big building
- Warden	- Principal
- Prisoners	- Students
- Boredom	- Boredom
	(They very quickly learn to use their first description as the basis for the second description.)

Fig. 7.3

By this time, the students will have figured out the process, and will be selecting characteristics of the school that make their case. When they have completed the comparison above, they will be quite satisfied that they have proved their point. Ask them whether they have been fair to schools? Are they certain their biases have not affected their selection of data? To make your point, ask the students whether they can think of anything else that they could use as a comparison for a school? After a little thought and a few suggestions, they might decide that other analogies might be a job or a business. Place one of those on the chalkboard, and have the students suggest characteristics for them. Again, they might come up with something like figure 7.4.

PRISON	SCHOOLS	BUSINESS
- Guards	- Teachers	- Foremen
- Cells	- Classrooms	- Places to work
- Lack of freedom	- Lack of freedom	- Lack of freedom
- Work without pay	- Work without pay	- Work with pay
- Big building	- Big building	- Big building
- Warden	- Principal	- The Boss
- Prisoners	- Students	- Workers
- Boredom	- Boredom	- Boredom

Fig. 7.4

Again, the students might argue that prisons are the better analogy because workers get paid, while students and prisoners do not. Ask the students to consider whether they have examined all of the points of comparison. Ask them to really think about where the comparisons are different instead of similar. Suggest some concepts for them to think about: purpose of the institution, reasons for attending, right to leave, discipline, holidays etc. Challenge them to make such a list (Fig. 7.5) and encourage them to discuss each item thoroughly:

PRISON	SCHOOLS	BUSINESS
Purpose - punishing people	**Purpose** - educating people	**Purpose** - providing services
Attendance - guilty of a crime	**Attendance** -need for an education	**Attendance** - earning a living
Right to leave - prisoners - completion of sentence	**Right to leave** - every afternoon - at a certain age - upon graduation	**Right to leave** - quitting time - changing jobs
Discipline - class discussion about the nature of discipline in prisons	**Discipline** - class discussion about the nature of discipline in schools	**Discipline** - class discussion about the nature of discipline in businesses
Lack of freedom - class discussion about the nature of freedom in prisons	**Lack of freedom** - class discussion about the nature of freedom in schools	**Lack of freedom** - class discussion about the nature of freedom in businesses
Holidays - none	**Holidays** - weekends, summer, Christmas, Easter, etc.	**Holidays** - weekends, annual, Christmas, Easter, etc.
- Work without pay - Big building - Warden - Prisoners - Boredom - Cells	- Work without pay - Big building - Principal - Students - Boredom - Classrooms	- Work with pay - Big building - The Boss - Workers - Boredom - Office

Fig. 7.5

As students begin to reconsider the parts of each whole, they may become less glib about each institution and really begin to think about the purposes and activities of each. When this happens, they may be better equipped to think about what schools are and what they do. They may end up concluding that neither jails nor businesses are a completely accurate analogy. What they will end up with is a much deeper conceptual understanding of social organizations such as jails, schools, businesses, etc.

By now you may have noticed that what started out as a compare and contrast thought process has really become an analytical thought process. Students began to do analysis when they began to think about what each part of the whole does. What is freedom in a jail, and how is it like or unlike freedom at school or at work? What is the relationship between freedom and the right to leave and the kinds of discipline found in each institution? When someone begins to examine the relationships among the parts of a whole, they are being analytical.

Analysis

Once students can categorize, classify, summarize, compare and contrast, they will naturally begin to analyse. Comparing and contrasting has now become an analytical heuristic. You will recall that we defined heuristics as those thought processes that enable the definition and solution of problems. Analysis is an important part of finding solutions. Heuristics are helpful because they organize information into patterns that help us see relationships and hence solutions. Students are not an exception to this rule.

Analysis is the pinnacle of this set of thought processes. Analysis has several roles. One is to understand how some aspect of reality actually works. For example, why is the Canadian parliamentary system organized as it is? Another role of analysis is to determine whether a particular point of view is accurate. Is it true to say that the parliamentary system is a very democratic system? A third role is to decide whether one choice is better or worse than another choice. Is gun control a good policy or would it be better to allow citizens freedom of choice on this issue? Analysis in a critical part of the decision making process. A fourth role is a problem solving role. What can be done about the rising crime rate? What are the causes of crime in our society? Trouble shooting is an analytical process.

The thought concept of analysis has the following parts:

- Label:

Analysis is the label for the analytical thought process described below.

- Attributes:

The process of analysis has the following critical attributes:

THOUGHT PROCESSES:

- Purpose:

To define the structure of a whole and describe the relationships between its parts;

(What is this thing all about?)

- Categorizing:

Dividing the whole being considered into its basic parts;

(What are the basic parts of this thing?)

- Comprehension:

Conceptualizing the main parts;

(How should I understand each part?)

- Classification:

Describing the organization of the parts within the whole

(How do all the parts fit within the whole?)

- Relationships:

Describing relationships amongst the parts of the whole.

(How does one part of the whole affect all the other parts?)

- Generalization:

The critical attributes can be generalized as a thought process in which the thinker defines the main parts of a whole, describes their organizational pattern, and their interrelationships.

This completes the analytical category of thought concepts. Their purpose, as we have discussed, is to break wholes into their constituent parts so that the relationships between the parts can be understood. However, analysis is only one part of the thought process. The other part is the creation of meaning. During and after, analysis thinkers have to ask themselves what the information is telling them. Some kind of meaning has to be constructed. Understandings derived from analytical thought concepts provide the basis for making judgments and drawing conclusions. We now need to examine the synthetical stream of thought.

THE SYNTHETICAL SET OF THOUGHT CONCEPTS

Synthesis is the process of combining parts and wholes into larger wholes. It is the reverse of analysis. An arch is a beautiful example of a synthesis. The arch synthesizes stones and shapes and forces into a self-supporting whole.

Fig.7.6

Each stone in the picture has been carved into a precise shape and carefully placed so that the stones are locked into position. The builders by conceptualizing an arch were able to synthesize a self-supporting structure. The function of each separate part is clearly much less than their function collectively. Until the stones were shaped and properly arranged, they were nothing more than a pile of stones.

The purpose of synthetical thinking is to increase understanding. In conversation we often use the phrase: "what does this add up to?" Implicit in this phrase is dissatisfaction with merely itemizing and describing something. We want to stand back and see how everything 'makes sense'. How do the parts combine to create a larger whole? Synthesis is the point at which we extend our thinking beyond factual information. We look at the information, we look at the context, and we catalogue the relevant concepts, and based on all of that we create some kind of meaning.

Synthetical thinking is risky because it is an extension beyond basic information. Metaphorically, if we think of the facts as the trunk of the tree, then synthetical thinking is going out on a limb. The farther out we go, the shakier our position. That is why it is important to construct a substantial trunk of information and pick a strong limb to head out on. There are many limbs to choose from, and some offer better support than others.

In general, a synthesis is a combination of seemingly isolated pieces of information into a coherent and comprehensible whole. The thought concepts of generalizing, inferencing, hypothesizing and concluding help the thinker create syntheses of one sort or another. Thinkers employ these thought concepts in sequence. Each thought concept produces a type of synthesis, which in turn can be used as the basis for more thought and yet another synthesis. An example of how this works in practice is the criminal justice system.

A crime has been committed, and the police investigate. A team of investigators attend the crime scene. Detectives and various forensic specialists gather information. Slowly a body of factual information is assembled. The detectives, in consultation with the forensic specialists, categorize, classify and analyse the data. They are looking for patterns which will eventually provide meaning (responsibility) for the crime.

It is at the pattern stage that detectives focus on synthetical thinking. They examine the body of information (clues) and ask themselves what generalizations are possible given the information available. As well, they will discuss what inferences might be drawn from the evidence. They may decide that an inference offers scope ("following a lead") for more investigation. It is likely that there will be more than one plausible generalization and inference. Each will need to be pursued to determine its accuracy. More data will be collected, and from that data more generalizations and inferences will be drawn.

Once all that has been done, the police begin to develop a hypothesis about who is responsible for the crime. (Police may refer to this as the theory of the crime.) When the police are satisfied with their hypothesis, they will take it as their theory to the prosecutors, where the theory and its supporting data is again discussed and analysed. If the prosecutors accept the hypothesis, charges will be laid and arrests made. At this point, the prosecutors have formally and publicly adopted a theory of the crime. It has become their conclusion.

Still, under our constitution the work done so far by the police and prosecutors is considered to be only supposition. The defendant is innocent until declared guilty by a jury of her or his peers. Defendants have the right to confront their accusers in an open and impartial court. It is the role of prosecution to present the evidence along with the generalizations and inferences they have made. They have to convince the jury their theory of the crime is correct beyond 'a reasonable doubt'. The defence has to convince the jury there is 'a reasonable doubt' about the prosecution's case. The defence does this by rebutting the prosecution's evidence, casting doubt on their generalizations and inferences, and by so doing discrediting the prosecution's theory. The defence may, if it chooses, present an alternative hypothesis/theory to explain the crime.

Once both sides have presented their cases, the jury, using the law as its criteria, has to assess all that it has heard and reach a conclusion. In some cases the jury's conclusion marks the end of the process. In other cases it does not. In an attempt to avoid mistakes and do justice, the criminal justice system has developed elaborate procedures to make sure all relevant thought concepts are used properly. Despite all the care, mistakes are made. An evaluation process called an appeal is used to determine whether errors have occurred. This is intended to be a final check on the performance of the criminal justice system.

Students already know and use many synthetical thought concepts intuitively. It is part of their culture, and many will have picked up thought concepts from those around them. Despite that, many students find it difficult to transfer these intuitive concepts to the formal, academic world. They need some bridges to help them do that. The first bridge is a series of concept attainment exercises so that they are clear about these processes conceptually.

One synthetical thought concept they do quite naturally is generalizing.

Generalizing

Generalizing is the process of examining aspects of reality, defining their characteristics, and stating a rule that applies to those characteristics. If you have seen cats, lions, leopards, and tigers eat meat, you might generalise by saying, "Animals of the cat family eat meat."

The thought concept of generalization has the following parts:

- Label:

    Generalization is the label for the synthetical thought process described below.

- Attributes:

    The process of generalization has the following critical attributes:

THOUGHT PROCESSES:

- Purpose: To create meaning by applying a general rule of some kind to the characteristics of a whole;	(What should I think about this?) (What are these things telling us?) (What does all this add up to?)
- Categorizing: Dividing the whole being considered into its basic parts;	(What have we got here?)
- Comprehension: Conceptualizing the main parts (ideas) (actual and implied);	(What are these things?)
- Commonalities: Defining the common elements amongst the parts;	(What is similar about them?)
- Synthesizing: Stating the pattern, rule, law, class that applies here.	(What 'sums up' these similarities the best?)

- Generalization:

The critical attributes can be generalized as a thought process in which the thinker conceptualizes the main parts (ideas), looks for commonalities, organizes them into a pattern and then states a rule which best describes that pattern.

The problem with generalizing is not that students do not know how to do it, but that they do not do it well. Making an accurate generalization requires careful attention to detail, because the small details can make or break a generalization. An important difficulty lies in the assumptions we bring to a generalization. Thinking about information is actually a screening process. The information on which we intend to base our generalizations is filtered and distorted by the assumptions which form our mental screens.

Racism is an example. Sometimes the generalizations we come up with have more to do with our assumptions than with reality. In learning to generalize, students need to learn that they have assumptions which affect their perceptions of reality. As students conceptualize the process of generalizing, they should also learn to evaluate their use of generalization as a thought pattern.

Typically, thinkers use some form of syllogistic reasoning to reach a synthesis. A syllogism can be defined as an argument which consists of two statements (premises) and a conclusion logically derived from the statements. All animals have four legs; this creature has four legs; therefore, it must be an animal. The accuracy of the conclusion depends upon the truth of the statements and the logical connection between the statements and the conclusion.

What would a legitimate generalization look like? Suppose students have been studying the culture of the Japanese. They might come up with the following generalization: the diet of Japanese people is different from the diet of Canadians. In this true? The students should be challenged to test their generalization. One simple, straight forward way of doing this is to learn to use syllogistic logic critically:

STUDENT SYLLOGISM	EVALUATION
Major Premise Japanese people eat rice, vegetables, seafood, and very little meat. **Minor Premise** Canadians eat potatoes, vegetables, meat, and very little seafood. **Conclusion** The Japanese diet is different from the Canadian diet.	Students would have to determine whether: - this is an accurate description of the Japanese diet; and whether, - this is an accurate portrayal of the Canadian diet; and whether, - this conclusion can be accepted as an accurate generalization.

Fig. 7.7

In this case, dietary data for the Japanese can be found; students can apply the generalization thought process to it and critically develop a generalization they believe to be accurate. They can repeat the process for Canadians. They then can compare their generalizations, and determine whether the two diets are basically similar or different

Generalizing can become more problematic with racist, prejudicial, or discriminatory statements. Suppose your students make the following generalization: "Students who attend a certain high school across town are all snobs." If this generalization is challenged, students will eagerly recount all the examples of snobbery they have encountered. As far as they are concerned, the case is closed: those students are snobs. The generalization should be challenged, and the students should evaluate their thinking. Provide the students with a syllogistic model and use it as the basis for a Socratic class discussion:

STUDENT SYLLOGISM	SOCRATIC EVALUATION
Major Premise: Snobbery is the belief some people are better than other people.	*(What is snobbery?)* - Is this a correct definition of snobbery? - What if the school has been very good at some things? Is it snobbery to refer to them?
Minor Premise: Students from that high school are always saying their school is better than other schools.	*(What have the students actually been doing: are they just being proud of their school, or are they 'putting down' other people?)* - How many students attend that school? - Have you talked to all the students? - What is a reasonable percentage of students who might fit the description of being a snob? - What percentage of these students conversation is spent in bragging about their school and in 'putting down' others?
Conclusion: Therefore, these students are snobs.	*(Based on the evidence, what can be reasonably said about these students?)* - Is this a reasonable generalization given your answers to the questions above?

Fig. 7.8

Syllogisms like these can be used as the basis for a class discussion. Initially, a class discussion is a good approach to use because it allows you, the teacher, to model the use of syllogisms as an evaluative process. The topic is not a particularly threatening subject for students, but it will be of interest because most students will have encountered one variation or another of this experience. Allow students scope to discuss the issues thoroughly. Ask the students to introspect about their behaviour. Do they have a tendency to brag about their school leaving the impression they are snobs? From here, you can move to issues such as nationalism and racism, and the effects these notions have on human understanding.

Inferring

Inferring is the process of examining aspects of reality, defining their characteristics, and stating a reasonable extension for them. If all the cars you see parked on a street face the same direction, you might infer that you are on a one-way street.The thought concept of inferring has the following parts:

- Label:

    Inferring is the label for the synthetical thought process described below.

- Attributes:

    The process of inferring has the following critical attributes:

THOUGHT PROCESSES:

- Purpose:

To create meaning by deciding how the characteristics of parts of a whole point to a certain conclusion;	(Where do we go from here?) (What is this trying to tell us to do?) (This looks bad, I think we should get out of here!)

- Categorizing:

Defining the characteristics of a whole;	(What is the situation like out there?) (What are the people like?) (What's wrong with you, you do not look well!)

- Comprehension:

Conceptualizing the main parts or ideas;	(You mean to tell me that they did what!?) (Are they easy to work with?) (Are you running a fever?)

- Classification:

Organize the main parts into a meaningful pattern;	(This situation looks dangerous.) (The morale in the office is really low.) (You really look ill.)

- Extension:

Stating the ideas, beliefs, conclusions which can be reasonably drawn from a situation.	(I think you should get out of there.) (You won't be happy working in that office.) (You had better go to a doctor.)

- Generalization:

  The critical attributes can be generalized as a thought process in which the thinker conceptualizes the main parts (ideas), organizes them into a pattern and then states the ideas, beliefs, or conclusions that could be reasonably drawn.

Inferring is a creative, intuitive process. The mind has the capacity to conceptualize and pattern information quickly, and to draw meaning from those patterns. Sometimes people have an uncanny capacity to draw good conclusions from seemingly very little data. Even though it is a largely unconscious process, a great deal of logic has been applied in deriving inferences.

The 'if this, then this' logical pattern is an important tool in making inferences. Card players use it all the time. "If three aces have been played, then the probability of an ace coming up has to be much less, so I will play this..." is the thought process. Students already know how to do some of this. What they need are experiences that allow them to define the concept of inferring and learn to apply it systematically to their thinking.

One way of doing this is to give students scenarios which describe small mysteries. One mystery students are perennially interested in is "what is going to be on the exam"? The honest answer to students is if they carefully looked at their notes the answer (inference) is fairly obvious. Returning to the "if this, then this" logic one might think that "If the teacher has spent a lot of time emphasizing certain topics, then it will be likely those topics will find their way onto the exam."

Challenge the students, in groups, to pick a subject from those they are taking. Ask them to think about the type of exams the teacher of that subject tends to give. Have the students come up with a generalization (model) of that teacher's exams. Then ask the group to spend some time studying their notes for the period on which the next exam will be based. Finally have them make up a syllogism which might look something like this:

Major premise:

This what an exam for this subject typically looks like.

Minor premise:

This is what the teacher has emphasized.

Conclusion (Inference):

This is the exam we predict the teacher will write.

Evaluation:

All the students have to do to test their inference is to wait until they see the next exam. The day following the exam, they can evaluate their syllogism to see what they got right. By the way, the student will likely get better marks on the exam because they are better prepared. In this case, they did more than just memorize. Be sure to encourage the students to analyse the reasons for their better performance on the exam as well.

Hypothesizing

The distinctions between generalizing, inferencing, and hypothesizing are subtle. Students will tell you that they sound like the same thing. The students are not entirely wrong. In the exam syllogism above, the students developed an inference. But that inference could also be adopted as a hypothesis by many students. Many of them will use the exam model they prepared as the basis for their studying. (For some, it may have been all the studying they did.) In effect, the students were saying (betting) that they had got the inference right. By doing that, they turned their inference into a hypothesis. The difference between inference and hypothesis is intent. A hypothesis is what you finally decide to conclude based on the evidence available to you at the time. You understand that you do not know everything, which is a risk, but you decide to accept your hypothesis as the best conclusion you can come up with at the moment.

- Label:

  Hypothesizing is the label for the synthetical thought process described below.

- Attributes:

  The process of hypothesizing has the following critical attributes:

- Purpose:

To create meaning by reaching a tentative conclusion, solution, decision, prediction, etc. about something;	(What should one believe, think, or do about something?)

THOUGHT PROCESSES

- Problem: Determining a reason or need for creating a conclusion, solution, decision, prediction, etc. about something;	(Why did something happen?) (Who is responsible for this?) (What can explain this?) (When should this be done?) (Where is the problem here?) (How can this situation be handled?)
- Categorizing: Defining the characteristics of a situation;	(What is actually happening here?) (Who did what?) (What do we know for certain?)
- Comprehension: Conceptualizing the main parts or ideas;	(It looks like.....?) (What kind of behaviour is that?)
- Classification: Organize the main parts into a meaningful pattern;	(What could explain all this?) (That behaviour could be explained by...?)
- Extensions:	
Generalizations	(Generally this type of situation means....?)
Inferences Stating the ideas, beliefs, conclusions which can be reasonably drawn from this situation.	(If this is what is going on, then we should expect....?)
- Synthesizing: Forming a proposition (belief, conclusion, decision, solution) that seems the. most probable	(The best way to deal with this situation would be to....) (The best solution is . . .) (This is what is going to happen...) (This is what I believe to be the truth.)

- Generalization:

> The critical attributes can be generalized as a thought process in which the thinker defines a proposition which adequately explains some aspect of reality, based on reasonable generalizations and inferences drawn from available information.

Synthesizing as a Thought Concept

The Nomenclature of Synthesizing

Synthesizing, theory, hypothesis, conclusion, model, and classification are often used interchangeably. These terms are all interrelated, but they do have somewhat different meanings and intents. We have already defined synthesis as the process of combining parts and wholes into larger wholes. In the sense of conclusion, synthesis means the formation of a larger and final meaning derived from the thought that has been done. A hypothesis, then, would be a tentative conclusion about the larger meaning of some aspect of reality. A hypothesis can also be a coherent set of ideas which began as a classification system. A hypothesis can also be expressed as a model of reality. If a thorough analysis confirms that the defining characteristics of the model and reality appear to be similar, then the thinker is in a position to reach a theory or a conclusion. A theory is simply a belief or conclusion that the model does accurately explain some aspect of reality. Based on that conclusion, the thinker makes some kind of decision.

Thinking Requires a Problem

The most beautiful thing we can experience is the mysterious.
It is the source of all true art and science.

Albert Einstein

The unexamined life is not worth living.

Plato

It is the unusual that triggers thought. The usual involves habitual thought patterns developed over time. Need demands thought: we want something and can't get it; something does not work as it should; there is a disagreement about something; or, there is a puzzling situation. These are the perennial problems of living. Despite their ordinary nature, they demand solutions or conclusions of some sort. Students face them all the time. What one should study is a potent example for students. When a meaningful problem is created in the classroom, students are motivated to think.

Unfortunately, we practice behaviours and accept assumptions which interfere with thinking. We love to 'jump to conclusions.' Students, like most of us, are threatened when their premature conclusions are challenged. Their response to such a challenge is "well, that's my opinion!" The modern social contract is implicit in that response. In social discourse, we believe everyone in a democracy has a right to an opinion. Challenging the opinions of others is somewhat disrespectful, because opinions are approximately equal in worth. And finally, the unspoken social contract: if you do not criticize with my opinion, I won't criticize yours. Live and let live, in other words. Such an attitude truncates thinking.

Too often students are given conclusions to questions they have not asked. Students may be lectured about a theory of behaviour which to the teacher and society seems absolutely critical to student well being. There are many examples: taking drugs is hurtful, adolescent sex is risky, driving carefully is important, post-secondary education is a necessity, and so on. As adults, we feel so strongly about these issues, we are afraid to make them problematic. By so doing we prevent students from thinking about issues and reaching their own conclusions.

But we worry, "what if they come to the wrong conclusion as so many kids appear to do?" We are reluctant to take that risk, so we harangue them. The irony here is if the conclusion appears as obvious as we think it is, why would students not see the obvious as well? By not creating opportunities for students to do their own thinking, we impose conclusions on them. It is important to realize that students are in different places with different pressures and needs to be reconciled. One conclusion does not fit all. Student reaction to conformity is to feel they have no choice but to rebel against this treatment. We create power struggles with uniformity. Student response will be to assume that since they live in a democracy, their conclusions are as good as anybody else's. Therefore, thinking is unnecessary.

Teachers who are working to foster a spirit of independent critical and creative thinking must motivate students to think. Teachers can do this by creating situations which give students reason to want to think. Students are like the rest of us. They will fall back on habitual responses if those will do. Students seldom think unless there is a clear need to think. It is uncertainty which forces thought.

Moral issues are among the great uncertainties of life. They are full of risks and problems. Students know this. Their lives are plagued with moral problems containing significant consequences. How do I respond to my boyfriend? What will he do if I say no? How do I respond to a silly and dangerous dare? Will my friends respect me if I refuse to take a dare because it is silly and dangerous? All of these issues are worthy of discussion in the classroom. If they are presented as hypothetical, problematic situations, students will think about them. If they sense that their thinking is being respected, they will reciprocate with respect. Then the notion that one person's opinion cannot be challenged because it has to be automatically accepted as equal to all other possibilities will be less likely to fly.

A classroom where thinking is the norm is one where everything is problematic in a friendly and supportive way. The little journalistic heuristic of who, what, when, where, why, and how should become a standard thought process in the classroom. Students should be encouraged to create problems as jumping off spots for their thinking. Then the conclusions they reach will be theirs.

The Role of Models in the Thought Process

A model can be a set of beliefs, a picture, a system, or a pattern which describes reality in some way. The ideas in a model should be coherent, and they should accurately represent reality. It is through analysis that the thinker evaluates coherency and accuracy. Do the relationships really interconnect with each other as thought? Do the characteristics of the model correspond to the characteristics of reality? It is really an exercise in comparing and contrasting? Earlier, we imagined some students who might claim that the prison system was a good model to explain the school system. We had the students do a compare and contrast to determine whether the prison model accurately reflected the reality of school systems. Only after the students had done an analysis of several models would they be in a position to come to a legitimate conclusion about the reality of the school system.

Conclusions Without Thought Are Not Conclusions

A conclusion has a degree of finality to it that inferences and hypotheses do not have. In everyday life, a conclusion is what is actually done. If one were shopping for a new television set, the first step is to survey the possibilities available. At some point you might decide that television set C seems to be the best choice. You might discuss your choice with others by suggesting that you believe C is the one you should get. At this point television set C is a hypothesis. However, when you buy it and take it home, it becomes your conclusion. There is a degree of finality to conclusions that hypotheses do not have.

Some conclusions are more final than others. In the television case, consumer laws and store policies allow for the possibility of rethinking purchases. After a week's trial (evaluation) you may decide you did not come to a good conclusion, return the television, and try another. Students need to understand, though, that there are certain conclusions which are much more final. Reckless driving has consequences which are deadly and final. Students must not be protected from these thought processes. They may claim and we may think they are too young to deal with these realities, the hard reality is that life holds everyone responsible for their conclusions.

Concluding

A conclusion is the end product of a chain of thought processes. Too often it is formed at the beginning. A conclusion formed early may be a generalization or an inference or an hypothesis, but it is not a conclusion. A conclusion presupposes the thinker has performed synthetical thought operations such as generalizing, inferring, and hypothesizing which were based on analytical thought operations. The end product is known as a conclusion, but in essence a conclusion is based on a model the thinker has concluded accurately portrays reality. As far as the thinker can see, this is the way reality operates and/or this is how the thinker ought to relate to reality.

- Label:

Concluding is the label for the synthetical thought process described below.

- Attributes:

The process of concluding has the following critical attributes:

- Purpose:

to create meaning by reaching a conclusion, solution, decision, prediction, etc about something;	(What am I going to believe, think, or, do about something?) (What must I believe, think, or do about something?)

THOUGHT PROCESSES:

- Problem: Determining a reason or need for creating a conclusion, solution, decision, prediction, etc. about something;	(Why did something happen?) (Who is responsible for this?) (What can explain this?) (When should this be done?) (Where is the problem here?) (How can this situation be handled?)
- Classification: Organizing the main parts of something into a pattern;	(What could explain all this?) (That behaviour could be explained by this system?)
- Synthesizing: Forming a proposition (belief, conclusion, decision, solution) that seems probable;	(The best way to deal with this situation would be to do the following things.) (The best solution is to do this.) (This is what is going to happen here.) (This is what I believe to be the truth.)
- Modelling: Creating a coherent set of ideas which describe something;	(This is what makes sense here.) (This is what it is all about.) (This is what I believe happened.) (The best explanation we can come up with is this model . . .)

- Analysis:

Comparing the parts of the model and their interrelationships with reality;	(Does this make any sense?) (Have I really understood what is going on here?) (Have I/We got it right?)

- Conclusion:

Concluding that the model is accurate and is something that behaviour can be based upon.	(This is what I believe to be true.) (This is what I am going to do.) (This will be my policy from now on.) (This becomes a value for me.)

- Generalization:

The critical attributes can be generalized as a thought process in which the thinker defines a problem, forms a tentative conclusion, and tests and modifies that conclusion until the thinker is satisfied the conclusion is a good approximation of the truth.

Simulated court cases are an excellent teaching technique to give students experience in using thought concepts. In preparing for the case, students have to collect data and perform analytical thought processes on it. They will also have to perform the synthetical thought processes of generalizing, inferring, hypothesizing, and forming conclusions. Exercises like these give students meaningful experiences using both analytical and synthetical thought concepts

Analytical and Synthetical Thought Concepts Are Interrelated

So far in this chapter, analytical and synthetical thought concepts have been considered as two separate streams of thought. This was done for definitional purposes. It was also done to demonstrate that one thought concept in a stream supports other thought concepts in the stream. There are close relationships between thought concepts in each stream. As we think, we use thought concepts in a hierarchical fashion.

However, we do not think that way. We do not work our way through the analytical stream and then follow that by thinking through the synthetical stream of thought. We use both streams simultaneously, and not necessarily in the order they have been presented here. We may start with one of the analytical thought concepts, and then shift over to a synthetical thought concept for a bit, and then move back to an analytical concept again. We will do this as many times as needed, and at very high speed. Most of the time, we are not conscious of doing it. We just do it. Diagrammatically, it might look like this:

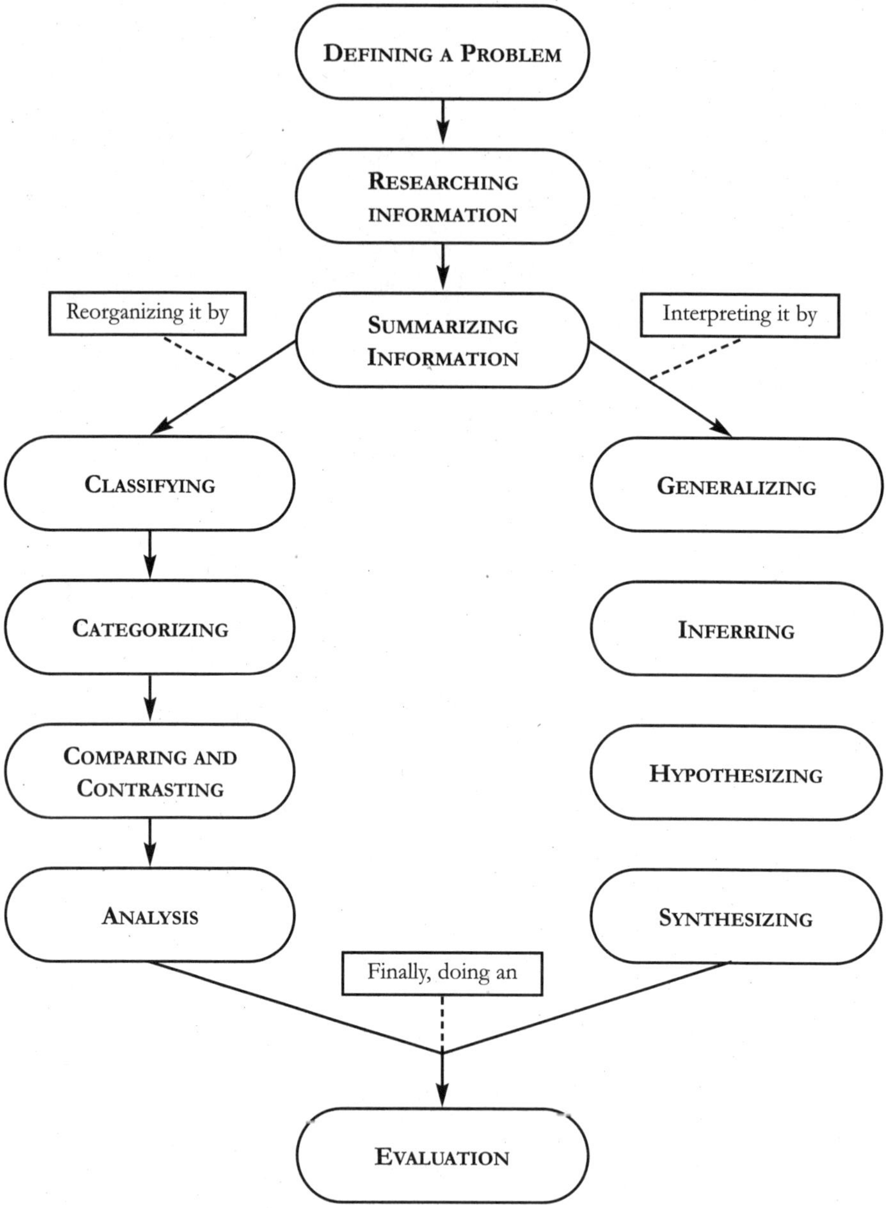

Fig. 7.9.

In this model there are some suppositions about thinking as a process. We have already the discussed the first supposition: the notion that not everyone will use thought concepts in this order. The second supposition is that thinking always begins with a problem of some kind. This is a fairly safe supposition, because most serious thinking deals with some kind of unknown which may be characterized as a problem. After that, it is anyone's guess as to what thought concepts a thinker might marshal, and in what patterns. The model of thinking above is intended only as an example of what might happen. As your students mature in their use of thought concepts, they will devise a personal set of patterns (attack skills) which meet their thought needs. That is to be expected and encouraged, because if they do not they will not have re-created those thought structures in their minds. Without that re-creation, their will be little transfer of thought concepts to their personal lives.

IMPORTANT CONSIDERATIONS IN PLANNING A SEQUENCE OF THOUGHT CONCEPTS

Thought concepts are not mastered easily. Students need time to assimilate them, apply them, and evaluate their worth. All of these steps are inherent to mastery. None of them are achieved by memorization. Mastery is achieved by directly manipulating information grounded in the students' reality using a thought concept. It is a serious mistake to assume that students will easily transfer a newly learned thought concept from a familiar situation to an unfamiliar situation. A different and unfamiliar situation makes a newly learned thought concept seem strange and not user friendly. It takes time for students to gain experience with thought concepts in a variety of possible situations. Barry Beyers argues that students cannot successfully master more than three thought concepts per year.[5]

Classroom time is limited and many demands are made on that time. There is simply not time to expose students to every situation, but time does need to be taken to make sure students receive a broad exposure of applications for the thought concepts they are learning. Given this reality, a scope and sequence of thought concepts has to be carefully thought through. The scope and sequence below is organized in a spiral sequence so that the thought concepts learned in the previous year serve as the basis for thought concepts in the current year. This approach allows students to practice and apply the previous year's thought concepts while learning the current years. Over the course of three or four years, students can master a sophisticated set of thinking tools. The chart above could serve as a starting point for creating a scope and sequence of thought concepts.

There are many research skills which fall under this category. Most of them have been listed and thoroughly discussed in other places. The purpose here is to discuss the pedagogy of critical and creative thinking skills. This is not to suggest that research skills are unimportant. Rather, the problem has been that critical and creative thinking skills have been taken for granted. Research skills are often taught without giving much attention to critical and creative thinking skills. The absence of critical and creative thinking skills while doing research leads to problems such as plagiarism and an attitude of 'going through the motions' by students. For example, the Internet has much to offer in the way of information and ease of research. For that reason, students should be made familiar with these and other types of research techniques. But the question remains: how are students to manage all of the information they uncover? Unless they have a full complement of critical and creative thinking skills, they will not be able to organize and comprehend the information they discover.

The chart above suggests an order in which these thought concepts could be taught. In the main, the thought concepts are arranged so that learning one thought concept will prepare the student for the next. It would be better to learn thought concepts from each stream rather than one stream at a time. That way, students can see how the two streams of thought concepts complement each other.

The creation of mental patterns of thought concepts is absolutely critical to the development of student thought processes. These simple patterns eventually become their attack skills. As they become comfortable with a thought concept, they will turn to it when they confront a problem. By learning thought concepts in sequence - where one thought concept clearly and logically supports another thought concept -they will begin to appear as useful problem solving tools. By doing this, students are creating personal problem solving heuristics. These heuristics will become more sophisticated as they master new thought concepts and add them to their heuristic patterns. In this way, the students will master a repertoire of problem solving skills.

Most thought concepts, provided they are grounded in the students' reality, are fairly simple and straight forward. There are two critical issues in their mastery. The first is transfer which we have already discussed in some detail. The second is being able to create a purposeful chain of thought concepts which will successfully address a problem or issue of some kind. Achieving that kind of thinking in students requires creativity and hard work on the part of the teacher. The key to this is to treat thinking skills as thought concepts. Each thought concept can, in effect, become a little Lego block which the student can learn to assemble into a variety of patterns as needed.

End Notes

1. In theoretical terms, heuristics are defined as cognitive strategies which help to simplify what would otherwise be complex judgmental tasks. The word heuristics comes from the Greek meaning "serving to find out or discover". They are also referred to as 'cognitive rules of thumb'. For example, doctors, when faced with a puzzling set of symptoms, are taught a heuristic: "when you hear hoof beats, think of horses rather than zebras".

People use heuristics all the time. Queuing is one quick rule of thumb that neatly solves many social issues of order and precedence in our public lives. Some people faced with a difficult decision make up a pro and con checklist with which they order all the pros and cons in an attempt to place a value on the relative worth of each choice. Another heuristic is double checking something before accepting it as fact. A problem solving heuristic is to divide a complex problem into a series of simpler sub-problems which are easier to solve.

2. Categorization is also the process of conceptualization. We discussed this process in *Chapter Six* in some detail. Most often, the thinker will be searching for a concept as a group in which to place the whole in question.

3. See the *Chapter Eleven* for a section outlining methods of teaching the concept of criteria, and its use as an evaluative tool.

4. I have placed summarizing in the analytical category because most of its thought processes require analysis. However, it also has elements of synthesis in the communications stage of its thought processes

5. Barry Beyer, "Improving thinking skills: Defining the problem", (Phi Delta Kappa 1984 Vol. 65 No.7) pp. 486-490.

Chapter Eight: Developing Independent Learners

Whom you change, you must love first

Martin Luther King

Table of Contents

INDEPENDENT THINKING AND LEARNING IS THE BASIS FOR INTELLECTUAL DEVELOPMENT

In this chapter, we will focus more on intellectual theory to examine some of the research and thinking related to the teaching of thought. We will examine some of the major theoretical points of view related to the issues of effective teaching and learning. Following this chapter, we will refocus on the classroom in an effort to discover how theory can more effectively inform classroom instruction.

Richard Paul argues people have both primary and secondary natures.[1] A primary nature, he suggests, is spontaneous, egocentric, and strongly prone to irrational belief formation. It is what we consider to be instinctual thought. A secondary nature, on the other hand, is something learned. Paul defines some characteristics of secondary nature: it includes a dislike of inconsistency in thinking; a love of clarity of thought; a passion for reasons and evidence; an understanding that everyone has a point of view; an insistence on fairness to points of view other than one's own; an acceptance that life has to be lived inferentially, because no human has a clear and direct pipeline to reality; and, an understanding that one can absolutely believe in the correctness and certainty of one's personal view and still be wrong. None of these characteristics comes naturally or easily. It takes time and practice to develop a secondary nature.

Developing Moral Autonomy

The problem is whether independent moral growth can be stimulated in the classroom. There is an inherent dilemma for those who advocate authoritarian solutions in dealing with the primary nature of students. By denying freedom to students, students are being given an escape from personal responsibility for their decisions. Students are able to hide from responsibility by believing they have no choices in behaviour. "The teacher hates me" so there is nothing I can do to improve my situation in the classroom. "I hate the teacher (because of some perceived injustice), so I will show him or her by failing the class." If you hang around adolescents for any length of time, you are going to hear this kind of rhetoric. Classrooms do create those kinds of conditions of irresponsibility.

If we assume the central purpose of schools is to prepare students to live independently in a free society, it is difficult to see how a classroom based on authoritarian assumptions can achieve this. That takes us back to philosopher Locke, and the notion of rule of law established by people who are willing to live under law they create for themselves. Such a social contract presupposes a social grouping of people who are able to independently assess the realities they face, and make the necessary adjustments to that reality. They know they are accountable for the mistakes they make. There is no one else to blame. It is through such processes that moral and intellectual growth can occur. This is the challenge for classrooms.

Fostering Intellectual Growth

Similar conditions pertain to more narrow academic studies as well. Such a challenge requires a careful assessment of the basic intent of the formal teaching carried on in classrooms. What are students actually learning from that teaching? For example, it has been widely assumed that a formal and largely abstract presentation of mathematical ideas is the most efficient method of teaching mathematics. In a study of Brazilian street children who were self-taught in mathematics, Carraher found that they often display an understanding of numerical principles and operations superior to those displayed by regular school children.[2] Regular school children apply algorithms in a rote way that street children do not.

Another study conducted to assess the impact of different instructional approaches found similar results. (Ruscio *et al*) This study, using three groups of people, compared the level of creativity after receiving one of two types of instruction. One group was instructed on how to make a paper model using a precise step-by-step algorithmic instruction process in which they followed a precisely defined rubric. The second group was instructed using heuristic problem solving strategies that were more general, flexible, and exploratory in nature. Both groups learned and remembered the same amount of information on the task. Both were equally able to meet the requirements of the task. The difference showed up in the levels of creativity and mimicry exhibited by each group. If the teaching objective was to teach students to accurately copy something, then the algorithmic method was successful. If creativity and the ability to transfer information by applying it to novel situations were the objectives, then the heuristic method was superior.

Developing Multilogical Thinking

The power of technology continues to grow in every area of human existence. As humankind becomes more and more powerful, the demand for responsible moral thought becomes more critical. We live in an era where significant decisions need to be made on a range of issues: is global climate change occurring; should the international rule of law be imposed on recalcitrant nations; are multicultural societies superior to unicultural societies; and many others.

Various responses to these questions are based on a myriad of different assumptions and inferences. Any response to an issue is bound to be controversial, because people will have developed conflicting, strongly held viewpoints, each based on a set of assumptions and inferences that are coherent, logical, and acceptable based on their assumptions. Richard Pauls describes these issues as being multilogical, because it is possible to construct a variety of logical constructs to use in responding to them.[3]

Those who construct a logical response to a certain issue tend to believe their response is absolute in the sense that there is no other realistic approach to the issue. In doing so, the temptation is to oversimplify an issue, leaving the impression that it can either be reduced to some piece of factual support which 'proves' it true or untrue, or that the opinion (ideology) supporting it is above reproach or question. In reality these issues are multilogical, meaning that more than one response to an issue is possible, depending upon the assumptions and the selection of evidence. Different value claims may be made based on inferences and assumptions needing to be questioned and explored in open dialogue. Do the different value claims contain truth and utility? Simply because someone emphatically and absolutely believes something to be true does not make it that.

Are we producing students who can critically analyze such multilogical issues? Research indicates that little is being done. Most student work in the classroom is rote, with very little thought being required (Boyer, 1983; Goodlad, 1983; etc). Teachers who actually do classroom work on critical thinking say that students react to the notion that problems and issues are multilogical with disbelief and unease. Multilogical thinking is outside their frame of reference. Throughout their lives, they have been led to believe absolutes exist: science will establish truth; certain ideologies are truthful and others are lies; and one's personal opinion is sacrosanct and above reproach.

This is sad, because students in our classrooms who are 15, 16, 17, 18 years of age will have to live with the consequences of decisions being made today. It is highly probable that future decisions will require a high degree of flexibility and creativity, accompanied with the ability to conciliate and develop consensus, which allow decisions to be made and implemented. In 20 years, these students will be on the threshold of decision making for society. In 20 years, the consequences of the decisions (or non-decisions) made today will likely be coming to fruition. How will our students respond? Are we preparing them to make difficult decisions filled with ambiguity and trade-offs?

Learning to Reconcile Conflict

Educators struggle with resolving the emotional mind with the rational mind. The Enlightenment bias was to exalt rationality and denigrate emotions. Emotions were pictured as being unruly, and reason orderly. The romantic bias was to exalt emotions as being warm and human, and to denigrate reason as being cold and calculating. More unilogical thinking. In picking our way through this perceived contradiction, we need to recall the emotional component of rationality. It is not one or the other; it is a partnership where two significant human abilities work in concert to help us respond to reality in productive ways.

Emotions focus our perceptions and predispose us to decisions. A justification for valuing one set of facts or ideas over other facts and ideas is not always clear. It has been assumed that an emotional predisposition toward something is necessarily bad. It is not. Those who lack the emotional capacity to "streamline decisions by eliminating some options and highlighting others" are unable to make reasonable decisions in a reasonable fashion.[4] We rely on our emotions to focus and concentrate our rational energies upon things important to us. At the same time, our thinking has to be reasonable. Reason says that there has to be some kind defensible relationship between reality and what we think. That relationship may be empirical, or it may be logical. In either case, there has to be coherence between our minds and reality Those who lack the ability to cohere emotions and reasons are either doomed to make bad decisions throughout their lives, or to fritter away their time on inconsequentials. Rational passions are often stored and expressed as values. More about that in the next chapter.

The issue here is not whether we have biases, but can we grow in them? We need rational, humane passions leading us in civilized directions. It is too easy to retreat into the comfort and safety of the isolation of personal certainties. The problem of emotional growth is the risk entailed in leaving private certainty. Many people are not willing to confront those kinds of risks.

C. Wright Mills argues that there are three categories of believers.[5] The vulgar believer is at the lowest level of belief. A vulgar believer is one who uses slogans and stereotypes to define a point of view with which they egocentrically identify. Those who do not completely accept their vulgar point of view are enemies who must be categorically rejected. Their ideas are unacceptable and must be rejected, less the thinking of the vulgar believer be contaminated with lies and distortions. Such enemies are not worthy of being recognized or debated. They are dangerous and must be ignored, at the very least.

According to Mills, some people grow in their belief systems and become sophisticated believers. A sophisticated believer may be willing to recognize the existence of other points of view, but only to refute them. Sophisticated and creative arguments may be marshalled, but nowhere in those arguments is recognition of the validity of other viewpoints. The object for a sophisticated believer in any debate will be to cunningly and wittily destroy the validity of the opposing belief. Egocentricity and defensiveness are still the driving motivations for the sophisticated thinker. Much time and effort is spent in creating apologetic justifications in an attempt to win others to their point of view. 'Be reasonable, do it my way' could be the theme for this thinking.

A critical believer is one who is willing to engage another point of view sympathetically, because the critical believer is able to recognize the weaknesses in his or her belief(s). They are not egocentrically attached to their viewpoint, and are willing to learn from other viewpoints. They welcome additional evidence and insight through exposure to thinking from other points of view. They accept debate as a dialogue whose intent is to create a richer and fuller understanding of a subject.

We cannot believe everything. Beliefs are necessary to our personal self-definition and necessary to growth in our personal, intellectual, social and moral growth. The key word here is growth. Students pick up beliefs from many sources (chauvinisms of all kinds, ideological beliefs, religious beliefs, etc.) and carry them around as unexamined 'baggage'. The role of schools is to help students grow in their beliefs rather than attempting to convince them their beliefs are wrong and should be discarded.

Adolescents want to become independent, and so they are interested in growth. They are motivated to distinguish themselves from their parents and others who may have authority in their lives. One of their criteria for independence is the right of self determination in areas such as personal beliefs. Often this takes the form of questioning parental, school, and church beliefs, as well as experimenting with other belief systems.[6]

As beginning believers, adolescents tend to be either vulgar or sophisticated thinkers. They can be quite defensive, because of their insecurity about being able to defend their beliefs. Someone who even mildly questions an adolescent about personal beliefs may be seen as a threat. The role of egocentric fear needs to be recognized and respected in this context. Fear gets in the way of growth, because students do not want to be humiliated or rejected for their beliefs, or worse yet: forced to conform to someone else's beliefs. It is only in a gentle intellectual community, where critical believers can demonstrate the potential of intellectual growth *vis a vis* beliefs, that growth becomes possible and desirable for the adolescent.

Richard Pauls points out that people reject dialogical discussion because their experience with debate has been primarily with vulgar and sophisticated believers. Such debates, rather than being a collective and mutually supportive search for truth, become an egocentric game of upmanship with a take-no-prisoners, win-at-any-cost attitude. Many people retreat from these exercises to the private solitude of their personal beliefs, vowing never to play this game again. Others learn to play the game very well. They can be counted upon to engage in a vulgar debate with competitive fury, determined to overwhelm any opposition they find.[7] It is not surprising that in past eras it was considered to be bad manners to discuss topics like religion and politics in polite company. A more modern method of dealing with the problem of vulgar debate is to make things politically incorrect. Certain topics are ruled off limits.

These social attitudes spill into the classroom. There is an implicit recognition of the notion of vulgar believers when educators argue that students should not have an opinion until they are knowledgeable enough to create a sensible opinion. It is not uncommon to hear teachers refer to classroom debate as 'blood on the floor' and view the whole exercise as a 'pooling of ignorance'. Students learn a great deal from dialogue; much more than they learn from debates. A simple distinction between debate and dialogue is to consider debate a competitive exercise in which winners and losers are declared. Truth and intellectual growth is secondary to winning. A dialogue involves sharing ideas behind points of view with the intent of expanding and enriching the viewpoint of each participant within the dialogue.

Students learn many things from this kind of dialogue. Most importantly, they learn to respect their personal opinions, and to respect those of others. They learn to understand and have confidence in their opinions. They learn to respect their intellectual competence in the 'to and fro' of dialogue. It is in this context that the egocentric need to protect one's intellectual turf has the potential to be reduced. The way is cleared for beliefs to grow from the vulgar level to the critical level. This process must occur before students are willing to become critical thinkers. There will be more about using dialogical thinking as a teaching tool later in the chapter.

Dialogue in the classroom is a win-win situation. Not only do students learn to trust themselves and others in dialogue, they also learn much more about the content of any topic they happen to be discussing. Dialogue forces students away from dependence upon verbatim memory to a dependence upon forming meaning so that they understand the gist of the topic. Dependence upon verbatim memory limits students to stereotypical responses in a dialogue. Gist frees students to respond to dialogue critically and creatively.

Purpose of Education

What do we want from schools? What do we need from schools? When we think about schools, we seem to develop contradictory social policy. We argue that we live in an era where the 'creative destruction' of the old is considered to be standard operating procedure. The shelf life of existing products, procedures, social roles, jobs, etc becomes increasingly shorter. That would seem to suggest there is a need for students who are trained in a heuristic approach to instruction so that they can cope with a world of 'creative self-destruction'.

Existing social policy towards schools seems to be one of strict accountability aimed at the furtherance of intellectual standards. The upshot of this approach in the classroom is an increase in algorithmic instruction. Rubrics have become one of the key words in the lexicon of instruction. Teachers feel called upon to make their teaching objectives more and more precise, so that the students 'get it'. Mystery, ambiguity, and the world of inferences are shunted aside in favour of success. Is that what we want? Is that what students who live in a changing society need?

This conflict between the goals of information and thinking and the goals of obedience and independence needs to be resolved. This can be a win-win situation. It is possible to have the best of both worlds, but in order to do that the whole issue needs to be unpacked and repackaged into a more productive approach to learning. There are a number of considerations that need to be addressed.

Redefining the Central Problem of Learning

Verbatim Memorization and Gist

Two basic beliefs about learning and thinking continue to drive educational thinking. The first belief is that information processing is not possible unless the thinker has a store of relevant information available to the short term memory. The second belief is that short term memory and the mind's information processing systems occupy the same area. The Integration Hypothesis, as this is known, infers information storage and information processing are competitors for the same limited capacity of the brain. The current educational paradigm of childhood cognition is based on the Integration Hypothesis. There are three steps in the paradigm. First, children are exposed to background information. Second, they are given some reasoning questions to focus thinking on the information. Finally, the mind of the student responds by encoding traces of the information into a temporary work space. These traces also serve as retrieval cues to guide the search through the long term memory for appropriate processing operations. When the processing operations are found, they are applied to the traces, and the student announces a solution. This is the theory, but there is remarkably little research evidence to support it.[8]

Research tends to support a model of cognition called the Parallel Retrieval Hypothesis.[9] This hypothesis posits that short term memory and information processing systems are separate and independent of each other. There is one limited capacity system for storing and retrieving information, and another limited capacity system specialized for processing information. These systems do not overlap, and they develop independently of each other. Under this model, information processing is not as dependent on memory as theorized under the Integration Hypothesis.

Thoughtful readers will be somewhat puzzled by the notion that information processing is not dependent on memory. How is it possible to process information one does not remember? Again, we need to examine some assumptions; in this case, they are about the relationship between knowledge and memory. The widely held assumption about knowledge is that it depends upon being able to recall verbatim memories of events or information. It is believed that reasoning proceeds by retrieving verbatim memories that are somehow attached to relevant concepts, and that together this information becomes the knowledge used by individuals as they think. Hence, attempting to think without information is not possible.

While it is true that we do store verbatim memories, we also use another system to store information. This type of memory is known as the 'gist' memory. Verbatim memories are defined as specific representations of the surface forms of specific inputs (objects, events, ideas, emotions, etc) held as traces in the mind. Verbatim memory allows one to specifically recall certain features or representations of communications, images, diagrams, events, etc. Gist memory is different. Gists are not strictly memory representations. They are better described as constructive inferences one makes and stores in the mind as one considers the reality of something.

When studying something, a thinker gathers and stores a number of impressions or representations that may initially be stored as verbatim memory. During the process of study, the thoughtful person also selects (or learns) relevant concepts and attaches meaningful interpretations to them derived from the current information being studied. The connections between selected representations and related concepts are used to create interpretations which become the 'gist' of a person's understanding. This gist is stored in the mind and is functionally independent of verbatim memory.

Gist memory is longer lasting, and functions after verbatim memory is lost. Constructive inferences about the gist of the material being studied are somehow more durable than verbatim memory. Over time, one may forget the specific representations of verbatim memory, but still be able to recall generalized impressions/inferences which are the gist of the reality of an event or an idea. Gist becomes the long term understanding of an aspect of reality. The diagram below lays out this process conceptually. (One way of helping students learn the gist of complex ideas is through the processes of concept webbing and mapping. By learning to create concept maps for themselves, students learn to create personal frameworks to use in forming their gists of reality. Concept webbing and mapping will be described in more detail later in the chapter.)

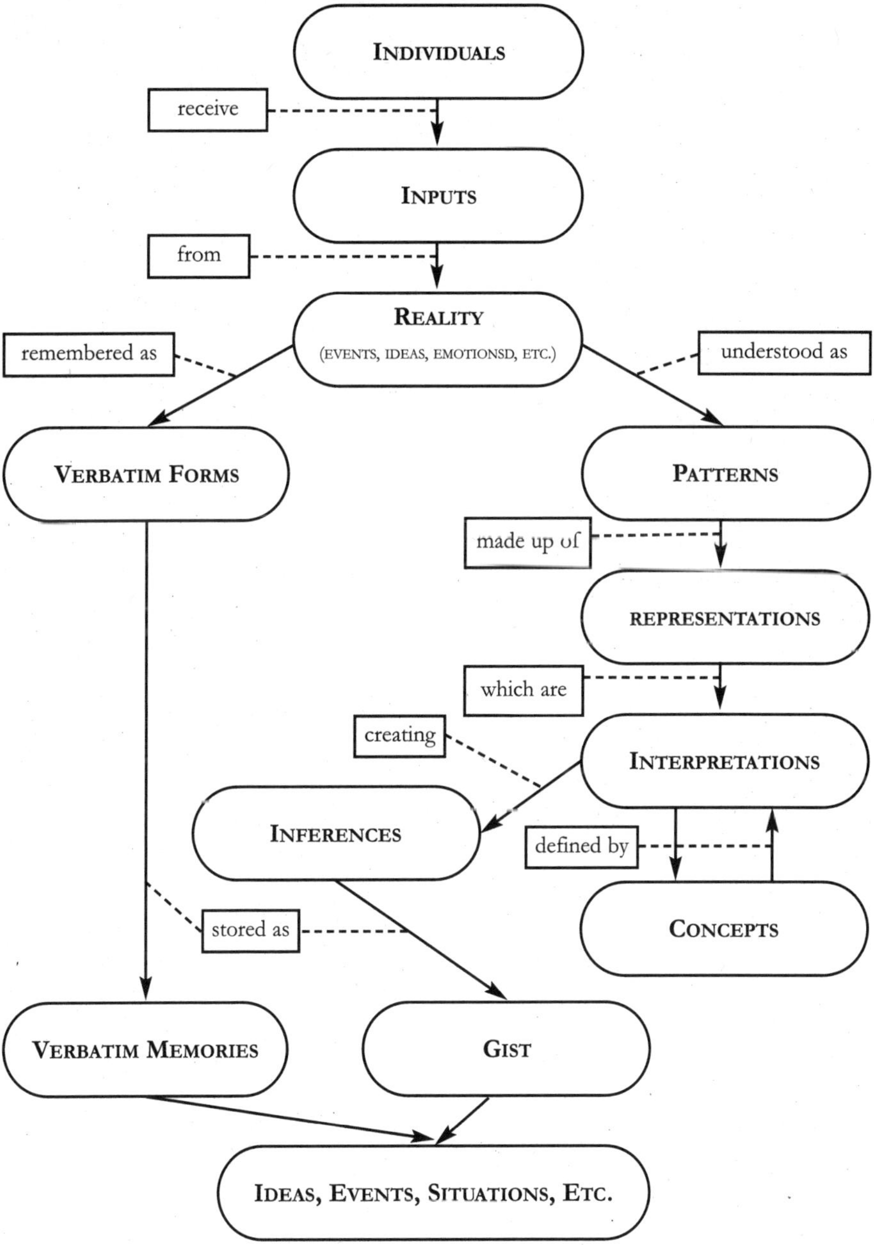

In the future, when the individual runs into a related problem, the mind may have two sources of information for thought. The thinker may turn to information stored as verbatim memory information for specific representations. More likely, the thinker will turn to information in the gist memory as a source of understanding to wrestle with a problem at hand.

The key here is to note the difference between rote memory and understanding. A verbatim memory may have information, but little understanding. At the moment, I can close my eyes and visualize the engine compartment in my car,. I can actually visualize quite a lot of it. None of that would help me determine why my car will not start. I can infer little from what I remember. A mechanic may have never seen the inside of my car and may not be particularly familiar with the model of my car. Yet she will have the gist of mechanical information in her mind that would enable her to generate a series of inferences that are more likely to solve my car problem than would my verbatim memories.

Many lines of research indicate gist memory is much longer lasting than verbatim memory.[10] Are mechanics able to remember specifically the inside of all the engine compartments they have observed? Obviously unlikely, and they do not need to. Because they rely on their mechanical gists, they have no need to remember each and every car engine. One can speculate about the sources of this phenomenon. Gist possibly becomes intimately tied up with the mind's conceptualization process. Gist becomes part of the conceptual understanding of reality. In a previous chapter, when we discussed the conceptualization process, we noted that there appears to be a difference between empty, abstract concepts, and concepts loaded with meaning. The latter are much more useful and comprehensible, because they stimulate the development of inferences.

It is possible that a thinker/learner builds concepts by relating them to specific representations of reality. A gist is something filled with meaningful concepts that generate inferences, which are useful, applicable and transferable to novel situations found in reality. In this way, gist becomes part of the mind's general response tactics to reality. This may be just another way of describing experience. The experienced mind is better able to define a problem and lay out alternatives for solution than the inexperienced mind. Experienced minds focus on the gist of a problem, rather than on rote understanding.

Research on human cognition offers support for the theory described above. Studies of chess experts indicate that they are not endowed with superior problem-solving processes or heuristics. What they do have is a vast network of specific knowledge related to chess in this case. It appears experts classify problems differently than novices according to the 'deep principles' they embody.[11] Chi showed that six year-olds who have a lot of dinosaur experience from which they have created coherent knowledge networks tend to sort examples of dinosaurs in a classic hierarchical fashion. Normally hierarchical sorting is not seen until age seven. Chi argues the naive performance of children stems from an immature knowledge network. As children grow in experience with a subject, they create more elaborate and coherent networks as a basis for their cognition.[12]

This takes us to the contradictions in knowledge and memory as related to thinking. In education, it has been widely assumed that thinking is not possible until students have committed to verbatim memory (memorized) a basic fund of information. Research now indicates people (students) begin to consider problems/issues long before they have heard all the information. Courts have long intuitively understood this, and warn jurors against coming to conclusions before all the evidence has been heard. (I suspect many jurors privately ignore this warning.) People form gists and revise them as they receive more relevant information while they proceed with their thinking. People also think about issues without necessarily having a lot of information. What they are doing is relying on their gist memories for thought material.

We sometimes dismiss this process as going off 'half cocked' or 'jumping the gun'. That may be the risk of early gist formation, but it seems necessary to the meta-cognition process in which the thinker asks him or herself questions: "What is this all about?"; "What am I to make of all of this?" or "where is this going?" Most good thinkers understand that these early gists will not be the final answer, and form them on a preliminary basis. This sense of gist formation appears to resemble the thought concept of hypothecation.

There are a number of benefits in learning to form gist memories. An important stimulus to gist formation is problem solving. First, problems motivate students to think. This is fairly obvious. Less obvious is the role problematizing has as a stimulus to gist formation. If students are unaware of a problem, or issues related to the information being presented, they have little incentive to become actively involved with the information. Gist formation requires active involvement, because the mind has to create inferences which are relationships between the information and concepts stored in the students' minds. With gists in place, students are much better prepared to engage in the transfer of learning. As will be described below, the formation of gist memory is critical to facilitating transfer of knowledge from one situation to another.

The Significance of Gist Formation for Independent Learning and Thinking

Again, as was the case with beliefs above, the issue comes down to the issue of stimulating intellectual growth: defined at this point as the ability to think and learn independently. Many traditional thinkers in education criticize the notion of inexperienced students being encouraged to rely on the gists stored in their minds as thought material. They believe student gists are likely to be inadequate. They probably are, as are the gists we store in our memories.

With some justification, students resent the implication that their own gists are inadequate. In their minds, the gists they create and store seem quite adequate to them. If they were not, they would have created others. The challenge for educators is to encourage students to form and reform gists as part of the ongoing process of learning, something we all have to do. This is where independent thinking and learning becomes life long thinking and learning. Gist formation and reformation is a life long process.

The other reality may be that in a rapidly evolving society filled with new technological and social ideas, the gists of educators may also be somewhat inadequate. It is not uncommon to hear comments (clichés about programming video cassette recorders, etc) that young people are more intellectually agile in dealing with modern technology than their elders. Be that as it may, we do depend upon a somewhat inadequate cultural transmission process to stimulate cultural growth.

It is probably a good thing that the gist of reality the next generation takes from their education is not quite the same as the gist of the older generation. It is more important for students to create their own gists rather than reproducing culturally standardized examples. The creation of new gists by the next generation is the source of cultural growth. If learning is to be meaningful and transferable, students must construct a personal set of gists based on reality as they perceive it. If students do not create their own gists, little of substance or longevity will be transmitted from generation to generation.

Inert Knowledge

A related problem is that of inert knowledge. Teachers are quite familiar with this phenomenon, even if the label may be new. A common classroom scenario goes something like this: A teacher carefully teaches a set of ideas. The teacher reasonably believes the information has been learned, because the teacher has tested her/his students. Student responses indicate they remember the ideas. Yet some time later, in another situation, the students behave as though they have never heard of the information. They do not apply the information to the situation unless prompted by the teacher. Even with prompts, students are unable and unwilling to use the knowledge they have 'learned'. The information does not appear to have any effect on the thinking or behaviour of the students.

When I attend seminars, lectures, or other functions of the kind, I am an inveterate note taker. It helps to keep me focused on the material, and as far as that goes, it is helpful. Occasionally, a seminar leader may say to the group in some frustration, "Work with me on this!" I suddenly realized that I had been floating along gathering information but not really focusing on the gist of the information. I was unlikely to use such information in my day to day life. Much of it would simply become inert and have no influence on my future thinking. On one level that may not be a problem, but on another level I may be seriously short changing myself by not creating a gist of information that could be useful in some aspect of my life. This is the problem of inert knowledge: stuff that just lies there in your brain out of reach for transfer to another situation.

Cognitive Dissonance and Activated Ignorance

Inert knowledge has a more damaging dimension. As all of us do, students form sets of ideas and beliefs as a basis for comprehending the world. People - including students - are reluctant to discard these ideas because they make sense, and because they are egocentrically attached to them. Beliefs are self-created, and people resent the suggestion that their beliefs - and by extension they themselves - are personally inadequate in some way. When new knowledge or beliefs appear to threaten pre-existing knowledge or beliefs, students are faced with cognitive dissonance.

Cognitive dissonance is the process of dealing with two or more sets of ideas that appear to be legitimate, but also appear to be incompatible with each other. The dissonance becomes greater if one of the ideas is something that has been 'bought into' by the individual and considered significant in some way. Individuals may do one of four things to reduce dissonance: change one's attitude, change one's behaviour, seek other support for one's beliefs, or reject as unimportant and immaterial dissonant cognitions.[13] The quickest and simplest solution is to reject the new knowledge in favour of existing beliefs. This is what Pauls calls activated ignorance.[14]

Activated ignorance prevents students from accepting (applying) new ideas being learned to other situations in their lives, because they already have certain preferred ideas for dealing with that situation. It is more comfortable to remain deliberately ignorant. This phenomenon can be seen in classrooms when teachers attempt to stimulate independent and creative thinking. The teacher provides some information, and teaches a problem solving or writing rubric for the students to apply in their thinking. Then the teacher poses a problem which is deliberately vague in an effort to stimulate independence and creativity. Students are encouraged to begin solving the problem. Nothing happens.

The students are uninterested in pursuing what they perceive to be a lose-lose situation: a lot of hard, uncertain work for low grades. Their strategy - based on activated ignorance - is to reduce the uncertainty and thereby increase the probability of higher marks. They begin to pick away at the independence aspects of the project until they have forced the teacher to create a precise rubric for the assignment which removes all uncertainty and all creativity. The upshot is that each student response to the assignment will look pretty much like the other responses being turned into the teacher, and the teacher is forced to give everyone a good grade.

Students are hesitant to adopt new strategies based on independence and creativity in favour of those tried and true strategies that brought them success in the past. For students, success in terms of marks will always trump success in terms of independence. The reality is that the basic rules of the classroom have to clearly and unequivocally change before students will give up their inert knowledge and activated ignorance.

The Nature of Intelligence and Its Implications for Instruction

Cognitive theory defines intelligence in three ways. Intelligence can be defined as the innate ability to learn, think and create. This viewpoint perceives intelligence as power, in the sense that one mind is capable of more powerful thought than another. Some theorists define intelligence in this way.[15] A metaphor would be to think of intelligence as a neurophysiological computer. The computers supporting different minds vary in capacity and efficiency. The power of intelligence is determined by the efficiency and precision of the neurophysiological 'computer' in our brains. From an educational standpoint, there is little that can be done to change the power of intelligence. Individuals have to accept and work within the constraints established by their genetic heritage.

Another definition of intelligence is to think of it as the breadth of knowledge of content (content defined as both knowledge of information and knowledge of thought processes) the individual has been able to accumulate. Content here refers to facts and know how. People who have accumulated a high level of content specific information are considered to be intelligent. Research on experts such as chess masters as compared to highly knowledgeable lay people indicates that knowledge of facts is not enough to intelligently and independently think critically and creatively about various domains.[16] People who are 'intelligent' in domains such as physics, mathematics, writing, athletics, etc need specific ways of organizing perceptions and attacking problems in order to think successfully about them.[17]

Hayes (1981) demonstrated that developing a content repertoire able to achieve excellence in a domain requires extensive practice on the order of ten years of work at eight to ten hour days.[18] Schools have devoted much time and energy to this approach of developing intelligence. Education has routinely placed its bet on developing content in students. The payoff has not been substantial.[19] Some people in one or two domains may be able to accomplish that amount of work, but students are not going to become sophisticated in all domains. Choices must be made about areas where they concentrate. The issue for schools is how to provide students with a useful general education in many domains, not with the goal of creating 'experts', but with the goal of helping students understand the gist of a domain.

A third approach to intelligence is to consider it as a tactic individuals use in dealing with reality. The ability of an individual to define a problem and set the conditions for its solution might be an example of tactical intelligence. Research has shown that mentally challenged students can learn to memorize as well as their peers provided they are taught appropriate tactics.[20] A study in which college students were taught a set of problem solving strategies found that their ability to solve mathematical problems markedly improved.[21] Good thinking is based in large part on the tool box of strategies an individual is able to apply to a given task. Research has found that classroom strategies that teach students to analyze and generate designs are very helpful in improving students' ability to think independently [22]

Intelligence is a complex amalgam of power plus content plus tactics. All factors are needed. The ability to independently think and learn about reality depends upon the power of one's neurological computer, the set of ideas and procedures one brings to a situation, and the tactics or strategies that one can use in attacking a problem or issue.

Education Should Focus on Teaching Tactics

As we have noted, little can be done to change the performance of one's neurological computer. Its performance appears to be pretty much fixed. Traditionally, education has focused on intelligence as content. Education has worked very hard to improve the level of content in students' minds. The payoffs from this approach have proven to be limited. Knowing the facts is not enough.[23] That leaves tactics as the best area for schools to pursue. Teaching for tactics is an area shown to have payoffs in terms of student performance and moral growth. Schools should concentrate on tactics, because that approach provides the best opportunity for education.[24]

Teaching Methodologies Are Critical to the Development of Independent Learners and Thinkers

There are two basic teaching strategies, which can be applied to the classroom. The traditional and predominant teaching strategy may be labelled the algorithmic paradigm. The other approach is known as the heuristic paradigm.

Algorithmic Teaching

The algorithmic approach to teaching advocates the teaching or learning of specific steps or rules that carry the teacher or learner along a straight forward path to clearly defined goals or objectives. The algorithmic approach may be most clearly seen as teachers help students prepare for an important examination. Students are naturally concerned about their performance, and desire to remove as much uncertainty as possible. Teachers, in an effort to create conditions for student success, provide precise descriptions to facilitate learning information, exact procedures for solving problems, and direct instructions for what to study and how to study. Students are directed to their notes and textbooks for all the correct answers, procedures, and methods they will need on the exam. Under the algorithmic system, teachers feel a professional responsibility to guide and support the learning of their students. Many teachers feel it amounts to little more than 'spoon feeding', but they feel powerless to do anything about it.

Despite some reservations about 'spoon feeding', most teachers would consider algorithmic teaching to be good teaching. Good teachers prepare lessons with clearly defined objectives and procedures which make learning simple and straightforward. Ralph Tyler might be considered the guru of this paradigm of education.[25] Mystery and uncertainty are eliminated, and precision and correctness are considered to be the critical values in algorithmic teaching. Teachers who do this well are considered to be professionally responsible educators.

Heuristic Teaching

There is another vision of education that might be labelled the heuristic paradigm. Adherents of the heuristic paradigm see learning as a personal process of knowledge construction. In the heuristic system, students learn by teaching themselves from experiences created by teachers who are concerned to stay out of the students' way as much as possible. These teachers make learning problematic, so that students have an opportunity to explore using problem solving strategies (heuristics) that are general, flexible, and exploratory in nature.

It is not possible for people to be experts in all the different issues confronting them, so they adopt heuristics such as 'seeing is believing' to guide their thinking. The theory of heuristics (which will be explained in more detail later in the chapter) holds that people naturally adopt problem solving strategies (heuristics) to help them function in a complex world. Heuristics may be thought of as simple 'rules of thumb' which people use to give direction to their thinking. An example would be something called the representational heuristic. This is a tactic that assumes an unfamiliar situation may have certain similarities to other more familiar situations. If similarities can be found, then those other situations may give direction as to how to proceed with the unfamiliar situation. People rely on many types of heuristics or rules of thumb to guide their thinking. People cannot fully research and evaluate every personal situation they face, so they learn to use intellectual short cuts (heuristics) as quick decision making guides.

Secondary school students also use heuristics. They have learned to use a variety of heuristics to help them manoeuvre through life. Their problem is inexperience hence a smaller bank of heuristics. They need opportunities to learn to use heuristics effectively. Unfortunately, many students check their heuristics at the classroom door because they seem counter-productive to success in classrooms. In some classrooms that is the case, but in others student heuristics are prized for making a significant contribution to the intellectual life of the classroom.

There has been a long term controversy between algorithmic and heuristic. Adherents of the heuristic paradigm accuse the algorithmic model of evaluation as teaching conformity by leaving the impression there is certainty in life. Heuristic advocates see algorithmic based student evaluation as being the major method of enforcing conformity. Evaluation is a powerful teacher, because for students the very definition of success lies in conforming to the expectations of the evaluation. Non-conformity represents failure, something which is not open to debate in the classroom. Certainty takes the form of correct answers. Certainty takes the form of learning a number of simple straight forward procedures leading to correct answers. Certainty takes the form of finding the correct answer to a problem in the back of the book. The algorithmic lesson seems to be that life is simple and relatively risk free if one conforms to the procedures of the classroom.

From the perspective of heuristics, it seems obvious that life is more than an algorithmic process. Most of the complex, multilogical problems students face in life do not have simple, clear cut answers. The really important questions in life are messy, and require balancing pros and cons not to get the best answer, but often to get the least bad answer. It is not unusual to choose between two good things knowing that despite whatever is chosen, there will be a sense of loss.

Algorithmic Tactics vs. Heuristic Tactics

Many in the education community would claim that they have been teaching for tactics. Most teachers would say they spend hours and hours of classroom time teaching writing skills, arithmetic skills, reading skills; the list can go on and on. And they are, but the approach they tend to use is algorithmic. Schoenfeld did a study of two groups of students. One group studied a series of worked out solutions to problems demonstrating certain problem-solving techniques. None of the techniques were demonstrated to this group. The other group studied the same solution with overlays demonstrating the tactics being used. Both groups practiced solving problems. The second group showed marked gains in problem solving while the first showed no gains at all.[26]

Problems in Moving from Algorithmic Instruction to Heuristic Instruction

This takes us back to the research cited earlier about the long term effects of using algorithmic methods of instruction as opposed to heuristic methods of instruction. Students socialized by algorithmic instruction which is reinforced by algorithmic evaluation will experience cognitive dissonance when they first experience heuristic instruction and evaluation methods. Teachers need to be aware of this, and to develop strategies to help students discover productive approaches to reduce their frustration.

The effects of activated ignorance, gist formation, and the limitations of inert knowledge, provide powerful guidance for the direction teaching needs to take. Initially, students will need help in moving away from strategies founded on activated ignorance. Cognitive dissonance can be either an obstacle or an important ally in stimulating students to grow towards independent thinking and learning. It has been shown that cognitive dissonance can be a powerful motivator of independent thinking, because in this case the dissonance demonstrates the possibility a particular learning strategy is inadequate.[27]

Whether students will continue to employ strategies based on activated ignorance or will turn to independent learning strategies depends upon the classroom conditions they encounter. If evaluation, in particular, is based upon a heuristic approach, and if students are helped to learn various heuristic techniques to guide their thinking and learning, then students will be more motivated to find productive alternative styles of learning.

Gist formation is an intellectual process critical to successful independent thinking and learning. Both depend upon the ability to transfer ideas learned in one situation to other situations. It is gist formation that makes that possible. This is why students must transfer their primary learning strategies from dependence on verbatim memorization (with its underlying intent of creating inert knowledge) to gist formation. Unless this shift occurs, much of what students learn in the classroom is doomed to remain as inert knowledge.

MISEMPHASIS ON FORMAL REASONING AS A LEARNING TACTIC

It turns out there are a number of obstacles to independent thinking and learning buried in this seemingly simple exercise. Schools responding to societal demands have accepted a powerful, implicit objective to teach students to reason formally. Formal reasoning is the process of developing arguments according to the rules of logic. Syllogisms are simple examples of formal logic in which the major and minor premise must relate to each other according to precise logical rules before a conclusion may be accepted as valid. In a formal reasoning exercise, all the premises are provided for individuals to use in reasoning. They are simply asked to draw a conclusion, with the correct answer clear and certain, provided that the individual has obeyed the rules of logic. The traditional paragraph structure taught in schools follows a simple syllogistic pattern. Essays follow a similar pattern, creating a large syllogistic pattern with a series of smaller syllogisms buried within the larger syllogism. Students are expected to learn to create and express - in literate form - a series of coherent syllogisms. They find this difficult to do.

People, including students, are notoriously bad at formal reasoning.[28] Formal reasoning is a highly abstract exercise. For young students (and this extends well into secondary school) who are primarily concrete thinkers, exercises in abstract thinking are difficult. Pure formal thinking abstracts reality into symbolism (numbers, letters, etc) which concrete oriented thinkers find difficult to manipulate. It is not that concrete learners cannot learn to reason abstractly, they can if the learning process is correctly conceived.

The problem of teaching formal thinking tends to become a motivational one. Many students find formal thinking exercises pointless (Many adults do as well).[29] They cannot relate the abstract ideas to any reality that meets their intellectual needs. Their difficulty stems from misunderstanding the rules of formal reasoning, which demand they reject empiricism and attend only to the precise wording of the problem and its premises. They continually attempt to be empirical instead of logical by substituting reality as they perceive it for logic. In their minds, they are being asked to accept unreasonable processes leading to illogical (unempirical) solutions. Because concrete thinkers have extreme difficulty either understanding or accepting formal thought, they are chronically unsuccessful at it.[30]

This is not to say that students should not be provided experiences with formal thinking. But it is to say that those experiences need to be grounded in the students' reality. It needs to at least begin with information with which they are familiar. Much like the learning cycle discussed in earlier chapters, a system needs to be applied in this situation as well. As students gain experience with formal forms of thinking, they will gain some understanding and confidence in using formal thought.

Still, formal thinking has real limitations in its ability to deal with what Paul calls multilogical problems.[31] Paul suggests that typical formal logic exercises are unilogical problems where a single, clear, concise answer is possible. Life is too messy for unilogical definitions of problems. Gigerenzer quotes a philosopher who was dealing with significant questions about some upcoming career choices. The philosopher as advised by a colleague to apply the rules of formal logic to his situation. The philosopher responded by saying "Don't be silly, this is serious stuff!"[32]

The Problem of Unbounded Rationality

Formal thinking assumes that people are capable of unbounded rationality. Unbounded rationality assumes that thinkers perform extensive research with one question leading to another until a mass of information is accumulated. The lines of research typically result in a variety of alternatives, each with a certain probability of occurrence. Each probability has to be calculated and compared, such that the most statistically significant probability is selected and applied. For most people living ordinary lives, this laborious process flies in the face of reality. They simply do not have the time or the intellectual energy to do thinking based on this kind of research. Families, jobs, and personal relationships simply demand too much time and intellectual focus for them to ever seriously consider spending hundreds of hours researching even the most significant and pressing of personal problems.

Long before I had any knowledge of the concept of unbounded rationality, I ran into it with misgivings during pilot training. Being keenly aware of the inherent dangers of flying, I was eager to know as much as possible about the many things that could go wrong. The training manuals I read were couched in terms of what a good pilot would do in times of crisis. For example, in the meteorology section, there were pages and pages of information on how to respond to bad weather. I attacked that information with great energy. Soon, I began to realize that if I were flying a little plane by myself in bad weather, I would not be able to review and respond to all the alternatives available to me in the training manual. It was not that I was practicing activated ignorance, but I was highly aware that in a stressful, dangerous situation much of the training manual's information could be inert.

Despite understanding my limitations, I still wanted to fly. So given those limitations, the question became one of how to proceed safely. That brought me to another set of concepts, one that at the time I could only intuit, because I was unaware of them. They are bounded reality and heuristics.

An example of bounded reality is that of a pilot in the cockpit of a little plane in bad weather. The reality a pilot is capable of handling is bounded by intellectual capacity and experience, as well as the constraints of time and all the other demands placed on a pilot in that situation. This applies not just to pilots, but more broadly to the human condition. We all live under constraints of bounded reality. We are not and will never be 'godlike' in our ability to survey all and understand all. We respond to little windows of information which provide limited - and sometimes biased - understandings with serious time constraints. Based on those windows, we must make decisions for good or ill. We have to respond to reality because not to make a decision is, in effect, to make a decision.

My solution to this dilemma was to adopt some rules of thumb. I now know these rules of thumb are formally called heuristics. They are intellectual shortcuts we employ to cut through the laboriousness of formal reasoning described above. My heuristics: never, never fly without checking the weather, pay strict attention to the weather as I flew, never press on into bad weather and land as soon as possible in the face of bad weather. My informal reason told me that prevention is always preferable to problem solving in a cockpit in bad weather.

THE ROLE OF HEURISTICS IN PRACTICAL THINKING

Humans seem to learn to use heuristics quite naturally. Animals also use heuristics to solve their survival problems. A mother bird returning to her nest of chicks has to decide which chick to feed, and be sure that all chicks get adequate nutrition. How does a bird do this? Obviously, it is not going to use some intellectual process of formal reasoning. The bird has to rely on some simple, reliable system that feeds every chick. It could simply be random chance or some simple 'fast and frugal heuristic' that guides her behaviour.

Students in the final semester of high school face a somewhat similar situation. There are an array of career choices available to them. A formal research and evaluation program takes more time than most students feel they can devote. Despite lengthy research, students may still find they cannot fathom the probable consequences of one career choice over another. Some probably adopt a heuristic and make a choice, while others become paralyzed by inaction. Sometimes this inaction can consume many years before a choice is made. It seems likely some people are either unable to find and employ useful heuristics, or are unwilling to trust their utility.

Heuristics Are Cognitive Rules of Thumb

In theoretical terms, heuristics are defined as cognitive strategies which help to simplify what would otherwise be complex judgmental tasks. The word heuristics comes from the Greek, meaning "serving to find out or discover". Another definition is 'cognitive rules of thumb'. For example, when faced with a puzzling set of symptoms, doctors are taught the heuristic: "when you hear hoof beats, think of horses rather than zebras".

People use heuristics all of the time. Queuing is one quick rule of thumb, which neatly solves many social issues of order and precedence in our public lives. Some people faced with a difficult decision make a pro and con checklist in which they order all the pros and cons in an attempt to place a value on the relative worth of each choice. Another heuristic is double checking something before accepting it as fact. A problem solving heuristic is to divide a complex problem into a series of simpler sub-problems which may be easier to solve.

Criteria Determine Suitability

Inherent in the process of using heuristics is the notion of criteria. Criteria are the standards that determine the acceptability or suitability of a choice. Most often, these criteria are simply assumed without much thought. Certainly in the case of the mother bird, the criterion of making sure that each chick gets the nutrition it needs will not be clearly spelled out, but that is the point of heuristics. The heuristic of queuing, for example, is mostly based on unconscious criteria having to do with fairness, good manners, concern for others, etc. In the case of young people trying to decide upon a career, their criteria might be success, interest, reward, etc. The central point in heuristics is that when the criteria have been met, the search for alternatives may end. If a young person finds a career offering a fair probability of success, appears to be interesting, and provides a sufficient level of reward, there is no need to look farther.

Ecological Rationality: Coming to Terms with Reality

In understanding the heuristic concept another concept, ecological rationality, needs to be considered. In formal rationality, the object is to maintain order between one's premises and the inferences one draws. We are taught that beliefs and behaviour ought to be coherent. This is always a major concern, especially in relation to the ethics of dealing with others. At the same time, people find that they also have to deal with the external disorder of their environment. Many people say: "You do what you have to do." This often sounds self-serving and possibly illogical. It may be, but it is also a rueful understanding there are events beyond one's control. "If wishes were horses, beggars could ride" is an old aphorism that recognizes the harsh realities of life. The intellectual relationship between a difficult to control environment and the individual human response to it is known as ecological rationality.

Fast, Frugal and Accurate Decision-Making

Ecological rationality recognizes that perfection is mostly not possible. Perfection usually comes at a large cost in terms of other things that have to be done in life. Limitations on personal time force perfectionists to apply heuristics to all the other things in their lives in order to make time for their passion. In dealing with the inherent disorder of life, people make inferences that they want to be fast, frugal and accurate. The problems of life demand swift and accurate decisions and we need heuristics which do that quickly and efficiently. At 5:30 p.m.. rushing home to make supper, an individual does not need to become engaged in a long, fruitless discussion about who should go through the checkout counter first; let's just get on with it. Frugal means finding solution that for problems which use the minimum necessary resources: intellectual, emotional, and physical. The third leg of the heuristic intellectual stool is accuracy. Accuracy means finding results, which respond regularly and predictably to selected criteria.

Homer-Dixon describes an incident where the engine in the tail of a large airliner exploded in flight. The explosion destroyed most of the controls in the tail of plane, making it almost impossible to steer. The plane was piloted by two highly experienced, professional pilots. They quickly discovered the problems they faced were becoming unmanageable. In such a situation, problems cascade; each problem triggering a series of consequent problems. They almost instantly faced information overload. Fortunately for them, travelling as a passenger was another highly experienced pilot who was able to lend a hand. With all of that experience and a little bit of luck, they more or less landed the plane.

The pilots had been tossed into a new environment where the traditional rules of aircraft control disappeared. They did not understand the new rules of the situation, because the standard cause and effect of pilot-plane behaviour was gone. An action by a pilot could precipitate an uncontrollable reaction by the plane. A new and mysterious ecological relationship between pilot and plane had been established.

The pilots were just reacting as best they could to the situation. Very early on, they discovered the plane could continue to fly, but they were unable to steer it. What alternatives were left to them?

Fundamental Rules of Heuristics

Heuristics have three rules. First, there is a stopping rule, which simply says there is a point in thinking where there is no further need to search for alternatives. Second, there a decision rule, which says stop looking when you discover something that works according to the criteria selected for determining success. This is also known as the satisfying heuristic: stop looking when you find something that works (is satisfactory). Finally, there is an information search rule, which also has three rules defining the search: 'take the best' is an option where a cue or alternative is selected based upon how often the cue results in correct or incorrect options. With 'take the last', the researcher examines cues used in the past that have been successful and picks the one used in the most recent decision. 'Ordered search' is a system whereby the researcher chooses the cue with the highest validity that has not been tried yet.

Returning to the pilots struggling to control a crippled airliner; they believed two control methods remained intact. The ailerons on the main wings seemed undamaged and controllable, and the power to the engines under the wings could be varied. Which control system should they use? Stability of the aircraft and steerability were two fundamental criteria that must evaluate what ever inference they came to. Two problems with aileron control were that it could potentially lead to instability and that it could not change the altitude of the aircraft. (As it turned out later, they could not control the ailerons at all.) Using the engines to control the altitude and direction of the aircraft seemed to fit the two criteria so, immediately the pilots stopped searching for more aircraft control clues and began concentrating on steering the aircraft to the nearest airport.

Their decision rule has to be based on their criteria about the plane's behaviour. They would have is to decide is how to go about their research without triggering a disaster. There are three heuristics which might be applicable to this situation. The 'take the last' heuristic is simply turning to the last strategy the pilots know of which worked well in a similar situation. This heuristic would be quickly rejected, because little in past experience was going to be helpful in this situation. The 'take the best' heuristic recommends searching for and taking the first option that can be found to work according to selected criteria. In this situation 'take the best' heuristic is a limited option because of the high risk of instability. The pilots likely turned to an 'ordered search' heuristic to discover what the plane was capable of in this situation. When they discovered there was little response to aileron control, but there was some response to judicious control of the engines, they immediately stopped experimenting with the controls. Their criteria were met and they turned their minds to the problem of landing the plane.

In terms of metacognition, the pilots had no idea of they were using heuristics. They may never have heard of heuristics, and certainly would not engage in a theoretical discussion of the thought processes they ought to employ in the situation. They could only react to the ecological realities of the moment.

IGNORANCE BASED DECISION BAKING

There are a wide variety of heuristics people may adopt, depending upon their circumstances. One major circumstance is making decisions with insufficient information. Ignorance is a part of the human condition that we all have to learn to deal with. This is particularly true for students. Ignorance is what makes them students. Yet they have the capacity to use intellectual tactics such as heuristics. They do it all the time in their personal lives. The issue is how to encourage students to use heuristics in their day to day classroom lives.

In previous chapters, we discussed the Learning Cycle in some detail You may recall that the theory of the Learning Cycle is based on the idea that students learn new concepts and concept skills more easily if they learn them while dealing with familiar material. This is a typical ignorance based heuristic tactic. Many heuristics have evolved to deal with ignorance based decision making.

Recognition Heuristic

When dealing with something unfamiliar, we turn to some basic heuristic tactics. One is the recognition heuristic. An illustration of this heuristic in operation is the Doctor Seuss story, *Green Eggs and Ham*. The recognition heuristic is the process of choosing between two alternatives, one known and one not. The known alternative contains the criteria being searched for. In the case of green eggs and ham, the criterion is acceptable taste. Ham fits the criteria, but green eggs are an unknown. When in doubt, choose ham because you know what you are getting. Users of the recognition heuristic simply assume that if one of two alternatives is recognized and the recognized, object contains the desired criterion, then choose that one. Advertising is heavily invested in persuading people to use this heuristic.

Representative Heuristic

Another example of ignorance based decision making is the representative heuristic. When an individual has to respond to something unknown, a useful tactic is to compare that unknown with something that is known that appears to have similar characteristics. Inherent in the known are the criteria by which the individual will determine whether the unknown is acceptable or not. An example might be deciding whether to go to movie A or movie B. Using the representative heuristic, the question then becomes whether the movies are similar to other movies that have been viewed and were found to be entertaining (the criterion). If movie A is said to be similar to another familiar and entertaining movie and movie B is not, then movie A might be selected over movie B. Certain features are selected from the known that appear to conform to features in the unknown and an inference is drawn about the unknown. The stopping rule is applied and a decision is made about the movie to attend.

Availability Heuristic

The availability heuristic is used as a tactic when the thinker is confronted with a reality about which little is known. The government has announced a new social policy. People have to decide whether they are in favour of it or not. They could use the availability heuristic to select anecdotes about the performance of this government in past situations. At the same time, they will also select criteria as a basis for judging government performance. The criteria might be cost, equity, efficiency, inconvenience, etc. If their available memory of the government's performance in the past was poor based on their criteria, they will likely reject the new policy. In general, thinkers use the availability heuristic to review their memories for examples that appear to be similar to the unknown in significant ways. If the thinker finds a memory of a situation that appears to be very similar, the next step would be to consider the criteria. If the criteria are positive or negative, then the thinker might well infer that the strange situation is acceptable or unacceptable, as the case may be.

Intelligent Decision Making

For Homer-Dixon the story of the damaged airliner and the pilots' response to it is a metaphor for all the systems we have created that have the potential to escalate out of control. Homer-Dixon argues that we must realize we can only deal with bounded reality, and because of that we need to understand our limitations. Homer-Dixon wrote *The Ingenuity Gap* to remind us we regularly interact with massive natural (environmental) systems and massive man made systems. Most times, we take them for granted.

Homer-Dixon is critical of the common belief that we have enough understanding of these systems to allow us to adequately control them under any circumstance. In a chapter entitled "Careening into the Future:, he talks about the ingenuity gap. He defines the ingenuity gap as the growing gap between the rising societal and environmental problems we face and the solutions we are able to generate. He worries about the lag between the growth of significant problems and the production of ingenuity needed to solve those problems.[34]

Homer-Dixon points out that there is more and more information in the world and that it is flowing faster and faster. Individuals in responsible positions are often called upon to be 'on top of" truly prodigious amounts of information.[35] In financial decision making, individuals are dealing with derivative models that require them to simultaneously juggle six computer screens of constantly changing information. It is the frontal lobe of the brain which mediates all this information so that effective judgments and decisions are made. The frontal lobes handle the higher order, judgmental mental processes. It is here that the mind takes in informational (objective) inputs from reality and blends them with the emotional (subjective) inputs based on personal experience and feelings.

Judgment is not possible without frontal lobes. Homer-Dixon cites an example of a postal clerk who suffered a serious frontal-lobe injury. Despite the injury, the clerk performed well on standard IQ tests. So well that the clerk was able to remain a member of Mensa, the high-IQ society. Despite his good performance on IQ tests, he was unable to sort mail. He could not do the necessary planning, organization and integration of complex information needed to perform the necessary complex sequential tasks.[36] The question arises: what do IQ tests tell us about the mental abilities of our students? How useful are the array of "meritocratic testing procedures (Scholastic Aptitude Tests, Graduate Record Exam, etc.) that we use to sort and assign people into categories" [37].

It appears that standard testing procedures do not adequately measure frontal lobe activities. These are the abilities which "we generally regard as essential to human intelligence and which make us truly flexible, adaptable, and surviving beings in a complex world".[38] Homer-Dixon concludes by pointing out that "although IQ scores correlate well with school grades they correlate weakly with measures of creativity and only account for about ten percent of variation in the success of individual in later life." He wonders what long term effects this kind of evaluation has for the production of ingenuity in a world increasingly dependent on ingenuity for survival.

Algorithmic education and IQ scores are used to justify each other. It is not only Homer-Dixon who is asking hard questions about algorithmic evaluation.

Sternberg and Kaufman are also questioning our approach to intelligence testing.[39] Algorithmic teaching methods coupled with algorithmic evaluation will not produce the kind of creative thinking needed in the future. Algorithmic teaching prepares people to live in the past not the future. Heuristic education offers a way out of the blind alley of algorithmic education.

The Significance of Heuristics for the Classroom

Most of the evidence cited so far indicates quite clearly that if independent and creative thinking is the goal of education, then heuristic teaching tactics are an important approach to consider in achieving this goal. Since we have a long tradition of algorithmic teaching, and since we use our past educational experiences to define 'good' teaching (using tactics like the availability and representative heuristics), we find it difficult to imagine classrooms based on a heuristic paradigm. We now need to look at detailed descriptions of the algorithmic and heuristic paradigms in actual practice in the classroom. In doing so, the major criteria for judging the effectiveness of teaching will be whether students are able to learn and retain significant pieces of cultural information, and to think and learn independently and creatively.

Problems with the Formal Logic Assumption

Teaching for independent thinking which tends towards the formal thinking model has real problems. It should be noted parenthetically that schools do not exclusively teach formal logical thinking. But the thinking behind standard school curricula is heavily oriented toward formal logic. The emphasis on formal reasoning is justified by the belief that an educated person is one who can think formally. Much of what educated people have to know and do in later life depends upon their capacity for formal thought. There is much truth to that, but it begs the issue of whether the current algorithmic approach to thinking is creating formal thinkers. There are indicators which suggest that it does not.[40]

There is a high degree of frustration at the lack of success young people have in learning to use formal thought processes independently. One modern response to this failure is to turn to rubrics as a intellectual crutch for students to lean upon. This represents an attempt to adapt the algorithmic approach in an attempt to salvage some semblance of success in the algorithmic teaching of formal thought. Rubrics can be a helpful tactic, but not if they are taught in an algorithmic fashion.

Students too often respond to rubrics taught as an algorithm with memorization as their basic learning strategy. They learn (or copy) rubrics and apply them to their assigned problems in stereotypical fashion. Rather than being independent and creative, their thinking remains rote and mechanical. The consequence is that students do not become independent thinkers. Rather, they continue to mimic what they believe their teachers want and later consign the rubric to the inert knowledge bin of their minds. Further, because their experience with formal thinking has been difficult, painful, and not all that productive intellectually, they find refuge in activated ignorance. Their belief that much of what they learn in school has little practical relevance to their lives has been confirmed. They have little intention of transferring what they 'learned' to other situations in their lives.

The Problem of Over Fitting

The algorithmic approach also provides other roadblocks to independent thinking and learning. Fact oriented teaching is actually counterproductive on a couple of fronts. The first is a concept known as over fitting. In our every day lives, we intuitively know that too much information can be a hindrance to understanding. Imagine you are trying to locate your friend's home in a suburb of a large and strange city. You stop at a service station, lost, and phone for directions. Your friend is a verbose individual who, while he provides directions, offers a travelogue of information for you to consider as you travel to his house. Of course, the travelogue is not helpful, and you would probably tell him to save it until a later time. At the moment, all you want are precise directions and turning points that will allow you to navigate to his house successfully. Your memory is not capable of handling the additional information. Your helpful friend is guilty of over fitting. So is education.

There is a fine balance between too little information and too much information. In the above example it was you, the student, who had a better handle on the proper amount of information than the teacher, your friend. On the heuristic level we use an aphorism where we talk about not seeing 'the forest for the trees'. This is an implicit understanding that we can lose the larger meaning in a welter of detail. At the same time we also use another heuristic, 'the devil is in the details' warning us to beware of missing important little details which have significant consequences.

History teaching can become a welter of detail with 'one damn thing happening after another'. Students can be completely overwhelmed by historical detail. They are left with little sense of any kind of big picture, or in other words, they cannot find the gist of the historical narrative. This often becomes very apparent as they research and plan an essay on some historical topic. It is not uncommon to see students paralyzed by indecision because they cannot priorize historical detail. Each historical fact seems as important as another.

This, of course, is a major problem for any researcher (not just in history). Carr, an eminent historian, commented on this when he noted that many people 'cross the Rubicon' every day.[41] Yet, in history the event of Julius Caesar crossing the Rubicon in defiance of the Roman Senate is deemed to be a much more significant historical fact than the fact hundreds of people every day cross the Rubicon on their way to Rome. The issue is how to assess meaning by making distinctions between significant and irrelevant data so as to eliminate the noise of excess information.

Research is as much a process of eliminating information as selecting it. The problem is that both students and teachers have a tendency to over fit. To be safe, students over fit by choosing everything. By so doing, they refuse the responsibility of summarizing. Teachers over fit because they feel they must fill up each teaching day with information. If your only tool is a hammer, then every problem is a nail. If the only teaching activity is the dispensation of information, then every problem is a lack of information to be solved by more information. The consequence of that is over fitting.

Frames of Reference Are Critical

Students can only make choices about information if they have a frame of reference that provides criteria for evaluation. The criteria inherent to frames of reference allow them to priorize and make judgments about information. If we ask students to critically evaluate an event or issue, then we must provide more than information. We have to help them develop some kind of basis for making critical judgments. Judgments do not happen in a vacuum, they happen when the critic has some predetermined criteria to use in evaluation.

The Acquisition Bottleneck

Currently, the approach to developing a frame of reference involves giving students a set of information, and asking them to write something about the information. The writing may be a class presentation, some journal writing, an essay, etc. It is hoped that in the research and writing process students will develop a frame of reference for themselves. That is usually a misplaced hope. What more often happens are varying degrees of plagiarism. Students, desperate to find something meaningful to say, steal ideas. For the students who have no sense of frame of reference as a concept, complete reliance on plagiarism seems the only alternative. Other students who vaguely recognize a frame of reference when they see one are able to engage more subtle types of plagiarism. But, plagiarism it will be.

The problem with this off-handed approach to teaching frames of reference is the acquisition bottleneck. Perkins notes "soaking it up" does not occur, because students are unable to develop thought frames without help.[42] Research shows quite clearly that students learn and retain more when they are helped to understand the underlying principles (or frames of reference) involved in the information being taught. This is really discussing the concept of gist. We are back to the notion of learning the gist of something, rather than memorizing information.[43]

This is where teaching needs to occur. Dissemination of information without helping students develop comprehensible frames of reference is a pedagogical waste of time. First, students need help in defining and understanding the underlying principles buried within information. Secondly, they need help in organizing the principles they have identified into coherent patterns or frames of reference. Once these two operations have occurred, students are in a better position to be critical thinkers. Then they have the possibility of becoming independent thinkers (after they are able to create and evaluate their own frames of reference).

Information is irrelevant without an evaluative frame of reference. In the classroom, much more time must be spent on the tactics of thinking than on the dissemination of information. Once they understand the tactics of research, students are as able to find information as the teacher. This is becoming more true as we move steadily into the information age of the internet and the digital storage of information. Information is not the problem. The problem is what to do with all the information. The problem is over fitting. Schools must help students learn various tactics in managing and evaluating information. Simply turning students loose on the internet to 'do their thing' will not achieve critical and independent thinkers and learners.

The Role of the School in Discouraging and Encouraging Independent Learning and Thinking

It is the classroom teacher who establishes the ground rules for learning in the classroom. Teachers do not feel completely free to respond to the needs of their students because they feel a responsibility to conform to the demands of the education culture broadly defined. Educational culture is based on a set of assumptions about learning from the prevailing educational paradigm. The most basic assumption schools and teachers accept is the algorithmic paradigm of teaching. In the algorithmic paradigm, there are many assumptions which need to be questioned *vis a vis* independent thinking and learning. Despite research that questions the practices of algorithmic instruction, many algorithmic practices are maintained or passed on to the schools unexamined. As institutions, schools chronically deal with the consequences of those assumptions. So far we have noted three: activated ignorance, inert knowledge, and an inability to transfer learning.

What research shows quite clearly is that there is a cause and effect between educational practice and student outcomes. But it may not be what was expected, depending upon the objectives of schools and teachers. If independence and creativity were the objectives, then there is a disconnection between objectives and outcomes under the algorithmic paradigm. If conformity and reproduction of the culture were the objectives, then there is a connection. In fact, students do respond to the educational methodology (teaching strategies) they encounter in the classroom. Students learn much more from teaching methodology than they learn from the actual content being taught. The content students absorb may become inert knowledge, the lessons from the teaching methodology certainly does not.

There is surprisingly little active concern about the consequences of teaching methodology in the educational community.[44] The education community in the broadest sense, schools, and teachers need to understand and accept the consequences of their approaches. It is not enough to claim they are creating independent thinkers and learners, and then continue to teach using traditional algorithmic strategies. Changes need to be made before students will respond with independence and creativity. The big question is what direction ought instruction to take? Some examples and directions have been established in this chapter. These themes will be explored in more detail in the next chapters.

End Notes

1. Richard W. Paul. "Dialogical Thinking: Critical Thought Essential to the Acquisition of Rational Knowledge and Passions". *Teaching Thinking Skills.* Ed. Joan Boykof Baron and Robert J. Sternberg. New York: W. H. Freeman and Company. p.130.

2. P. Carraher, T. N. Carraher, D. W. Carraher, and A. D. Schliemann. "Mathematics in the streets and in schools". *British Journal of Experimental Psychology.* 1985. Vol. 3. pp. 21-29.

3. Paul. p.131.

4. Antonio Damasio. *Descartes' Error: Emotion, Reason and the Human Brain.* New York: Grosset/Putnam. 1994. As referenced in Golelman, Daniel. *Emotional Intelligence.* New York: Bantam Books. 1995. p. 28.

5. C Wright Mills. *The Marxists.* New York: Dell. 1962.

6. Edgar Z. Friedenberg. *The Vanishing Adolescent.* Boston: Beacon Press. 1964. p. 9.

7. Paul. p.130.

8. C. J. Brainerd and L. L. Gordon. "Development of Verbatim and Gist Memory for Numbers". *Developmental Psychology.* 1994. Vol. 30 No. 2 p.164.

9. Brainerd & Gordon. p. 164.

10. C. J. Brainerd and V. F. Kingma, "The Memory Independence Effect: What Do the Data Show? What Do the Theories Claim?" *Developmental Review.* 1992. Vol. 12. p.181.

11. A. DeGroot, "Perception and memory versus thought: Some old ideas and recent findings". *Problem Solving.* Ed. B. Kleinmutz. New York: Wiley. 1966.

12.. M. T.H. Chi, J. E. Hutchison, and A. F. Robin. "How inferences about novel domain-related concepts can be constrained by structured knowledge". *Merrill-Palmer Quarterly.* Vol. 35 pp. 27-61.

13. L. Festinger. *A Theory of Cognitive Dissonance.* Evanston Ill.: Row, Peterson. 1957.

14. Paul. p.134.

15. E H. J. Eysenck. "Introduction". *A model for intelligence.* Ed. H. J. Eysenck. New York: Springer-Verlag. 1982. pp. 1-10.

16. DeGroot, 1966.

17. M. T. Chi and E. Rees. "A learning framework for development". *Contributions to Human Development.* Vol. 9. pp. 71-107.

M. Chi, P. Feltowich, and R.Glaser. "Categorization and representation of physical problems by experts and novices.". *Cognitive Science.* 1981Vol. pp. 121-152.

18 J. R. Hayes. *The Complete Problem Solver.* (ERIC: ED234995).

19. D.N. Perkins. "Thinking Frames: An Integrative Perspective on Teaching Thinking Skills". *Teaching Thinking Skills.* Ed. Joan Boykof Baron and Robert J. Sternberg. New York: W. H. Freeman and Company. p.45.

20. J. Baron. "Intelligence and general strategies". *Strategies for Information Processing.* Ed. G. Underwood. London: Academic Press. 1978. pp.403-450.

21. A. H. Schoenfeld, "Measures of problem-solving performance and of problem-solving instruction". *Journal for Research in Mathematics Education.* 1982. Vol. 13, pp. 31-49.

22. Bolt Beranek and Newman Inc.. "Final Report". *Project Intelligence: The development of procedures to enhance thinking skills.* Cambridge, Mass: Bolt Beranek and Newman Inc.

23. Chi, *et al.* 1981.

Feltovich & Glaser. 1981.

J. H. Larkin. "The role of problem representation in physics". *Mental Models.* Ed. D. Gentner and A. L. Stevens. (Hillsdale N.J.: Erlbaum. 1983.

Schoenfeld, 1982.

A. H. Schoenfeld and D. J. Herrmann. "Problem perception and knowledge structure in expert and novice mathematical problem solvers". *Journal of Experimental Psychology: Learning, Memory, and Cognitions.* 1982. Vol. 8. pp 484-494..

Hayes, 1981.

24 Perkins. p. 45.

25. Ralph W. Tyler. *Basic Principles of Curriculum and Instruction.* Chicago: The University of Chicago Press. 1949.

26 A. H. Shoenfeld. "Explicit heuristic training as a variable in problem-solving performance". *Journal for Research in Mathematics Education.* 1979. Vol. 10. pp. 173-187.

27. L. Festinger and J. M. Carlsmith. "Cognitive Consequences of Forced Compliance". *Journal of Abnormal and Social Psychology.* 1959. Vol. 58. pp. 203-210.

28. H. A. Simon. "Invariants of human behaviour". *Annual Review Psychology.*) 1990. Vol. 41. pp 1-19.

29. I have chatted with adult learners taking logic classes at a university level. Many of them cannot see any utility to processes they are studying. Many high school mathematics students will make similar claims. They might be more motivated if they could see how the information they are learning could be applied to their personal reality in some way.

30. William Damon. *Handbook of Child Psychology.* New York: John Wiley & Sons. Inc. p.804.

31 Paul. p.131.

32. Peter M. Todd and Gerd Gigerenzer. "Précis of Simple heuristics that make us smart". *Behavioral and Brain Sciences.* Vol. 23. 2000. p.729.

33. Thomas Homer-Dixon. *The Ingenuity Gap.* Toronto: Alfred A Knopf. 2000. p. 11.

34. Ibid, p. 23.

35. Ibid p. 208.

36 Ibid p. 219.

37 Ibid p. 219.

38. Ibid p. 219.

39. Robert Sternberg. "How Intelligent Is Intelligence Testing?". *Scientific American Presents: Exploring Human Intelligence.*

C Wright Mills. *The Marxists.* New York: Dell. 1962. Vol. 9, No. 4. Winter 1998. pp. 12-17.

Robert Sternberg and James Kaufman. "Human Abilities". *Annual Review of Psychology.* Vol. 49. 1998. pp 479-502.

40. Damon. p. 804.

41. E. H. Carr. *What is History?* London: Penguin. 1961.

42. Perkins, p. 47.

43. Brainerd and Gordon p. 164.

44. In general, it is fair to say that beyond the production of textbooks, there is little formal institutional support for teaching methods. The design, production, dissemination of, and accountability for teaching methods (technology) for use in the classroom is at a low level relative to the work being done in other industries. The reason for this is the pervasiveness of the algorithmic model: why is it necessary to design a myriad of different ways to tell people what to know and think? The unspoken answer is that there is no significant reason beyond making classrooms 'fun', so why bother? The other attitude is that it is up to individual teachers to research and develop these tactics. Any teacher worth his or her salt can do this. Compare that to the team approach to developing tactics in other industries.

CHAPTER NINE: THE ROLE OF HEURISTICS IN INDEPENDENT THINKING

TABLE OF CONTENTS

Issues in Creating a Community of Scholars in the Classroom

In educational literature, there is discussion about classrooms as communities of scholars as the critical precursor to independent learning. Such rhetoric sounds great in theory, but in practice it has proven to be a difficult goal to attain. Large classes filled with unmotivated students - bringing their problems and attitudes with them, which limit their interest in voluntary learning - are common. There may be salutary exceptions to this generalization, but by and large students have little interest in learning beyond doing the minimum to get the grades they deem necessary. Given these realities for many parents and educators, the straight forward, reasonable conclusion is to impose learning upon students using an algorithmic methodology.

The issue to be pursued in this chapter is whether substituting a heuristic based teaching program for the more common algorithmic teaching programs will encourage the creation of communities of scholars within classrooms? Despite the problems found in many schools, it remains remarkable, really, how many students remain committed to independent learning. This is where the initial potential lies. This chapter will discuss ways of exploiting and expanding that potential.

Paradigm shifts often hinge upon taken for granted assumptions. Two shifts in assumptions need to occur. Shift one is to give up memorization and all the evaluation systems based upon it as the primary learning strategy (of course, this is not a small issue). Shift two involves rebalancing power related to freedom and choice for students in classrooms. Most teachers (and society) would react with misgivings at notions of classroom freedom: "What would I do?" "How would I maintain control?" and "The students will never learn anything; it will be a shambles!" To traditional information disseminating teachers, the new paradigm appears to be a looming dark chasm of disaster into which all will plunge. It appears to be a nightmare of discipline problems and low achievement.

What is being overlooked is how maintaining traditional forms of education causes many discipline problems in classrooms.[1] Students resist information dissemination because they intuitively understand it does not meet their needs - at least when it is presented in an algorithmic form. They know they are being overwhelmed with information, and their personal heuristics are telling them their first order of business is to make sense of what they have before gathering more information.[2] When one listens to the complaints of students, the refrain sounds something like this: "Why are we learning this; how will it help me live my life?" These comments are often interpreted as laziness being rationalized, but it is more than that. It is saying that learning, at the least, should have personal meaning, and better yet personal utility.[3]

The Central Issue for Education is Tactics

The reality of paradigm change can be quite different. It is already happening to some extent in many classrooms, and those teachers who are practicing it are not prepared to return to the old ways. As mentioned earlier, the educational technology already exists to make a community of scholars a practical reality. What remains to be done is to let go of unproductive assumptions and get on with the task of creating classroom societies.

Educational technology offers many techniques which can be used to create heuristic based classrooms. Some are currently being used, albeit in a piece meal fashion, with the dissemination of information being the primary objective.[4] The objective needs to change, making information the means to independent learning and thinking rather than the end.[5] When that paradigm shift occurs, many existing techniques will become much more successful in the classroom. At the same time, new techniques will be developed which will be very productive in developing independent thinkers and learners.

Understanding Power

Teachers must understand that power, defined as the ability to control the behaviour of others, can be approached from two basic points of view. The more traditional approach is the zero sum approach. The zero sum viewpoints see power as a scarce commodity coveted by the powerful and the powerless. Sharing power means the person sharing is losing power in favour of those who are receiving power. Given this reality, power sharing is a struggle with winners and losers. A zero sum view of the classroom sees the teacher holding a limited amount of power. That power involves the power to assign marks, control the learning agenda, restrict student freedom, etc. If some of that power is transferred to students, they in their immaturity will misuse it, and they will be extremely reluctant to return it to the teacher. So good discipline means that the teacher must maintain strict control of power, and assign it to students on a strictly limited basis, usually as a reward for good behaviour.

There is another view of power which may be labelled empowerment. In this view all members of a community together create power. Power is the concerted action/behaviour of people working together for a common purpose. Ultimately, no one has power over another as suggested by the zero sum view. Rather, people agree to pool their powers for personal wellbeing, however defined.[6] Empowerment views power as something that grows through personal relationships rather than something that is scarce. The more power is shared in working toward a common goal, the more power is created.

A classroom in which students are energized and mobilized toward the achievement of a goal of some kind is full of power. Students in this situation have large amounts of power, but so does the teacher. What is interesting is that neither a student nor teachers really appreciating the reality of their power. They are so busy enjoying their lives, it does not occur to them to count who has how many units of power. For people functioning under an empowerment social regime, power in the zero-sum sense seems irrelevant.

Much of student evaluation has been a zero-sum tool to force student compliance in the classroom. Evaluation will have to change before classrooms of scholars are possible. Gone would be testing for information. Information based questions would be seen as being irrelevant for a couple of reasons. One is that all of this kind of information can be researched as needed. Secondly, necessary and useful information would be quickly and permanently stored in students' minds as gist. Information not so stored was likely deemed to be irrelevant for one reason or another. A heuristic classroom would allow students to make those decisions. (They do so anyway in algorithmic classrooms, either by forgetting it, assigning it to inert knowledge, or ignoring it through activated ignorance.) All that is being given up is the power to attempt to impose knowledge on students.

What is being gained is an evaluation system which becomes a learning tool for students. They use evaluation to determine personally whether they are approaching the achievement of their goals in any meaningful way. Evaluation in this view essentially concerns the careful consideration about the work they have done (process and product) in producing something (products, ideas, communications, etc). Over the course of time, as their interests evolve and mature, they will share and evaluate many things. Student centred evaluation is only possible when the competitive threat of failure and its related public humiliation is at least lessened if not removed.

As pointed out earlier in this book, mystification is a great problem for students. It gives students a feeling of powerlessness. In that sense, mystification is a great enemy of empowerment. Mystification is actually a zero-sum power concept in which bits of information are doled out by an all-powerful leader.[7] The reverse of this process, empowerment, would say that information must always be demystified by grounding it in a reality students can appreciate. All this is saying is that children, like adults, use basic heuristics to make sense of reality. We have mentioned three: the recognition heuristic, the representative heuristic, and the availability heuristic. When students are trusted to employ their personal heuristics in learning, then they are on the road to empowerment. In fundamental terms, this is the basis of the heuristic paradigm. On the other hand, the algorithmic paradigm is always in danger of mystifying and tumbling into zero-sum power relationships.

The Tactics of Learning Are the Goals of Education

A necessary task in developing classrooms of scholars is to create curricula which proceed from heuristic assumptions rather than algorithmic assumptions. Such curricula would be focused on learning tactics rather than the accumulation of information. Tactics would become the end of learning, and information would become the means. Goals and means would now be reversed.

With a little research and thinking, it would be possible to get a handle on children's age-related interests on a variety of things. Children/students are somewhat predictable. Their interests appear and disappear in predictable fashion. Those interests often appear in concert with the development of certain cognitive skills. Some examples: children at certain ages love dinosaurs and will voluntarily spend hours working with them; at certain ages children love class inclusion exercises (Jane Doe, 127 Regent Street, Toronto, Ontario, Canada, Western Hemisphere, World, Sun solar system, Milky Way Galaxy, etc., etc.); students in adolescence love to discuss social relationships because relationships are such a delicious mystery; many students at various stages of their lives love cars, computers, music, art, movies, animals, sports, etc.

Is it possible to rethink the disciplines of mathematics, the sciences, social sciences, philosophy, literature, etc from the viewpoint of the heuristic paradigm, and discover respectable learning objectives which could meet the needs of students and society? It is, particularly if one is prepared to give up pre-packaged algorithmic objectives for heuristic objectives. If one looks at a history of the evolution of mathematics and science, it is already there. If one looks at history itself as a series of social experiments from which societies sometimes learn something, then one can see the process of heuristics working throughout history. Why not let students in on the process and harness all that intense curiosity about how things work? For example, rather than teaching geometry as some kind of formal thinking exercise, why not teach it as a heuristic process of learning the relationships of shapes, much as the ancient Greeks did in their sand boxes?

Whether a community of scholarship is possible in the classroom depends at bottom on respect between teacher and students. Unless there is a mutuality of respect, it is hard to see a scholarship community evolving. Students need to feel they have the respect of their teacher. Mistakes, shortcomings, and inadequacies all need to be respected as the ground of the human condition. Because also mixed up in that human condition is talent, brilliance, and insight all struggling to be born. Respect requires everyone in the community of scholarship to search diligently for those small indicators of talent. They are there, they are tentative, and they will quickly run for cover if they are not honoured.

Teacher leadership in a community of scholars needs to be dynamic and upbeat without being dominating. This is a very fine line to follow. It requires teachers who are imaginative and stimulating and who know when to 'shut up' and 'get out of the way'.[8] Such teachers are not wimps who cannot demand respect. Rather, they are people with high levels of self-respect who have little difficulty in giving respect to others. Of course, teachers are not perfect, and have their share of inadequacies. Students are more aware of that than most. What student's prize in leadership is honesty, and the ability to admit mistakes and move on in a constructive manner. By doing so, teachers create a positive role model for students to follow.

The Face of Teaching in Classrooms Using a Heuristic Paradigm

We have already discussed some of the social dynamics necessary to create a heuristic centred classroom. Much research work has been done on developing effective social dynamics for classrooms. That work is absolutely critical and needs to continue, but there is another issue needing serious consideration. What educational purposes do social dynamics serve in classrooms? The obvious purpose is to develop those social skills which will allow children to function effectively in society. Another purpose is learning to use social skills as a means to learn independent thought. The purpose of this book is to look at the development of thought processes in the classroom. The central purpose of schools is to prepare young people intellectually and morally as well as socially.

Important as social relationships are, they are not the focus of this book. Parents and society continue to expect schools to turn out students who are intellectually capable citizens. The central issue of our time is which paradigm can do a better job of that: the algorithmic or the heuristic? The research cited in this chapter clearly suggests that the heuristic paradigm is the better approach.[9] Let us say again, it is not a question of whether students learn important bits of information.[10] They will under both paradigms. Research clearly supports that.[11] The issue is whether information is enough. Again, it is clear that information by and of itself is not enough. Students need to be able to think and learn independently. They do not get enough of that from the algorithmic paradigm.[12]

Heuristic Teaching Strategies

The remainder of this chapter will be a fairly detailed and specific discussion of what teachers can do in their classrooms to move from an algorithmic paradigm to a heuristic paradigm. Earlier in this book we spent some time discussing the significance of patterning as a concept. At this point, we need to return to the notion of patterns. Students must understand we assume reality can be patterned and by understanding how to create and use patterns, they can learn to think critically, creatively and independently.[13] Teachers need always to work on developing this sense of coherent patterns in reality.

Without repeating many of the ideas already discussed around conceptual thinking, it is important for teachers to help students come to understand that concepts are the basis for our understanding of the patterns of reality. Concepts and their interrelationships form the gist of any understanding. By understanding concepts and their interrelationships, students are learning and remembering the gist of what they are studying. It is gist that they carry in their minds and manipulate into various patterns (or models - more about that later) as they think about something.

There are some important thought techniques centred on concepts that teachers can develop with their students. One is known as concept webbing, and another is concept mapping.[14] We have used concept maps in a couple of places in this book already. The simpler technique is concept webbing, and that would be good place to begin with students.

Concept Webbing as a Heuristic Activity

In general, educational activities should be presented to students as thinking tools which are helpful in thinking about complex topics. As part of any introduction to new learning and thinking strategies, students need to know there are methods (heuristics) which make the complex simpler and more transparent. When a new strategy such as concept webbing is introduced, teachers should adopt a heuristic approach.

Typically heuristic approaches begin with problems or issues so students can immediately see the need for a thought strategy. Any presentation should take advantage of the inherent ability of students to employ heuristics. If the objective is to encourage independence in learning and thinking, then it is critical to work with the students' natural heuristic abilities. In the specific case of introducing concept webbing, the heuristic of availability is a natural intellectual support for students.[15] Students can be challenged to suggest some general topics they know something about and would be interested in exploring in some detail. They may suggest a range of topics from movies to sports, to fashion, to relationships, etc. Pick one that seems acceptable to most and is fairly straight forward as a learning tool. I will choose sports for my example, understanding that it may not be a good one for many classrooms.

Explain that you are going to demonstrate a way of exploring a large topic such as sports. Place the word/concept in the centre of the chalkboard and then ask them for ideas (concepts) that relate to it in some way.

Fig. 9.1

Ask a student to write ideas from students around the central concept of sports. The students, of course, are brainstorming ideas. As they do that their ideas can be placed in a web around a central concept. This approach allows students to keep track of their ideas (concepts) and do a preliminary arrangement (pattern) of the concepts. The class might develop a diagram something like the one below:

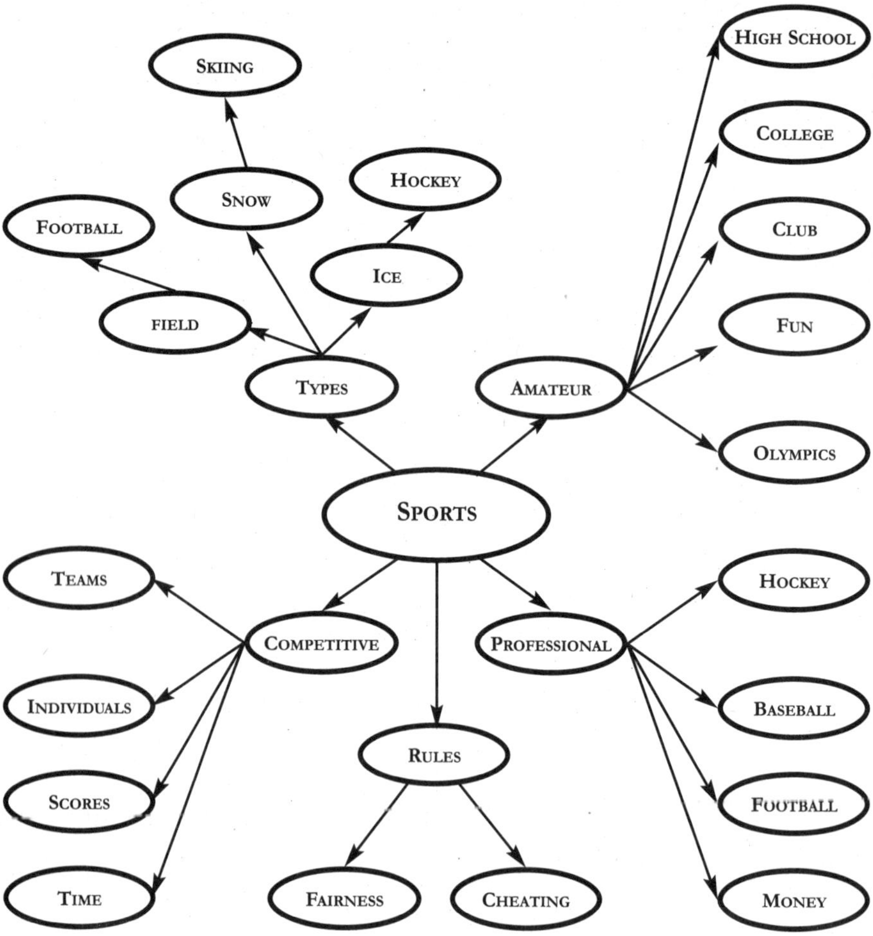

Fig. 9.2

By this time, students will be independently expanding their gist of understanding of the topic under discussion. They will also be using their personal heuristics (recognition, representation, availability) to gather more personal information about the topic. As the web expands students will be in an increasingly better position to discuss the topic. Opinions will be stated and reacted to. As the discussion process proceeds, the heuristics of availability, recognition, and representation will bring more ideas to the discussion and web creation. They can now see the basic framework (pattern) of the topic, and they can see some of the relationships between the topic components (concepts). As students discuss their concept webs, more ideas will be generated, leading to more concepts for the web.

This would be a good point to introduce the importance of relationships between the concepts. Usually these relationships are expressed as verbs and occasionally as adjectives and adverbs. Relationships between concepts need to be tested for their accuracy. Briefly stating the relationship between concepts in the concept web is one way of determining the validity of the relationship being suggested. In turn, when all the relationships have been examined, one is in a better position to trust the validity and coherence of the pattern being expressed through the concept web. Challenging students to evaluate the words being used to describe relationships between concepts makes it a much better thinking exercise. It is through exercises like these that an intellectual ethic can be established in the classroom which has the potential to transform it into a community of scholars. After students finish, the concept web might look something like the example below:

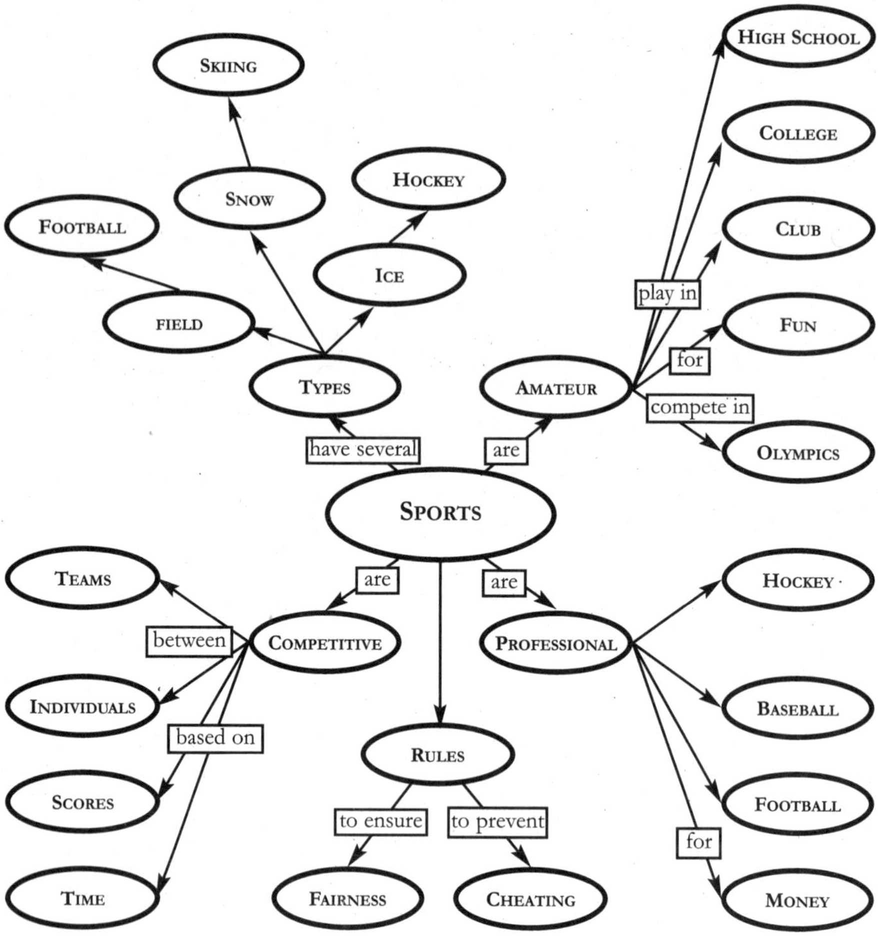

Fig. 9.3

Learning the Gist of Thought Concepts

As students proceed with a heuristic exercise like concept webbing, they unconsciously perform a number of thought concepts. They categorize, classify, summarize, analyze, infer, and model. All of these thought concepts are inherent to the brainstorming, web building process. Starting at the end of the concept webbing process, we find students are capable of creating models. (It is important to emphasize here that models developed in classrooms will look different than my example, and will certainly vary from classroom to classroom.) Their model resulted from the various inferences they drew as they considered concepts within the framework of sports. For example, what should be the proper relationship between professional and amateur athletes and the Olympics? Some might infer that professional athletes should not compete in the Olympics. Others might draw quite different inferences. Students will likely have opinions/inferences about the suitability of allowing professionals to compete, or preserving it as the pinnacle of amateur sports. This debate could quite easily lead to the development of competing concept webs or models.

Returning to the beginning of the process of considering issues using concept webbing, we can observe students quite naturally performing thought concepts such as categorizing and classifying. Thinking conceptually about an issue forces students to create broad categories. In our example, some categories were types of sports, characteristics of participants (amateur, professional) competition, rules, etc. As the students generated their conceptual categories, they were also classifying (patterning) the categories in their webs. By classifying the categories, the students then naturally began to analyze the relationships between the categories. Any discussion of a conceptual proposition becomes an analytical discussion because analysis by definition is a consideration of relationships between categories. For example, are rules necessary to the success of any sporting endeavour: why or why not? Finally, the whole endeavour of webbing can also be called a summary; in this case, a summary of sports.

The important thing for teachers to understand is that students are mostly unaware of their mental activities. One might argue that if students are able to perform these thought concepts naturally, then it does not matter whether they are consciously aware of their abilities. But if we wish to equip them with an intellectual toolkit to which they can consciously and purposely turn to in novel situations, then we do need to make them aware of what they are doing. If they are to be able to transfer thought concepts from one situation to another, then students need to have some awareness of their thought processes.

As students perform a thought concept, they and the teacher should develop a practical definition and note it for the future. The important thing is that students develop in their minds the gist of the thought concepts they employ. As their thought concept gists develop, they will be able to refer to them much more easily. For quite a while teachers should be sure to emphasize each thought concept as it pops up in the intellectual activity of the classroom. "We were doing categorization and classification, but now we are doing analysis." We need to hear these kinds of comment often in the classroom. It may even become something of a joke among students. That is actually a healthy sign, because if students can joke about it, they likely have assimilated the gist of the thought concept(s).

There is another critical process that must also be stressed. Thought concepts are not used in isolation. They are used in a pattern with one thought concept, providing information to be used in turn by other thought concepts until a conclusion has been reached. Thinkers create routines to think about issues and/or in solving problems. In the sports example described above, the routine ran roughly in the following order: categorizing, classifying, analysis, inferring, and modeling. It is likely that heuristics such as concept webbing are successful thought strategies, because they stimulate a richer array of thought concepts than would be the possible without a supporting heuristic. Different heuristics will stimulate different patterns of thought concepts. This is an important reason for developing a variety of heuristics with students. Later in the chapter, we will be looking at other heuristics.

Linking Thought Concepts into Purposeful Patterns

As students work with a heuristic, it is critical they realize they are using concepts in a linked fashion to achieve a goal of some kind. Students must be made aware they are using thought concepts as part of an overall purposeful routine. As teachers and students identify the thought concepts being used, they might also develop a thought concept check list. This list could be added to as students learn and use more concepts. Such a list could be placed on a side board of the classroom and used to monitor the thought concepts being used. As students do exercises like concept webbing with related discussions, they could use the check list to keep track of the thought concepts employed. Students could be challenged to take turns in monitoring: a kind of play-by-play overview of a class discussion. Rather than using checkmarks, they should use numbers so they become aware of the patterns in their thinking. This would help them to learn to develop personal thought routines which they can adapt and transfer to other situations.

Effective thinkers facing challenges are able to develop productive thought routines in an ad hoc manner which varies from situation to situation. As students become self-aware of the thought concepts they use, it is important that they not learn them in a lock-step, algorithmic process. Students need to learn that thought routines are adaptable and self-correcting heuristics which change as their needs change. We are back to the notion of ecological rationality. Earlier we noted that any intellectual relationship between a difficult to control environment and the individual human response to it requires a creatively reasoned response. As the environment changes, so must the thought patterns of the thinker change. Plug-in, formulaic thinking becomes stereotypical and out-of-touch with the processes of reality. Remember that thought concepts become tools in the students' personal intellectual took kits to be used in a variety of ways as reality requires.

As a community of scholars, the classroom should practice using a variety of heuristics so as to stimulate a variety of thought routines. If students and teachers consciously keep track of the pattern of thought concepts being used in each thought routine, students are likely to learn a more heuristic approach to their thinking. This kind of heuristic self-awareness is an important pre-cursor to independent thinking.

Inferencing

Students are typically weak at inferencing[16]. The idea of looking at a piece of information and checking through one's personal store of information (gists) in order to find something which can be related to the first piece of information is something that many students have little experience with. This is a critical ability to gain if one wishes to become a successful thinker. Initially students may need some guidance in learning to make inferences.

There are a number of simple approaches or heuristics teachers may use to demonstrate how to discover inferences. Seeking relationships among the components of a piece of reality is one place to start. This is why, in concept webbing, it is so critical for students to state relationships using verbs or modifiers to connect concepts. Such relationships in and of themselves are inferences. The student has to generate the connection between concepts out of his or her personal experience. This automatically forces students to turn to their heuristics of availability, recognition, and representation. Another thinking tactic would be to ask students to consider what concepts can and cannot be added to their conceptual model? Does a certain idea/concept fit: why or why not? Another simple heuristic is the "who, what, when, where, why, and how (W5)" heuristic. Challenge the students to pick one of the question words and use it to form a question. Why......?; when.....?; etc. By doing this, the students can explore new patterns of ideas.

What role(s) might the teacher play in these situations without becoming algorithmic in their teaching? Returning to a further consideration of the concept web/model on sports, the teacher could initiate a discussion by asking; "What about ice dancing? Where should it go in the sports model?" A question like this could encourage students to begin to think independently about the nature of sports and the nature of the arts. This would help them develop a distinction in their minds between arts and sports. Another question leading to a similar distinction is to ask whether professional sports are work or fun? Such a question would challenge students to more precisely define work and sports. In both cases, the important thing is to encourage students to explore by creating and evaluating inferences as part of their thinking and exploration.

The fundamental issue for teachers is to help students learn to create conditions that make it possible to think independently. At the same time, while students are thinking about various topics, they are also learning the gist of information, thought concepts, communications skills, and social skills. Under the heuristic paradigm, learning objectives are no longer limited to memorizing information objectives. They encompass a much vaster potential for learning. The potential can be expanded as students learn to apply other heuristics to their concept webs

Achieving Transfer

Once the idea of concept webbing is established with students, the teacher should provide them with opportunities demonstrating how to use concept webbing as a heuristic to explore other issues. A teacher might wish to encourage students to think about a topic such as the environment. Rather than give students information, the teacher can place the word environment on the chalkboard and ask students to contribute related concepts and build a concept web. Students could either suggest or write in the concepts they believe are germane to the central idea of environment as the discussion proceeds.

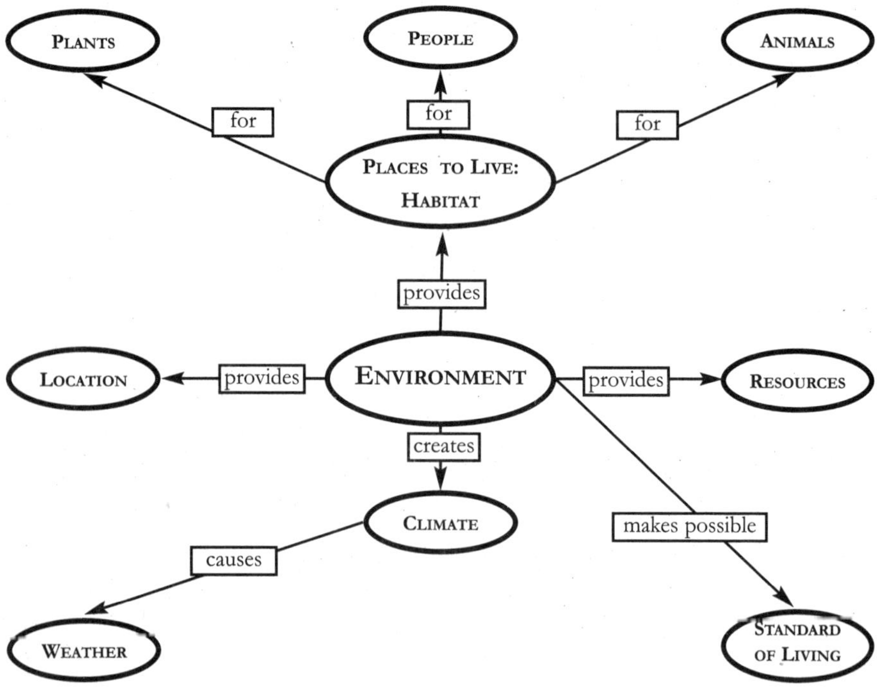

Fig. 9.4

This might be a probable first response by students. It is simplistic, and in some respects, inaccurate and misconceived. But it is a place to start thinking, both in terms of being critical and being creative. As guide to a community of scholars, it is not the teacher's role to provide precise answers and conclusions. That immediately tumbles the teacher into the algorithmic mode of teaching. The leadership of the teacher needs to be much more Socratic in approach.

The teacher has to use a variety of heuristics to help students think and learn independently. We will not be able to explore all of them here, but we can explore a few and see where they take us. A simple tactic to begin with is to ask 'what is missing?'; are some significant aspects of the environment and its interrelationships missing from the concept web? Simple questions could point students to areas they could explore which would help them expand the number of concepts they have to consider. Ask them to consider how environmental problems would relate to the concept web? Concepts like extinction of species, pollution, shortages (water, oil, etc) and climate change might be areas to explore. If the students feel there is a gap, but they do not know which concepts might be available to fill it, then they have the nucleus of a research program. As each new concept arises, the students should be challenged to fit them into their web somehow.

Heuristics Expedite Thinking

It is important to inform students of the heuristic they are using to expedite their thinking. It is not necessary to use the term heuristic if the term seems cumbersome. Still, it is important for the development of the gist of thought concepts in the minds of students that they be made aware they are using thinking strategies, shortcuts, rules of thumb, etc to support their thinking. As part of the gist development process, students need to have a label of some kind for the mental processes they are performing. Students need to understand the gist of these strategies, and to add them to their intellectual tool kits for use in other areas. Giving each heuristic a simple label helps students keep track of them. For example the heuristic outlined in the above paragraph might be labelled 'find the missing concepts'. The heuristic below might be called the 'double check' heuristic. Students and teachers should also track the thought strategies they are using in class so that students can personally evaluate their effectiveness.

Students will always retain the power to accept or dismiss a heuristic or thinking strategy. If the heuristic strikes the student as being meaningful and useful, the student is more likely to retain and use it. If the heuristic appears difficult and makes more work than it saves, it is unlikely to survive in students' intellectual lives. It is important for heuristics to be used enough to give students opportunities to understand their gists, and to be able to use them with facility and success. If facility and success are achieved, then the heuristic will become incorporated in the student's intellectual toolkit.

Returning to heuristics that teachers may use in the classroom, a straight forward heuristic is to simply double check or question the propositions (the suggested relationships between concepts) proposed in the students' concept web (model) above. The students might ask themselves whether the propositions they have suggested are completely true. For example, in the concept web on the environment above, there is a proposition suggesting people are dependent upon habitats. Some might question whether modern societies are in fact dependent on habitats. They could argue modern science allows the manipulation of habitats as needed. Others could disagree, noting that despite science, humankind remains ultimately dependent upon habitats for their livelihood. The dialogue between these two points of view would be a powerful learning exercise for students to pursue. It is important for students to learn to criticize the propositions they construct by asking themselves whether a proposition may be somewhat less than true or overlooks some important issue. This might be referred to as the 'dialogical thinking' heuristic.

Another simple heuristic students could adopt is the 'devil's advocate' heuristic. Students could create an imaginary other person to play the role of devil's advocate. It is the responsibility of this imaginary person to question and suggest alternative propositions to the proposition the student is considering. This may not mean students have to abandon the proposition they were originally considering, but it may mean that there are some conceptual qualifications or alternatives which can be added to the concept web. The imaginary devil's advocate might claim our use of the environment has not always improved living standards. Sometimes our treatment of the environment lowers the standard of living. The thinker now has to consider how to work the concept of pollution into the concept web.

Another heuristic would be to reverse the causation, which could become known as the 'old reverse causation' heuristic. It could work something like the following. The proposition that the environment makes possible a standard of living is reversed by some people to say that improving the standard of living makes a better environment possible. Is that true? What are the implications of such beliefs? Another example would be to ask whether plants create the environment. Is this true and what are the implications of such a perspective? Research and discussion could result in new concepts and propositions being added to the students' concept web.

In the course of discussion, students may possibly begin to disagree with each other about how to view the environment. They may not quite understand why they disagree and as a result they cannot define their disagreements. The problem here may be that they are making certain unconscious assumptions about the environment. Because of their lack of personal awareness, they are unable to confront each other openly about their points of view. All of this is leading up to another heuristic which might be labelled 'challenge the basic assumption' heuristic. One way of illustrating that for students is to redo a concept web by making some other concept the central organizer. In effect, that is beginning one's logical thought processes by a different set of assumptions.

Informal Teaching of Formal Thought

We are now encroaching on formal thought here. We are approaching some issues of logical thought through the back door, so to speak. The problem for many students with logical thinking is that it becomes too abstract, especially when they have to hold an array of propositions in their minds. Concept webbing allows students to build and rebuild logical constructs in a concrete manner. The teacher might do a concept attainment lesson on logical constructs using concept webs as examples of logical constructs. Most students can look at a proposition linking two concepts and offer some kind of critique of the implied logic. Changing the central concept of a concept web allows students to rethink their logic one proposition at a time.

Let us suppose that two groups of students see the environment from conflicting points of view. One group sees the environment as a source for a high standard of living for humans. Another group might argue the environment is the source of life (a habitat) for creatures (including humans). Both could be challenged to create a new concept web with what they would consider to be the central concept. Two possible examples follow:

Construct A

The starting points for concept webs may be located in a variety of places. Typically they are in the middle of a web as they are in the example below. Begin with standard of living and then follow the relationships throughout the web.

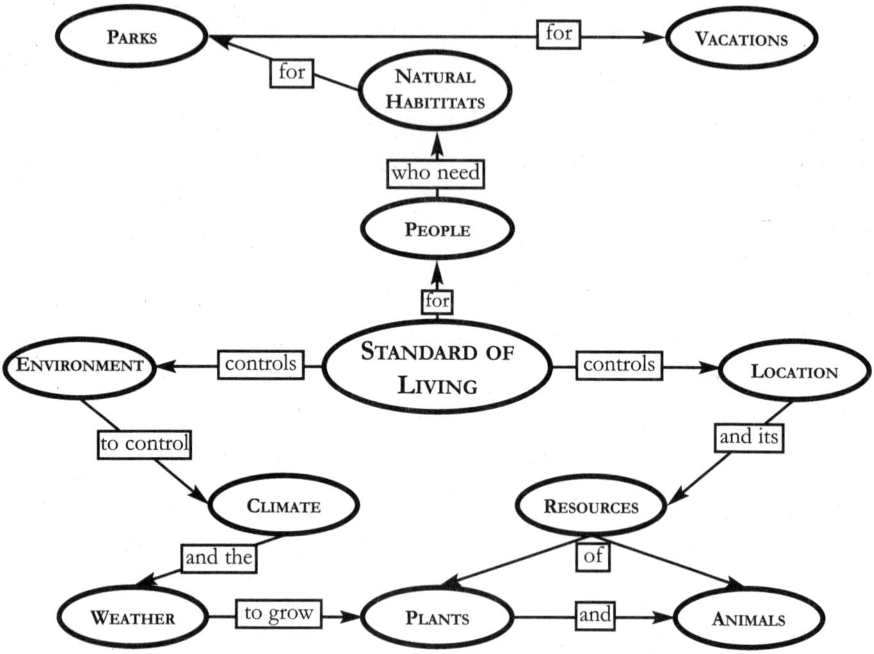

Fig. 9.5

CONSTRUCT B

In the example below, the arrangement is slightly different. In this case, the starting point is the concept 'environment', and one can then logically follow the relationships throughout the web.

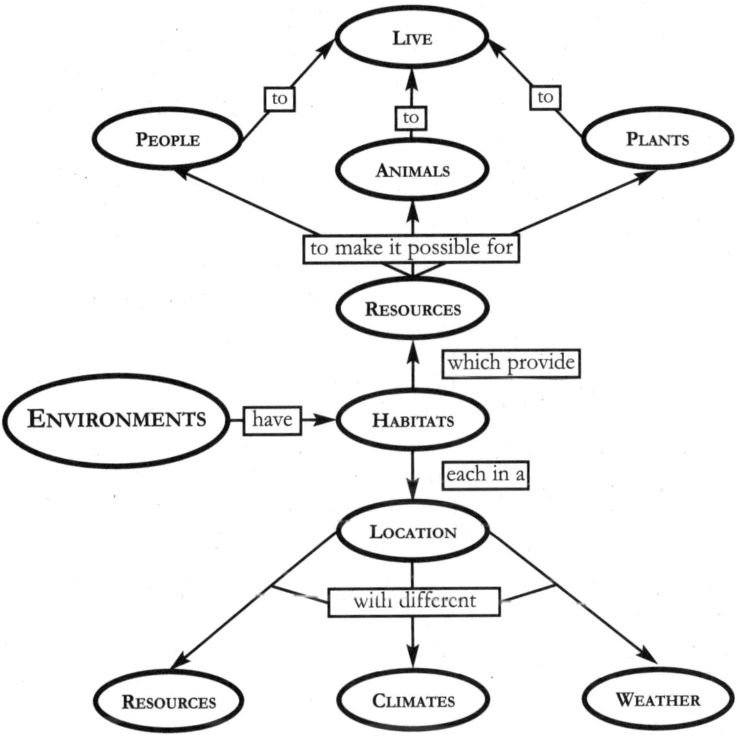

Fig. 9.6

What has been concretely illustrated here is what Pauls refers to as multilogical issues.[17] Each concept map has a particular logic which is questionable to some and acceptable to others. Students need time to discuss these two points of view and opportunities to create other points of view based on different assumptions as they develop their understanding of the environment.

Concept webbing has the potential to become a primary heuristic for students. In classrooms where this approach has been practiced, students have readily adopted concept webbing as a thought strategy to help them learn, think, research and write. We will take up each of these specific objectives in more detail in succeeding pages.

The basic assimilation of information (gist) is more effective, because students are dealing with an appropriate amount of information. Using concepts to facilitate the summary of information reduces the problem of over fitting. By learning to select fundamental concepts, students are forced to create and use the gist of the information they receive. As pointed out earlier this type of learning is much more likely to last than the verbatim memorization of information.

Achieving Multiple Learning Objectives

By engaging in these heuristics, several learning objectives are being achieved at the same time. The first, the gist of environmental understanding, is being broadened and deepened. There is no doubt that the students are picking up more environmental information at the conceptual and the factual levels. Secondly, students are learning to use thought concepts in practical hands-on situations as communities of scholars. If the thought concepts they repeatedly use are identified and emphasized as they work their way through various concept webbing exercises, students will develop personal gists for many of those thought concepts. Thirdly, if students are shown, they use thought concepts in patterns as they practice a particular thought routine, they can begin to understand how purposeful thinking consists of a pattern of different thought concepts, all of which they can understand and apply. Fourthly, students can begin to understand that heuristics are a way of initiating thought routines which in turn organize thought concepts into different patterns to achieve different conclusions. It resembles a *Lego* game, in which a variety of blocks can be assembled into different patterns to create different models and conclusions (the synthesizing thought concept).

Heuristics provide thought paths which young thinkers can naturally follow and achieve success. They also give students permission to think independently. Too often, students have the idea there is a predetermined conclusion they should reach. If students believe that, then they will be reluctant to think independently because they may not come to the correct conclusion. Achieving success in thinking is also important here. Success informs students that work can have a payoff, and that they are competent. It is success that motivates students to continue the sometimes onerous process of learning to think..

Concept Attainment Heuristic

At this point ,the teacher might introduce the concept of ecology, since it has not arisen so far. This could be a concept attainment lesson in which the teacher leaves the central concept oval blank and begins to build a series of propositions around the oval through discussion with students.

It would not be a good idea to present the concept web as a *fait accompli* to the students. That will simply turn into an algorithmic, memorization exercise. Rather the teacher must work with the students and develop each proposition in discussion with the class. The teacher might begin with the concept location and work with the students to develop the proposition that locations have climates and resources. Then the propositions of temperature, rainfall, water, soil, etc would logically (empirically) follow.[18] With that in place the students should then begin to think about concepts related to the food chain. What is the basis for the food chain, and how do all the concepts interrelate?

Once the basic web is in place, ask the students to begin to speculate on the central concept. There are a number of approaches that could be used here. One would be to remind the students of the basic elements of a concept: critical attributes, generalization, and concept label. Explain to the students that surrounding concepts are the critical attributes. Given those critical attributes, ask the students to suggest a generalization that might logically follow. Students now need to do some generalizing in this situation. You might remind them of the generalization concept, and then ask for some examples based on the concept web they have been discussing. During a class discussion, the students might decide on a generalization that seems most acceptable. Then the students could attempt to come up with a word (label/metaphor) summarizing the generalization.

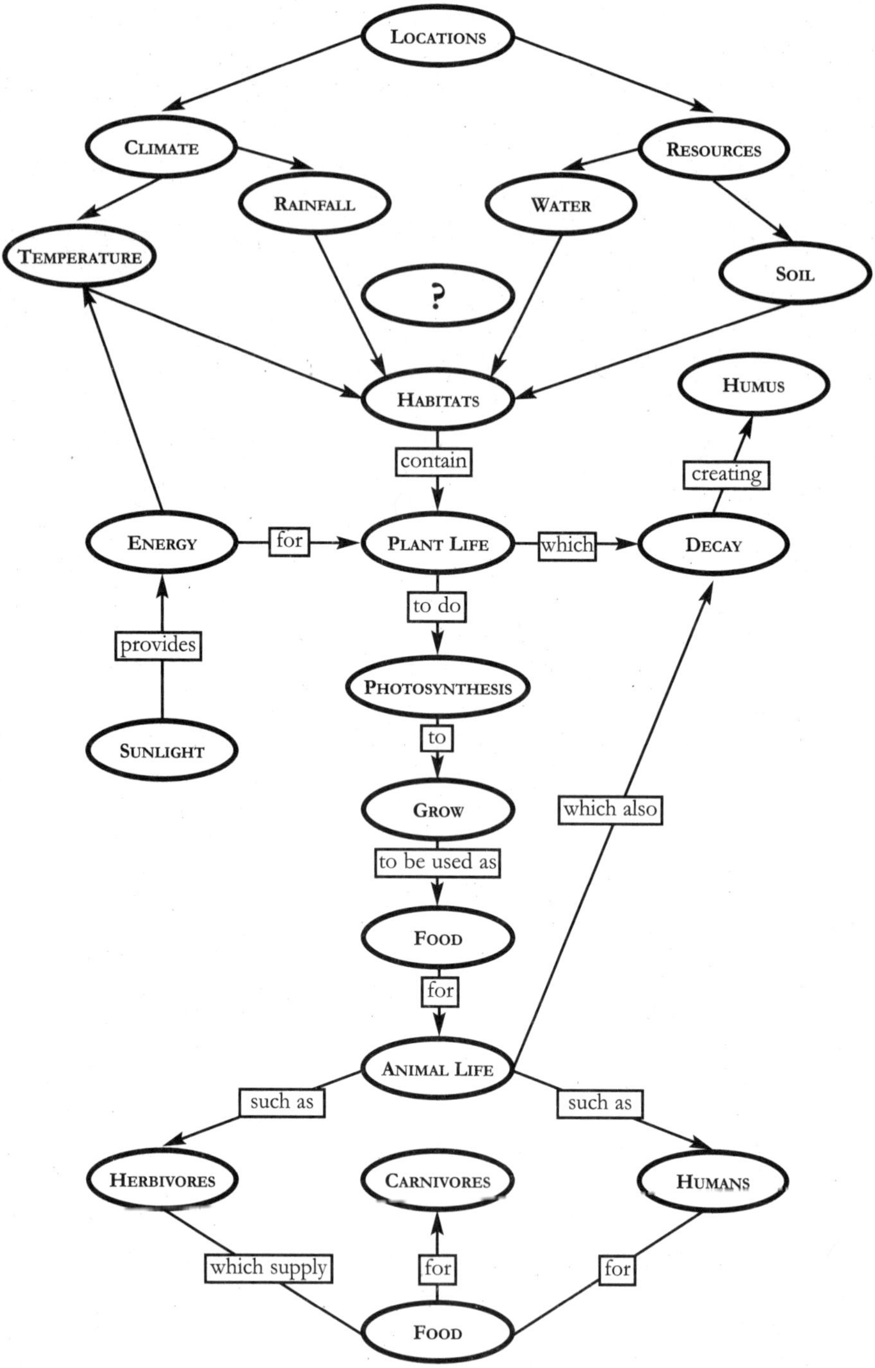
Locations
Climate
Resources
Rainfall
Water
Temperature
?
Soil
Habitats
Humus
contain
creating
Energy
for
Plant Life
which
Decay
to do
provides
Photosynthesis
Sunlight
to
Grow
which also
to be used as
Food
for
Animal Life
such as
such as
Herbivores
Carnivores
Humans
which supply
for
for
Food

Fig. 9.7

When the process is done, the students might attempt to give a label to that missing concept. They will have many of the critical attributes from which to work. The students may not be able to come up with a label, but they should be able to define the generalization for ecology.

This might be a good time to remind students they are replicating the process of developing new labels for concepts. For example, words like biology, psychology, geology, etc could be examined. They could learn that *logos* is the Greek word for 'study'. Ask them whether they think the concept web represents a logos situation. What kind of word might they coin by using 'ology' as the stem for their new word? Students need to understand this pattern so they can see how the larger community of scholars operate. Someone might then remember they heard the word ecology somewhere and ask whether that is the missing word. They, then, could learn the Greek word *oikos,* meaning 'household', and from there begin to think of ecology as a metaphor conceiving the environment as a complex household. The implications of this metaphor could be starting point for discussion.

Concept Webbing/Mapping Is a Heuristic Activity

If you have been following the evolution of the concept webs used as illustrations, you may have noticed that they appear to be moving from a circular display of concepts to a more linear display. This is the fundamental difference between concept webbing and concept mapping. Concept webs leave an impression of wholeness, in which relationships are displayed in a more or less static pattern. A snapshot of reality fixed in time. Concept maps provide a connotation of a journey, with a beginning point and an ending point. Concept maps typically begin with a key concept, and trace the development of significant relationships between concepts through to a conclusion. Concept maps may be similar to concept webs in the sense that some concept maps may be circular (cyclical), and so the destination (conclusion) can be the starting point. Concept maps attempt to provide a sense of direction, a flow of ideas with a starting point and an ending point.

Both methodologies have their advantages and disadvantages. Concept webbing is a good method for establishing an initial understanding (the gist) of a piece of reality. It is a way of getting the concepts and their relationships right, and determining where the knowledge gaps may be. Concept maps represent a thought process whereby the thinker begins to critically and creatively think about an issue. In concept mapping, the thinker begins to take on a point of view (hypothesis) and organize support (analysis) for that point of view. So concept maps lead one to conclusions about reality. In that sense, they synthesize a specific model of reality which may or may not be accurate

Let us take a couple of the biology concept webs we developed above and reconfigure them into concept maps. You may recall that earlier we noted concept webs could be reconfigured to show different points of view on an issue by changing the central concept of the web. The first examples below show contrasting views of the environment depending on whether standard of living or the environment should be considered the key concepts. This, of course, is a fundamental issue facing our society.

Construct A: 'People' as the Central Concept

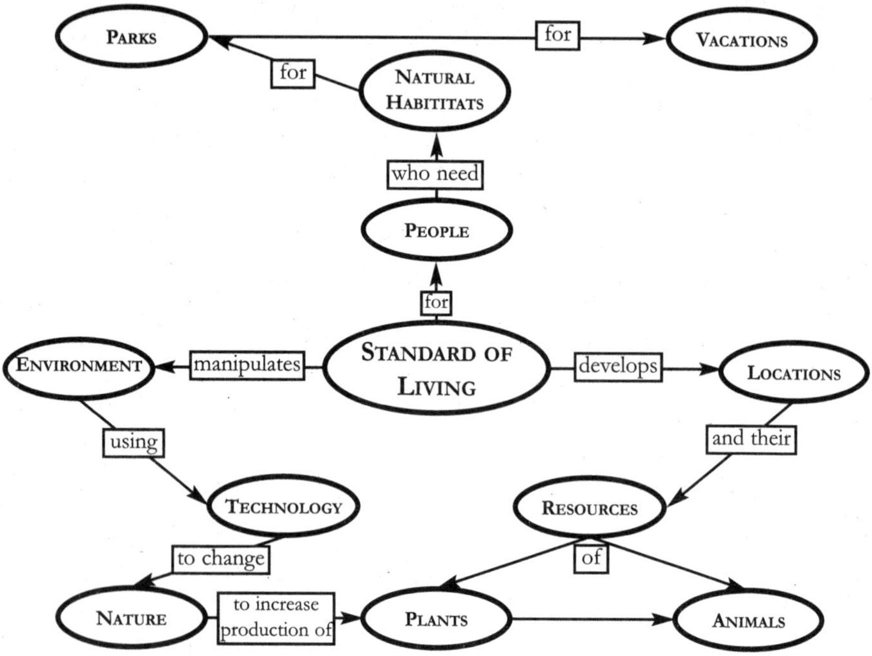

Fig. 9.8.

Because of the concepts selected, This concept web has an implicit point of view. It is also a borderline concept map, because it has begun to construct a linear argument: that by developing a high standard of living, people can manipulate the environment to make it more productive, and thereby increase the standard of living for people.

As students think about this argument, they may gather more information and they may want to defend it against those who disagree with it. One way of doing that is to develop their ideas into a concept map. In doing so, the students would have to decide what would be the logical starting point for their argument. In the map I am about to construct, people and their ability to control the environment would be the starting point. These relationships would constitute the first two levels of the concept map:

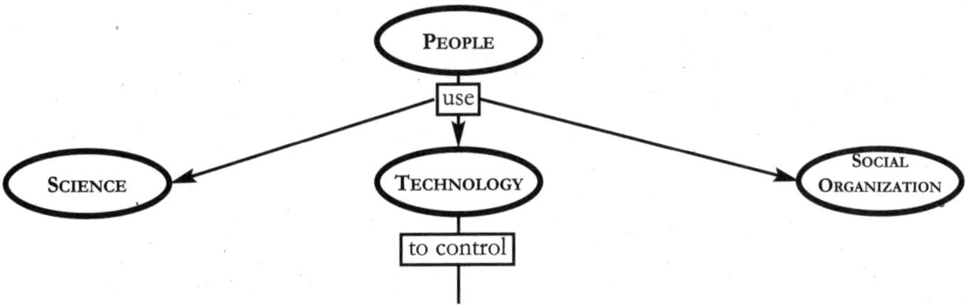

Fig. 9.9

The thinker could then go on to think about what is being controlled, and how that control occurs:

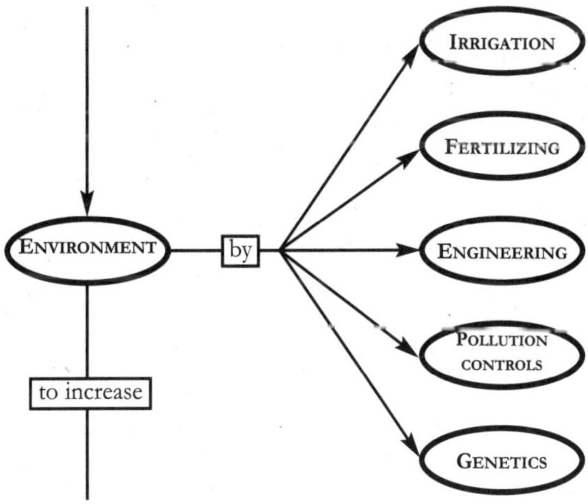

Fig. 9.10

Here, the thinker begins to refine the argument somewhat. Obviously, the point of all of this is to increase the standard of living. But there are more concepts to consider than just material consumption that are important, of course. Other concepts to consider could be reducing the amount of resources consumed in producing material goods, and reducing the level of pollution in producing and consuming goods.

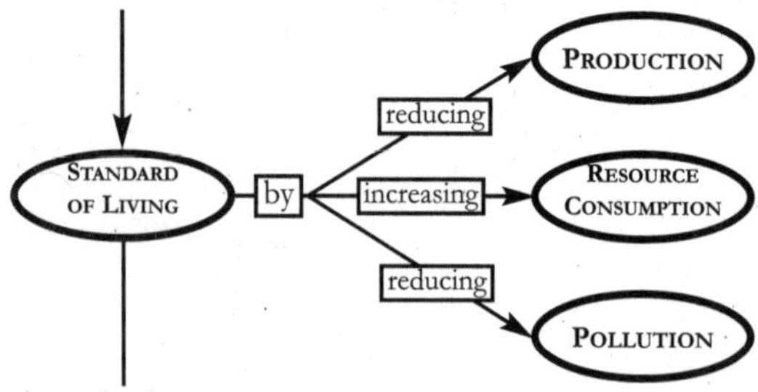

Fig. 9.11

The conclusion to this concept map would be to suggest that the net effect of science and technology would be to improve the standard of living of people by reducing drudgery, improving the environment and improving health standards.

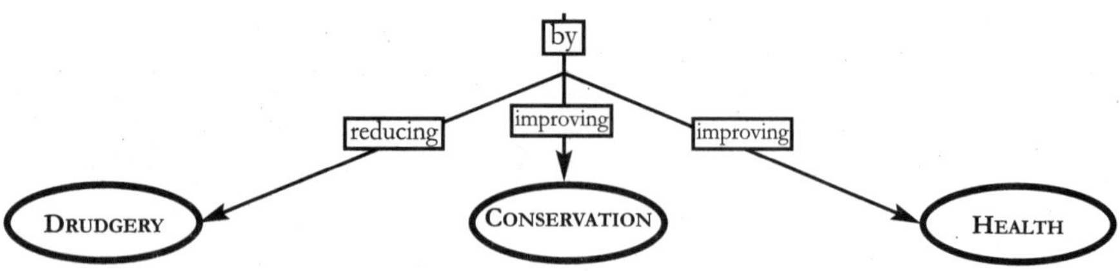

Fig. 9.12.

All of this can be put together into one concept map that expresses a point of view about the relationship between science, technology and the environment.

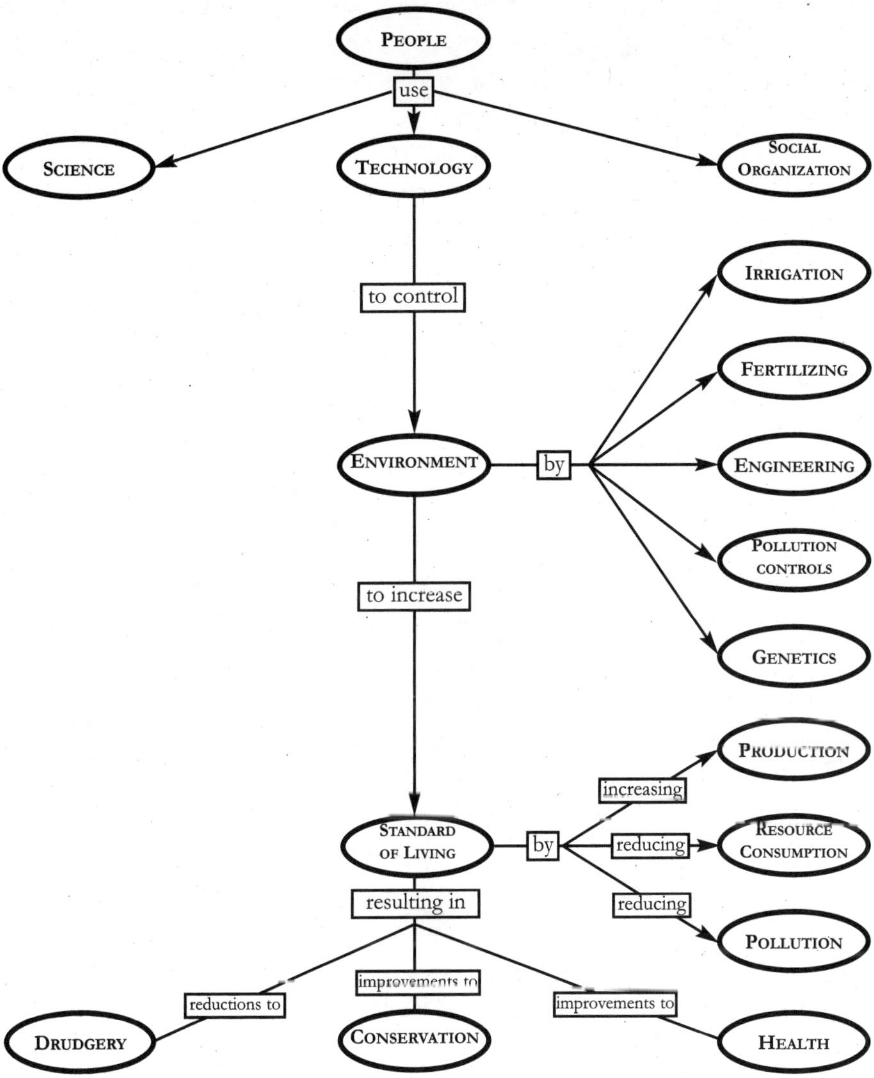

Fig. 9.13

Dialogical Thinking

That people should be considered the central concept of the environment is a point of view held by many and disputed by many. Some students will argue the point of view that habitat as outlined in the concept web below, and later developed into a concept map is a more accurate reflection of current environmental reality.

As important and stimulating as this debate might be, the really important issue here is the intellectual and moral growth of all students as they learn to independently critique intellectual positions they have grown up with. Again we see in heuristic teaching that students are capable of achieving multiple learning objectives. Besides all the thought concepts students are assimilating in this process, they are also assimilating the dialogical nature of intellectual thought. Students from both points of view (people and habitat) will have to deal with the other point of view in some intellectually honest fashion. As students go down this road it becomes increasingly difficult to maintain a narrow intellectual focus which excludes other points of view.

CONSTRUCT B: Habitat Is the Central Concept

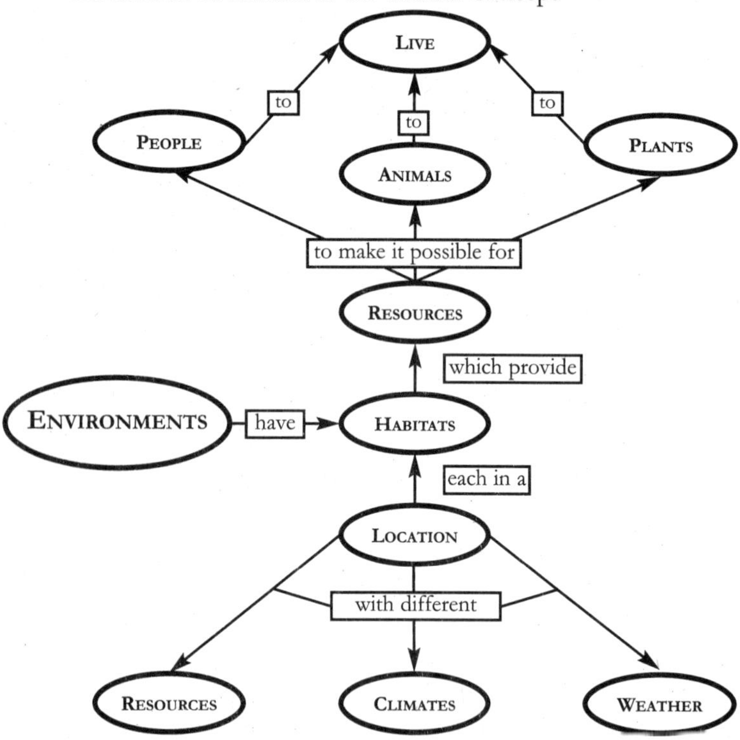

Fig. 9.14

As students do more research and think about on environmental issues, they will collect more concepts. These concepts have to be assimilated into the students' existing framework. Piaget noted that the process of assimilation will only work for a time. As students gain more concepts they will have to accommodate the new conflicting concepts by developing a more sophisticated structure to deal with a more complex reality.[19] Concept mapping is one way of helping students to do that.

Below are a couple of concept maps that might be developed by students as they think their way through environmental issues:

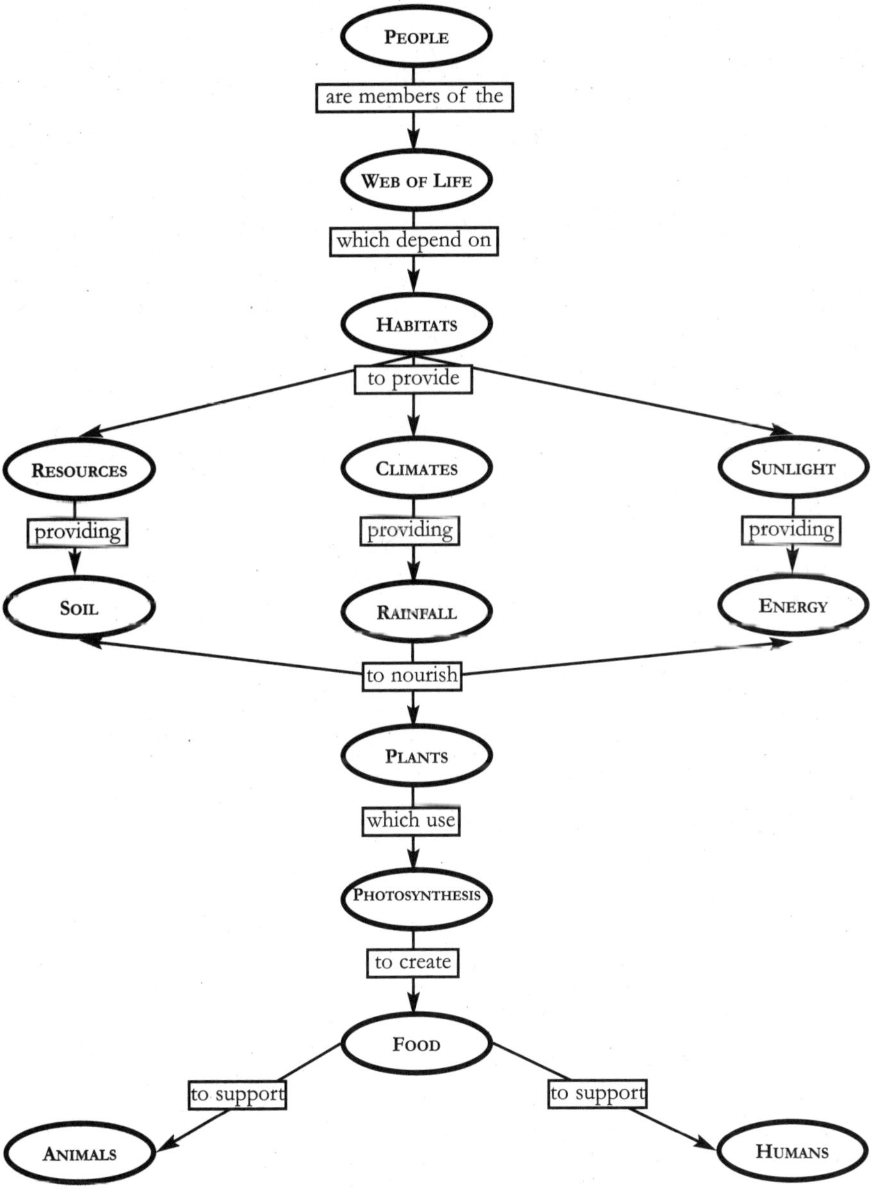

Fig. 9.15

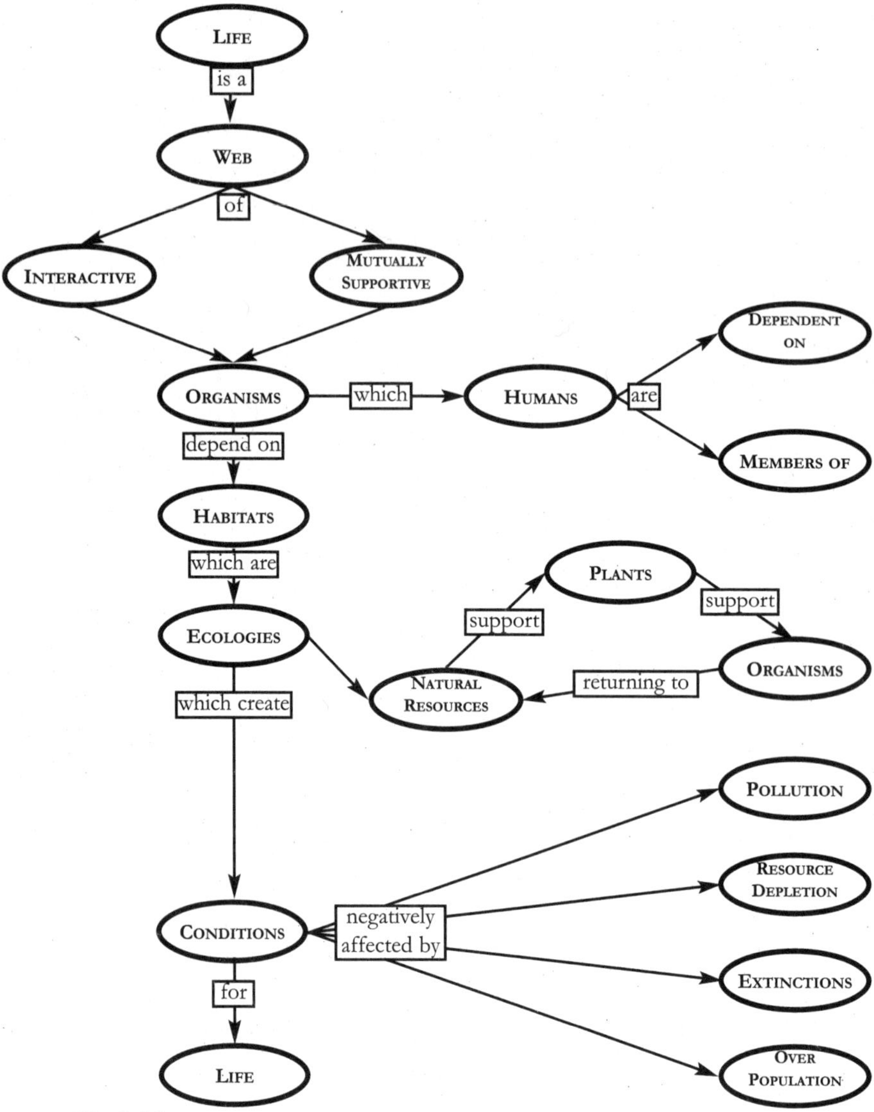

Fig. 9.16

Concept mapping is a useful tool to be used as part of a heuristically planned unit. Students may have gone through a number of exercises designed to stimulate thought about an issue. Some of the exercises may have been simulation gaming, synectics, discussion groups, concept webbing, thinking frames, dialogical thinking, etc. (All of these strategies will be discussed in some detail later in the chapter.) As students proceed through these exercises, they will be accumulating concepts. At some point, it is useful for students to gather up all of their concepts and organize them into a pattern. Concept webs/maps are a good vehicles for doing this.

Resolving Issues of Information Overload, Overfitting, and Activated Ignorance

Earlier we discussed the problems of information overload in the form of overfitting, which results in the formation of inert knowledge and activated ignorance. Concept webbing and mapping help students to intellectually move beyond these issues, because they lead to the formation of gist knowledge rather than verbatim knowledge. Because of that, students gain the confidence to begin using heuristics and thought concepts that allow them to think independently and creatively.

Concept webs and maps are themselves heuristics, because they are a good rule of thumb for dealing with complex, abstract issues. Suppose students have been involved with a series of activities relating to a historical issue. Such an issue might be revolution, for example. As students proceed in their thinking about revolution, they accumulate concepts (economic, political, social, and cultural) related to revolution. As well they also gain historical information, possibly from a variety of societies which have undergone revolution. At some point, students will have gathered enough information to be at risk of overfitting. If teachers are not careful, student response may well be activated ignorance: "What's the use of all this revolution stuff anyway!?"

This will particularly be the case if students are called upon to do some kind of independent thinking without the support of some kind of heuristic. If students are introduced to concept webbing/mapping heuristics, they will be in a much better position to organize their concepts on revolution into a pattern (web) with which they can begin to draw inferences by using thought concepts. Teachers could ask students to go through the notes, classroom materials, and source to find and list the concepts they have used. Students, as a class or in groups, could then select a central concept (which may in this case be revolution) and organize a concept web as was done in the earlier examples.

The Natural Use of Thought Concepts

By creating concept webs, students create concrete representations of their abstract thought. Because the representation is concrete, many things have been simplified for them. First, the capacity of the short term memory is limited. If students are asked to hold large amounts of information in their short term memories as well as manipulate it with various thought concepts, they will be unable to do so.[20] The mental capacity is just not available. But if they have a concrete representation, they can move from their verbatim memory to their gist memory to think about the issues at hand. Secondly, they are now in a much better position to see the need for thought concepts. By doing concept webs, they accomplish the categorization and classification of information. They can easily recategorize their information by reorganizing their concept webs. As they do that, they are reanalyzing the relationship between and within the concepts.

Thirdly, they will begin to form opinions (hypotheses) about the issues with which they are dealing. It is at this point that they wish to move from a concept web to a concept map. By doing so, they are beginning to synthesize ideas. This is normally held to be a very high order of intellectual activity, something assumed to be normally beyond adolescent thought. By using concept maps, students are capable of reordering their concepts into a planned, purposeful and coherent exposition of ideas. When they have completed their map, they will have synthesized a model of reality. It may not be correct, but that is not the point. Science has long recognized that all scientific models are falsifiable. The students' models will be falsifiable as well. In the sharing and discussion of their models, they will come closer to 'truth'. It is at this point that the students will be doing dialogical thinking. More about that later.

KNOWLEDGE IS A HUMAN CONSTRUCT

The notion that knowledge is a human construct is an important idea for students to understand. By using a heuristic approach, students demonstrate that they have the capacity to participate in the process. Students should also begin to understand that knowledge construction is an endless process. We have noted there are many different ways of organizing concepts, and many concepts can continually be added to a concept web. In fact, the search for missing concepts will turn into an important research objective. Students could be challenged to ask themselves what significant concepts are missing from the web they have developed. Then they can begin research aimed at finding other significant concepts. By doing so, they may find information which will change their view of any given topic.

Heuristics for Writing

We have discussed concept webs as research organizers, but they can also serve as organizers or heuristics for writing. If a student has a topic which requires some written exposition, a concept web can serve as productive heuristic. First, students can use webbing as a brainstorming heuristic. As they think, read, and discuss the topic, they can jot down concepts that they discover or that occur to them. Often one concept leads to another as the propositions and relationships take form. The web itself becomes a concrete reality, for students because a web holds information, visually leaving students' minds free to search for other ideas. The web will stimulate the availability, recognition, and representative heuristics for the students.

Research Heuristic

Eventually students will run out of ideas, and then they may wish to revise and reorder the web. It is here the individuality and creativity of individual thinkers will be displayed as they begin to establish their own patterns of thought. Still, at some point the students might begin to realize there are gaps in their webs which need to be filled by research. Now the students have the beginnings of a research program. They can go to information sources searching to fill specific needs. With a concept web background, they will find it easier to interpret and infer from the information they find as they research. It will fit into a pattern of thinking they have already established.

Students can be shown how concept webbing can be a good way of summarizing information as they research. Rather than writing down large amounts of research information, students can list the concepts they find and then arrange them into a mini-concept web they believe reflects the gist of information they found.

Rather than attempting to retain verbatim information, they are now retaining the gist of the information. It is the gist that will serve their research purposes. By concept webbing their research information, students will find they can summarize it without plagiarizing. Then they can consider how their mini, summarizing concept webs can be fitted into the larger webs (patterns of ideas) they are considering.

For example, students might be researching the impact of pollution on the environment. As they read their research material, they might select certain fundamental concepts. Initially they might only make a list of the concepts, but as they do more thinking about the concepts, they might decide to create a concept web or possibly a concept map. Students can describe how the concepts interrelate and ultimately how they fit into the larger concept web on the environment. As the students research, they can amass a variety of mini-concept webs which help them understand the complexity of any topic they research.

Paragraphing Heuristic

One the research phase is over, the students can then turn their attention to the writing phase. Now a concept web can serve as a heuristic for organizing an essay. This can actually be demonstrated in concrete form to students. See the example on the next page. It might be simpler to consider these first as a process for writing paragraphs.

The standard rubric for teaching students how to write a good paragraph is the topic sentence, supporting sentences, concluding sentence model. It is important for students to get the gist of this rubric. If they truly understand the rubric's gist, they are then in a good position to understand the fundamental rubric for writing essays. The problem is that too often paragraph rubrics (as well as essay rubrics) are taught algorithmically.

Concept webbing allows teachers to help students develop their understanding of paragraphing heuristically. Using concept web example (see below), teachers could ask students to think about where they would start if they were to write a paragraph based on this example. Students might conclude that the central idea of the web is habitat. (If they do not, students could recreate the concept web with another concept at the centre. They then could follow this writing exercise using a different concept web.) They then can also see that the ideas (concepts) surrounding the web all provide more information about habitats. Each of these ideas would be part of a supporting sentence. Then students would have to think about what their conclusion (important inference) about habitats might be. Because the concept web has coherence, any paragraphs they write will likely be coherent as well.

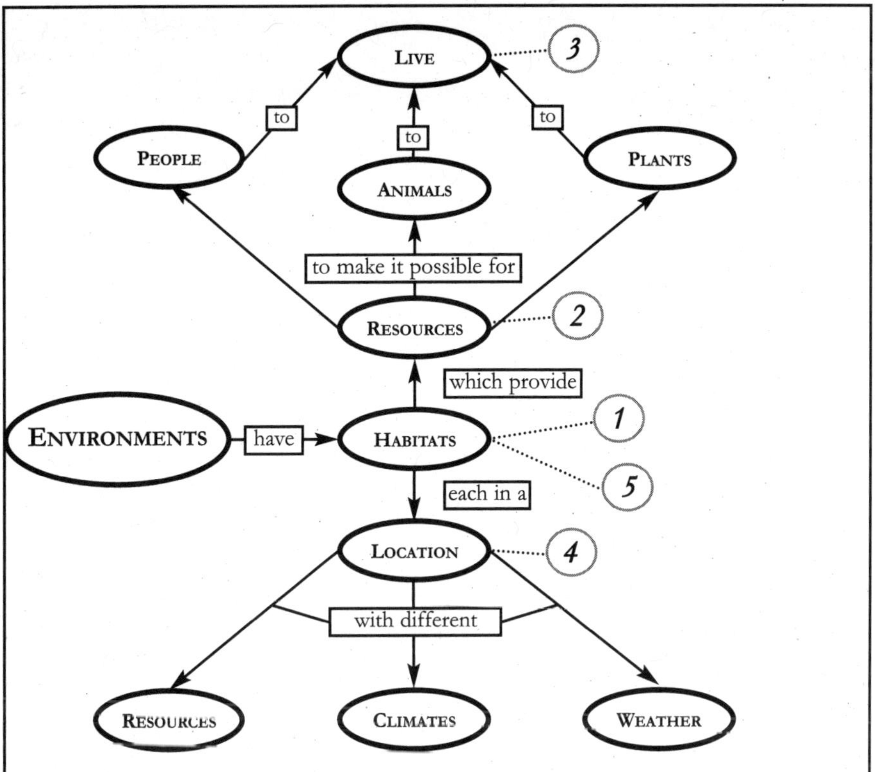

Topic Sentence:

1. Habitats are . . .

Supporting Sentences:

2. Resources are important . . .
3. Life is not . . .
4. Locations change . . .

Concluding Sentence:

5. Life cannot exist without . . .

Fig. 9.17

Essay Heuristic

A similar approach can be taken with essay writing. In the case of essay writing, concept mapping would likely be a more useful heuristic. Students may well begin their research and thinking with concept webs, but they will likely find that a concept map will transfer more easily into the essay format. Again teachers need to help students understand the essay rubric. As with paragraphing, this should be done heuristically rather than algorithmically. A good place to begin would be to review the elements of a good paragraph with the students. Encourage the students to explain the purpose and function of each element. By doing so, students will increase their gist understanding of the concept of paragraphing.[21]

Challenge the students to think about the problem of writing longer pieces than a paragraph. Efficiently organizing longer pieces is the question students should think about. Display a concept map of ideas (better, develop one with the students) and ask them to think about how they would describe the information contained in the concept map in prose form. Allow the students to think and discuss the problem. Suggest they could use their knowledge about paragraphing as a heuristic. An example of this process is illustrated below.

1. Thesis of the essay
2. Supporting Paragraph
3. Supporting Paragraph
4. Supporting Paragraph
5. Supporting Paragraph
6. Supporting Paragraph
7. Supporting Paragraph
8. Supporting Paragraph
9. Supporting Paragraph
10. Supporting Paragraph
11. Supporting Paragraph
12. Supporting Paragraph
13. Concluding Paragraph

Fig. 9.18.1

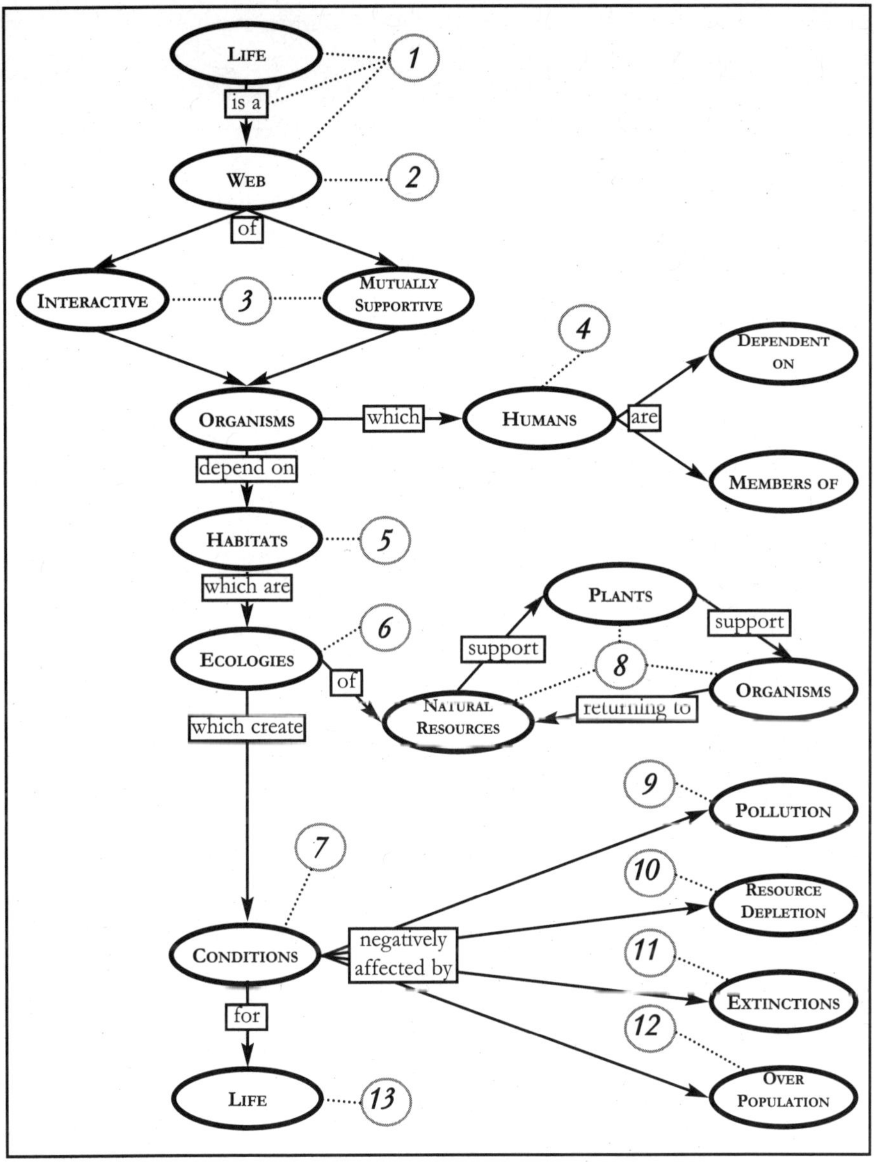

Fig. 9.18.2

The important thing here for students to realize is thar they now have a plan or a framework for their writing. More importantly, this is a outline/model of reality they have constructed for themselves. If there is to be independence and creativity in thinking, students must construct the model themselves. Anything else is algorithmic teaching and thinking. If the approach has been heuristic, students are likely to be comfortable with the ideas they are writing about and have a clearer idea of where their thinking is going.

Once they get to the actual writing stage, they will be in a better position to concentrate on designing paragraphs because they can see the complete scope of the essay. They can be more confident in their decisions about the message of their essay. One paragraph will derive from the others thereby constructing an argument that has some logic and coherence.

Adolescent Angst while Writing Papers

For those of you who have counselled adolescents in writing assignments, you are likely familiar with adolescent writer's block. Young people can be paralyzed by a blank white page demanding a response. They are paralyzed for a number of reasons. They cannot find a place to start because they cannot see the whole. They have a nagging feeling they are missing something significant which will make them look foolish and earn them a low grade. So, they attempt to assemble all available information in their consciousness as well as think about and plan their paper. They cannot do it because their verbatim memory is overloaded, and they lack meaningful gist to serve as a basis for what they want to say. They feel they are in a situation where they have lost control. Concept mapping eliminates much of that trauma because it establishes a meaningful framework from which to work.

There is another type of adolescent writer who is filled with verbosity. Any and every idea is written down in some kind of stream of consciousness which lacks direction, logic, and coherence. After reading the piece, the reader is left with frustrated incomprehension: "What was that all about?" Verbose writers need the direction and discipline of concept mapping which insists there must be a relationship between concepts before they can be mapped. Concept mapping forces the verbose writer to develop a set of logical relationships before starting the writing process.[22]

LIFE LONG HEURISTICS

Concept webbing and mapping have the potential to be powerful personal heuristics which students carry with them for the remainder of their lives.[23] Those teachers who have carefully developed webbing and mapping with their students find both independent thinking and independent writing are enhanced. For many students essay writing is a torturous exercise with very little payoff. Many students have no idea of what constitutes a good essay. Students like heuristics because they take the uncertainty and drudgery out of writing. With a concept map the reality of good essay writing becomes much clearer and precise.

There is a minority of students who have disabilities of one kind or another which make it extremely difficult for them to write formal sentences, paragraphs, and essays. They are otherwise intellectually capable and fully understand the material they have been taught. These students are often penalized by modern evaluation systems which demand students display their knowledge by writing short paragraphs, reports, essays, etc. For many of these students, concept webbing and mapping is a device which allows them to demonstrate their depth of knowledge. It may also help them make gains in their ability to write more formally.

END NOTES

1. E. Boyer. "High school: A report on secondary education in America". New York: Harper and Row. 1983.

J. I. Goodlad, A place called school: Prospects for the future, (New York: McGraw-Hill 1983).

T. B. Sizer. *Horace's Compromise: The dilemma of the American high school today.* Boston: Houghton Mifflin. 1984.

2. Raymond S. Nickerson. "Why Teach Thinking". *Teaching Thinking Skills.* Ed. Joan Boykof Baron and Robert J. Sternberg. New York: W. H. Freeman and Company. p. 32.

3. E. M. Glaser. "Critical Thinking: Educating for responsible citizenship in a democracy". National Forum. 1985. Vol 65. pp. 24-27.

4. I am now speaking specifically about secondary schools, although many of my comments also apply to Middle Years education as well. Kindergarten and primary education have made real strides toward heuristic based instruction. Unfortunately, from grade four on, the information/algorithmic paradigm increasingly dominates teaching.

5. Edys S. Quellmalz. "Developing Reasoning Skills". *Teaching Thinking Skills.* Ed. Joan Boykof Baron and Robert J. Sternberg.. New York: W. H. Freeman and Company. p. 95.

6. This is not always a benign, constructive approach to power. In this situation, people can be coerced in subtle always to acquiesce to the group or to individuals within the group. Peer pressure is a type of empowerment pressure where young people 'go along' in order to be accepted by the group.

7. Teachers who teach in this style are often very caring of their students. It is the algorithmic paradigm they have accepted that makes teachers feel they are doing the right thing by doling out information in logical pre-digested form. In their view, this is the only way students can absorb 'complex' information.

8. Vern Hembrow. " A Heuristic Approach Across the Curriculum". *Language Arts.* Vol. 63. No. 7. Nov. 1986. p. 674.

9. Ayelot Meron Ruscio and Teresa M. Amabile. "The Effects of Instructional Style on Problem-Solving Creativity". Creativity Research Journal. 1999. Vol. 12 Issue 4. p. 251.

10. J. Easley. "A teacher educator's perspective on students' and teachers' schemes: Or teaching by listening". Unpublished paper presented at the Conference on Thinking, Harvard Graduate School of Education.

11. D.N. Perkins. "Knowledge as Design: Teaching Thinking Through Content". *Teaching Thinking Skills.* Ed. Joan Boykof Baron and Robert J. Sternberg. New York: W. H. Freeman and Company. pp. 46-47.

12. Richard W. Paul. "Dialogical Thinking: Critical Thought Essential to the Acquisition of Rational Knowledge and Passions". Teaching Thinking Skills, Ed. by Joan Boykof Baron and Robert J. Sternberg. New York: W. H. Freeman and Company. p.130.

13. There are, of course, major philosophical implications to these assumptions. Initially, students need to become comfortable with the notion of patterning. Later, as they better understand the patterning process, they will realize there are a variety of patterns possible. Still later, they can be introduced to theories like Chaos Theory which suggest that patterning is not always as clear and precise as we would like it to be.

14. Joseph D. Novak and D. Bob Gowin. *Learning How to Learn.* New York: Cambridge University Press. 1986. pp. 15-40.

15. In a classroom developing into a community of scholars, both teacher and students need to be supported in their intellectual activity. Devices such as concept webbing do that. The teacher needs to select approaches that allow for clear and precise modeling of the thought processes students are expected to learn.

16. Paul A Klaczynski and Gayathri Narasimham. "Representations as Mediators of Adolescent Deductive Reasoning". *Developmental Psychology.* 1998. Vol. 34. No. 5. p. 865.

17. Richard W. Paul. "Dialogical Thinking: Critical Thought Essential to the Acquisition of Rational Knowledge and Passions". *Teaching Thinking Skills.* Ed. Joan Boykof Baron and Robert J. Sternberg. New York: W. H. Freeman and Company). p.131.

18. Teachers might begin to make the distinction here between logic and empiricism. The two often coincide, but not always, so it is important to help students understand the difference conceptually.

19. Barry J. Wadsworth. *Piaget's Theory of Cognitive Development.* New York: David McKay Company, Inc. 1971. pp. 14-15.

20. D.N. Perkins. "Thinking Frames: An Integrative Perspective on Teaching Cognitive Skills". *Teaching Thinking Skills.* Ed Joan Boykof Baron and Robert J. Sternberg. New York: W. H. Freeman and Company. p. 49.

21. Most of these activities are really concept attainment activities. It is important that students understand paragraphs and essays as concepts of writing. As concepts, paragraphs and essays have critical attributes, generalizations and labels.

22. For a more detailed discussion of concept mapping see Novaks and Gowin. This little book gives a wealth of information on the development of concept maps and their use in the classroom.

23. It is in this sense that life long learning becomes meaningful and practical. Life long learning does not just mean being prepared to learn new things at every stage of one's life. It should also mean learning things that will have useful application throughout life.

CHAPTER TEN: INDEPENDENT THINKING

TABLE OF CONTENTS

FRAMES OF REFERENCE DIRECT THINKING

No one thinks in a vacuum. Our thinking is an extension and elaboration of the ideas we understand. Extending thinking out of the range of the known into the unknown is not an easy process. We depend upon frames of reference to provide a basis for thinking. Frames of reference can be both a help and a hindrance. They help by providing a set of assumptions and a structure to guide and direct our thinking, much like the concept webs and maps we discussed in the previous chapter. Frames also have the capacity to limit our thinking by acting as blinders to other aspects of reality. The limiting power of thought frames is very powerful. Because of that power, the ability to reconceive frames of reference imaginatively and to refocus on other aspects of reality has been restricted to a few people, and for those few it is further restricted to one or a few fields. The first step in freeing one's thinking from the control of frames of reference is to understand frames exist and they do control our responses.

Sources for frames of reference can be found throughout our culture. In fact, culture itself is the overarching frame of reference in which we live. Within cultures are other frames of reference, known as world views. World views have a profound impact on how people perceive and think about reality. Within world views are other frames of reference, sometimes referred to as paradigms. These are somewhat narrower frames of reference guiding perception and thought. We can refer to scientific paradigms or religious paradigms among many others. Each is a frame of reference containing sets of assumptions about reality, and procedures for discovering more about reality. Those accepting the scientific paradigm may discus the scientific method as a way of discovering information, while those accepting a religious paradigm believe prayer is the best way to discover truth. Closely related to paradigms are ideologies of various kinds, which also provide sets of assumptions to guide perception and thinking. At a more personal level, we select models (media, myths, heroes, etc) to emulate and guide our thinking about issues. The subtle aspect of all these frames is how little we question them. It is more usual to simply accept them with little conscious thought.

In current popular culture, people worry about whether they are thinking in or out of the 'box' (frame of reference). Implicit in this concern is the concern that world views, paradigms, ideologies, models, tradition, habits, etc have the power to limit thinking. The belief is that independent and creative thinking require the ability to understand and discard the 'box' as being limiting. The contradiction here is that one cannot think without a frame of reference, because thinking has to be based on a set of assumptions. Whenever assumptions are accepted, a frame of reference (box) has been created. The issue then is not so much thinking outside of a frame of reference, but being aware of the frame of reference being used so that one can critically evaluate the advantages and shortcomings of its assumptions.

Creativity is enhanced by Frames of Reference

The reality is that creativity is enhanced by the structure and discipline of a frame of reference. We have seen that already with examples such as concept mapping and webbing. The structure of the two systems are freeing rather than limiting. Students are able to see the shortcomings and possibilities inherent to the frame of reference they have created. They are able to see the relationships among the parts of the frame of reference. Based on all of this, they are in a much better position to search for more information (if needed) and to draw creative inferences based on the information and its relationships that they have already assembled.

At the same time, they are able to critically evaluate the frame of reference they have adopted/created. This is the real issue surrounding 'thinking outside the box'. The real issue is whether one can critically evaluate the box being used as a platform for thinking, not whether one can discard the box entirely.[1]

Understanding the Impact of Frames of Reference on Thinking

Students need to be aware that they use frames of reference to support their thinking. Pauls argues that the primary role of the school is to help students learn to understand the frames of reference they encounter, and then learn to critically evaluate them.[2] Pauls further argues that teachers need to teach in the 'strong sense'. By that, he means that teachers should teach so that students both understand and learn to critique the prevailing frames of reference they find in their social environment. This is not an easy thing for students to do. Students will have accepted many prevailing frames of reference as being truth. They will have a vested interest in some of them, and may have developed emotional capital in defending them.

One way of defending a frame of reference is to assume it is reality rather than a frame of reference, and demand that it be accepted as reality by everyone. In this way we convert beliefs into self-protecting truths. People who do this are resorting to activated ignorance to protect themselves from unwanted points of view. Of course, the problem with this is that it limits any ability to imagine alternatives outside of an accepted frame of reference.

Some of those frames become personal biases or prejudices, which people (students) are reluctant to abandon. Like all of us, students find it a struggle to gain a wider perspective on issues in their lives. If students are to be helped to become free and independent thinkers, they must learn to think via heuristic processes rather than algorithmic processes. Students must learn thinking skills in the context of dealing with the reality of the frames of reference within which they live.

The Limitations of Algorithmic Teaching

Students who learn through algorithmic exercises tend to gain the impression the frame of reference they have learned is not open to criticism because it is reality. In the student's mind, a frame of reference remains outside the realm of criticism because it is the only way of thinking about something. In this way, independent and critical thinking is cut off. Students will either assume there is no other frame of reference to be learned, or they will become hostile to or fearful of new frames of reference. They will use whatever thinking skills they have to rationalize and justify what they already believe. Their learning skills simply trigger various forms of activated ignorance. In terms of C Wright Mills, they may move from vulgar thinking to sophisticated thinking, but not to critical thinking.

As a community of scholars, the classroom needs to accept this challenge as fundamental to the learning process. Eastley suggests that children need to learn to solve the problems they encounter independently. He believes that even the most monological of problems can and should be approached dialogically.[3] Students should work on problems in small heterogeneous groups, where in the process of solving a problem, they learn to convince each other and to understand the other. It is through dialogical discussion that students discover they have views, and those views have strengths and weaknesses. This is how they learn the contrast between their views and the views of others. They learn personal wellbeing and friendships can survive the give and take of dialogical discussion. They may also discover that it is an interesting and useful process. In this way, a community of scholarship becomes real and meaningful to students. When this happens, students develop a growing self-discipline making growth to intellectual independence and creativity possible.

Eastley would have teachers choose and present appropriately challenging problems and tasks to students. Teachers should train group leaders to facilitate dialogical exchanges. Teachers should serve as moderators/facilitators of class discussions. In this way, students can discover their own activated ideas. If a process of discovery and evaluation is not facilitated in the classroom, many students will become and remain invincibly ignorant when putting knowledge into action. Unless students learn to question their assumptions while young, their biases, stereotypes, distortions, illusions, and misconceptions cannot be dissolved with the purging power of dialogical exchange.

More Heuristic Teaching Techniques

The remainder of the chapter will be a discussion of the variety of ways in which teachers can deal with the issues raised here. We have already touched on dialogical thinking which will be defined and discussed in more detail below. There are a number of other techniques which lend themselves to heuristic teaching, and as such work well in classrooms aspiring to be communities of scholars.

The concept of paradigm is a critical to understanding the source of frames of reference. As a source of problems for communities of scholars, paradigms offer a wealth of material for dialogical discussion. Perkins describes a model that students can learn heuristically, and which will help them become learn to critically analyze frames of reference.[4] This is a necessary skill for a community of scholars.

There are a wide variety of framing possibilities used to structure ideas. One we have already discussed in some detail is the use of concepts to organize and pattern ideas, thereby creating a frame of reference. Matrices are another way of using concepts to analyze relationships between ideas. Metaphors and similes are powerful frames of reference. Too often, these are considered to be mainly literary devices, and studied solely in that way. They are extremely important of course, but it is important to understand that words in the language, especially English, are powerfully metaphorical. To take one simple example, references to the colours black and white can be filled with metaphorical allusions which easily construct a frame of reference. Students need to learn to notice and critically analyze the choice of metaphor being made in rhetoric. Synectics is a whole study to the application of metaphor to learning. Social structures themselves provide frames for thinking and behaving.

People find it extremely difficult to stand back and critically view the social constructs within which they are behaving. One way of helping students learn to do that is through simulation gaming. A simulation game, as are all games, is simply an imaginary frame of reference that all members of the game temporarily agree to accept. In one sense, it is no different than going to a movie or play, etc during which people temporarily suspend their disbelief. Students need to understand that they suspend disbelief on many more things than games and entertainment.

DIALOGICAL THINKING

Propagandistic Thinking

Have you ever listened to a sophisticated argument being made with articulate rhetoric? As you listen to the argument, you become increasingly uneasy. There is something wrong with what is being said, but you cannot decide why you are uncomfortable. The logic seems acceptable, but the conclusions are dubious. Such arguments are often predicated on a set of emotional assumptions. Propaganda operates this way. It attempts to make it easy for the listener to just 'go along' with the argument and its premises. The listener is carefully guided away from any alternative explanations which could sway people to alternative arguments. If situations like these are difficult for adults, they 'make adolescents crazy'.

As listener and thinker of information, the problem for the critical consumer is to imagine alternative frames of reference. A practiced propagandist carefully establishes a frame of reference, and then attempts to block any consideration of other frames of reference. So, if a pro-environmentalist writer is constructing an argument the writer's frame of reference will assume that the only issue worthy of consideration is the protection of the environment. Nothing else matters. The same sort of rhetoric occurs on the side of those arguing from a narrow economics perspective. If the economy does not grow, then all is a disaster. There is no other reality allowed in this situation. Of course, none of these issues are black and white. They require establishing priorities, drawing balances, reconciling contradictions, etc. None of which propagandists want to consider.

Concept of Thought Frames

If students are to develop into critical and independent thinkers, then they must understand the concept of thinking frames. Earlier, we considered this notion to some degree when we discussed the idea that the central concept in a concept web establishes the basis, direction, or frame of the concept web. Change the central concept and the concept web will be significantly changed. Students will not have much problem understanding that. Where they do have problems is in imagining another frame of reference to think from, while placing a frame of reference that they are particularly partial to on hold. Both of these problems need to be dealt with in the classroom.

Multilogical Thinking

Students need to gain experience with what Richard Paul calls multilogical issues[5]. The environment and all its related issues are multilogical problems. Any issue that has more than one point of view supported by arguments based on empirical reality or logic is a multilogical issue. Most of the issues we face in life fit this definition. Students are constantly faced with a multilogical reality. All of their lives they will need to confront this reality.

Thinking is simple when one can construct an argument based on a single set of assumptions. The illustrative example we have been using is the question of humanity's relationship to the environment. One set of assumptions would say that the protection of the environment must be considered supreme, since all organisms including humanity are dependent upon it. The fate of humanity depends upon the fate of the environment. This seems so self-evident; it is not questioned by many. Based on those assumptions, one can construct a logical, coherent case for investing heavily in the protection of the environment. Another set of assumptions would suggest that the environment is for the service of humankind. Humanity has a responsibility to develop the environment such that it is made productive enough to raise the standard of living for everyone. One only has to witness the suffering during a famine to believe that the wellbeing of humanity is critical. By providing people with a high standard of living, people can learn to make the environment more useful ,and in many cases improve it. These two points of view are seen by many as being so sharply contradictory to each other such that if one is accepted then the other must be untrue.

The Concept of the Dialogical

The reality of epistemology is that contradictory sets of beliefs about something can both be true. In this example, both the needs of the environment and the needs of humanity are paramount. The environment must be preserved, and humankind has the right to exist. There are many such contradictory realities in life. These kinds of dilemmas are dialogical in the sense that one truth cannot be accepted at the expense of the other. Unfortunately, much popular thinking is predicated on simple non dialogical thinking. The belief seems to be that one point of view is completely correct, and all others must be discarded. Part of the problem is that which C. Wright Mills noted when he pointed out that some people are not critical thinkers.[6] Non-critical thinkers want to believe there are simple non-contradictory answers to all problems.

By introducing students to concept webs as discussed above, conditions have been created which will make it easier for students to understand the need for dialogical thinking. Previously we have developed concept webs, and then concept maps outlining arguments espousing a strong environmental point of view and a strong economic development point of view.

Heuristically, a dialogical reality can be established for students by helping them construct logical arguments using concept webs. As illustrations, we have already done so by creating a concept map which describes the environment as one of interactive habitats and organisms which are mutually self-sustaining, and another concept map which describes how humans use the environment to raise the standard of living of society. Students must be allowed to construct these viewpoints for themselves. By allowing students to develop the arguments heuristically, they will have a much richer and deeper understanding of the significance of each argument. Then it becomes much more difficult to dismiss a contrary argument simply because a student disagrees with it.[7]

The Dialogical Clash: Developing a Heuristic for Writing Dialogical Essays

Dialogically speaking, the real issue is how to encourage students to confront the basic viewpoints within each argument. In other words, they need to be sure they understand the gist of each argument. If students are working from concept webs and maps, much of this work will have already been accomplished. They need then to construct each argument based on their analyses of the concepts in their webs and maps. There is a model on the next page *Fig. 10.1*, which shows how that might be done. What it suggests that students do is write out the two arguments side by side, so that the theses of each argument, the supporting information (paragraphs) and the final conclusions of each argument can be displayed side by side for comparison. Students need to be encouraged to write both arguments as convincingly as they can. The temptation always exists to make one argument the 'loser' by omitting or skewing the supporting evidence. Students need to understand this moves the exercise from dialogics to propaganda

Viewpoint A

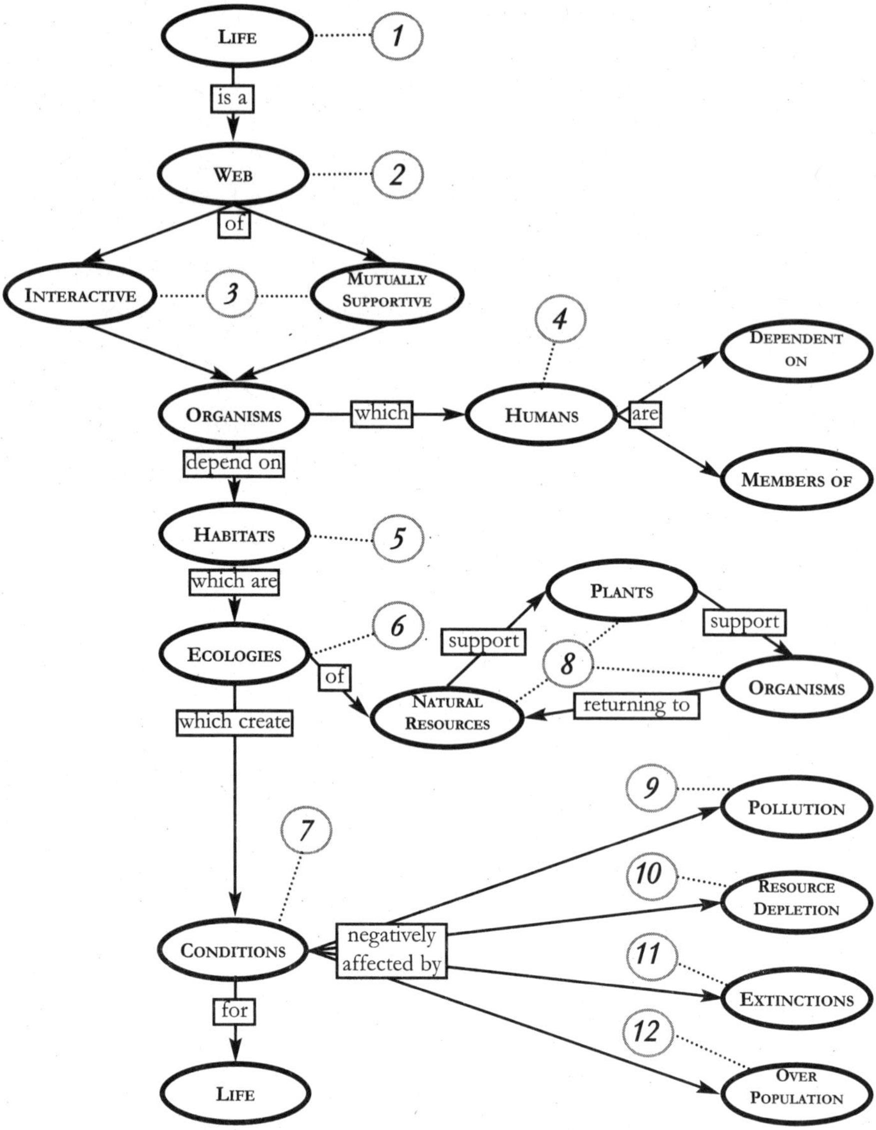

Fig 10.1

VIEWPOINT B

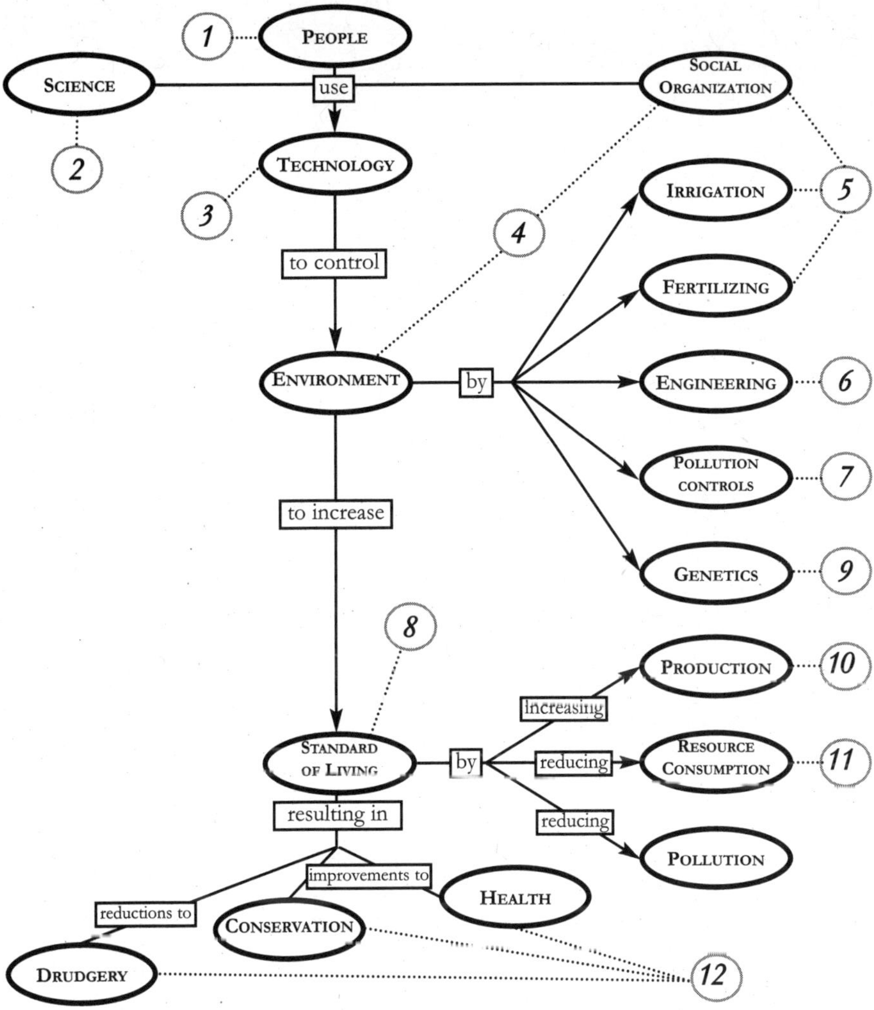

1. Thesis of the essay
2. Supporting Paragraph
3. Supporting Paragraph
4. Supporting Paragraph
5. Supporting Paragraph
6. Supporting Paragraph
7. Supporting Paragraph
8. Supporting Paragraph
9. Supporting Paragraph
10. Supporting Paragraph
11. Supporting Paragraph
12. Supporting Paragraph

Clash of Ideas: using values and questions to evaluate points of view

13. Concluding Paragraph

<table>
<tr><th>A</th><th>Viewpoints A & B</th><th>B</th></tr>
<tr><td></td><td>1. Purpose or thesi of the essay</td><td></td></tr>
<tr><td>1. Paragraph on the thesis of viewpoint A</td><td></td><td>1. Paragraph on the thesis of viewpoint B</td></tr>
<tr><td>2. Supporting paragraph on the role of webs in nature.</td><td rowspan="11">Comparing, analyzing, and evaluating the various supporting paragraphs</td><td>2. Supporting paragraph on the role of science in understanding relationships between nature and humanity.</td></tr>
<tr><td>3. Supporting paragraph on the interactive/relational nature of life.</td><td>3. Supporting paragraph on the role of technology and the environment.</td></tr>
<tr><td>4. Supporting paragraph on humanity as part of nature.</td><td>4. Supporting paragraph on the role of social organization on the environment.</td></tr>
<tr><td>5. Supporting paragraph on the nature and role of habitats in nature.</td><td>5. Supporting paragraph on effective development of the environment.</td></tr>
<tr><td>6. Supporting paragraph on the nature and role of ecology for nature and humanity.</td><td>6. Supporting paragraph on controlling pollution</td></tr>
<tr><td>7. Supporting paragraph on the role of ecology in creating conditions for life.</td><td>7. Supporting paragraph on the role of use of genetics</td></tr>
<tr><td>8. Supporting paragraph on the relationship of natural resources, plants, and organism..</td><td>8. Supporting paragraph on issues related to increasing standard of living.</td></tr>
<tr><td>9. Supporting paragraph on the effects of pollution.</td><td>9. Supporting paragraph on the effects of increasing production.</td></tr>
<tr><td>10. Supporting paragraph on the effects of resource depletion.</td><td>10. Supporting paragraph on the problem of resource consumption.</td></tr>
<tr><td>11. Supporting paragraph on the effect of extinctions on ecological relationships.</td><td>11. Supporting paragraph on a constructive approach to pollution.</td></tr>
<tr><td>12. Supporting paragraph on the impact of over population</td><td>12. Supporting paragraph on how science, technology, and social organization can improve standard of living</td></tr>
</table>

Fig 10.1a

13. Concluding paragraph on sustaining life.		13. Supporting paragraph on improving life for people.
14 Statement of basic values/criteria that should be used to evaluate viewpoints A & B.	Selection of the primary values/criteria to be used in coming to a resolution of this dialogue.	14 Statement of basic values/criteria that should be used to evaluate viewpoints A & B.
	Concluding paragraph which resolves the dialogue in some way.	

Defining Evaluative Criteria

The risk for students in being scrupulously fair is that dialogical thinking results in the thinker become paralyzed with inaction. Because both arguments seem correct, students waffle back and forth between arguments, and end up with some kind of trite conclusion based on compromise. It is at this point that students need to move out of the frames of reference established by both arguments and ask themselves what they believe to be important. In other words, they need to think about the fundamental criteria they want to use to evaluate arguments in this situation.

Thinkers need to have criteria they can use to make decisions in these situations. These criteria are the fundamental values the individual believes must prevail in any situation.

These values can be economic, political, social, philosophical, moral, etc. Such a framework could be established in discussion with the students, and could be referenced whenever needed. It could also be modified and added to as other dialogical situations arise. By creating this framework, students will become more confident in their ability to manage dialogical discussion.

For example, in the dialogue on environmental issues displayed above, students could choose to apply some of the following values as criteria:

- economic
- political
- social
- philosophical
- moral
- biological
- etc.

- high standard of living;
- freedom of choice
- having a place to live;
- a purpose for living;
- respect for life;
- truth about biological reality

Students need to be encouraged to think and debate these criteria, and then be able to construct a reasoned argument for accepting one value over another. Again, this is dialogical because it is likely that most values selected will be acceptable in that all have the potential to be constructive in the right circumstances. So it is not a case of dismissing a value as wrong, but a case of determining what value(s) would be most suitable for the situation.

Developing Personal Values

This is not relativism in the sense of saying: "well, my opinion is good as anyone else's opinion" or "one opinion is as good as another". Rather, it is a process of determining what one's opinion should be based upon. In a sense, it is an attempt to reach out to major ideas that might be used to support one's point of view. There may be two stages in this process. Firstly, it is a case of deciding upon the best set of fundamental assumptions to be used in dealing with a narrow but pressing aspect of reality; in this case, the environment. For adolescents, this may be the first time they have seriously considered what they believe related to specific contexts like the environment. After they have honestly and seriously considered their value assumptions for a specific case, they may discover they are preparing a ground of assumptions which will ultimately become part of a personal ideology. This process takes them to the second stage of value formation where they develop an ideology they can refer to throughout their lives.[8] Again, we are talking about life long learning as preparation for making a lifetime of decisions in a caring, thoughtful manner.

At this point, students could create a values framework or matrix which would have the ultimate purpose of becoming a personal ideology.

VALUES	related to ARGUMENT A	related to ARGUMENT B
ECONOMIC	- all parts of the environment are equally valuable	- certain parts of the environment are more valuable than others
POLITICAL	- the environment and its parts should have rights	- only people have rights
SOCIAL	- the entire environment (world) should be considered our home (habitat)	- The environment is owned by property owners who determine its use
PHILOSOPHICAL	People and other organisms are equals	- People have the right and the responsibility to control the environment
MORAL	- The present generation is responsible to future generations for its use of the environment	- The environment should be fully available for use now for the benefit of people

Fig. 10.2

The matrix above is for illustrative purposes only. Such a framework should be developed in the classroom in heuristic fashion. Students should be challenged to decide for themselves what their values are. The role of the teacher is to make suggestions for the students to consider. But it is they who will have to decide what they believe. This frame work would not be intended to be a final product: ever. Rather, it could be an ongoing, developmental heuristic, made up of criteria students could refer to as they deal with the myriad of dialogical issues in their lives.

Developing and Applying an Evaluation Heuristic

Once a values matrix has been developed, it could be used as a set of criteria (a screen) to evaluate the arguments in the dialogic on the environment above. One approach to that is to ask the students to reform the values they have developed into questions. The process of reforming statements into questions is a simple heuristic that students can use to move quickly into an evaluative mode of thought. The following questions are examples of what might be prepared:

- Are some parts of the environment more important (useful, valuable, significant) than other parts?
- Do all organisms have an equal right to exist (eat, reproduce, be free in their territory, etc.)?
- Does ownership of property provide owners with certain rights and privileges?
- Does human intelligence give humans special privileges/rights/ responsibilities?
- Does the existing generation owe a responsibility to future generations?

Obviously, these are not the only questions that could be asked. Each of the above questions could also be asked in different forms, which would affect the conclusions drawn for each question. Students need to understand that the way they ask questions will determine how they evaluate and draw inferences about their topic. One way of helping students see this is to have a question brainstorming session. Again, students are learning that they can develop heuristics which make it easier for them to apply thought concepts to their thinking. Brainstorming is a well known heuristic used in many situations. One can create a slightly different heuristic by linking the question formation heuristic described above to the brainstorming heuristic. In doing so, students are learning to develop chained thought processes that are so critical to sophisticated critical and creative thinking. Students should think of as many ways as they can of asking questions about the values they have selected. Then they have to decide which of the questions are the most significant to use in their thinking about the topic.

On this basis, students will be able to decide what they believe and thereby conclude about the topic. In the concept map of the environment, dialogue near the bottom (see page 363) reference is made to a clash of ideas. There is more than one clash of ideas in this dialogue, but a major one is the question of whether the environment has significance independent of human need. Students who accept the idea that human need and control is paramount would likely be willing to conclude that the purpose of the environment is to serve human need. Those who believe that humans are simply one of many organisms inhabiting the environment, each having significance, may be more reluctant to conclude that the only purpose of the environment is to serve humans. Defenders of either viewpoint would have marshalled arguments they believe would clearly demonstrate the supremacy of the environment or the supremacy of human need.

UNDERSTANDING REALITY THROUGH DESIGN

We cannot comprehended reality in totality. Humans get around that limitation by selecting certain aspects of reality to stand for the whole. In effect, they design a model of reality which they believe is an accurate replica of the real thing. The model comes to stand for the whole. An example of that is the environmental dialogue above. Each side of the dialogue created an environmental model they assumed to be accurate. Then, criteria were selected with which to evaluate the models. On that basis, they would come to some kind of conclusion about how to deal with various environmental issues.

What is important to understand is that these mental machinations do not change reality in any way. It is what it is. Reality does not have design; it is our models of reality which have design. We can believe what we like about reality, reality is incapable of caring. It is we who have to adapt the design of our models in the interests of criteria like accuracy, responsibility, consequences, safety, accountability, etc. Accuracy, responsibility, and so on are values used as evaluative criteria to test mental models for validity. Students need to understand that knowledge in this sense is a human construct which only approximates reality.

Paradigms and Design

The notion that knowledge is a constructed approximation of reality makes people uncomfortable. They react to the inherent uncertainty of epistemology by adopting broad conceptions of reality that we now label paradigms. Paradigms are culturally acceptable sets of ideas, beliefs and values which define the various ways in which reality can be interpreted. Cultures, at every stage of their history, generate a broad consensus about how reality ought to be understood, and then design models of reality which conform to that consensus.

Paradigms govern our understanding of spirituality, nature, society, politics, economics, etc. For example, Western medieval society was dominated by a Catholic paradigm which carefully defined relations between humanity and the sacred and secular environments. E. M. W. Tillyard describes the Elizabethan model of the universal order as a chain, a series of corresponding planes, and a dance. Taking the notion of a chain as a model, with angels at the foot of God's throne at the top of the chain, humans in between (with both Godlike and animalistic tendencies), animals below humans, and at the very bottom, inanimate objects.[9] The underlying assumptions of the medieval model defined how reality was perceived by the medieval mind. Those assumptions became a paradigm which explained medieval religion, politics, economics, science, and art within society. For example, because the Ptolemaic geocentric model of the universe fitted well with the medieval model, it was, for centuries, accepted as an accurate description of the universe.

The medieval paradigm became accepted as the natural design of reality. It did not occur to most people to question the design defining the 'natural' order of the universe, society, or the sacred domains. Such ideas were held to be heretical and beyond question. Initially, it was only a small, courageous group who dared question aspects of the medieval paradigm. Over time that group grew larger, until there was an intellectual renaissance in which many of the medieval paradigmatic assumptions were re-examined, and in some cases discarded. Naturally many people were highly reluctant to leave the old paradigmatic assumptions behind for something that seemed, at best, strange and risky.

Members of modern society can be mildly derisive of the struggle people in the past have had in discarding old paradigms and developing new ones. We like to pretend a couple of things. One is that our thinking is superior to the thinking found under old paradigms. Second, that our thinking is less controlled by dominant paradigms than it was in times past. Still, there are certain paradigmatic assumptions about reality we are reluctant to question. Some examples: the belief that science has the capacity to discover truth; the notion that the market place acts as an "invisible hand" efficiently directing our economic decision making; the belief that the majority should rule, even though there is plenty of evidence to suggest that majorities do not always make the best decisions.[10] The problem with these ideas and others like them is not that they are wrong; the problem is they are only partially correct. When applying the methods of science or economics as algorithms to understand reality, the inferences/conclusions derived need to be scrutinized carefully for their veracity. They cannot be taken uncritically as truth. It is somewhat ironic that even while we criticize our forbears, we tend to follow similar patterns of thinking.

Understanding and thought always occur in a framework. A way of looking at this has already been discussed in some detail when we considered the familiarity and representative heuristics. You may recall that the familiarity heuristic is a rule of thumb which holds that events easy to recall are more likely to occur than those that are not, and the representative heuristic holds that the probability of something being true or occurring increases the more it fits an "existing cognitive stereotype".[11] It is the concept of an existing cognitive stereotype that is the issue here. A cognitive stereotype contains those concepts, ideas, beliefs, and values that individuals hold to be true or untrue. They provide a framework by which the thinker selects elements from reality and make judgments (decisions) about them. The source of a cognitive stereotype is largely drawn from the surrounding cultural paradigms in which the individual lives. The problem for independent, critical and creative thinking is our tendency to uncritically adopt many ideas from our paradigms and use them as a frame of reference to understand reality.

Independent thinking cannot be independent until the thinker has the ability to stand back and question their frames of reference. Conceptually that is not possible until the thinker understands that thought is based on paradigms. Subjects like history, political science; economics, etc need to be taught from the perspective that the reality they describe is based on an intellectual design. A certain intellectual design or model may well have much of significance to offer, but it is also likely to have limitations. Students cannot become independent thinkers until they have some sense of the design assumptions underlying the disciplines.

Let us return for the moment to the content/tactic debate which we discussed in some detail earlier in this chapter. The problem with an emphasis on content is that it seldom allows much time for consideration of the frames of reference assumed in the content being taught (intellectual design, paradigms, ideology, etc.) . The emphasis in content teaching tends to centre on the acquisition and retention of information at the expense of discussion about the validity of the frame of reference inherent to that content. D. N. Perkins argues that the emphasis in teaching has to shift to tactics, because that is the only way to help young people become independent thinkers.[12] An important part of that process is to make students aware of thinking frames or as we have been discussing paradigms.

Knowledge by Design

Perkins argues that understanding any piece of knowledge or any product of human intellect involves viewing it as a design: a structure shaped to a purpose.[13]

He further argues that understanding involves being able to answer four design questions about the product of human intellect:

- What is it purpose or purposes?
- What is its structure?
- What are model cases?
- What arguments explain and evaluate the object?

Perkins argues that these four questions used as a heuristic can help students learn to independently understand a wide array of knowledge.[14]

These four questions will become a heuristic only if students continue to turn to them at future points in their lives. To make this a reality, students must be given opportunities to apply these design questions in meaningful ways. Such a heuristic might be labelled the design heuristic.

Essentially, the notion of design being fundamental to understanding human or intellectual reality is a conceptual notion. Students need to come to understand the underlying concept of design in the creation of human reality.[15] Thus the initial teaching of knowledge by design is a concept attainment activity. Starting with the concrete, Perkins suggests that students consider the design issues surrounding common household objects. He suggests students begin the concept attainment process with a simple example like the thumbtack. The intent at this point is to help students attain the concept of design and appreciate the utility of using the design questions. In the process, students will begin to understand and assimilate the questions. The important thing is for students to learn to carry on the process independently.

A concrete example and the design questions create an analytical situation in which students can employ the questions to create an analytical matrix for understanding the inherent design of objects and ideas, thumbtacks being one simple example of the process. It is important that students be made aware that they are doing the skill concept of analysis here. An analytical discussion of thumbtacks using the design heuristic might follow these lines:

- Purpose:
    To hold objects in place on bulletin boards, walls, etc;
- Structure:
    Wide round head attached to a short pointed prong;
- Model cases:
    Different types of thumbtacks could be displayed and compared;

Arguments

- Explanatory:
    The head is wide to push the tack comfortably
    and hold papers in place,
    The short shaft allows the tack to penetrate easily,
    The point allows easy penetration;
    The shaft provides friction to hold the tack in place;
- Evaluative:
    Thumbtacks are cheap, handy, and easy to insert,
    They can create holes in walls and are sometimes hard to remove;
    They can get lost on the floor and stick in floors and soles of shoes or, worse yet, in someone's feet.

This would give a basic analysis of the design of thumbtacks. Perkins points out that this discussion could be extended to consider the physics of thumbtacks (points are inclined planes; the purpose of points is to concentrate pressure: all of this could be calculated within a science class).

Heuristics, Metacognition, and Independent Thinking

Other objects could be analyzed as well so that students could begin to assimilate the four design questions. It is important that students begin to understand that the objects created by humans for use by humans are all products of design. Of course, this statement should be challenged in class: is it really true that all human thought and production has design? Students should be challenged to take that question very seriously. Can they find something that does not fit the design model of human thought and productivity? Eventually they might discover they will be using the four design questions to discuss the concept of design:

What is the purpose?

- What purpose does design serve in thought and production?

What is the structure?

- Are patterns the structure of design?

What are model cases?

- Examples with clear design and those with unclear design.
- Do unclear examples ultimately exhibit a design?

What arguments explain design?

- Why do human constructs always have a purpose?
- Why does purpose need a pattern?
- Why do we need examples to understand a reality like design?

What arguments evaluate design?

- Are humans able to create without purpose?
- Are humans able to understand without order?
- Are humans able to test models such as design without examples?
- Are humans able to explain reality without recourse to a pattern?

A discussion such as the one outlined above introduces students to the concept of epistemology. It may not be necessary to label this discussion as such, but it is important that students have it. It is also important for teachers to realize that the structural support of a heuristic like that of Perkins' creates conditions where students are capable of such a discussion. Independent thinking requires metacognition: the capacity to step away from one's thought processes and examine and evaluate them as if they were another's thoughts. More importantly, all independent thinking must have elements of metacognition, because metacognition also encourages the thinker to question the surrounding frame of reference.

Perkins believes design questions are basic to understanding the intellectual processes of humans. One way of helping students through this process is to help them create analytical matrices based on these design questions. Students need to understand that a matrix allows them to categorize and classify information thereby preparing it for inferencing. Again, students need to understand that creating a heuristic using the design questions, and a matrix makes the use of thought concepts easier. In a class discussion, have the students design a design question matrix that might apply to a variety of ideas. Such a matrix might look like the following:

DESIGN QUESTIONS: EXAMPLES & INFERENCES

- What is the purpose of . . . ?
- What is the structure . . . ?
- What are model cases (examples) of . . . ?
- What arguments:
  explain . . . ?
  evaluate . . . ?

Fig. 10.3.

Students could initially practice with this matrix using the thumbtack example above. Soon they would need alternate examples as a way of testing and deepening their understanding. Some concrete examples they might begin with are scissors, telephones, automobiles, etc. Of course, this is only preliminary to applying the concept of design to more abstract and profound issues. The issue for independent thinking is whether the students will transfer this heuristic to other areas in their thinking.

The design heuristic can be used in a wide variety of situations. It is important that students be allowed to use the design heuristic in a sufficient amount of situations to make them comfortable with it, and to see its usefulness in their thought processes. A typical adolescent critique of the classes they take begins with the observation that there is no point to the classes they are taking. They are unable to see how subjects like mathematics, science, etc have any relationship to their lives. Part of the problem is that they do not understand the relationship between understanding mathematics and understanding reality. In other words, they do not understand the design function of mathematics.

For example, the concept of number base in mathematics seems somewhat abstract and abstruse. Students could be challenged to think about the design of number systems. They might begin with the base ten system. The teacher might begin with some discussion questions that would stimulate the students to think about the design of mathematics. The issue is to do this heuristically so that students begin to think about mathematical design.

A teacher guided class discussion might proceed as follows:

- Is it possible to count without the invention of numbers? Suppose someone asked you to tell them about the "Xs" below:

XXXXXXXXXXXXXXXXXXXXXXXXXXXX
XXXXXXXXXXXXXXXXXXXXXXXXXXXXXXX
XXXXXXXXXXXXXXXXXXXXXXXX
XXXXXXXXXXXXXXXXXXXXXXXXXXXX
XXXXXXXXXXXXXXXXXXX
XXXXXXXXXX
XXXXXXXXXXXXXXXXXXXXXXXXXXXXXXXXXX
XXXXXXX

- What can you tell them without numbers?
- How many different things could you say with numbers?
- What is the purpose of numbers?
- Why have we found it so important to have a system of numbers?
- Is there a basic design to our numbers? If so, what is the purpose of that design?
- How many numbers are there in our number system:
- An infinite number?
- Ten?
- How can both answers be correct?
- How do we use ten numbers to create an infinite amount of numbers?
- How does a tally system of counting work?
- Suppose you are counting pennies from a very large jar and the phone rings. By the time you are off the phone, you have forgotten your count. What can you do to make sure you do not lose track of your count?
- What number would you choose to make a tally: 2, 5, 7, 10, other?
- Do we make tallies in our number system?
- What number did we choose to make a tally on?

- Why did we choose the number ten? - Why not six, twelve, or some other number instead of ten

- Would there be problems if the base of a number system were a prime number like three or seven?

- It has been said that the notion of zero as a number is a very great mathematical invention.

- Why do we need a symbol/word for nothing in mathematics?

- How is it used in our number system?

- Explain the Roman numeral system.

- Why is it used very little in modern society?

- Place some numbers in the Roman system on the chalkboard and ask the students to use them in performing the four number operations.

- Place the same numbers on the chalkboard in base ten and ask for the four number operations.

- In a class discussion, decide why one system is so much easier than another. (Do not accept familiarity as a basic explanation).

- What are other possible number systems?

- Can you create other number systems?

- What might be the advantages and disadvantages of each?

- What number system is used by computers?

- Why is a binary system ideal for computers?

- Why has the metric system of measurement replaced the imperial system?

After a general discussion of the above questions (and others) ask the students to use both the information that they have collected and the design heuristic to analyze the base ten number system. Their work might look like the example below:

DESIGN QUESTIONS	EXAMPLES & INFERENCES
WHAT IS THE PURPOSE OF A NUMBER BASE SYSTEM SUCH AS THE BASE TEN SYSTEM?	- We have a chosen a number system with 10 digits: 0, 1, 2, 3, 4, 5, 6, 7, 8, and 9. - Why did we choose to use a base system? - Why did we choose the base ten system?
WHAT IS THE STRUCTURE OF THE BASE TEN SYSTEM?	- The base ten system is structured to use only ten numbers in varying combinations to express any number. - In counting, when the ten numbers have been used, they are grouped as ten and the same ten numbers are repeated and regrouped as needed; - the base ten structure is a tally system based on ten: - ///////// becomes ///////// on the tenth number; - adding another number creates ///////// plus / (or 11) and so on. - 0,1,2,3,4,5,6,7,8,9 becomes one group of ten (10) on the tenth number - adding another number creates one group of 10 plus 1 or 11. - the tallying process may continue infinitely: two groups of ten equalling 20, ten groups of ten equalling 100, and so on. - Zero as a number is important to a base system of numbering because of its ability to hold a place value: the value of one changes from 1 to 10 to 100 to 1000 simply by adding zeros to the right of the number
WHAT ARE MODEL CASES (EXAMPLES) OF DIFFERENT NUMBERING SYSTEMS?	- The Roman numeral system is a system based on tens but it is not a base system because it does not use the concept of zero as a place holder. - The base two or binary system is a base system which only has two numbers 0 and 1. - Other base systems can be created at will. Examples could be the base five system or the duodecimal (base 12) system
WHAT ARGUMENTS EXPLAIN THE BASE TEN SYSTEM?	- We selected the base ten system of numbering because counting began as a one to one ratio between human fingers and reality. - Each number concept (e.g. // = 2 or /// = 3) was given a defining label (as words and symbols). - As calculations proceed, place value allows groups of ten to be formed and reformed as needed in order to express the needed numbers.

cont'd . . .

cont'd . . .

WHAT ARGUMENTS EVALUATE THE BASE TEN SYSTEM?	- It was very difficult to do any kind of advanced arithmetic such as multiplication and division in the Roman numerical system because of the lack of place value. - Base systems lend themselves as tools to perform different arithmetical computations. - The binary or base two system worked well in computers because 0 could be expressed by switching off and 1 could be the switch on. - The base ten system has been incorporated by the metric system of measurement to create a system of units that can easily be converted by adding or dividing by ten. - The Imperial System of measurement based on a base ten system of counting while using a variety of other bases (12" = 1 foot) is much more difficult to convert from inches to feet to yards, etc.

Fig. 10.4

Understanding the Role of Perception, Paradigms, and Ideology in the Social Construction of Reality

Many students will neither understand nor care about the notion that an understanding of reality is based upon design. I can hear many high school students saying "so what?" The 'so what' is the fact that reality, particularly social reality, can be strange and confusing without a grasp of the concept of design. A popular defence against uncertainty among adolescents is to feign a cool and rejecting cynicism that pretends not to care. Teachers wishing to teach concepts related to design should expect this form of activated ignorance.

A response to the 'so what' question is to remind adolescents they are as human as the rest of us, and react as negatively to chaos and uncertainty as do other humans. A jumping off point for this kind of discussion is to ask the class to consider their responses to chaos and uncertainty in important areas of their lives: personal relationships, home life, education, or jobs might be some major categories they could consider. Ask the students to create scenarios describing examples of personal chaos and uncertainty, and then ask them to discuss their strategies for dealing with these situations. Students might even apply the design questions to their strategies. By doing so, they may begin to understand how much they use design in their personal lives.

Heuristic teaching requires that students be given fundamental reasons for learning the processes of design in thinking and understanding. If students have some background in concept webbing/mapping by now, they will already be aware of some possibilities in patterning and designing reality. They will have a heuristic on which to build a deeper understanding of design. One of the most fundamental reasons students can discover is that they 'do' design themselves without giving it much conscious thought. Students need to be helped to see that this is just one more tool in their intellectual toolkit.

Living in the human condition means that everyone has to work at ordering chaos and making the arbitrary predictable. Students might have a better understanding of the relationship of this statement to their personal lives by now, but they may not be very clear about how it works at the societal level.

This is where the study of history can be so helpful, but it must be done heuristically. To accomplish this, history needs to be accompanied by a study of psychology and philosophy. These may seem like strange bedfellows, but to truly understand the historical process, students need to examine the relationship among historic events, human behaviour, and human thought. History programs can be developed which examine the underlying patterns of Western society. (This, of course, could be done with other societies and traditions.)

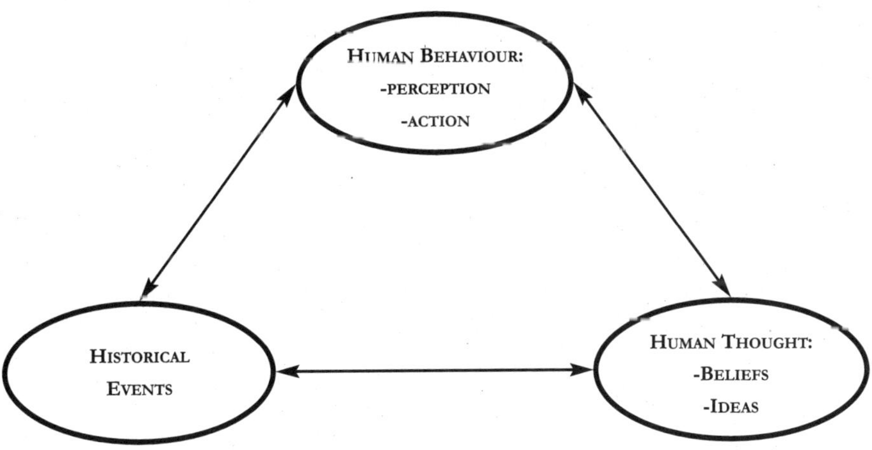

Fig. 10.5

History often appears to be random, arbitrary, and chaotic. It is very easy to become lost in a welter of seemingly unrelated events. Historical understanding can be helped by having some kind of structure or design from which to view the events of history. This is not to claim that history is predictable, or that this particular approach holds any key to understanding the direction of history. It is to claim that students find analytical structures useful tools for organizing historical information and as a springboard to creating inferences. It is wrong to think that students can analyze and infer without a structure. No one can. Professional historians also use structures to think with (learning various philosophies of history is part of their training).

Analytical structures are never completely adequate, if only because they are based on a set of assumptions. They will inevitably highlight certain aspects of reality at the expense of others. Students need to understand this: they need to have experience in evaluating the structures they have selected for use, and the inferences (conclusions) they derive from those structures. This topic will be discussed in more detail later in this chapter, and in the next chapter. In fact, as students become comfortable with the design analysis, there is no reason they could evaluate the simple structure above for its validity. If they found it wanting, they could make the appropriate changes.

There are many periods of history which could be used to illustrate this process in the classroom. Earlier, we examined the intellectual transition from Medieval society to Renaissance society. This is a good example, because it illustrates how the development of new philosophies led to new perceptions of reality, and new forms of behaviour. All of this resulted in new historical events. Within a century, Italian and Northern European societies were markedly different. One can also see this process earlier, albeit more slowly, in the failure of Classical civilizations, and the growth of new philosophies and perceptions of reality out of the wreckage of those civilizations. Christianity and Islam are two examples. Following the Renaissance, historical events like the Reformation, the Enlightenment, the political revolutions, and the growth of liberalism in the nineteenth century are examples of changing thought and perceptions that redesigned society. Handled heuristically, these events can be fertile ground in building an understanding of the tremendous design changes presently occurring in our time.

Conceptually, students need to be aware of the role of human psychology in the historical process. Before they can do that, students need to understand how their psychology affects their reaction to events around them. A good place to begin is with the concept of human perception. They are probably unaware of how slippery the issue of perception can be. 'Seeing is believing' is a traditional heuristic. There are two traps to fall into here. One is the more obvious trap of believing what we see. Most of us, including adolescents, have enough experience with life to be somewhat sceptical of that heuristic. Despite our scepticism, we are still gullible. Advertising and propaganda are powerful examples of that. The other more subtle trap is seeing what we believe. We find it more difficult to understand that we impose our mental models of reality on reality without questioning the validity of doing so. This is one of the serious problems with heuristics. The representative and availability heuristics lead us to see what we believe to be true. Students need experience with this process before they begin to understand how much they depend upon their beliefs to reduce chaos and increase predictability in their lives, even though this strategy can lead to false conclusions.

Students need to have a variety of experiences which examine the quirks of their perception process. Any good psychology text will contain a chapter on perception which outlines a variety of perception tests students can undergo. It is beyond the scope of this book to examine them all, but here are a few examples and some possible inferences that might be drawn from them. A very simple example to begin with is a puzzle where one is challenged to join all nine dots below with four straight lines, without lifting your pencil:

Fig. 10.6

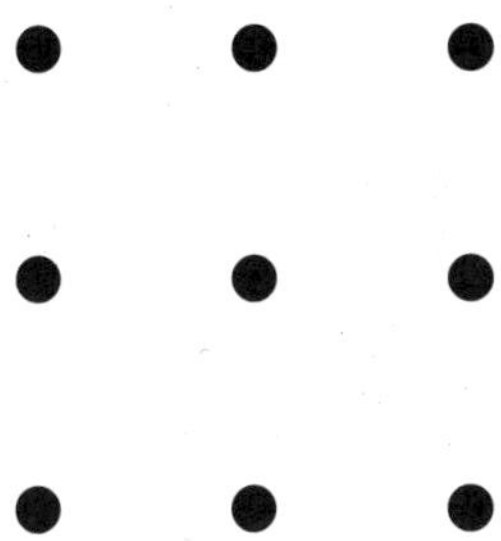

Those of you who have attempted this puzzle will know that what makes it difficult to solve is your assumption about the rules of the puzzle. Most people assume that there is an invisible border (indicated by the outside dots) which cannot be crossed. Based on the assumption of a border, most attempts resemble figure *10.7*

Fig. 10.7

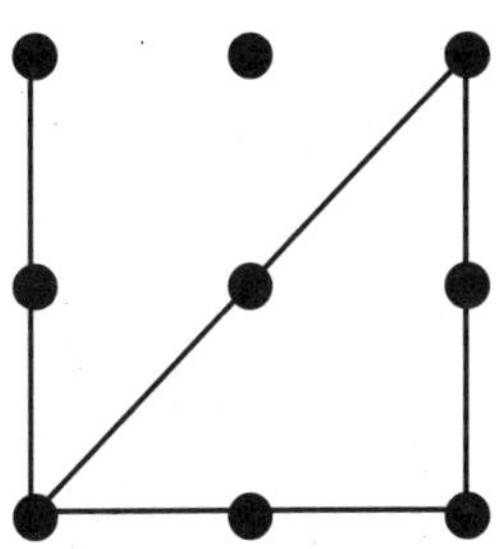

Many variations of line patterns like this can be attempted, but inevitably the nine dots cannot be joined by four lines. As the old saying goes: 'you can't get there from here'. What you have to do is figure out your faulty assumption and abandon it. Of course, the faulty assumption is the invisible border that you dare not violate. But what are the possibilities if you do? The example below shows how the puzzle might be solved:

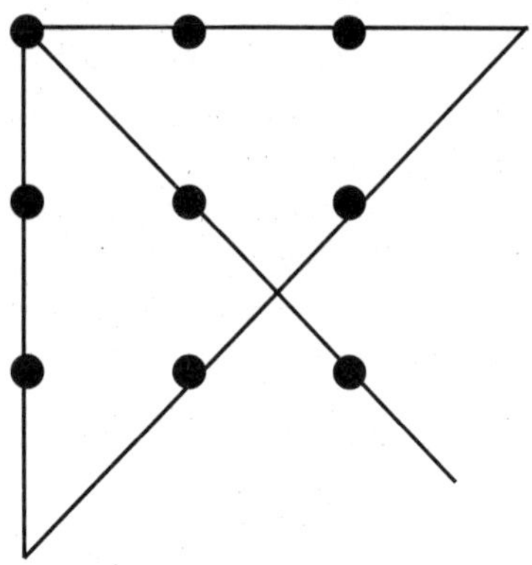

Fig. 10.8

With the benefit of hindsight, the solution seems obvious. The real question is why it is so difficult to find the faulty assumption. A possible answer is that we have been taught to obey borders. More than that, we have been taught to expect borders. So, we approach this problem with a set of unconscious assumptions (a framework) which dispose us to perceive the problem in a non-productive way. One possible source of this framework (one of many) is that we were taught to colour within boundaries as small students. Staying within the lines becomes an unconscious assumption about intellectual reality. Generally speaking much of intellectual reality (pictures, diagrams, pages) all provide us with definite boundaries. This page has a clearly defined margin which is obviously there even though it is not defined by lines. We have learned to obey what we cannot see. Human perception is highly influenced by assumptions and circumstances. Some simple illustrations and possible inferences that might be drawn from the illustrations follow.

It would be helpful for students to be introduced to the perception process itself. Again, this is somewhat beyond the scope of this book, but in general terms the students should understand that the perception process is at least a two stage process. The five senses gather pieces of information and send them to the mind, where the mind reassembles the pieces of information into coherent wholes based on its assumptions about reality (for example, our minds can organize the nine dots above to indicate a boundary). A simple example to discuss is the perceptual mechanics of viewing film or television. Students need to understand that in the case of colour television, they are viewing three rapidly moving dots in the primary colours. Since the mind cannot receive information as rapidly as the television is providing it, the mind stores a memory of past images while it is receiving the current image. The result is the perception of a smooth coherent image that is perceived as gradually evolving, rather than being a series of disjointed rapidly moving dots, which is the reality of the situation.

Student's books (and movies or moving pictures) have used this principle by displaying small pictures of figures in the upper left hand corner of each page. Each figure is redrawn slightly from page to page. By riffling the pages rapidly, the figures in the picture appear to move. Again, students need to understand that the mind remembers one image as it is receiving another and assembles rapidly moving images into a whole, and thus perceives movement when none is there. For a short time, we are prepared to accept this reality. The issue is becomes how long should we accept these media realities as being real?

The other important concept students need to consider in this context is the willing suspension of disbelief. They need to realize that they voluntarily agree to believe what they are seeing. Movie, television, plays, etc all depend upon our agreement to suspend our disbelief. The more we suspend disbelief, the more realistic the performance becomes. Very small students suspend disbelief so thoroughly that the viewing experience can become extremely rapturous or extremely frightening. This phenomenon provides advertisers and propagandists with extremely powerful tools to persuade people to certain points of view. We have had many bad experiences with the suspension of disbelief in the twentieth century, and now in the twenty-first century.

Noam Chomsky has written extensively on this process, which he labels "manufacturing consent"$_{16}$. Chomsky argues that governments deliberately set out to create conditions of belief which will cause people to consent to governmental policies and decisions to which they might otherwise object. There are many historical examples of this process that could be explored. Adolf Hitler is probably the most infamous one, but there are many more.

It is critically important for the students' independent understanding of history that they realize past historical events, like present historical events, are made by people whose perceptual processes are similar to those in humans today. Consent had to be manufactured in the past as well. Historical people were once present people, and had to deal with information and uncertainties as people do today.

Some Ideas on Using Heuristic Methods in the Presentation of Historical Events

I have been arguing that students need to assimilate the gist of information before they can think independently about that information. It is true that students need to have information to think with. But they need to gain that information in ways that allow them to create gists.

Simulation Games Are Heuristics[17]

An important teaching and learning heuristic is simulation gaming. Many people know it as role playing, and while that is an important aspect to simulation gaming, there is more to it then that. An effective simulation game has three major aspects to it. First, it has to have a scenario of some kind which establishes the problem(s) or issue(s) students are faced with. The scenario, initially, will sketch out the basic situation in which the students find themselves, and a basic outline of issues which have to be handled in some way. It is important to note that successful simulations work on a need to know basis. Information is supplied as students' understanding increases, and related informational need grows.

Secondly, students find themselves assigned to some kind of roles. The roles provide students with a point of view and a perspective from which to assimilate information. The roles may represent archetypes selected to present different viewpoints. They generally represent various sides of an issue that have the potential to come into some kind of conflict, depending upon how the roles are played by the students.

Thirdly, the information itself is an important part of a simulation. In effect, it is a role as well. In their roles, students may believe they have control of events based on the information they have assimilated, but information is always incomplete and contradictory, making events seem unpredictable and arbitrary. This process is exacerbated by the contradictory and unpredictable ways other roles will view and use information.

Fourthly, simulations must have a process of interaction among the roles: the clash, so to speak. This may be a conference, a court case, a project to achieve something, a debate, etc. It may be an exploration to solve a mystery by finding information. A simulated archaeological dig could be an example. There are many alternatives to choose from. The important consideration here is to choose a structure that initially provides guidance for students as they learn their roles and the issues, but becomes less obtrusive as students become more competent to direct events in the simulation. Simulations act as a heuristic by providing a structure which initially motivates and guides, and later provides a platform that allows students to generate their own creativity.

Fifthly, a good simulation will always contain surprises as reality impinges on the course of events in unpredictable ways. It is here that students learn to flexible and creative as they modify their plans to deal with a new and unexpected reality.

Finally, a simulation must have a debriefing period, giving students an opportunity to step back from the game and the roles they played, to introspect about their contribution as they analyze and evaluate the events of the simulation. This is actually a metacognitive process where students consider their thought processes in the context of the reality they have had to react to. It is also paradigmatic in the sense that a simulation game acts as a paradigm or 'box' that defines reality for the students. They need to understand that for a time they willingly 'suspended disbelief'.

Debriefing simulation games provide students with practice examining and evaluating their behaviour in paradigmatic contexts. In broad terms, this can be a definition of the structure of a simulation. In the next pages, we will consider an example of one. In this sense, simulations are also heuristics, because they enable students to assimilate large amounts of information. As students work through the simulation, they are guided to categorize and classify information in their minds.

Issues Related to Effective Heuristic Teaching

As teaching strategies, simulations are often seen as taking up too much classroom time. This criticism takes us back to considering fundamental issues of pedagogy. The real issue is learning to think, not learning information. Many history teachers who teach information algorithmically are concerned that while students may learn one or two historical events from simulations, they will have an inadequate grasp of other events, and thereby miss the broad sweep of history. There may well be some truth to that, but there are a couple of responses that need to be noted.

One response is that long term learning depends upon learning the gist of information. It is unlikely that students will learn the gist of history simply by learning information about large numbers of historical events. Research is clear: verbatim memorization is not nearly as effective as learning gist.[18] If all that happens is verbatim learning, students will not have gained a broad and thorough grasp of history either. It is a serious dilemma for teachers of history.

The important thing to understand is that the human mind does not classify only according to intellectual ideas. The mind uses emotions, relationships, aesthetics, and morality as classification systems as well. Information classified as emotional gist is very affecting and long lasting. It provides meaning and significance to what might otherwise not seem very relevant. This is the problem with a purely intellectual, abstract presentation of historical data. It lacks the capacity to be engaging and affecting.

The second - and even more important - issue is helping students learn to think about history. Large amounts of historical information are readily available. Every year, a wide variety of media provides more information than any single person can absorb. The real issue is learning how to think about that information. Historical information may be useful, but it can also be highly misleading. Historical information comes packaged as a design. That means a writer has done the selection, classification, and inferencing. The historical package being perused may or may not be acceptable; however, the real point is whether the student of history has any capacity to make judgments about the package. Providing a student with the intellectual tools to do that is the real point of teaching history, not the mere collection of information.

AN ILLUSTRATION OF HEURISTIC TEACHING USING SIMULATION AS A TACTIC

World War One Simulation, Part One: Stumbling into War

Let us return to an actual example of a simulation game to see what it might look like in the classroom. The example being used is drawn from Saskatchewan Learning.[19] This simulation is based on the events leading to World War I. The game simulates a mythical conference in which students role play the great powers and a few of the minor powers who played a significant role. In the conference, students have to resolve some of outstanding issues bedevilling international politics in the early Twentieth Century. The game consists of preparatory activities, the conference itself, and finally resolving the consequences of decisions made at the conference.

As their roles are distributed, students are introduced to the basic historical scenario of the early twentieth century. The major roles are the United Kingdom, France, Germany, Austria-Hungary, and Russia. The smaller countries are Italy, Turkey, and Serbia. Students are given thumbnail sketches of each country: recent history, geographic location, and brief overviews of each economic and military status. Depending upon the size of the class, there may be three or more students representing a country. They are actually role playing the cabinet (chief minister, foreign minister, economics minister, etc). This activity is intended to give students a basic conception of the concerns of each country.

Now students begin a more in-depth analysis of the situation facing their respective countries. Usually students will work as a team.[20] One student will study their country's recent history; another will examine the geography and economics of the country, and a third may examine related security issues. By this time, students realize that as members of cabinet they have a fiduciary responsibility for the wellbeing of their people. The point of this exercise is to allow each cabinet to assess their country's strengths and weaknesses, and those of other countries. Each cabinet needs to decide who are threats and who have the potential to be allies. Based on the information they gather, they begin to develop a foreign policy. Students rapidly realize they are not self-sufficient in trade or in defence, which means they need to find allies who will support their foreign policy goals in trade and defence. At the end of this session, countries may have formed alliances in an attempt to augment their security.

Once a preliminary foreign policy has been established, the student cabinets representing each country have an opportunity to meet informally with other countries. The first objective of these meetings is to assess whether a country has the potential to be an ally, or ultimately a threat in some way. After a period of negotiation, countries may form alliances based on the needs they perceive. The alliances can take a variety of forms, but usually they define the commitments each country is prepared to make to each other in terms of trade, defence and foreign policy.

In this game, there are some overriding issues requiring international discussion and agreement. There has been an arms race, there are disagreements over territory and trade routes, there are past injustices that have not been resolved, etc. Periodically in international affairs, groups of countries meet to try and resolve their differences. At this point in the simulation, a formal conference is convened to allow the powers an opportunity to resolve their outstanding issues. One of the first issues that will have to be resolved is voting privileges. Usually, each great power has a vote, and the lesser may or may not have one. That is left up to the students to determine. It is unlikely there will be a tie, so issues will be decided one way or another. One of the possible items in an alliance agreement is some accord to support each other in votes at the conference.

Eventually there will be winners and losers at the conference. The alliance systems formed by students are usually asymmetrical, guaranteeing that some alliances will have more votes at the conference than others. As the conference members debate the issues, events outside of the conference are occurring. It is the role of the teacher to introduce these outside events. They are based on historical incidents, and can have a major impact on the conference. The last of these will be the surprise assassination of Archduke Franz Ferdinand, heir to the throne of Austria-Hungary, by a Serbian nationalist society. Typically, this will have a profound effect on the attitudes of the students as they scramble to react to the news of the assassination.

After the assassination, all the student groups are forced to carefully consider their options, and to determine the best way to protect their sovereignty. Foreign policies will become much harder as countries become more insecure. Usually this means that Austria-Hungary will demand the right to impose sanctions which are intolerable to the sovereignty of Serbia. Russia will usually support the Serbs, whom they consider to be their Slavic brothers. If this occurs, then Germany - who is most often Austria-Hungary's ally - will agree to support Austria-Hungary. This leaves the United Kingdom and France to consider their options.

This situation develops rather rapidly, forcing other countries to react to protect their sovereignty. One reality of international decision at this point in history is the perceived need to mobilize militaries quickly, so that a country does not begin a war at a disadvantage. There is great pressure on the leaders of countries to move precipitously. The students may not want to declare war on each other, but feel compelled to do so by events. Usually, they declare war.

Debriefing Simulation Games: Returning to the Principles of Intellectual Design

Students will have developed a set of personal heuristics and gists based on their experiences in the simulation by now. They need an opportunity to think independently about their experiences using critical and creative thinking skills such as analysis, inferencing, evaluation, etc.

At this point of the game students have enough experience with international issues and processes and historical background, they could learn from viewing actual film footage of world war one. One example is the film *The Guns of August*, based on Barbara Tuchman's classic discussion of the causes and events of World War One.[21] There are other good films and information sources describing the war and its aftermath.

It is useful for students to compare and contrast their behaviour in the game with the historical record. As students watch the film, it should be paused to allow students opportunity to compare and evaluate what they have seen. Discrepancies between the game and the historical record should be thoroughly discussed. During such discussions, it should be emphasized that rather than considering the discrepancies as mistakes, the 'mistakes' indicate the potential of history to take different courses. Every historical player in the summer of 1914 had the potential to make a difference in the course of history. Students at this point could take some time out to compare the events of 1914 with other international crises to determine whether alternative course of action could have happened. The Suez Crisis of 1956, the Cuban Missile Crisis, and the First and Second Gulf Wars are examples that students could examine.

Using Various Heuristics to Stimulate Independent Thinking

It is not enough to present history as a series of events and to leave it at that. This statement equally applies to the presentation of history through techniques such as simulation games. Students need to be aware that history is always seen from a point of view. Often that point of view has not been subject to a conscious examination, in the same sense that the unconscious acceptance of boundaries surrounding the nine dots in the puzzle had not been examined. As students discuss historical events, they also need to participate in exercises which will help them examine the unexamined assumptions of the historical players, as well as the students' own unexamined assumptions. Through this process, students should begin to develop a set of metacognitive heuristics they can apply throughout their lives. A highly significant form of life long learning.

As noted above, a simulation game can be seen as design and as a heuristic. Both of these notions make it possible for students to get the gist of whatever event they might be studying. If the intent is to provide students with the gist of a historical event such as World War One, then via the excercirse - playing a simulation game, viewing a film such as Tuchman's *Guns of August*, and based on that do some background reading on the history of the event - one might argue that students would have accumulated sufficient information to have a basic sense of the role of World War One in history.

However, in a heuristic classroom, many students might be appalled and angry at the blood shed World War One represents. By now they should be asking evaluative questions about the event. They will wish to think about it in more depth than they have done so far. Heuristics can be useful beginning points to critically evaluate historical events. A number of useful debriefing exercises can be designed to help students develop a critical thinking process to apply to a historical event. Below are a number of examples of heuristics that might be developed and applied to historical events. In no way should the list be considered definitive. It is intended to be an example of what could be done with imaginations and creativity by the teacher. The important thing about all of them is their capacity to be heuristic rather than algorithmic.

The Drama Heuristic

History is often presented as if it were a drama with an introduction, middle (action) and a conclusion. The courses of historical events are portrayed as if they had some kind of inevitability about them. Descriptions of the causes of World War One do not leave the impression there are any alternatives to the 'Guns of August' in 1914. Yet it is important to understand that there is no predetermined historical outcome, despite the impression left by dramatic accounts of historical events in students' minds. Nor is there any neat closure with the "hero riding off into the sunset to live happily ever after". According to Arnold Toynbee, the reality of history may be characterized as: "[some historians believe that history] is just one damned thing after another."[22] As soon as World War I was completed, humanity embarked upon another series of events one of which was World War II. And of course the stream of events did not end there. The perception of discrete historical events are picked up from years of watching dramatic accounts of historical events (stories and movies about history do this all the time) and in doing so, assimilating dramatic design as a structure for understanding history. In this sense the dramatic form becomes a heuristic used to define our thinking about history.

A modern case in point could be our evaluation of the Kennedy presidency. The assumed dramatic design for John F. Kennedy's tenure in the White House was the movie Camelot. The events of his presidency, including the assassination, were seen through the romantic lens of the Camelot story. It was not until much later that the public (including journalists) was able to escape that illusion and take a more critical look at the Kennedy years. The dramatic design becomes a mental framework, which students unconsciously use to understand historical reality. Teachers need to be aware of that so they can help students evaluate their preconceived historical frameworks.

Using drama as a heuristic tool does not have to be a negative exercise. The dramatic heuristic can be used to help students of history see history from a different perspective. World War One can be critically evaluated using the dramatic heuristic as an analytical tool. For example, students could look at *All Quiet on the Western Front* for its portrayal of events and the players within the events.[23] It would be important for students to understand that both the book and the movie were highly controversial, with the book being banned in many places for its unsympathetic portrayal of the war. This would be a way of introducing students to the concept of mind set and its role in shaping our perceptions of events.

Students could usefully apply the design concepts outlined above to these historical accounts:

- what was the purpose of the dramatic account?
- what was the structure of the dramatic design employed?
- what are some model cases of accounts of World War One (pro-war and anti-war)?
- what arguments explain and evaluate historical accounts of World War One?

This approach could be used to evaluate many examples of current events. Students could find examples of current decision making, and begin to use the design questions as an evaluative heuristic.

The Rumour Heuristic

The formation of public opinion is another concept students should become aware of. Noam Chomsky refers to these ideas as the manufacture of consent. In modern societies, especially democracies, those who hold political power may find it expedient to embark upon a course of action they believe the general public would not approve. The response of the powerful is to design a public relations campaign to persuade people the proposed public policy is acceptable. More often, events occur which frighten the public in some way. The fear is exacerbated by a rumour mill (occurring in the media, coffee row, call-in radio programs, etc). which may be augmented by other events or more rumours over the course of time. The public demands action, and the political leadership find it expedient to use these events to persuade people to accept certain policies they might other wise not accept.

A simple game can be played to demonstrate the power of misinformation. It is an example of people receiving incomplete information, and then using their personal heuristics to create what is to them a reasonable representation of what they heard. Ask a class to arrange themselves into a line around the perimeter of the classroom. Give the person at the head of the line a short passage to read, and then whisper what they read to the next person in line. Each person will repeat the message in turn, until the last person in line has heard the message. Have the last person repeat out loud what was heard so that everyone can compare it with what they heard. When that is done, have the first person reread to the class the actual message. Invariably, there will be distortions because of mishearing or misunderstanding the message as it was passed down the line. Even if an individual did not quite hear or understand the message, the individual is required to pass something on to the next person. This forces the person to improvise, based on what would seem reasonable according to their beliefs and understandings.

Students should consider how this compares to the way in which they receive information in their personal society, and what they do to the information as they pass it on. All of us who have lived in compact societies such as schools, offices, and other small communities have been quite amazed at the power of the rumour mill to distort information. We have the concept of the urban myth where people come to firmly believe quite strange ideas. 'They' - as in 'they say..........' - can carry a lot of weight with people.

At the end of this experiment, students can discuss historical issues such as racism and prejudice. Why was/is it so hard to make gains in addressing race and prejudice? What arguments did slave owners use to justify the right to own slaves? Why are we so fearful of strangers, and why do feel justified in allowing that fear to goad us into mistreating people we do not know? There are many historical examples. 'Yellow journalism' - the extreme nationalistic, jingoistic, inflammatory journalism practiced by newspapers during the run-up to World War One - is considered to be a cause of World War One by some historians. Political leaders were so afraid of public opinion; they did not dare to appear conciliatory in their foreign policy. Canadian examples might be our attitudes toward immigrants over the course of our history, or the treatment of the Japanese during World War II. Students might examine the evidence used to justify the Japanese internment. Were there real grounds for internment, or was this just hysteria fed by rumour and self-interest?

A research project for students debriefing the World War One simulation would be to ask themselves these sorts of questions about the formation of public opinion. They might start by asking themselves whether they were stampeded into war in their simulation. Why did they not stop and offer some compromise that might stimulate negotiation? The students certainly should look at the kind of war propaganda that is extant at the beginning of all wars. Could they withstand the hysteria, or would they acquiesce?

Heuristics of Perception

Students need to understand that the context in which we perceive something can have and enormous effect on the way we perceive it. Psychology texts have many examples showing the effect of field and ground relationships on our perception. One can surround a colour plate with other colours, and change the perception of the central colour quite dramatically. We judge the size of objects based on their surrounding context. There are clever examples showing dramatic changes in the perception of the size of the an object simply by moving the object from context to context. Movies, television, and the stage all use lighting and music to heighten and change one's perception of the events on stage or screen. All of these effects can be used by the propagandist to affect people's perception.

Hitler's rallies are good examples of the manipulation of perception. Both Joseph Goebbels and Albert Speer, Hitler's chief lieutenants, quite candidly discuss the techniques used in their memoirs.[24] Speer explains that rallies were always held at night under enormous floodlights.[25] He describes how floodlights were used to create gigantic columns in the night sky. He goes on to describe the careful attention to the design of uniforms and symbols. Music, chanting, and the mass marching of large arrays of soldiers all were carefully orchestrated for their effect. The effect was augmented by the careful use of public address systems to give people the perception they were part of a great movement with its own momentum. People had the feeling they were part of a wonderful history that was being created.

The Heuristics of Gaming

Another concept students should understand is mental set. Throughout our discussion, we have been examining sources of mental sets. All of the perception examples listed above may result in the creation of mental sets. Mental set may be defined as the expectations we have created about reality. Those expectations very much determine what we expect to see. The attack on Pearl Harbour and the resulting war against the Japanese certainly created a mental set which made people much more willing to accept flimsy evidence based on prejudice and rumour. Mental sets have the power predispose people to think in certain ways.

We like to play with mental sets and humour is a good example of that. The preamble of a joke is intended to create a mental set: an expectation of what ought to happen. The punch line provides an alternative conclusion which does not match our expectations or mental set. Sometimes these jokes are funny (and harmless) and other times they pander to our prejudices. Humour is a fertile ground for understanding the assumptions of a society, because it is so firmly based on cultural expectations.

Everyone has mental sets that they turn to for guidance when choices and decisions have to be made. Mental sets are obviously useful, because they provide us with guidance for our behaviour. Without them we would be like small students reliant on others to provide guidance. As with all the other examples we have discussed, it is important to understand we have mental sets and are capable of standing back and examining them. Students need to be aware of their use of mental sets in various situations so they can think about them.

Games are a system for creating mental set. If one thinks about the design of games, they all tend to follow a basic structure: they have a simple clear objective (throwing a ball through a hoop supported ten feet above a court); it establishes a set of rules about how one goes about performing the actions of the game (the ball must be bounced every time the player takes a step); and it has a system for measuring the achievement of the objective (points earned for each time the ball goes through the hoop). Of course, games become much more complex than this basic structure, but all the rules still tend to define and guide these three components of the game structure.

Hence when someone invites you to play a game of basketball, if you know the game, you will have a pretty clear idea of what to expect. The game has created a mental set which triggers all sorts of expectations about behaviour. Like the issues related to drama discussed above, games create a mental set about the perception of reality. Games are an intellectual design of reality. They also become metaphors for understanding the behaviour of individuals within society. This occurs because games create expectations of behaviour. Some of those are expectations are related to team work, competition, sportsmanship, aggression and the like. The mental sets of games transfer from games to other areas of life. They also transfer back from life to games.

There are historical examples which indicate the role of games in affecting the choices of people in historical events. Very dramatic examples come from the battlefield. In war, young men (historically) have been asked to go out and perform behaviours which have a high probability of maiming or killing them. One would expect that a natural instinct for self-preservation would interfere with that process. In some cases it does, but in many others soldiers sacrifice their lives. It would be useful for students to speculate on the reasons for this self-sacrificing behaviour. Students could be offered a number of explanations. The standard explanation is patriotism and nationalism, the notion that the loyalty and love for their country of young soldiers creates a mind set of self-sacrifice for the greater benefit of the county. That may well be true.

However, there are other explanations. One was offered by General Wellington after the Battle of Waterloo. He is reputed to have said that the Battle of Waterloo was won on the playing fields of Eton.[26] Is Wellington correct in suggesting that athletics creates a mental set (or heuristic) of team loyalty, self-sacrifice, competitiveness, etc. that pre-disposes young men to become good soldiers?[27]

In World War One, soldiers could only survive on the battlefield by digging trenches to protect themselves from machine guns. The attack strategy of trench warfare was to ask soldiers to charge out of their trenches and run across an open empty space toward the trenches of the enemy in an attempt to overwhelm the enemy trench. The enemy had machine guns, which they used quite efficiently to kill the charging soldiers. It soon became clear the casualty rate resulting from this strategy was enormous. Yet young soldiers continued to participate. One very telling symbol in this situation occurred before the attack, when the young officers would kick a soccer ball towards the enemy trenches and say "The enemy has our ball, go and get it back".[28]

The important point here is that a mental set has a design which can be analyzed as any other design is analyzed. A mental set has a purpose and a structure which can be analyzed and evaluated. From the safety of the classroom, one might question the behaviour of those soldiers, but one needs to understand they were attempting as best they could to respond to a bad situation. When they examined their personal heuristics, the response they got was they must be good team players. It would be seen as 'incredibly bad form' for a young man to let his side down. Anything else was cowardice, and that accusation was worse than death.

The problem is that most people of the time could see no other alternative. Lord Bertrand Russell argued passionately for pacifism, and went to jail for his contribution to the debate. The mental set of the day could not allow for independent thinking on issues related to war and peace. Concepts such as nationalism, sovereignty, national security, economic wellbeing had a powerful hold on the public imagination. These concepts (and others like them) were arranged into a coherent pattern which clearly defined the options available. Powerful militaries, alliances, and the will to wage war in the name of national security formed the national mental set. Lord Russell's vision was completely outside the bounds of an acceptable mental set, and therefore not something worthy of rational consideration. A collective mental set such as this is a paradigm.

The Impact of Paradigm and Ideology on Thinking

It is time to discuss the overriding sources of mental sets: paradigms and ideology. The two are similar in their effect on mental set, and in many ways are linked. But there are also important differences. Students need some background on them, so that they are capable of doing a design analysis of them.

Paradigms are a coherent pattern of ideas, beliefs and values which provide society with a widely accepted gist of reality. They change fuzzy, contradictory, unpredictable reality into something seemingly more understandable and predictable. Paradigms provide the broad assumptions on which to base decisions. In the case of our discussion example, World War One, paradigms define how to respond to threats to national security. Ideologies are competing sets of ideas, beliefs and values, often within the same overall paradigm, about how to proceed in more specific terms. Ideologies may vary on strategies, speed of action, the treatment of people in situations, etc, but remain generally agreed on the overall paradigm. For example, in the United Kingdom prior to World War One, there would have been much ideological discussion about the best foreign policy to follow, and later some discussion on how best to wage war. But there would be little discussion on whether empire, the monarchy or a foreign policy based on a powerful navy was a good thing. Those issues were paradigmatic and therefore beyond the bounds of rational discussion, as Lord Russell discovered when he was brought to trial for disagreeing with the established paradigm.[29]

Returning to the concept of perception again, one can set experiments which show the effect of paradigms on the mind set of young people playing games. A few years back, a cross-cultural experiment was performed using a game as a device to test the mind set of young Aboriginal and American students toward playing games.[30] The game was quite simple. Players sat around a board with a hole in the centre. The object was to pull a peg into the hole. Opposing pairs of players each had a line attached to the peg, and had to pull against each other as they attempted to move the peg into the hole. A player who was successful in getting the peg in the hole was rewarded with candy.

The Navaho children played the game in a very cooperative mode. Each Navaho child took a turn at getting the peg in the hole and receiving some candy. Their concept of the game seemed to be how efficient they could be in increasing reward. The American children saw the game very differently. They were highly competitive and worked hard to prevent other players from getting the peg in the hole. Either they did not perceive the Navaho children's system of increasing reward, or they preferred competition to reward. In both cases, the basic mental set about how to play the game was quite different. The source of the overriding mental set has to do with paradigms and ideology.

Without doing an anthropological analysis of Navaho and American cultures, there is evidence here that different paradigms are at work. American children are socialized into a competitive game paradigm. Most games they play have an element of competition designed to test their ability to perform well under pressure. Individuality requires that one learn to stand up for oneself despite the adversity. Winning is an important expression of individuality. The Navaho culture, with its paradigm of community values and cooperation, is much less concerned about individuality. Group success means the individual has also been successful.

The important thing to note about paradigms is their pervasiveness. While there is some debate about the format of games in American culture, the reality is that the creators, manufacturers, and consumers of games all have essentially accepted the same game paradigm. Everyone 'knows' what a proper game should look like. This is especially true for the creators of games. Manufacturers believe a game, that does not fit the competitive stereotype will probably not be all that successful in the market place. To some degree they are correct, because when consumers (adults and children) come to buy a 'new' game, it still has to fit their concept of game.

Paradigms as a Source of Heuristics

Our heuristics are closely connected to the paradigms under which we live. The world often appears to be chaotic and arbitrary. Never more so than during a visit to a busy toy store during a shopping expedition, a couple of days before

Christmas. Mostly we have been discussing life and death issues related to war. Paradigms play an important role there, but they also play an important role in the day to day decisions of life. Assumptions related to health, business, and social interaction find their roots in paradigms. Should one go to a modern medical clinic for medical advice, or should one go to someone who uses a variety of herbal remedies for treatment? Do you consider the market place to be the most efficient way of distributing goods and services within an economy? Can you imagine an alternative and its consequences? Would you turn down a promotion and a transfer to a more lucrative job because it would interfere with your relationship to the extended family? For many people, these questions would seem puzzling because the answers are obvious. Of course one would go to a modern medical facility with the latest science and technology. Of course the market place is the most efficient allocation system. And, of course one would take the promotion and the move. Why would you even ask?

The paradigms of modern society do provide us with acceptable answers. In some cases, war or the threat of war may be justified. What gets really confusing is when the paradigms themselves are questioned. The problem is not so much that the paradigm(s) may be wrong. The market system of allocation has its successes. The problem for independent thinking and related critical and creative thinking is that paradigms have the power to foreclose debate. They do this firstly by carefully limiting the perception of its adherents. For the Navaho and American children, they could only think of one possible way to play the game. Then they provide us with coherent explanation (model) of reality. Science has the power to explain and solve all the mysteries of reality. And finally, paradigms predict the future by proclaiming good and bad choices for us. 'Chemo' is the best treatment for a cancer patient. The toy recommended by the toy store is the one your child will like, thereby avoiding disaster Christmas morning.

Paradigms need to be confronted before independent thinking is possible in the classroom. They need to be confronted with concrete, practical approaches young people can understand and appreciate. In confronting paradigms, the issue should always come as a heuristic. The Question of why vast numbers of people were sent to die on a battlefield is the focusing issue. The welter of historical detail should come as a consequence of students wrestling with historical events. As students immerse themselves in the issue, the historical detail will emerge. In this way, the confrontation of paradigms will be heuristic rather than algorithmic, because the students will want to respond with their points of view.

In our discussion above, all the examples noted were intended for use in the classroom. All the examples discussed share the fact that they are about decisions young people could see themselves having to make.

The Design of Paradigms

Returning to teaching history for a moment, students need to think about paradigms and design. They need to look at the design of the prevailing paradigm and ask themselves the basic design questions:

- what is the purpose of the paradigm?
- what is its structure;
- what are model cases; and,
- what arguments explain and evaluate the paradigm?[31]

World War One Simulation Part Two: Dealing with the Realities of War

As decision makers, students typically discover they have embroiled themselves with a modern industrial war. in the initial round of the World War One Game. Most students began the game believing they could find a better way of settling international disputes and avoid war. At the same time, students - like the leaders of the day - have little conception of the horrors of modern warfare. Few of us do. The point of this second phase of the simulation would be to confront modern warfare from the standpoint of paradigms and their impact on decision making. When societies are faced with realities such as war, what are the assumed constraints restricting their examination of the alternatives available to them? As students embark upon this phase of the simulation, they are likely to discover they have not considered all the alternatives. Some alternatives were likely summarily dismissed as being unthinkable (more likely, other alternatives simply did not occur to the students). At the end of this phase of the game, students need to ask themselves why this was so.

A heuristic approach to this issue would be to re-arrange the classroom seating such that the protagonists of the war sit far apart from each other. If it is possible, erect some kind of physical barrier between the groups to make it more difficult for them to see and communicate with each other. Also, students should have large maps of the Western and Eastern fronts, as well as maps of the North Atlantic Ocean and the North and Baltic seas so they can track and plan military operations. They should make small, movable symbols indicating the location of armies and fleets. Discussion between the groups should be limited and only done through cryptic messages that are unofficially slipped from one side to another.

The basic groups of the first phase of this simulation should be retained, but the groups need to reorganized somewhat. There would be three war rooms: Britain and France; Russia; and Germany and Austria-Hungary. Group members of Serbia should be assigned to Russia. Members of the Turkish group should go to Germany and Austria-Hungary and the Italian members should go to Britain and France. Each of Britain/France, Germany/Austria-Hungary, and Russia would assign two individuals (a political leader and a general) to be in charge of the country's response to the war. Two students should be made editors of newspapers, and their role is to inform the public. The remainder of the students will be the public, whose role is to supply soldiers, taxes, and loyalty to the nation. The soldiers should have no voice.

The leaders of the respective sides would meet in their central war rooms where the events of the battlefield would arrive as 'dispatches'. The political and military leaders would have to discuss their response and send 'orders' to the military commanders in the field. At the same time, some information may be sent to the press in the form of press releases. The student editors would have to decide what information, and how it would be shared with the general public. The public would have a formal opportunity to vote on the leadership of the government at stated periods of time.

It would be the role of the teacher to prepare the dispatches for the governments. The teacher could also provide some suggested alternatives from which the student leadership could choose. These could quite closely follow the events of the war. The dispatches might roughly follow these events:

Dispatch Content from the Teacher	Alternatives Available to Students
- In early 1914 the dispatches could display the successes and failures of a cavalry approach to warfare.	- Continue using cavalry? - Digging Trenches for protection? - Finding a mechanized alternative to horses? - Other responses?
- In early 1915 the dispatches could display the casualty rates resulting from traditional Nineteenth Century military tactics - Dispatches could discuss the need to find a response to the power of the machine gun and modern artillery.	- Digging trenches for protection? - Finding a mechanized alternative to horses? - Other responses?
- The dispatches could display the reality of trench warfare. - Long trench lines of soldiers separated by an open space of approximately 100 metres (No Man's Land) - Dispatches reporting the casualty rates and the success/failure of the military operations.	- Search for alternatives to defeat the enemy? - Mass attacks across 'no man's land'? - Huge artillery barrages on the opposing trenches? - Increase recruiting drives and put women to work in factories? - Other responses?
- Dispatches could report the growth of Submarine warfare and eventually the sinking of the RMS Lusitania. - Dispatches could describe the threat/success of submarine warfare on the flow of resources across the Atlantic and its significance to the war. - Dispatches could describe the growing need for men and matériel on the Western Front. - Dispatches could discuss the question of how to involve the U.S.A. in the war.	- Play up the tragedy of the Lusitania to increase public support for the war and to persuade the U.S. to join the war? - Play down the Lusitania attack as just one of the risks of war? - Other responses? - Continue developing submarines to halt completely the North Atlantic trade? - Develop ships able to carry out anti-submarine war effectively? - Other responses?
- Dispatches should report: - the high casualty rates and the very high expenditure of ammunition in the mass attacks. - Every where on the front are shortages of soldiers, ammunition, (matériel) hospitals, medicine, etc.	- Increase propaganda to persuade the public that the war is just and can be won? - Make military service compulsory? - Increase war production on the home front? - Encourage women to work in factories? - Other responses?

cont'd.

cont'd.

- Dispatches should also report: - the growing disillusionment and mutiny in the ranks of armies. - the risks of disillusionment amongst people on the home front as family after family loses loved ones.	- Rush more troops to the front in an attempt to overwhelm the enemy? - Increase work on motorized alternatives (tanks) to the cavalry? - Increase development and deployment of air planes? - Increase the level of propaganda among the people and the military? - Court martial deserters and cowards? - Couple over the top mass attacks with a two day artillery barrage to destroy enemy trenches and armies? - Other responses?
- Dispatches reporting the effect of the new mass attacks: - Field generals reporting they now realize there can be no quick strategic victory. - Mechanized tanks are still too clumsy and unreliable to be effective. - At this time there does not appear to be any feasible technological defence against machine guns and artillery	- Resort to a war of attrition: the country that runs out of soldiers and materiel first loses? - Increase recruitment drives for more soldiers? - Increase propaganda on the home front (We must continue fighting or the sacrifices of all the dead soldiers will have been in vain.)? - Increase the production of matériel? - Work to encourage/prevent the U.S. from joining the war? - Other responses?

Fig 10.9

It would be the role of the decision makers to determine how they would respond to these dispatches at every stage. They would be allowed the full range of responses, ranging from all out war to suing for peace. The decision makers would not be told this, other than they have the option of 'other response' from those they have been given. The given responses are based on the standard national sovereignty paradigm, governing relations between nations. They would have to make decisions based on their assumptions and related paradigms. It would be up to them to decide when and on what basis the war would end.

Analyzing the Design of Paradigms

One might begin the debriefing of part two with an examination of the war strategies and the casualty lists consequent to those strategies. The students should attempt to be both the responsible decision makers and dispassionate historical observers of the war. As responsible decision makers, they need to consider the moral implications of facilitating the deaths of so many people. What justification can they use to justify such a slaughter? As dispassionate observers, they should be asking themselves why some other less bloody alternatives could not have been found?

Students should look at the design of the situation they found themselves while within the simulation. Using the design questions, they should ask themselves what assumptions were being imposed upon them by the simulation. at This point, the teacher could help the students see that a as a game, simulation imposes a set of ideas, beliefs, and values on the players. The players can always reject the ideas, beliefs, and values of the game, but by so doing they are rejecting the game. Most people are socialized to be reluctant to do that. They may question the interpretation and application of the rules, but seldom the rules themselves. In this sense, simulation games are metaphors for paradigms. Paradigms define the rules for the 'game' of life. And, as such, people are reluctant to question those rules because it seems to question the purpose of life itself.

Students could begin to look at the simulation as a paradigm, and then use that as a platform to define and examine the paradigm controlling and guiding the conduct of World War One. Ask students in groups to attempt answers to the four design questions. After they have completed their initial discussions, have them share their ideas with each other in a general class discussion. As they decide upon a conclusion, have one of the students note the conclusion on the chalkboard. The response below are some of the possible responses the students might make:

What were the purposes of the simulation?

- to provide a heuristic which would guide the behaviour of students and thereby learn the realities of modern warfare.
- to act as a paradigm controlling and directing student perception and behaviour as they dealt with unfamiliar reality.

What was the structure of the simulation/paradigm?

- Students were divided into sets of antagonistic countries.
- The antagonistic countries were kept isolated from each other.
- Each country was organized in an authoritarian, top down manner.
- Information was restricted, and distributed to people as it suited those in authority.
- Those most affected by the decisions being made by authority were denied any meaningful voice in those decisions.

What are model cases of this simulation/paradigm (How might this simulation/paradigm be altered)?

Alternatives one and two are the ends of a continuum of political power.

ALTERNATIVE #1 AUTHORITARIAN

- Restrictions on the behaviour of Generals could be reduced, so that they have even more power to be ruthless and thereby win the war.
- Information should be completely restricted, so that people do not know the costs of winning battles.
- Strict laws must be passed that discipline both the public and the soldiers to be obedient and completely focused on victory.

ALTERNATIVE #2 EXTREME DEMOCRACY

- Information must be completely open to the people (and the soldiers), so that they know what decisions were made and what the consequences of those decisions were.
- Decision makers must be held accountable for the decisions they make.
- The people and the soldiers must be free to accept or reject the decisions of their leaders according to the dictates of their consciences.

What arguments explain and evaluate the simulation game system and the two model system described above?

Arguments explaining the systems:

The first model system is a military dictatorship.

- Duty and service to the state is the most important value.
- People are frail and fearful, and so must be disciplined and guided by the structures of the state: military, police, government, churches, schools, newspapers, etc.
- Security is much more important than freedom.
- The simulation system the students could be labeled a limited democracy
- This system is based on a paradigm which says that on occasion self-defence becomes more important than freedom of speech.
- The survival of the state (sovereignty) is the most important value and all other values must take second place to that.
- Accordingly, values like nationalism, patriotism, self-sacrifice, duty, etc are more important than freedoms and human rights.
- The end (survival of the state) does justify the means (the deaths of soldiers).

The second model system is a true democracy.

- Freedom and human rights are the most important values of society.
- People must be kept informed and given accurate information that will allow them to make meaningful choices about the behaviour of their society
- The state is the servant of the people.

Arguments (in the form of questions.) evaluating the model systems:

- Which model system best fits with the underlying paradigm of the history of World War I as recorded in most history texts?
- What are the beliefs and related behaviour of the model systems?
- What are the beliefs and related behaviours of the figures involved in World War I?

- Where is the best fit?
- What does not fit?
- Which model system best fits with the paradigms of the students?
- How would the students advocate dealing with the events of World War I if they were involved and responsible for the decisions?
- What beliefs and related behaviours underlie the decisions of the students?
- Which paradigm has the best fit?

After students have had an opportunity to consider the paradigms related to World War I, they will be ready to do a conceptual analysis of the overriding paradigm(s). Teachers and students brainstorm and list the major concepts playing a role in the thinking of the players in the lead up to the war, and its conduct. The teacher can also suggest concepts, and do concept attainment lessons as necessary; Students would begin to zero in on national self-defence as a justification for war. Through discussion, they might begin to see that the system of nation states results in a paradigm that presents national security as the dominant value in international relations. An analytical approach that would be useful here is concept webbing of the relevant concepts. Later, students might begin to do concept maps.

World War One Simulation Part Three: Dealing with the Consequences of World War I

The students then may simulate the Peace Conference at Versailles in 1919, where they decide how to conclude the war. Here they have the choice of being magnanimous or vindictive. After they make their choices, they can review the consequences of the actual Treaty of Versailles, and evaluate the decisions made in Versailles in 1919.

This simulation could use a conference format. The students could retain their country groupings, or they may elect to change countries for this round of negotiations. By this time it could be left up to the countries to establish the conference format they deem would be best to follow. Some format issues could be:

- who should (should not) participate?
- voting procedures?
- purpose of the conference?
- what power should the conference decision making processes have? (i.e. Should the conference decisions be binding on the participating governments or does national sovereignty take precedence?)
- determining the agenda for the conference.

In planning for their conference, students should also consider what issues they deem worthy of consideration at the conference. In effect, they would be planning the conference agenda. Some examples of issues they may consider worthy of discussion:

- responsibility for the war?
- reparations - who should pay for the war damages?
- future of prewar empires - who should be responsible for countries and areas of the world?
- prevention - what mechanism(s) can be created to prevent another catastrophe like World War I?
- what should be the response to the Russian Revolution of 1917?

Each country may agree or disagree with the list of conference topics selected; they may reserve the right to bring up any issue at any time. Once some of the basic decisions about format and agenda have been completed, students would then be responsible for negotiating a peace treaty that would settle World War I.

The Final Debriefing: Pulling Ideas Together Using the Various Thinking Tools Discussed So Far

At the end of this series of simulations, film studies, and reviews of history, the students will have collected a great deal of historical information. The simulation games have created a heuristic which make it virtually impossible for the students not to have assimilated the gist of this era. My experience with using simulation heuristics is that students who have played the game many years ago can still recall the game, its issues, the positions of the protagonists, the decisions they made, and finally the consequences of those decisions. The simulation heuristic is much more powerful in creating gists than lectures could ever be.[32]

In discussing the causes and effects of World War One, it would be helpful to gather a list of the basic concepts students have learned and used in the preceding exercises. The list might contain concepts like nation state, sovereignty, standard of living, international trade, nationalism, jobs, patriotism, national security, international relations, armies, navies, national power, aggression, conflict, balance of power, alliances, empires, industrial revolution, etc.

The class could be divided into groups, and challenged to concept web the class list of concepts. (They would be free to add other concepts they believe to significant.) Once each group had created a concept web, they would share their view of international relations with each other. At some point, they should understand that these concept webs actually represent paradigms governing the basic assumptions of international society in the early twentieth century.

Let us suppose a group of students developed a concept web which resembled the following concept web:

THE INTERNATIONAL SYSTEM OF NATIONAL RELATIONSHIPS

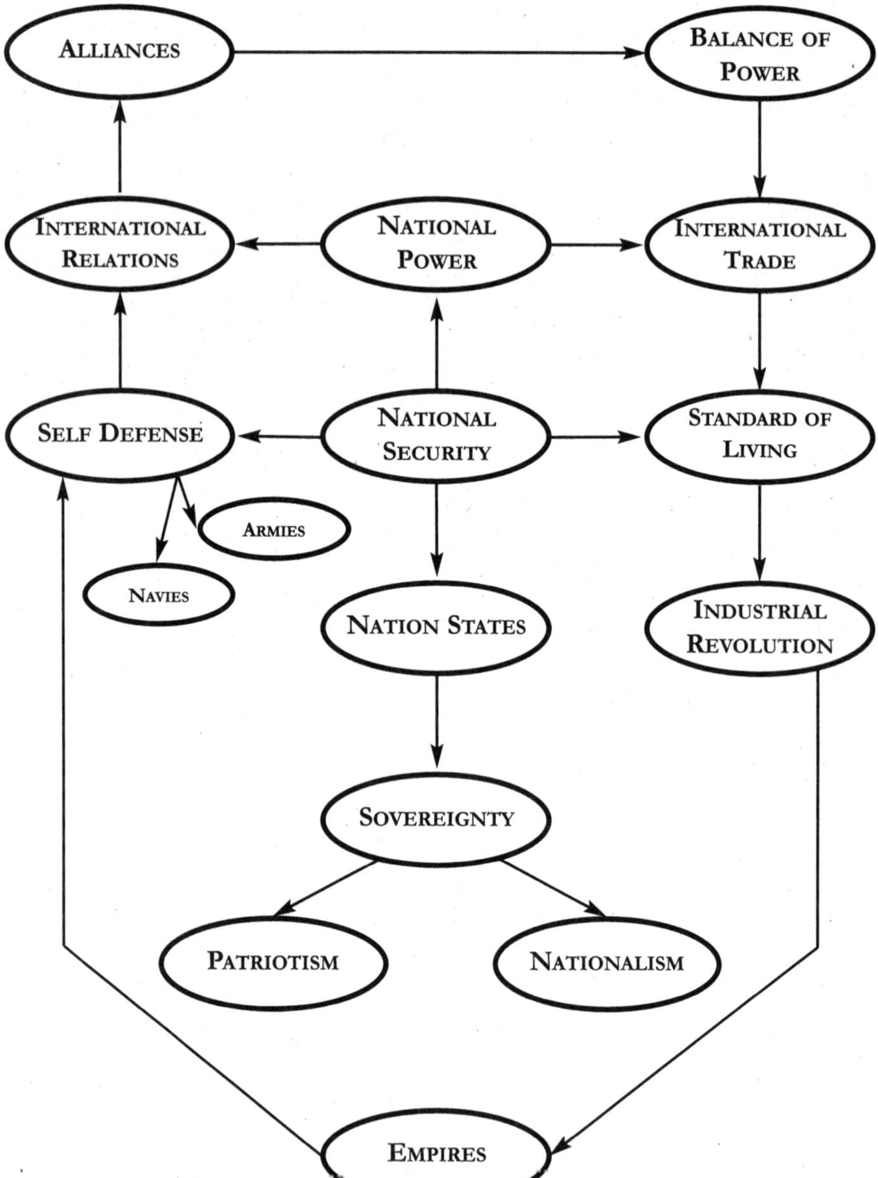

Fig. 10.10

With a basic paradigm of international relations defined, students would be in a position to apply the design questions to it. As may well happen in a classroom, there can be competing perceptions of what the nineteenth century paradigm of international relations actually was. That is not an unusual situation in the academic/intellectual community. What that does for the classroom is set up a dialogical discussion in which the four design questions can play an analytical role. Given the background students would have accumulated by this time, they would be in a position to develop preliminary responses to the four design questions applied to the international system as it existed prior to August, 1914.

The four design questions are:

- what is it purpose or purposes;
- what is its structure;
- what are model cases; and,
- what arguments explain and evaluate the object.

1. What was the purpose of the international system of relationships? Students could list a number of possible hypotheses using the stem "The essential purpose of the international system was to":

- maintain peace?
- provide security?
- maintain sovereignty?
- provide procedures for relating to each other?

2. What structures (and their related assumptions) within the international system were perceived by the students as they played the various simulations, researched the history, and discussed its implications. Some conclusions they might draw are:

- the most important issue for each country was the protection and furtherance of its sovereignty.
- each country employed representatives (diplomats) to meet and negotiate with others, but there was no formal, binding system for negotiating and settling differences between countries;
- there are a few voluntarily accepted rules about the treatment of each other's representatives;

- there is no international agency with authority to hold nations accountable for their behaviour;
- each country establishes a military to protect its interests;
- each country enters into alliances to gain the support of others in protecting its interests.
- a power balance may be established in which countries are reluctant to attack each other out of fear of successful retaliation
- regional power vacuums tempt nations to impose their power in that area

3. What are model cases of international systems? Based on their simulation experience and some of the associated research and discussion, students should be able to describe:

- the balance of power international system as it existed prior to World War I.?
- the League of Nations as conceived in 1919.
- United Nations?
- Pax Romana, Pax Britannia, Pax Americana
- Globalization

At this point students may wish to do some research on models with which they may be unfamiliar.

4. What arguments explain and evaluate the various cases of international systems? This could be done in several ways:

- In answering this question, students could be challenged to use the concepts they have gathered to critically evaluate the model cases of international systems listed above.
- Students, in discussion, should be encouraged to develop a list of evaluative criteria they believe could be fairly and constructively applied to the different cases they have defined.
- Groups could select one of the models above and do some historical research and a critical evaluation of it.
- There are a number of ways students could share information with each other about the cases:

- The class could hold a symposium in which each group presents its findings (conference style)[33]
- A report to some authority like the External Affairs Department of Canada, or the Secretary General of the United Nations, etc.
- It could be published as an academic paper on world international relations.

KNOWLEDGE IS A HUMAN CONSTRUCT

The Patterned Nature of Thought

Below is a concept web which summarizes thinking as we have been discussing it. If this were a seminar with an audience of teachers, it would be possible to develop this concept web through discussion. That would be the preferable option, because the web would reflect the contributions of all the participants. It would be a model of how they presently view the thinking process. In book format, the concept web looks much more fixed and inflexible than it is intended to be.

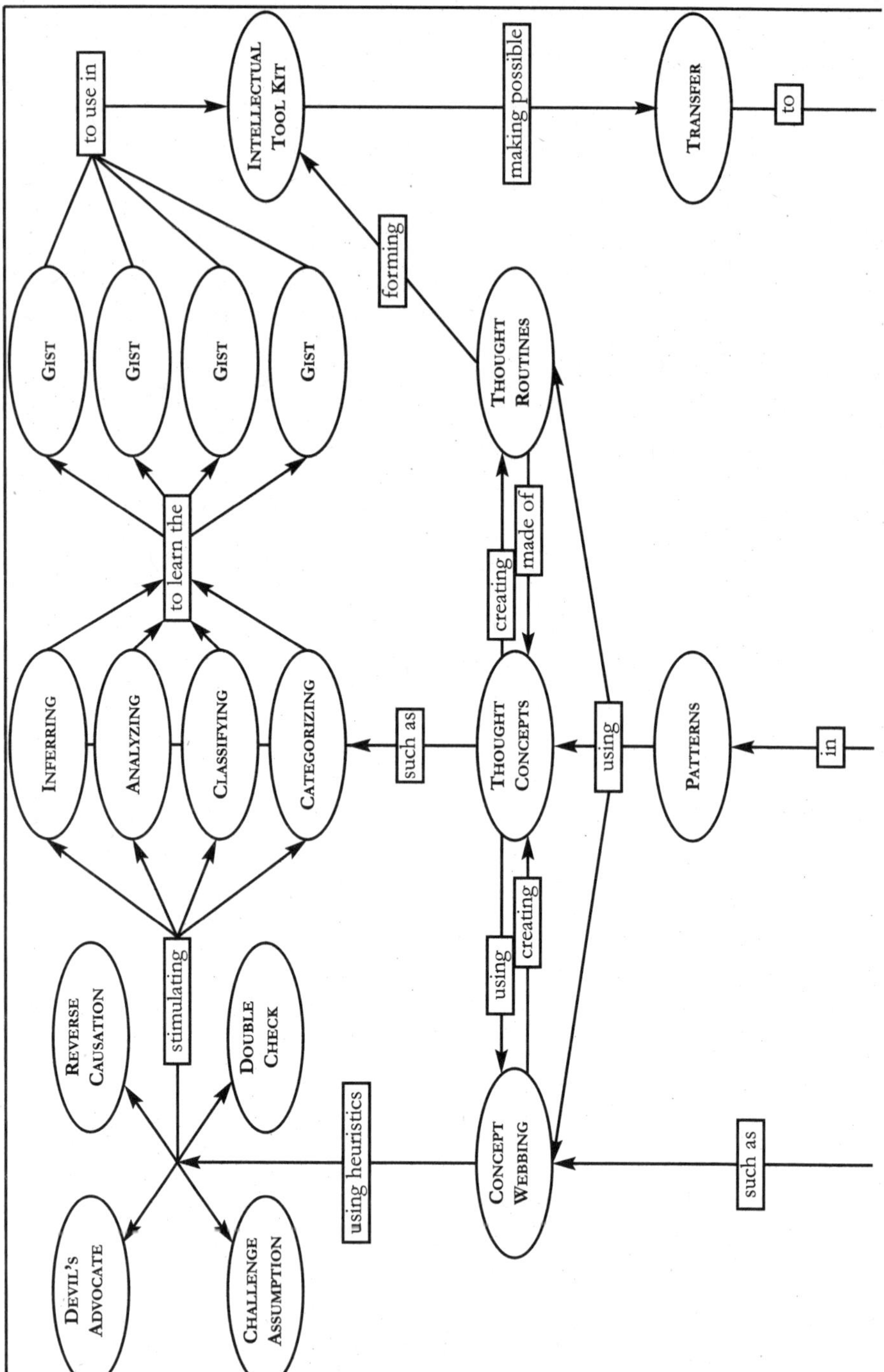
to use in
Intellectual Tool Kit
making possible
Transfer
to
Gist
Gist
Gist
Gist
forming
Thought Routines
to learn the
creating
made of
Inferring
Analyzing
Classifying
Categorizing
such as
Thought Concepts
using
Patterns
in
stimulating
Reverse Causation
Double Check
using
creating
using heuristics
Concept Webbing
such as
Devil's Advocate
Challenge Assumption

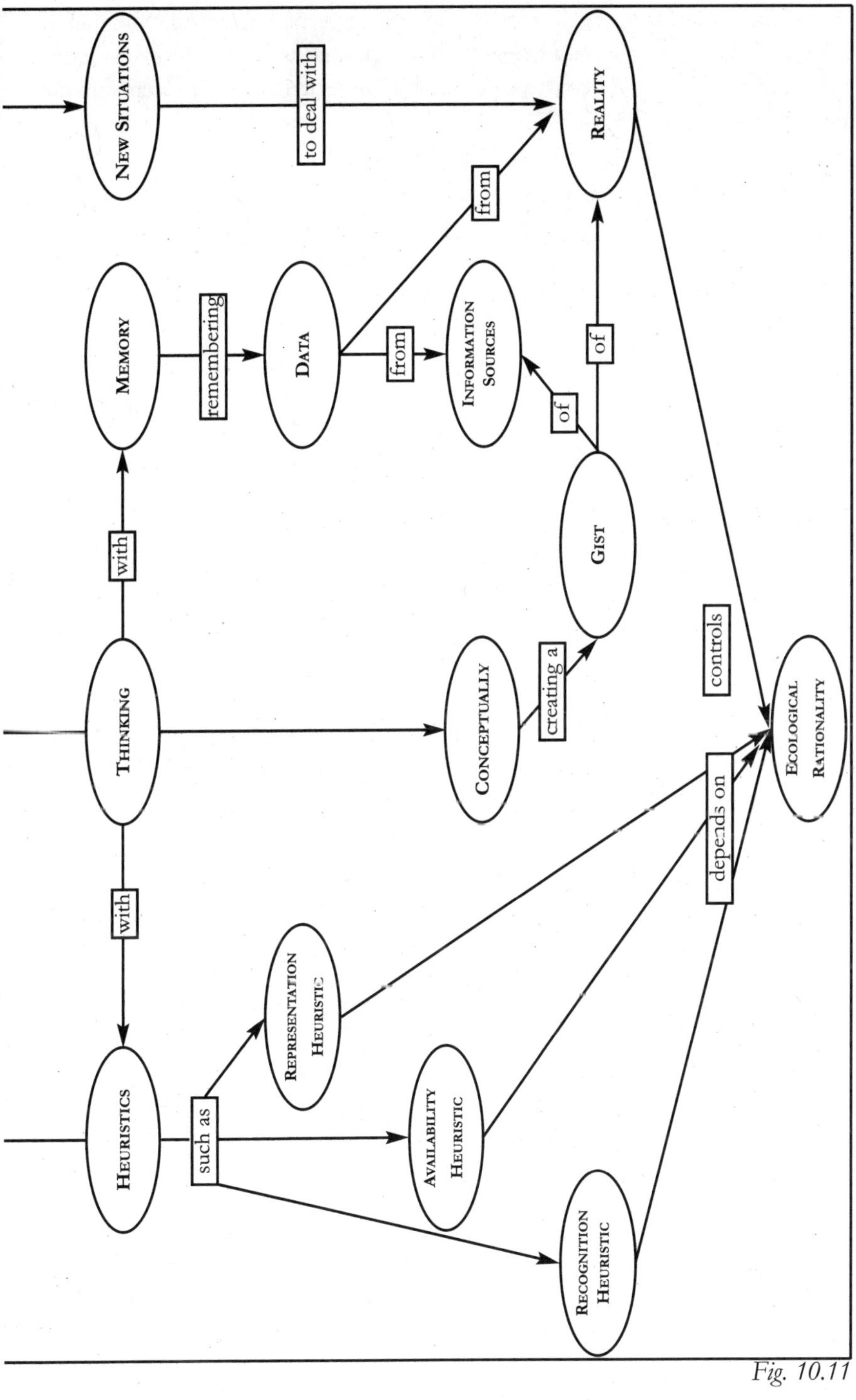
New Situations
to deal with
Reality
Memory
remembering
Data
from
Information Sources
from
of
of
Gist
Thinking
with
with
Conceptually
creating a
controls
Ecological Rationality
depends on
Heuristics
such as
Representation Heuristic
Availability Heuristic
Recognition Heuristic

Fig. 10.11

What the web above does is illustrate the patterned nature of thought. While every thinker's personal pattern will vary from what is described by the concept web, each thinker has developed a personal pattern of thought concepts unique to their experiences and needs. Most thinkers are unaware of having such a pattern, or that they are applying it as they think.

There are a couple of implications of this for education. The first is that learning to think requires learning to use a number of operations in conjunction with each other. It is like music: one note played over and over again is not particularly musical. Nor are notes played at random. Musicality is a patterned playing of notes. Thinking is similar. Teachers have to help students of thought learn to use thinking elements, just as students of music learn to use musical notes. It helps students conceptualize their thinking when teachers encourage students to create webs like the one above that model their thinking. The fundamental purpose would be to make students aware of their thinking. They could begin to understand their capacity for thought, and begin to analyze and expand their ideas about thinking. In this way, students can learn to introspect about their thinking, and thereby learn to be more self-evaluative about their thought processes.[34] It would be wonderful for students to begin to realize what absolute wonders their minds are. They should be encouraged to respect and honour their capacity for thinking for the marvel that it is.

END NOTES

1. This is really the process of metacognition, or thought about thought. In this context, students are capable of metacognition. It is a critically important process for them to learn and use.

2. Richard Pauls. "Critical Thinking and the Critical Person". *Educational Resources Information Center (ERIC).* ED 273 511 p. 6.

3. Monological problems are those problems with a single set of clearly defined assumptions that can be used to develop a clear, widely accepted conclusion. On the other hand, multilogical problems have a variety of acceptable assumptions which can be applied, therefore allowing a variety of acceptable conclusions to be derived.

4. D. N. Perkins. "Thinking Frames: An Integrative Perspective on Teaching Cognitive Skills". *Teaching Thinking Skills: Theory and Practice.* New York: W. H. Freeman and Company. 1987. p 47.

5. Richard Pauls. "Critical Thinking and the Critical Person". *Educational Resources Information Center* (ERIC) ED 273 511 p. 5.

6. C Wright Mills. *The Marxists.* New York: Dell. 1962.

7. In *Chapter Eleven,* we will be discussing issues related to dialogue on contradictory and valid moral claims. One of the tenets of dialogue is listening and appreciating the point of view of the other side. This is the process of dialogical reasoning, and is a fundamental skill for the resolution of conflict.

8. We will discuss this process in more detail in the chapter on values.

9. E. M. W. Tillyard. *The Elizabethan World Picture.* New York: Vintage Books. 1963. p. 25.

10. Adam Smith. *An Inquiry into the Nature and Causes of the Wealth of Nations.* Library of Economics and Liberty. Retrieved November 29, 2006 from the World Wide Web: http://www.econlib.org/library/Smith/smWN13.html.
1 V.9

11. Steven Schwartz. "Heuristics and Biases In Medical Judgment and Decision Making". *Applications of Heuristics and Biases to Social Issues.* New York: Plenum Press. 1994. p 52

12. D.N. Perkins. "Knowledge as Design: Teaching Thinking Through Content". *Teaching Thinking Skills.* Ed. Joan Boykof Baron and Robert J. Sternberg. New York: W. H. Freeman and Company. p 45.

13. Ibid p.64.

14. Ibid p.64.

15. This issue was discussed in detail in Chapter Five.

16. Noam Chomsky. Various interviews by various journalists. http://www.chomsky.info/interviews/1992----02.htm.

17. Simulations and simulation gaming are used by many organizations as a heuristic. They are able to portray concretely the interrelationship of a complex set of events and concepts so that thinkers can grasp the gist of the complex and use that gist as a basis for making informed judgments about issues related to the situation being simulated.

18. C. J. Brainerd and V. F. Reyna. "The Memory Independence Effect: What Do the Data Show? What Do the Theories Claim?". *Developmental Review.* Vol 12. 1992. p 181.

19. Saskatchewan Learning. Grade 10 *History Activity Guide.* Unit Five, Activity One. http://www.sasked.gov.sk.ca/docs/history10/activity/unit5/u5index.html.

20. As they gain experience with various educational methodologies, students react differently than inexperienced students do. In this instance, experienced students have learned most of the fundamental rules of simulation gaming, which allows them to anticipate what they need to be organized and prepared for success in the game. There is also a sense of anticipation, because students have learned to expect the uncertainty and crisis that challenges their thinking. Teachers with experienced students will need to administer less and less direction and guidance

.

21. Barbara Tuchman. *The Guns of August.* Presidio Press. Reprint. 2004).

22. Ferenc M. Szasz. *History News Network.* George Mason University. (http://hnn.us/articles/1328.html)

23. Lewis Milestone. *All Quiet on the Western Front.* Film. 1930.
There are actually two versions made; , if one can find a copy the 1930 version would be preferable to the 1979 film.

24. Alan Bullock. *Hitler: A Study in Tyranny.* New York. Harper & Row Publishers. 1962. p.379.

25. Bullock,p.380.

26. Professor. W. Selwyn. *Waterloo, a Lay of Jubilee.* Second Edition.

27. The distinction between these concepts becomes fuzzy. A mental set may be defined as a predisposition to accept certain, beliefs, behaviours or situations. An heuristic is a rule of thumb about how one ought to think and respond to ideas, situations, etc. The two will work in concert in many situations.

28. Martin Middlebrook. *The first day on the Somme : 1 July 1916.* Harmondsworth : Penguin. 1984. c1971.

29. Law is based on prevailing paradigms. This particularly true of laws which are established to protect the state from perceived threat.

30. Navaho/American game. See Sheldon Williams Collegiate for the book of reading in which this was described.

31. Adapted from Perkins p.64

32. Edward Nordhagan. *Balance of Power: World War I Simulation.* Non-published document 1972. I chose this simulation as an example because it is one that I first began using 30 years ago. I know students who played the game thirty years ago, and I have discussed their memories of the game. I have often been impressed at their level of memory concerning something that far back. It is unlikely they would not remember a lecture on the causes of World War I for thirty years.

33. What is meant by this is that the students should present their ideas as if they were seated at a conference table, rather than the more artificial didactic approach of students standing in the front of the class making a presentation.

34. The formal term for this process is metacognition or thought about thought. Most educational thinkers believe students cannot achieve this until they become mature formal thinkers. The concept web heuristic by making thought more concrete will undoubtedly hasten the process.

Chapter Eleven: Why Is Independent Thinking Important?

Logic is the morality of thought, and morality is the logic of action.
Jean Piaget[1]

Table of Contents

THE NEED FOR MORAL THINKERS

Why should independent thinking be considered one of the most significant goals for education? This is the question begged when independent thinking is selected as the central goal of education. What makes independent thinking so critical to the education of students? There are several answers.

Moral Autonomy Depends Upon Independent Thinking

One might begin an answer by noting that liberal democratic societies require people who can be autonomous, and autonomy is not possible without the ability to think independently. The problem with independent thinking and autonomy is dealing with the moral dimension of autonomy. Humans are social creatures, which means that their behaviour potentially can profoundly affect the lives of others. One dimension of morality is the treatment of one another in our relationships; therefore, autonomy must have a moral dimension to it.[2]

There are two fundamental poles to the spectrum of moral human relationships. One can simply accept the will of the group and follow its dictates. This end of the moral spectrum is heteronomy, in which individual morality is synonymous with the morality of the group, whatever that might be. The other end of the moral spectrum is autonomy, in which the individual independently chooses a moral stance from which to conduct her or his relationships.

It is one thing to argue that individuals must be morally autonomous so they are capable going their own way, morally speaking; it is quite another for them to live in a society, and play a role in the collective decision making of society. The collective will of people has a moral dimension as well. Of course, morally autonomous people can speak out in disagreement with the collective will and try to effect changes to that will, but at some point change may not be realized, and the morally autonomous individual will have to decide how to live with that.

Of course there are many possible moral stances that can be adopted. Humans have an enormous capacity to rationalize self-serving behaviour into acceptable moral codes. In a free, pluralistic society, it is difficult to impose a one size fits all moral code on everyone. People who have assimilated crude versions of post-modern attitudes will simply resort to the heuristic of free speech to justify their rejection of moral codes they disagree with. High school students are no different.

Such social phenomena impose a serious burden on moral education in the schools. Students reject moral stances they disagree with by stating to the teacher: "that's just your opinion.". It does not matter whether students actually verbalize the comment. It is powerful enough for them just to think it. This does not mean that students are autonomous. Paradoxically, many of them are heteronymous and simply reflect what they believe is the acceptable (cool) moral stance of the group with whom they want to be accepted.

Curricular Implications for Schools

Moral autonomy for individuals and for groups creates a nexus of educational opportunities for schools. Despite - or maybe in some cases because of scientific and technological progress - individuals continue to be faced with seemingly intractable moral problems. Many of these problems are current and relevant to the lives of high school students. Schools need to understand that the moral problems high school students find most interesting are the controversial ones, because society has not yet developed a coherent, established point of view on them. These are issues adolescents are more likely to be grappling with as well.

The Need for Moral Autonomy

Given these social realities, it is not surprising that the development of moral autonomy in young people is a controversial issue. Some see it as a dangerous and questionable notion. One challenge would come from some social conservatives who see this as liberalism and a steep slippery slope to social disaster. To them, liberalism has connotations of *laissez-faire* freedom, and a moral relativism in which anything goes. They believe such an approach to education to be socially and morally untenable in a civilized society. Other social conservatives realize conservatism is a minority viewpoint, which they see as a bulwark against the many foolish points of view allowed in a morally relativistic society. Given their minority status, they and their children must become morally autonomous so they can use the tools of independent thought as a conservative corrective to the ills of society.[3]

Despite the risks inherent in facilitating independent thinking, it is difficult to see how citizens can pick their way through the intellectual minefields of pluralistic societies without independent thought. All groups of citizens with a point of view find they need independent thought and argumentation as a means of protecting and extending their moral perspectives. Survival in the intellectual market place requires autonomous moral choosers. The development of an effective moral autonomy is one of the main themes of this chapter.

MORAL EDUCATION CAN BE EFFECTIVE EDUCATION

A second answer, one made throughout this book, is to say that independent thinking is a very effective learning tool. Students learn and retain more when they are placed in learning circumstances which encourage them to think their way through to their own conclusions.[4] Happily for teaching, students enjoy considering and debating open ended moral issues, provided the discussion is relevant and a dialogue. Adolescents find moral and ethical issues intriguing, because they offer scope for a wide ranging, creative dialogue. They also like moral issues because they shed light on issues and choices that bedevil adolescent life. Modern society has been constructed so that adolescents often lack opportunities to discuss moral issues with peers, family, and members of adult social institutions.

Self-fulfillment Is Enabled by Moral Growth

Self-fulfillment is another reply to the question of whether independent learning is a satisfactory goal for the education process. In the first chapter, the question was asked whether students should be educated for the benefit of society or for the personal benefit of the student. This is a complex issue, because it is difficult to separate the student's benefit from that of society's. An analogy might be helpful here. There is little question about the need for everyone to contribute to society, usually by holding a job of some kind. There is also little question that people have a dual loyalty while being employed. On the one hand, people work in order to earn the resources that allow them to share in the benefits of society. On the other hand, employees are expected to be loyal to and work for the well-being of their employer. A third notion is the idea that work should be personally fulfilling. When employees complain about the lack of fulfillment, they are often referring to a lack of independence in the form of personal decision making responsibility for doing their assignment. Some management theory suggests that without self-fulfillment, the employee loses his or her edge and becomes less and less productive.

Society tends to remain doubtful about the notion of independence in schools, citing the immaturity of young people as a reason for the lack of independence. Yet if you poll high school students and ask them what they consider to be the greatest shortcoming of high schools, they will point to regimentation. When high school students continue this line of thinking they will point to the freedom they see in being an adult and having a job. Yes, students are being unrealistic in many ways, but it does point to a fundamental reality about the aspirations of high school students.

Self-fulfillment is difficult to satisfy in an institutional setting, whether the setting is the work place or the school. It is essentially the same problem of reconciling the needs of the institution and the needs of the individual. Inherent in self-fulfillment is the need for personal growth. For human beings, hope is defined as potential for growth. Regardless of circumstances, people need to believe tthat here is hope for something better as a result of what is being done in the present. It is appalling to see the hopeless cynicism, frustration and rage crashing down on a high school class when students collectively can see no possibility of hope for that class. They can quickly decide what presently exists is unacceptable, and they are helpless to do anything about it. As student control diminishes, their sense of wellbeing and self-fulfillment diminishes, which in turn diminishes their attitude toward the class. Student attitude toward the efficacy of a class depends to a large extent on whether they believe they can generate an effective response to the demands of the class. From a student perspective, good classes are those where they feel they have some control of their destiny.

Learning to Take Personal Responsibility for Moral Growth

Student attitudes toward their personal responsibility for creating a community of scholars depend upon their sense of self-fulfillment. This applies to students as well as workers. Students and employees who feel unfulfilled tend to resist responsibility for their share of the problems in their communities. In some cases, they feel justified in doing whatever they can to exacerbate the problems they find themselves in. That may take the form of vandalism, insubordination, non-cooperation, etc. Often the behaviour can be self-destructive. Occasionally one hears a student say something like: "I hate that teacher so much, I don't care if I pass that class".

Blaming the victim is not the answer. If the response of institutional leadership is negative and blaming occurs, a vicious circle is easily established where discipline becomes increasingly authoritarian and the response becomes increasingly rebellious. Both sides lose respect for the other and the opportunity for growth is lost. This brings us to the major reason for independence in learning. Independent learners have the potential for all kinds of growth: intellectual, social, moral, etc. This chapter focuses on moral growth as being the most critical need in a democratic, pluralistic society.

Stimulating Moral Growth

Stimulating growth, especially moral growth, has been a long time concern for both the institutions of education and the institutions of the state. We did a brief historical review of some of the approaches to stimulating moral growth in the first chapter. It seems clear from the vantage point of the twenty-first century that free and independent people who are held accountable through the rule of law for their behaviour are more likely to achieve moral growth. Still, this remains a controversial point of view. Modern societies and educational institutions embedded in them have had their problems in successfully stimulating moral growth. Schools have struggled with many approaches to moral growth without coming to a widely held consensus on what works.

There has always been the temptation to resort to authoritarian tactics to force people to be good. Over the centuries, schools have repeatedly fallen into that approach with mixed success. For some, military schools with a 'boot camp' approach to discipline is seen the approach to use in inculcating moral behaviour. Criteria used by these institutions to define moral behaviour tend to be values like obedience, discipline, loyalty, honour, hard work, etc. At the other end of disciplinary spectrum would be the so-called free schools. These schools placed a high premium on personal freedom and responsibility. The belief was that moral growth will occur when students are free to experiment and learn from the consequences of those experiments. From each other and over time, they would learn the need for a social contract derived by consensus from those living under it. Criteria defining moral behaviour from this perspective would include values related to self-discovery, self-fulfillment, self-worth, freedom to be oneself, freedom to do what one chooses, etc.

Authoritarian and free schools have somewhat fallen out of favour. Schools by and large attempt now to be democratic in the sense of being authoritative rather than authoritarian. A democratic school believes in both accountability and freedom. Democratic schools, particularly in their approach to discipline, work to find a balance between accountability and freedom. Not surprisingly, different schools come up with different balances. In theoretical terms, democratic schools hold that students ought to be given freedom according to their maturity. Their maturity determines what they can be accountable for. For democratic schools, the values of responsibility, accountability, freedom, respect for self and others, etc. determine moral behaviour.

Like independent thinking, morality is personally chosen and not coerced. A very stringent test of successful moral growth is to examine the moral behaviour chosen by individuals when they feel free to decide what behaviour they will adopt. Another test is the ability of senior students to accept responsibility for the well-being of the school and classroom. Do senior students accept more responsibility, have more self-discipline, have more personal initiative, and offer more leadership to their school and community? Finally, what role has the school played in whatever moral growth that has happened in many cases? The reverse question needs to be asked as well: what role does the school play in the non-successes?

Relationship between Independent Thinking and Moral Growth

Part of the problem for schools is the limited influence they have on students[5]. So, where does this leave school programming related to moral behaviour? Actually, it leaves it in much the same place as its relationship to encouraging independent thinking among its students. Schools have to create conditions where students want to do both. It may be possible to teach independent thinking without moral thinking, but for the reasons cited above, it is not possible to teach moral thinking without teaching independent thinking. Students need to be independent thinkers in order to be autonomous moral choosers. Students have moral autonomy when they are able to make appropriate moral choices both when they feel free to do as they wish and when they are being pressured to do something they believe to be wrong, foolish, dangerous, or all three.

Values Serve as Criteria for Regulating Behaviour

By adopting values, people create sets of personal standards to use in measuring personal performance in some way. In this sense, values become criteria to both judge performance and outcomes. Criteria are rules or standards for making a judgment. A criterion can also be a predetermined test to gauge whether an outcome is what was intended. Values serve as our personal criteria for making and evaluating decisions in our personal and social lives. Values stimulate the often unspoken question arising after a decision is made: "has the action carried out as a result of this decision met the standards of my pre-chosen criterion (value)?"

Values Define the 'Practical' Realities of Life

Values are practical notions about how to live one's life. If an individual has truly assimilated a value such that it directs behaviour, then that value will appear to be 'common sense'. If such a value is questioned, the response may be one of disbelief at being questioned about the obvious. If the questioner continues the challenge, the response may well become defensive and dismissive.

For the sake of discussion, cultural/societal life may be categorized as personal life, social life, religious life, intellectual life, economic life, political life, and enforcement practices. This is not an exhaustive list, but it does cover some of major areas of society. So far we have confined our discussion of values to those standards which control behaviour. There are others. A range of standards could be beliefs, values, norms, and taboos. Together, all of these factors create a complex pattern of control within which people live their lives. It is against this background that peaceful societies operate.

These factors are not absolutes. They are balances, which vary from culture to culture and society to society. For example, players on a football team exist in a very competitive environment. They compete with each other for places on the team, and they compete with other teams for success. Yet they also cooperate with each other. Teamwork is just another word for cooperation. Players have to learn to balance cooperation with competition to achieve success.

Societies also have to balance values. In political terms, all societies have to balance order and freedom. People expect to be safe on the streets and roads. They place a high value on safety. In traffic, safety requires a high degree of order. At the same time, people drive cars to increase their range of choice: in other words, to have freedom. People who drive are also placing a high value on freedom. To maintain peace on the streets and roads, there must be a delicate balance between the values underlying freedom and order. An angry, frustrated driver is certainly not peaceful, and more certainly is a menace. Order becomes a question of finding the proper balance between competing values.

The same problem exists for the values related to equality and hierarchy. People have different skills, talents, and capital. Some skills, talents, and capital are rewarded more than others, resulting in an unequal distribution of wealth. Those with valuable skills tend to support the value of rewarding merit. Those who are poor tend to support the value of sharing. How is a balance to be maintained between those who have much and those who have little? This issue has caused much strife in societies over the centuries as they struggle to balance the rights of those who are wealthy against the rights of those who have little.

Considerations for Teaching Values

Values issues can be a good place to begin a discussion of peace related (human rights) issues. Value related issues are inherently motivating for students, because they are usually seen as significant to their lives in some way. Value oriented issues may be very powerful teaching devices in the learning environment, provided the discussion is based on respect for the intelligence and the morality of the students.[6]

Goals of the Values Component of Peace Education (Human Rights)

The overriding goal of values education is to help students move from moral heteronomy (the notion that one should believe various moral and ethical beliefs of society) to moral autonomy (Individuals have the capacity and responsibility to evaluate and select a set of values to follow). It is important to note here that moral autonomy does not mean individuals divorce themselves from religious traditions or other sources of values. Rather, what it implies is that morally autonomous people carefully consider religious or other values and adopt them on some reasoned or spiritual basis of acceptability. This is another aspect of independent learning discussed earlier.

Independent learning from the values perspective should result in young adults who are able to make independent moral judgments about their personal behaviour and that of the society in which they live. Values or moral education should give young people the motivation, skills and knowledge necessary to make good moral judgments. Since all of us often find sorting out moral issues confusing and complex, it should not be surprising that young people also have these difficulties. A second goal for peace (human rights) education is to create an attitude of sceptical open-mindedness among students that will make them amenable to thinking about values, unwilling to make up their minds about an issue too early, and willing to carefully test their conclusions before finally accepting them.

The Moral Nature of Young People

Some critical considerations related to the needs of students in developing moral autonomy. It must be remembered that young people are moral beings who need and absorb values to give purpose and direction to their lives. As mentioned before, they are interested in understanding and discussing the application of values to issues of concern to them and their society.

Developing moral autonomy is a life long process. Each person must take responsibility for their personal moral growth. Moral growth begins early in a child's life:

- In playschool, moral growth takes the form of learning to play cooperatively.
- In kindergarten, it takes various forms such as taking turns, sharing, and developing empathy for the rights and feelings of others.
- Throughout the years of elementary school, moral growth continues to expand as the children learn to understand rules and then learn to make rules so learning and play will be more satisfactory. (If one listens to ten year olds on the playground, their conversations will often consist of discussions about the rules of play often punctuated with the cry "That's not fair!")

- Adolescents recognize the importance of coming to terms with societal values, because they are now capable of abstract thought. They now understand values as ideals rather than rules. For many adolescents, ideals are much more difficult and demanding than were rules.
- Idealism allows adolescents to see shortcomings in themselves and society. This can provide an impetus to work out values positions for themselves. This results in the development of moral autonomy.
- Adolescents also know that understanding and finding an adult role in society where they can have some measure of independence is a critically important goal for them.

If values education is to be successful, the approach taken in any learning environment must respect the needs and goals of adolescents. If the approach does respect adolescents, then the discussion of values related issues can be a powerful learning experience. Value conflict is inherent to life and young people need to learn to resolve value conflict for peaceful living. (They usually learn value conflict tactics through modeling.) Young people will accept help in learning to take responsibility for individual and societal value decisions if they feel respected. If the issues are meaningful and relevant, young people will be motivated to constructively deal with issues such as social injustice, (economic, political, social) racism, environmental degradation, etc.

Approaches to Teaching Values

A fundamental problem for values education is the process of imparting values to students. Over the years, there has been much debate about the most effective way of accomplishing that goal. In general terms, three basic approaches to teaching values have been used: indoctrination, values clarification and the self-discovery of values.

Indoctrination

Indoctrination of values is the traditional practice of telling students what they should believe. It has been seen as the simplest and most direct method: just tell them and they will know. In practice, this has the shortcoming of easily becoming a harangue to people who are either uncaring or uncomprehending.

Values have both an emotional component and a rational component. It is possible for students to understand a value and not care (lack empathy) about it. In this situation, a lecturer is simply 'tuned out' by students, who continue to practice the values they care about. Other students may want to empathize with the value, but may not understand its significance at the emotional, existential level. After receiving a lecture, students may encounter variations of situations requiring the application of the value and simply not understand its need or how to apply it. Student intentions may be laudable, but their ability to apply the value is lacking.

Values Clarification

For a time, values clarification was a popular approach to teaching values. Advocates of this approach argued that students had assimilated values but did not know that they had done so. Some of the assimilated values might be negative, destructive values based on chauvinism, racism, narcissism, etc. Such values needed to be identified and 'clarified'. The assumption was that negative values could be confronted and eliminated so that constructive moral growth could occur.

The notion behind values clarification was to put students in stressful situations where politically correct beliefs would drop away to reveal students' true value positions. A controversial example of this approach were the so called 'life boat' exercises. A typical exercise would have groups of students pretending they were adrift in a lifeboat carrying too many passengers. Someone had to be sacrificed to save the remainder of the group. Who was it to be? The group had to make a collective decision. In one variation, the students would role play assigned lifeboat characters in an attempt to make the situation less personal. Other variations insisted students play themselves.

In either case, this approach presents serious ethical problems because the exercises create high levels of both personal and social stress. Hostility, anger, rejection, and self-criticism were usual effects of the exercises. Students can become so defensive that it becomes difficult to carry out the rational evaluation of behaviour which is basic to the values clarification process. Students begin to attach negative emotions to values clarification activities that warn them never to voluntarily approach this topic again. Such a situation hardly contributes to life long, independent learning about values.

Self-discovery of values

Self-discovery of values is a third approach which attempts to find a middle road between indoctrination and values clarification. The fundamental assumptions of the self-discovery approach are respect for the dignity of students, and respect for their ability to think for themselves. The strategy is to begin any discussion of values by grounding the discussion in the reality of students. Scenarios and case studies describing situations meaningful to students are discussed, so students can see the relationships between decisions, behaviour and values. Gentle role plays can be used to create scenarios which allow students to discuss the role values play in guiding behaviour. In both approaches, the critical learning process stems from the class discussions probing values issues. Such a discussion needs leadership from a teacher who can guide and elucidate the discussion without being intrusive or domineering.

People - especially young people - may not realize they are adopting certain values. Values are often absorbed more than they are consciously adopted. We may watch and admire the behaviour of someone and decide to copy their behaviour. A decision may have been made to believe something, but we are not very conscious of it, and we may forget the process entirely. Through some kind of mysterious alchemy, we now are beginning to understand as heuristics the decision remains until it is dredged up by some circumstance in the future.

There are many sources of values. Probably, the primary source is the family. Many family values are picked up so early in a child's life, the child tends to regard them as certainties rather than beliefs. Religious beliefs are another source of values that can have a powerful effect on behaviour. As a child matures, the peer group, various models (athletes, societal groups) may provide values to her or him. Adolescents go through an idealistic phase where they spend a lot of time searching for the perfect solution which conforms to their idealistic values. They are also become very intolerant of those whom they believe are not living up to certain value standards. Their search for the ideal often causes them to reject family or traditional values as being lacking in some way.

The exploration of the role of values can be guided by models of learning. The Learning Cycle for Concept Attainment discussed earlier can be modified to perform a similar teaching function for values.

Learning Cycle for Values

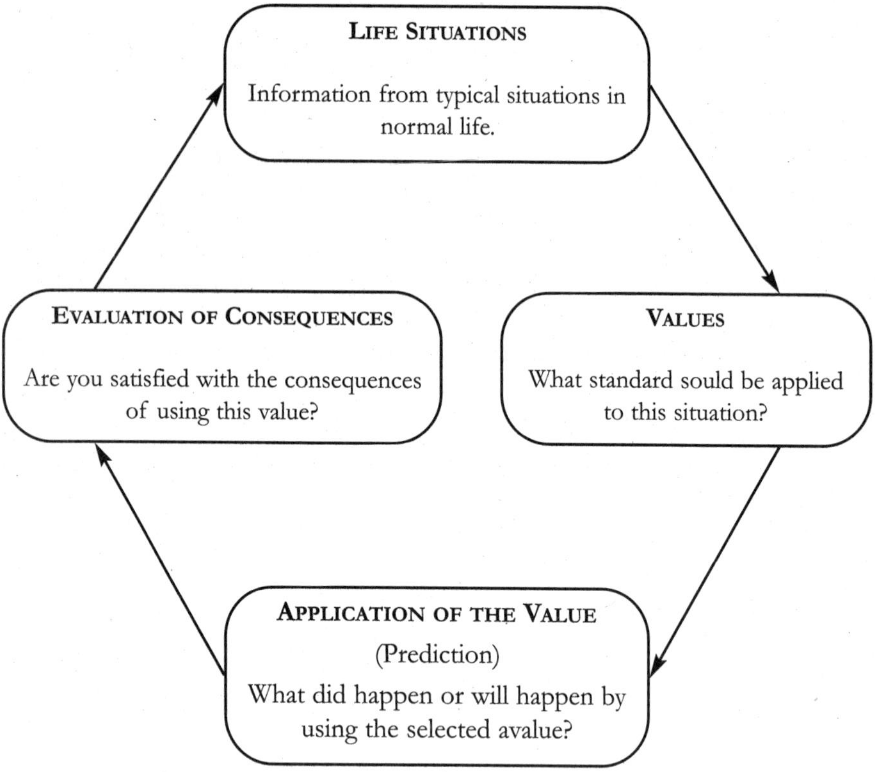

Fig. 11.1

This approach to values has mixed results as well. It has the benefit of being a good model for discourse on values related topics, because of the potential it provides for learning respect for different points of view, and for encouraging a dialogical approach in resolving differences in points of view and resolving values based conflict. The problem with this approach lies in its student centeredness. The problem is similar to the problems values clarification theorists had run into. Students resist values education, because it can appear irrelevant to reality as they perceive it. They dislike looking at catalogues of values which they either do not understand or can see no relevance to. They enjoy discussing moral situations which are values based, but they are less enthusiastic about looking at a variety of values and applying them to these situations.

DEVELOPING A PERSONAL SELF-AWARENESS OF MORAL REASONING

Students are products of a pluralistic society, and have assimilated many pluralist values and resist a 'one value fits all' approach because their heuristics tell them they have a better approach. Students have a lifetime of experience to draw upon in dealing with day to day moral issues. With some justification, they believe that they have experience because they have successfully handled (or seen handled) similar social situations somewhere in their past. You may recall that heuristics may be defined as intellectual rules of thumb. Moral thinking also uses rules of thumb which powerfully affect reasoning about moral issues. These rules of thumb can be found under categories such as courtesy, justice, morality, social relationships, sportsmanship, driving, conversation, business, and politics, to name a few. Each category contains a range of rules that have a specific application within the category, but in general terms contain the similar approaches to accountability for personal behaviour within society.

If one looks at sub-cultures such as that of adolescents, one would also find rules of thumb related to the treatment of others and personal accountability. Of course, not all of these rules of thumb are positive. Some of them can be highly negative and destructive. For example, some marriage relationships suffer under very destructive rules of thumb about power relationships between husband and wife. All of these relationships form the personal experiences of students sitting in classrooms, particularly senior students who are verging on adulthood.

The values clarification perspective is correct when it suggests that heuristic rules of thumb need to be considered by young people as they do moral reasoning. Some time does need to be spent in the classroom raising the awareness of personal rules of thumb. However, in doing awareness raising, respect for the dignity of students has to be the fundamental rule of thumb for educators. This brings us to one of the most basic moral rules of thumb: Do unto others as you would have them do unto you. None of this is rocket science (another heuristic) morally and ethically speaking. It is about day to day interpersonal relationships.

In helping students to conceptualize moral heuristics or rules of thumb, teachers could use a discussion grid *Fig. 11.2* to help students identify personal heuristics and evaluate their impact on their moral thinking:

Category of Social Relationship	The Social Ecology of the Situation	Heuristics: The Rule of Thumb Determining Response	Criteria: What Do You Want to Achieve? What defines success for you in this situation?
Participation in Sports			
As a player	Being involved in very rough play	**Retaliate** by playing rougher than the other players	winning? - pride? - courage?
		Ignore the rough play	- win by playing smart? - let the other players take the penalties? - focus on the game plan?
As a fan	Watching rough play	**Cheering** a successful rough check of an opposing player	winning? - pride? - excitement?
		Booing the play of the players	- to watch skilful play? - to watch sportsmanlike conduct? - excitement of skilful competition?

Fig. 11.2

The figure above is a description of participation in sports as a category of relationships with which most students would be familiar. The social ecology heading in the second column could also have been called a scenario, because it briefly describes a situation any participant might find her or himself. The next column refers to the rule of thumb that thinking participants adopt as they decide how to respond to the situation. At the same time as participants are doing fast and frugal thinking, they assume a set of criteria which determine when a suitable response has been found. Heuristic reasoning occurs very quickly and is quite unconscious. Fans in the stands mostly do fast and frugal thinking using self-serving criteria as they watch and analyze the play in front of them. The analytical chart (Fig. 11.2) attempts to slow down and unpack the process in a kind of freeze frame format similar to what film makers do.

When the material used is something as familiar as sports and cheering for one's team, students realize their beliefs in freedom of speech and their respect for the opinion of their peers. Such an approach gives them the capacity and support to hold a contrary position to a school based values analysis. More importantly, it gives them the capacity to begin independent thinking about moral issues. What they do is examine their bank of heuristics, and *voila:* they have an answer which has worked for them in the past. They have no reason to doubt that their heuristics will work in the future: all of this is a working definition of fast and frugal heuristics. This is where the work for teaching really begins.

The Role of Heuristics in Moral Reasoning

Moral growth remains the fundamental problem in all of this. Students are not finished products, and like others (including adults) are prepared to use pluralistic arguments in self-serving ways. Students are morally a work in progress. In the last chapter, we discussed heuristics as helpful methodology in dealing with the complexities of life. Like any tool, heuristics can be helpful or hurtful, depending on how they are used.

A dependence on heuristics (which we all have) becomes problematic when our thinking arrives at the evaluation stage. Since heuristics are so unconscious, they do not get a rigorous examination. Indeed, they are used because they allow for a 'fast and frugal' approach to problem solving, relieving the thinker of having to do a detailed analysis in order to arrive at a conclusion.[7] Research and personal experience shows the use of heuristics does lead to reliable conclusions.[8] Students may not know about research on heuristics, but they do know the reliability of their personal experiences. Given these attitudes, they are reluctant to do a rigorous self-examination of their application of values. It seems pointless.

Those who do values education and are interested in moral growth will have to respond to the heuristic phenomenon in some way. There is research on the effect heuristics have on the thought processes of people as they grapple with complex social, political and moral issues. This research can provide some insight into effective values teaching.[9]

The Effect of Bounded Rationality on Moral Reasoning

What we can know and consider at any point is bounded by the capacity of our minds. Citizens in a democracy face a large information overload problem.[10] They are expected to participate in social/political decision making, be good employees, raise families, and be responsible for their personal wellbeing in a variety of ways. Each of these responsibilities requires a large array of information and the forgoing list of responsibilities is by no means complete. Yet research indicates most people do not read newspapers or watch news related television extensively.[11] How do people who are ill-informed on a wide range of issues organize their ideas on those issues? People rely on judgmental heuristics to compensate for their lack of information.[12] Judgmental heuristics are intellectual shortcuts (rules of thumb in the last chapter) used to help individuals organize information and simplify the choices they face as they make decisions. Heuristics demand little information and yield dependable answers.

Heuristics create significant implications for teaching moral reasoning to students. What is the systematic interaction between the decision rules people use in reasoning about their choices and their political sophistication? It turns out that the relationship between principle and policy is only weakly linked.[13] The example cited in the research report argues that people may be in favour of the principle of racial equality, but would not support any policies to correct inequality. Research shows the relationship between principle and policy is no stronger among the well educated then it is among the less well educated.[14]

When researchers examined the reasoning of their subjects, they discovered that the "metaphor of a chain of reasoning" appears to be misleading.[15] Research indicates that people do not systematically work their way from the general to the specific. A theoretical view (one held by educators) of political and social reasoning suggested that a logical reasoning chain can begin with an ideological (principled) position or an emotional predisposition (affect), and use either as a basis to attribute reasons for a problem or problems leading to an opinion. This explanation seems a reasonable explanation of reasoning, but it was found to be wrong.[16]

Rather, people start at the beginning of an argument, immediately jump to a conclusion, and then begin to fill in the intermediate steps.[17] A logical reasoning construction follows this pattern: dislike A; blame A; and look for reasons to refuse support for A. An affect reasoning construction follows a shorter pattern: dislike A; refuse any help for A. There is no intermediate step in affect driven reasoning. Analysis in the logical reasoning and the affect cases appears to consist of an implicit explanation for the situation. For example, if the explanation consists of blame, then the conclusion will involve blame in some way. Dislike an ethnic group, blame it for its problems, and refuse to support any offer of help to it.

As noted above, people face problems of information overload. For most people, the information related paradox they face is not a problem of knowing too little, but a problem of not knowing enough.[18] This paradox is compounded by the unlikely expectation citizens will have formed clear opinions on a wide variety of issues, and are able to formulate carefully thought out opinions whenever there might be a demand for one. Citizens are much more likely to form opinions on the fly in response to situations as they arise. People do this because their working memories cannot hold information from their long term memories plus current information from the senses, and at the same time use all of that information to create a chain of reasoning. The more novel the situation, the more likely an intellectual bottleneck will be formed, forcing people to turn to heuristics as a way of making their intellectual tasks more manageable[19]. Given the inexperience of adolescents, it seems reasonable to assume they are even more likely to depend upon heuristics as intellectual crutches.

Fast and Frugal Reasoning

Let us return briefly to the role of heuristics in thinking. You will recall we discussed the use of fast and frugal heuristics particularly in chapter eight. In that chapter, we pointed out that there are a wide variety of heuristics that can be used, and we demonstrated the use of a few. Returning to the situation described in the above paragraphs, we can ask the question: what kind of heuristics do people use to help them make decisions about unfamiliar issues?

It is highly unlikely that students are aware of any thought processes they use automatically and unconsciously. Indeed, they are likely to scoff at the whole notion. Remember the point of heuristics is that they be fast and frugal. They are used because they deliver quick and accurate conclusions; they do so with a minimum of information and thinking; and they are ecologically valid in the sense that they deal with some reality the thinker has to respond to.

Below is a brief catalogue of heuristics that are likely to be employed. Students may not use the same heuristics, and they will not use those listed here, at least not initially:

Availability Heuristic[20]

- Making judgments based on what is available from an individual's experience.
- This is an ecologically valid clue for judging frequency; because in general, frequent events are easier to recall or imagine than infrequent ones.
- I will not vote for political party A because I can recall political party A making many bad decisions when it was in political power.

Representative Heuristic[21]

- Making judgments about some aspect of reality, influenced by what appears to be typical among the various examples found in the situation.

- This is an ecologically valid clue for judging the similarity of something novel by comparing it to other representative examples in one's experience.

- Movie maker X has made a new movie, and the prospective viewer decides it should be worth attending because the other movies she has made have been entertaining.

Recognition Heuristic[22]

- In determining which of two objects has the higher worth, if one is recognized and the other is not, then infer that the recognized object is more appropriate.

- In making judgments about the significance of one new object over another, an ecologically valid clue is to select the object that is more recognized over the less recognized.

- Singer A is better known than singer B. Infer that singer A is a better singer.

Take the Best Heuristic[23]

- In choosing between two options, choose the option which has a characteristic with the highest validity according to your selection criteria. If that discriminates between the options, stop looking. If not, try the next most valid clue until one is found that allows you to choose between the two.

- Using a minimal number of valid characteristics is an ecologically valid approach to making a choice.

- A young woman is considering how to respond to several young men in her office who appear to be interested in some kind of relationship. She is looking for someone with the potential to form a long term relationship. Her initial choice is a young man who talks about wanting to have a family.

Take the Last Heuristic[24]

- When responding to an unfamiliar problem, people tend to begin with the last successful strategy they used on another problem that appears to be similar.

- Using the last thing that worked in a similar situation is an ecologically valid approach to searching for solutions. If it is a solution, stop looking; if not, try the next thing and stop when something is found that works.

- Your computer is not working properly, you respond by trying the thing you last did when the computer 'sort of' behaved the way it is presently behaving.

Likeability Heuristic[25]

- When you like the source of a request, you will tend to do what is requested

- The acceptance of likes and dislikes is an ecologically valid clue for making choices.

- You are trying to decide which of two closely equal products to buy. You like one salesperson and not the other. It will be easier to buy from the likeable salesperson.

Dessert Heuristic[26]

- In determining whether a group in need should be helped, the following criteria determine the response:

- What is the source of the need?

- Does the need have an internal or an external causation?

- Whether or not a group is responsible for their misfortune is an ecologically valid clue for determining an appropriate response to their plight.

- Your response to the question of whether people plagiarize because they are lazy or because they do not know how to research a paper will guide your response to the issue of plagiarism.

In the course of normal day-today experiences, people do not have time to do detailed research from which they can draw systematic conclusions. Rather, they will turn to heuristics like those above - and others - for fast and frugal guidance in what to think or do about the various situations they encounter. This is a significant component in the informal, non-systematic thinking people have to engage in. Most times it works well by providing quick and appropriate responses to situations. Sometimes it does not.

Heuristics and Biased Thinking

One area where heuristics may be too easily applied is in the area of moral thinking. Can moral thinking based on the application of heuristics be the equivalent of prejudiced thinking? It would seem reasonable to suggest that thinkers who have grown up in an environment of prejudice potentially could apply heuristics based on prejudice to their thinking. In order to deal with this possibility, moral thinking, at some point requires some level of systematic, evaluative thinking. The problem with evaluating the role of heuristics in thought is they that work so far behind the scenes, consciously; people are unclear about how they arrive at their decisions. This in turn makes it difficult for them to understand their moral responses, and more importantly, track the moral consequences of their behaviour.

A Case Study on Human Relations

- *This is a true story. There was a man once who had a dog that barked at night. That dog barked and barked, and kept neighbours up at night. This man did not seem to care. He did nothing to stop his dog barking. So a group of neighbours talked about this problem - they could not sleep because of the barking dog. One man said "I know what to do," and without knowing what he would do, and without asking what he would do, the community gave its assent.*[27]

This story illustrates the application of fast and frugal heuristics, the use of values as criteria, and the need for some systematic thinking in moral decision making. I propose to approach this story using heuristic methodology, rather than an algorithmic.[28] Returning for a moment to the issues of teaching thinking, it is important to remember some critical issues. Thinking requires an issue of some sort as a reason to do any kind of independent thinking, hence the use of heuristic teaching. Teaching independent thinking requires that students be introduced to the idea of using chained reasoning. In other words students have to be able to assemble a series of thought concepts in a linked, intentional process leading to some kind of conclusion. Teachers can best teach this process by stacking their objectives (heuristics, criteria, moral decision making) so students can observe the various thought concepts being applied in a coherent process.

Since this is a story of normal human relationships within communities with which students have some experience, they will immediately begin to draw conclusions about the story using personal heuristic thought processes. In order to respond to the implicit issue or problem here, students automatically turn to personal experience for the information they need. This process will not be a very conscious one until they need to review their conclusions about the situation.

The concept web below (*Fig. 11.3*) is a visual, organizing heuristic to help students track the heuristics they automatically employ in determining their response to the man with the barking dog.

Figure 11.3 diagrams relationships between what people perceive is happening in the environment (barking); what is happening in the minds of the perceivers as they evaluate the owner's behaviour, and as they predict the unknown response of the owner. Missing from *Fig. 11.3* are the heuristics students employ as they think about their responses to this situation.

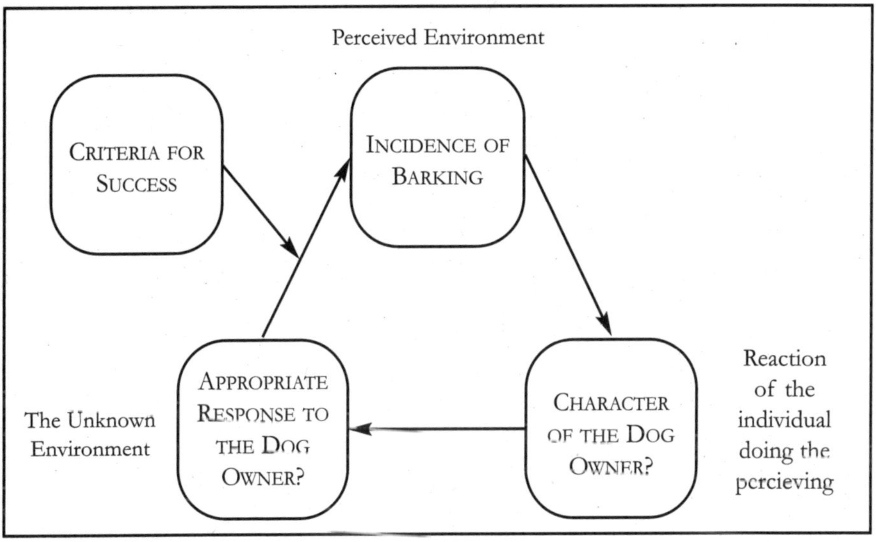

Fig. 11.3

In a class discussion, students could be challenged to suggest how they might approach this situation. The teacher could lead a class discussion beginning by asking students to think about the problem the dog owner seems to have with his dog. As the students make their observations ask them to explain the basis for those observations. Their explanations could provide some hints about the heuristics they are employing. Their answers and the probable heuristic could be placed on the chalkboard beside the "Incidence of Barking" box. Somewhat like the example in *Fig. 11.3,* the basis for the student's observations will likely be some version of the heuristic that they have used to reach their observation.

Now have the students offer a one word characterization of the dog owner. Once that has been completed, ask them to suggest what they would consider to be a pair of appropriate responses by the community to the dog owner. Ask the students to consider each pair and pick the most appropriate response. By doing this, students are forced to use their experience to create choices and their heuristics to select the best choice. Ask the students to explain why they selected a certain response over another. Again, this is an attempt to draw the heuristics that they are working from from the students. All of this could be placed on the chalkboard somewhat in the manner of *Fig. 11.4*

Applied Heuristics and student conclusions

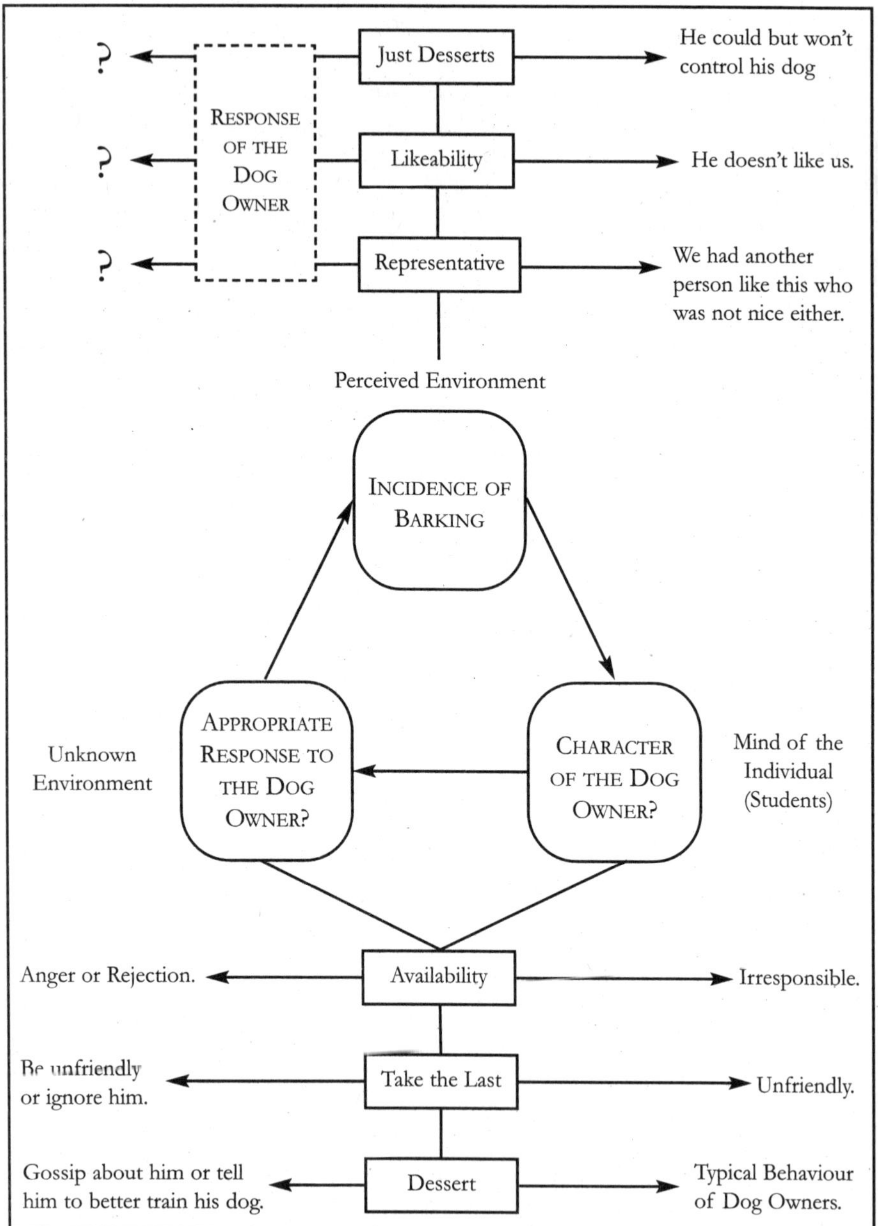

Fig. 11.4

When this section of the concept web is completed, ask students to reflect on what they assumed their main basis (criterion) was for success in this situation. You could initially solicit suggestions for discussion, or offer the following as a stimulus to discussion:

- Feeling superior to the dog owner?
- Winning an argument with him?
- Having his dog seized?
- Having the dog stop barking?
- Some other criterion?

Ask students to predict the dog owner's response to their approach to him. Do they believe it will be successful: would it be if they were the dog owner? After students have had an opportunity to think about the consequences of their criteria for success, ask them whether selecting different success criteria from those they assumed would change their approach (heuristics) toward the situation?

Now ask students to read the remainder of the story:

The man went and talked with the owner of the dog. The man did not talk about the dog. He talked about the neighbourhood; about the weather; and, about how the owner was. And the man asked if he could come back and visit. And he did, and they talked about the neighbours, and so-and-so who has been sick and needs rest, and . . . Before long, that dog did not bark at night anymore. Nothing was ever said about the dog, or the problem of barking at night, or angry upset neighbours.[29]

Ask the students to look at the situation from the standpoint of the Man-Who-Knew-What-to-Do (MWKWD) about the barking dog. Ask them to list what they think his criteria for success were. Then ask them to speculate on what he thought about the barking dog problem and the dog owner.

The Impact of Heuristics on Self-awareness

Moral reasoning is something done by people who base their thinking on two fundamental constants. The first constant is the personal. People make moral choices based on beliefs about their capacity to respond. The second constant is the social circumstances people find themselves in. Peoples' responses depend upon their social experiences. Students are no different. More about both can be found below.

By the time adolescents are able to form moral intent, they will have accumulated a bank of experiences which in large measure are used for self-definition. Moral intent is a significant part of self-definition. Students are often reluctant to try something new or rise to a challenge that seems well within their capabilities. The concept of heuristics may help explain the source of their reluctance to attempt new things. For example, the reluctance of many students to give up memorization in favour of independent thinking is explainable in terms of heuristics. Suppose students are offered a choice between a fact oriented multiple choice exam and an open book exam where they would have to respond to some issue with which they are unfamiliar. In considering their options, students would use fast and frugal reasoning via heuristics to determine their response.

> TAKE THE LAST HEURISTIC: The last time I did a multiple choice exam the wording of the questions was so confusing, I got a terrible mark. Multiple choice - no thanks!
>
> AVAILABILITY HEURISTIC: When I do open book exams I never understand the questions, so I cannot find anything in the text that seems like the right answer. Open book exams - no thanks!
>
> REPRESENTATIVE HEURISTIC: Every time I do an open book exam I get a lower mark than I do when I write a multiple choice exam. You can keep your open book exams!

Note how students interpret the social ecology of examinations from a personal perspective, and select criteria which determine the suitability of responses they get from their experience. In this case, marks received are the self-selected criterion, which determine whether a suitable response has been found. Marks received indicate when to stop searching for alternative responses. It is possible for students to select other criteria such as creativity, challenge, novelty but none of these meet students' basic social ecological needs for success and survival in the school and the home.

The point here is that past experience heavily influences the approach of students to current experiences whether it is music, art, athletics, public speaking, leadership, etc. In one sense, this is hardly surprising, but in another it is important because it is something students should become aware of and be encouraged to respond to as part of their intellectual awareness. Without some personal self-awareness of the heuristics they use, and the mostly unconscious evaluative criteria they apply to the heuristic process, students will have a limited understanding of their behaviour. With self-awareness, they may decide to change nothing about their lives, but at least they would have some opportunity for change.

Heuristics, Self-worth and Metacognition

Heuristics probably play a similar role in students' personal beliefs about their self-worth. When faced with personal choices which depend upon their personal self-worth criteria, and their personal histories, fast and frugal thinking will provide students with consistent responses, either negative or positive, about their potential. If students have an opportunity to become familiar with the notions of fast and frugal heuristics and satisfying criteria, they would be in a better position to judge the responses they receive from themselves about themselves. Then they would have the choice of rejecting the heuristic based response and attempting something else. This in itself could become a heuristic for students: should I 'second guess' myself on this issue? This would be an important addition to the intellectual tool kits of students.

FAST AND FRUGAL THINKING AND MORAL AUTONOMY

An example or two involving justice issues can demonstrate how moral heuristics might play out in the classroom. Students, many of whom are now receiving pay cheques, complain about the many deductions they see there. They are often annoyed at the amount of money deducted for income tax. If any defence of an income tax as an important and necessary social relationship is injected into the conversation, students quickly generate heuristics as they do fast and frugal thinking in search of ideas to attack the notion of an income tax. Such a class discussion can be tracked using an analytical model shown in *Fig. 11.5*.

CATEGORY OF SOCIAL RELATIONSHIP	THE SOCIAL ECOLOGY OF THE SITUATION (SCENARIOS)	HEURISTICS: THE RULE OF THUMB SELECTED TO DETERMINE A PERSONAL RESPONSE	CRITERIA: WHAT DO YOU WANT TO ACHIEVE? WHAT DEFINES SUCCESS FOR YOU IN THIS SITUATION?
DISCUSSION OF THE PRINCIPLE OF PAYING INCOME TAX			
WHO SHOULD BE TAX PAYERS?	High School Students who are working part time? Parents who earn middle class incomes? Business people? People on minimum wage incomes? Retired people on pensions?	**FAIR IS FAIR HEURISTIC** - Everyone should pay their share. **JUST DESSERTS HEURISTIC** - People are poor because they earn low wages and cannot support themselves. -Student live at home and do not need to support themselves. -Some people work hard, start businesses and create jobs. -Those that make lots should pay lots of taxes.	- Just taxation: Everyone should pay their fair share. - Justice means people should pay based on their ability to pay. - Justice means everyone should pay the same amount. - Students should be encouraged to work part time by reducing their taxes. - Students should be discouraged from working part time by increasing their taxes. - People should be encouraged to invest in business.

Fig. 11.5

The issue for moral thinking is to move students from reliance on heuristics as the basis for their moral reasoning to a consideration of overarching moral principles as criteria for moral decision making. Students should be encouraged to begin thinking about the moral principles that they believe should hold jurisdiction over society. In thinking about this, students could be challenged to describe a society under the sway of the moral principles they select. This question has the potential to encourage them to consider the consequences of any moral principle selected. It is important to remember that students, as they pursue moral questions, will constantly refer to their personal heuristics to support the fast and frugal thinking they do as they select one moral principle over another. For example, when people reason about issues related to injustice, the Just Desserts heuristic (which says people should be treated according to their level of personal responsibility for their predicament) will bias individual attitudes for or against just treatment of the class of individuals in question.

As a check on their moral thinking, students could then look at government spending as the flip side of taxation. Does this change their point of view in any way? What moral principles would they subscribe to when they look at taxation from the spending side? Again, students should be encouraged to look at the consequences of the moral principles they espouse. Would those principles result in the kind of society they would like to live in?

<table>
<tr><th>CATEGORY OF SOCIAL RELATIONSHIP</th><th>THE SOCIAL ECOLOGY OF THE SITUATION (SCENARIOS)</th><th>HEURISTICS:
THE RULE OF THUMB SELECTED TO DETERMINE A PERSONAL RESPONSE</th><th>CRITERIA:
WHAT DO YOU WANT TO ACHIEVE?
WHAT DEFINES SUCCESS FOR YOU IN THIS SITUATION?</th></tr>
<tr><td colspan="4">DISCUSSION OF THE PRINCIPLE OF WHO SHOULD BENEFIT FROM INCOME TAX COLLECTED?</td></tr>
<tr><td rowspan="2">WHO SHOULD BE TAX PAYERS?</td><td rowspan="2">High School Students?

Parents who earn middle class incomes?

Business people?

People on minimum wage incomes?

Retired people on pensions?

People who cannot work for one reason or another?</td><td>FAIR IS FAIR HEURISTIC

- Tax dolars should help everyone as equally as possible.

-Tax dollars should only be used for people and things that need them.</td><td rowspan="2">People should not be encouraged to become dependant on others.

- Society should help those that need help.

- Charity is best done by private inndividuals and the government.

- It is wrong to tax the hard work and initiative of individuals.

- There are things only governments can do, and governments should have the resources to do them.

- Students should be discouraged from working part time.

- People should be encouraged to invest in businesses.</td></tr>
<tr><td>JUST DESSERTS HEURISTIC

- People are poor because they lack the ability and/or the opportunity to find well paying jobs.

- People are poor because they do not improve themselves.

-People are poor because they do not try to improve themselves.

-People who make lots of money are best able to pay taxes.</td></tr>
</table>

Fig. 11.6

Moral autonomy depends upon the ability to candidly and critically introspect about the reasons for one's personal behaviour. Moral autonomy also depends upon personal courage in resisting unacceptable moral stances from peer groups and other agents of society. Since society is a collectivity of individuals, the morally autonomous thinker must be aware that heuristics play a significant role in the collective intellectual processes of people in society. These processes powerfully affect the moral autonomy of individual members of society.

One needs only to look at election campaigns to get a sense of that. Theoretically, election campaigns are a process in which the different points of view usually expressed by political parties are presented for consideration and choice by the electorate. In practice, the presentations are carefully crafted to appeal to the heuristics of the voter. For example, attack ads use the Take the Last Heuristic as a tactic, hoping that the last thing voters remember about a particular candidate is something nasty. Political slogans and metaphors attempt to capture the political agenda and in effect become a social heuristic. History is replete with successful examples of slogans hijacking public debate by elbowing aside other points of view. When this happens the slogan has successfully defined common sense for a majority of citizens.

The problem for people who are only able to rely only on fast and frugal thinking is the loss of flexibility in their thinking. Students and adults when faced with a slick 'spin doctored' argument are often at a loss as to how to respond. Spin doctors are clever enough to construct arguments based on typical heuristics from the culture. Slogans such as the "War on Terror" are effective because they correspond to heuristics such as Take the Last, Representational and Availability. When people hear propagandistic slogans, the heuristics they are likely to use are also likely to provide information reinforcing the slogan. Much of what they hear and see in the media and what they remember from the media suggests there is some kind of omnipresent danger 'out there'.

When a slogan can accomplish that, it also has the capacity to foreclose thought about alternative approaches to an issue, and thereby limits dialogue about the issues. Moral thinking and discussion must be dialogical if only because a dialogical approach to issues is inherently respectful of other points of view. Since moral issues are complex and multilogical, the search for meaning requires sharing from a variety of points of view. Sharing is more likely to occur when it is done in an atmosphere of mutual respect.

Understanding and Evaluating Moral Claims

People grow up with some kind of moral code, which they have assimilated from family, community, and social groupings of one kind or another. For most people, these kinds of moral codes have an ideological cast, mostly from a political or religious perspective. These ideologies contain a variety of value claims which are used as criteria to define responses to social reality in one way or another.

Recall that C Wright Mills argued that peoples' beliefs can be placed at one of the vulgar, sophisticated or critical levels of thinking.[30] Mills argued that people whose belief systems were at the vulgar and sophisticated levels react defensively in their approach to ideas that appear to contradict their point of view.[31] Their response tends to be one of winning a debate, rather than a dialogical approach focusing on finding as much truth as possible. Much of partisan political belief falls into the vulgar and sophisticated levels of thinking.

The problem for most people is an inability to refine their value claims so they become critically defensible. Before moral thinking can be autonomous, people have to form moral stances which they have critically reviewed and which they feel secure enough about to allow critiques from others who may have a somewhat different moral code. In C Wright Mills' terms, the individual moves his or her personal ideological construct from the vulgar to the critical, and by doing so comes to feel comfortable and secure enough to enter into dialogue with others.

Moral Reasoning

To some extent, moral reasoning requires that people up their complete reliance on fast and frugal thinking. It is not practical to say people should completely give up fast and frugal thinking given the exigencies of life. The pace of life would become unacceptably slow without fast and frugal thinking. Having recognized that reality, it is critical that students be able to perceive those issues of a moral nature which require more than fast and frugal thinking, at least in an initial contact with the issue. The wellbeing of students and those around them depend upon their success at being able to make these distinctions.

Empathy and Moral Criteria

Moral issues can be very subtle since they involve consequences for other people in the present and into the future. Sometimes it is difficult to perceive the moral dimensions of an issue. Moral thinkers develop empathy both for the wellbeing of others and for themselves. Empathy encourages people to take the necessary second look, which may reveal the moral issues at stake in various situations. Still, empathy is not enough. One may be empathetic and yet miss the critical moral issues.

Moral perception requires the application of criterion referenced thinking. Such thinking is based on the understanding and application of those widely accepted rules or standards (criteria) used to provide consistent bases for making judgments about some aspect of reality. Moral thinkers use moral criteria to identify the moral component in the many situations they encounter in life. But the use of criteria does not stop there. When the thinking of a morally autonomous person moves on to decide upon appropriate actions and goals, moral criteria are used to define both ends and means.

Moral Reasoning as the Basis for Making Moral Choices

For educators, there are two issues are paramount in teaching moral reasoning. The first is motivating students to want to reason morally, and the second is to provide students with an effective methodology to do it. Empathy plays a large role in the formation of motivation. Empathy is more likely to be encouraged and developed when moral scenarios are used with which students can identify. While empathy is important, students also need to be critical thinkers, not in the sense of being callous but in the sense of being able to look at situations realistically and clearly to see what is actually there not what they or believe is there. Students need to be familiar with the variety of logical procedures that enable people to be objective in their moral decision making. Most students will have to learn these procedures. It is tempting to approach the teaching of these procedures algorithmically, because they are in some sense algorithms. Such a temptation should be resisted, because while the procedures are important, what is more important is the willingness to personally adopt some of the procedures and use them as part of the life long learning process.

Syllogisms are the Building Blocks of Moral Argumentation

Moral reasoning will build on the various independent thinking procedures developed in previous chapters. A heuristic teaching approach would be to turn to syllogistic reasoning as a place to begin a consideration of moral reasoning. Students already use truncated forms of syllogistic reasoning. They hear truncated syllogisms everyday of their lives. Deductive syllogisms (See *Chapter 7*) are a natural jumping off point in moral reasoning, and in much of our thinking about other non-moral but otherwise significant issues (one could argue that all issues are moral in one way or another). People constantly generate major premises in a variety of forms such beliefs, opinions, or points of view about something. One hears people use premises in this sense, as in: "I think that was a really bad idea." Other sources of deductive premises are thought concepts such as generalizations, inferences, hypotheses, and theses. (See *Chapter 6* on thought concepts). People routinely use their personal heuristics to generate generalizations about one thing or another. Many of the major premises people use are in reality value claims used to justify points of view on moral issues.

A Heuristic Teaching Approach to Moral Reasoning in the Classroom

An actual example of something controversial, the possible legalization of marijuana, could be used to begin a conversation with students about relationships between acceptable social policy, personal choice and moral behaviour. Students could be encouraged to think about this complex and controversial set of interrelationships as laid out in *Fig 11.7*:

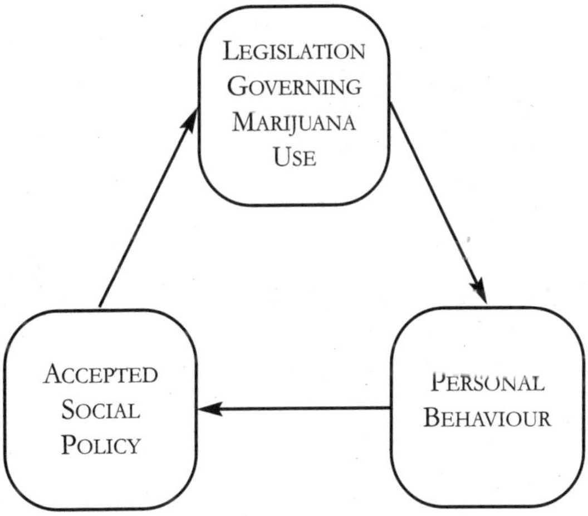

Fig. 11.7

Generating Major Premises/Moral Claims

This could begin as a class discussion about the propriety of legislation restricting the behaviour of citizens of a country. Out of necessity, discussions of this nature have to spend time generating (brainstorming) ideas about the issue. Students will not have spent much time formally thinking about the issue. They need time to collectively gather their thoughts and share their ideas in 'piggy back' fashion.

At this point in the information gathering process, students will turn to their personal heuristics for information, both as background and support. What the teaching process should hope to accomplish is to help students understand and respect the utility of both heuristics and formal moral reasoning. The use of personal heuristics (rules of thumb) contributes to the creativity, personal independence, and freedom of thought of each individual. The formal moral reasoning in this exercise can contribute to the need for the personal accountability of one's thinking and behaviour and the need for careful collective thinking, so that social policies generated are more helpful than hurtful to society.

In the course of discussing this issue, it is possible major premises or moral claims like the following might be expressed by students. Often the moral claims will be expressed as questions or in some other form, which lacks clarity. Students should be encouraged to reformulate their viewpoints into value claims without having them misrepresented:

- So, what's wrong with smoking a little pot?
  (There is nothing wrong with smoking marijuana.)
- Some people have to use marijuana as medicine.
  (People have a right to use marijuana if they need it for their health.)
- Marijuana is addictive and leads to other drug use.
  (Marijuana should remain a controlled substance because of its health risks.)
- Government does not have the right to tell people how to live their lives.
  (People in a free society have the right to decide how to live their lives.)
- If cigarettes are OK, then what is wrong with smoking marijuana?
  (Legislative double standards reduce respect for government.)
- Governments never pass laws that get it right.
  (Legislation ought to improve society, not make it worse.)

This could be something of a typical response from a senior high school class. Their responses are likely to be biased in favour of individual freedoms, and somewhat sceptical of interference by outside authorities. In order to set up a dialogue about legalization, the teacher might ask students to imagine what the value claims are of people who are not in favour of legalization. Again, students should be able to turn to their personal heuristics to retrieve some possible responses.

Note: It is important that this exercise remain within student intellectual control as much as possible. The teacher's role here is to be an unobtrusive road map, guiding students from one stage of the moral reasoning process to another. The teacher should not define the road map now. That can be done later, as a kind of reminiscence of how the whole "legalization of marijuana" discussion was handled. That way, students are more likely to see the general train of thinking and understand how each stage contributed to the final moral decision.

Returning to the marijuana discussion, students might generate the following ideas:

- Buying marijuana makes motorcycle gangs more rich and powerful.
  (Contributing to criminal behaviour is wrong.)
- Marijuana smoking can cause cancer just like cigarettes do.
  (It is wrong to allow people to do something like smoking marijuana, because of the serious health risks involved.)
- Governments can tax marijuana like they do with alcohol, and make lots of money.
  (This is a good way to raise money to do other good things in society.)
- Smoking marijuana and driving is as dangerous as drinking and driving.
  (It is wrong to allow people to do something that will make the highways even more dangerous.)
- People would rather smoke pot than deal with the problems in their lives.
  (It is wrong to encourage people not to deal realistically with their problems.)

Discussions such as the marijuana discussion above could be wider ranging by including other categories of moral issues. For example, students might be interested in exploring similar social policy issues such as prohibition, regulation of tobacco production and use, etc. The teacher could be helpful in this situation by suggesting broad categories of social situations and then encouraging students to suggest related major premises (moral claims). Some examples of social situations on which students might have opinions to offer are driving, medicine, military, sports, advertising, dating, jobs, money, government, etc. Students could be encouraged to create a concept web of moral issues they believe are of consequence, and use them as a springboard for moral explorations.

Using Minor Premises to Evaluate Major Premises

Unsubstantiated major premises are easy; the work begins when one has to generate valid minor premises to test the claims of major premises. Minor premises are the criteria against which major premises are evaluated. Facts are usually the first criteria used to evaluate whether a major premise is accurate factually. In terms of the facts, does the major premise make accurate predictions; is it valid and can it be said to be truthful? If the syllogism fails the fact test, it is over for that syllogism. If it passes, then it is ready for more testing.

Complex multilogical problems like the legalization of marijuana issues usually contain a variety of value claims. In this case, there are also value claims about the ability of government to legislate wisely, people's rights to free behaviour ,and claims about taxation policy. These issues are valid, and could/should be pursued by students as they consider the legalization issue. For now, we will look at the narrower issue of the health effects of marijuana. In the classroom, students should be encouraged to decide for themselves what the critical value claims are. They may decide there are one or more overriding value claims, and the other are subsidiary. In this case, the two value claims create a dialogue because they are contradictory.

People should be allowed to smoke marijuana because it is not harmful to their health.	**It is wrong to allow people to do things like smoke marijuana, because there are serious health risks involved.**
-Evidence supporting the major premise -Evidence contradicting the major premise	-Evidence supporting the major premise -Evidence contradicting the major premise

Fig. 11.8

Factual Evaluation

At this point, students need to do some research to discover what the factual evidence says about the health impacts of using marijuana. What do the facts say about the health effects of marijuana use? Are predictions about health effects accurate and valid? Do the facts support any conclusion that could be taken as truth about marijuana use? It should be noted here that this approach provides students with a precise framework to use as a guide for their research. The syllogism provides a system (in the sense Perkins uses it: see *Chapter Ten*) that guides student thinking.

When students have completed examining the factual minor premises, they should have an opportunity to examine and discuss (evaluate) what they know about the legalization issue so far. In their opinions, do the value claims pass the fact tests? If they do, they could move on to the next minor premises. Let us assume for the sake of argument that one does and one does not. The value claim "It is wrong to allow people to do things like smoke marijuana because there are serious health risks involved" is found to be factually acceptable while the value claim "People should be allowed to smoke marijuana because it is not harmful to their health" fails the factual test. In this procedure, the first value claim could go on to be subjected to the logic tests.

Note: The teacher could set this entire procedure up as a dialogical exercise as well as a moral reasoning exercise. In that case, students could be in two large groups, one group in favour of legalization and one group against it. Both groups could then pursue their moral reasoning to its logical conclusion. The students in favour of legalization could now think about succeeding moral claims related to government policy given that marijuana appears to have health risks. An example of such a value claim might be "People in a free society have the right to decide how to live their lives." Students could begin to test this value claim against various minor premises.

Logical Evaluation

Logic is the next criteria to use in evaluating a major premise such as "it is wrong to allow people to do things like smoke marijuana because there are serious health risks involved" or "people in a free society have the right to decide how to live their lives". Logically, does the major premise make sense, does it seem reasonable, do the supporting premises relate, and do the conflicting premises relate to the major premise in some way? If the syllogism fails the logic test, then it will have to be revised in some way or be discarded. If it passes the logic test, then it is ready for other tests.

Evaluation by Democratic Political Criteria

Many major premises have the potential to affect other people. If it does, then these people may have legitimate concerns about its impact on them. The reality of this situation is that the major premise will have to pass democratic political criteria before it will be acceptable to society. For example, the rule of law tests: Is the proposed policy constitutionally legal; will everyone be treated the same under this policy; have those with concerns one way or another been given the opportunity to clearly express their viewpoints on the issue; will a majority of citizens accept and support the policy; and will the policy meet the requirements of the Charter of Rights and Freedoms?

Both value claims on the legalization of marijuana will face very serious tests here. For example, how should a government proceed if there are two strong minorities, one in favour and another opposed? How should issues like safety on the highways be factored into this discussion? Students from both sides of the issue should be encouraged to use the broad issues above as a template for generating as many social policy questions as they can think of. It would be useful to hold a brainstorming exercise here where students 'piggy back' on each other's ideas. These questions should then be used as tests.

Students might produce something like that found in *Fig. 11.9.*

	People in a free society have the right to decide how to live their lives.	**It is wrong to allow people to do things like smoke marijuana because there are serious health risks involved.**
Will everyone be treated the same under this policy?	Yes, because everyone is free to choose whether they want to use marijuana or not. No, because non-smokers in public places will be affected by second-hand smoke. No, because people who drive may not have the opportunity to determine the safety of their trip.	Yes, because no one can legally use marijuana. No, for those people whose medical issues are helped by the use of marijuana.
Have those with concerns about this legislation been given the opportunity to clearly express their viewpoints on the issue?	No, because the bias of the political culture has consistently denied those in favour of recreational marijuana use a fair hearing.	Yes, because there has been a public debate about the health hazards of tobacco and marijuana for the past thirty years.
Will a majority of citizens accept and support the major premise?	No, because polls suggest that a majority of people continue to be opposed to the use of marijuana and tobacco.	Yes, because polls suggest that a majority of people would continue to support a legal ban on marijuana use.
Does the premise meet the requirements of the Charter of Rights and Freedoms?	Yes, because the Federal Government has the right to make and enforce this law and because no group in this legislation is singled out for special treatment.	Yes, because the Federal Government has the right to make and enforce this law and because no group in this legislation is singled out for special treatment.

Fig. 11.9

Students should hold a class discussion in which they evaluate the results of the political tests above. Has the "People should be free . . . " value claim passed the political test? Can it be substantiated that cigarette and marijuana laws constitute an unacceptable infringement on freedom? As far as the " It is wrong to allow people to do . . . " value claim is concerned, has the government received the political right to continue to deny people the right to smoke marijuana?

Students will have to come to a decision as to whether the two value claims have passed the political tests.

Once the political tests are out of the way, students will have to determine what the underlying moral claims of both value claims are. The first moral claim might be that governments do not have the right to unduly limit the freedom of their citizens. The second moral claim might be that governments have a right to protect their citizens from dangerous substances. Each moral claim needs to be subjected to moral tests to determine their moral validity.

PRINCIPLE TESTING THEORY

Four moral tests are used to examine the underlying moral principles involved in any proposed action. They provide students (and others) with a good beginning point for practicing moral evaluative procedures.

The Universal Consequences Test

The first moral test is the Universal Consequences Test.[32] This test asks what society would be like if everyone practiced the behaviour advocated by a moral claim. If it is wrong for everyone to adopt the behaviour based on a moral claim, then justice would say it is wrong for one person to adopt the behaviour as well. It may appear not to matter if one person throws garbage onto the street, but it would quickly appear to be wrong if many people did so. Therefore, the individual may not throw garbage on the street either.

If the moral claim in question passes the Universal Consequences Test, then it can move on to the next moral test. But if it fails the Universal Consequences test, the moral claim must be abandoned and a different moral claim needs to sought. The new claim would also have to be subjected to this and succeeding moral tests.

The New Cases Test

Suppose one is confronted with a situation where the facts suggest a certain moral claim can be used to justify one's behaviour. Someone has been convicted of first degree murder, and one's moral judgment leans toward the moral principle of equivalency. The moral claim might be that a person who murders must forfeit his or her life. The New Cases test requires the seemingly acceptable moral principle used in the first case be subjected to other similar and relevant cases, in order to determine whether it remains acceptable in the new situation.[33] If it seems wrong in the new case, it is likely to be wrong in the first case as well. The new case has to be vulnerable in the sense that it should be something one cares enough about to make one more critical of the moral judgment used in the first case. An individual may be strongly in favour of capital punishment as a deterrent to crime, but disagrees with it being applied to a member of his family. The new case, the family, is vulnerable in the sense that the individual cares much more about the person known than those unknown. The moral test is whether the moral principle should rightly be applied to his family. If it is wrong in that case, it is wrong in the other case.

It is important to understand that a principle may not necessarily be acceptable, despite having passed two moral tests. In terms of acceptability, all we can do is subject moral principles to as many moral tests as we can conceive. If it passes all those tests, we may tentatively conclude it is acceptable. Acceptability pertains only as long as a moral claim continues to pass moral tests.

The Role Exchange Test

The Role Exchange test asks individuals to imagine how they would feel if they were being hurt in some way by the unthinking moral claims of others.[34] Suppose your car will not start and you really need to get down town for a job interview. Your brother's new car is sitting on the driveway and the keys are in the house. Your brother is very concerned about the care of his new car. You wonder if it would be alright to borrow it for the morning, but he cannot be reached for permission. The moral test here is: how would you feel if it were your car? If you believe that the treatment you propose to inflict on others would be morally wrong if it were inflicted on you, then it must be assumed such treatment is morally wrong for everyone. If you would worry about potential damage to the car, and would feel disrespected at someone taking it without your permission, then you must extend the same respect to someone else. When you feel morally wronged by a behaviour, you must assume someone else would feel morally wronged as well.

However, suppose the issue was not for your personal convenience, but a life or death issue involving someone else, then the situation may be morally different. Suppose a neighbour had a heart attack and your brother's car was the only feasible way of rushing the heart attack victim to a hospital, the use of your brother's car without permission may be morally justified.

The Role Exchange test is often stated in the form, "How would you like it if someone did that to you?" This somewhat misstates the test, because the issue here is not whether you think a certain treatment is likable, but whether you think the treatment is morally justified. A child may not like receiving a vaccination by needle, and you do not like it much either. It may still be morally justified, because the intended consequences of the treatment are morally justifiable.

The Subsumption Test

As noted above, moral tests can quite readily show whether a moral judgment is acceptable in a given situation. What is more difficult to demonstrate is whether a moral judgment is completely acceptable based on the tests it may have been subjected to.[35] Principle testing theory, which we have been discussing, states moral principles must be subjected to the most rigorous versions of the most rigorous moral test available. Only if it passes all those tests might it be considered morally acceptable.

When the three moral tests are completed, one test, the Subsumption Test , remains to be applied.[36] The Subsumption test demands that in responding to a situation calling for a moral decision, one begins the testing process by selecting the most inclusive moral principle applicable to the situation. The inclusive moral principle becomes the major premise of a syllogism that must be subjected to a minor premise. Based on that relationship, one draws a conclusion that becomes a moral judgement about the situation in question. This is the first step in the subsumption process. The second step involves using the moral judgment derived in the first step as the major premise in a second syllogism and subjecting it to another minor premise in order to draw another conclusion or moral judgment. If the final moral judgment is consistent with the overriding moral principle you began with, then that principle can be considered to be sound. In other words, if the final moral judgment appears to be subsumed by the beginning moral principle, the moral assumptions appear to be consistent and coherent, making it likely the moral principles and related judgments are morally acceptable.

Let us examine two related examples of the subsumption process to see how it works out in practice. In the first example, suppose someone argues that gun control is good social policy for a society to adopt. The moral principle societies are safer with gun control becomes the major premise of a syllogism. The factual test or minor premise states societies with fewer guns have lower murder rates. The moral judgment or conclusion drawn from the first syllogism is murder rates can be reduced by limiting access to guns. So now we have created another moral principle which needs to be tested by a second syllogism. The major premise (moral principle) of this syllogism is societies with fewer guns have lower murder rates. This major premise needs to be tested by factual information (minor premise) to wit: With fewer guns available people are less able to kill other people. Therefore, it is socially good to limit peoples' access to guns. These syllogisms demonstrate that the final conclusion/moral judgment is consistent or subsumed by the initial overriding moral principle that societies are safer with gun control.

One needs to examine a second, similar example where the final conclusion is not subsumed by the initial moral principle to see how this works out in practice. Suppose someone presents a moral claim that having the right to own guns contributes to a safer society. This becomes the major premise and needs to be tested by the minor premise. The minor premise might remain the fact that societies with fewer guns have lower murder rates. The person arguing this syllogism might conclude it is wrong to take guns from people despite a high murder rate. The moral judgment "it is wrong to take guns from people despite a high murder rate" becomes the major premise of a second syllogism. Testing the major premise against the minor premise we get: people want guns to protect themselves from people who have guns. The logical conclusion from this syllogism is that it is necessary to limit access to guns within society to prevent people from killing each other. When one compares the final moral judgment with the initial moral principle we encounter a logical contradiction. The moral principle holding that the right to own guns leads to a safer society does not subsume the moral judgment that it is necessary to limit access to guns within society to prevent people from killing each other. There is something wrong with either the moral principle or the moral judgment, and the situation will have to be rethought before it can be considered morally acceptable.

Applying Principle Testing Theory in the Classroom

We now return to the issue of whether the two moral claims made earlier are acceptable: "people in a free society have the right to decide how to live their lives" and "it is wrong to allow people to do things like smoke marijuana because there are serious health risks involved". Students can be introduced to Principle Testing Theory using the material they have already worked with and developed. As an initial exercise, students could be given a template to work from so that the amount of information they have to hold in their working memories can be limited. The following template could best be developed in a class discussion using simple examples, at first, to introduce the four moral tests conceptually. It is likely that students will be some what familiar with them, with the exception of the subsumption test. They will almost certainly be using some of them as moral rules of thumb (heuristics) in their day to day lives. What they will be less familiar with are the systematic evaluation procedures used in the theory.

Returning to the dialogue about the role of government in peoples' lives, each side of the dialogue could be challenged to apply the moral tests to their respective value claim. The class might do a test or two in a class discussion to develop some examples before attempting the process on their own. Their results might look something like Fig. *11.10*. Each group could prepare a set of syllogisms using each test and then present their moral tests to each as part of a symposium on the issue. After the initial discussion, each side should redo the moral tests, but for the moral claims of the other side and them re-discuss their results.

MORAL PRINCIPLE A People in a free society have the right to decide how to live their lives	**MORAL TESTS**	**MORAL PRINCIPLE B** It is wrong to allow people to do things like smoke marijuana because there are serious health risks involved.
Major Premise: Would I want to live in a society where people are given the right to decide what they can or cannot do? **Minor Premise:** I know that people regularly do things that hurt themselves and others. **Conclusion** I would be very afraid that I could not protect myself or my family in this kind of situation. Pass/Fail for this test?	**ROLE EXCHANGE TEST** If I were in the situation being described here, how would I feel about the treatment I would receive? *The rule of thumb:* Do unto others as you would have them do to you.	**Major Premise:** Would I want to live in a society where people are concerned about protecting each other from behaviours that are dangerous? **Minor Premise:** People can become over zealous and interfere in peoples lives when they have no reason to interfere. **Conclusion** " I would want the right to protest against unwarranted interference in my life. Pass/Fail for this test?
Major Premise: What would society be like if everyone had the right to decide what they can or cannot do? **Minor Premise:** There are people who are prepared to use criminal behaviour to get what they want. **Conclusion** People need structure and guidelines to make them accountable for their behaviour. Pass/Fail for this test?	**THE UNIVERSAL CONSEQUENCES TEST** A moral principle cannot be acceptable unless the consequences of acting upon it are acceptable. (Coombs). *The rule of thumb:* What would happen if everyone did this?	**Major Premise:** What would it be like to live in a society where governments have the right to decide what is good and bad for their citizens? **Minor Premise:** " Governments are made up of people with all the abilities and limitations of any other large group of people. **Conclusion** Politicians and governments do not have greater knowledge of what is good for people than do people. Pass/Fail for this test?

cont'd

cont'd

Major Premise: Drivers on streets and roads should have the right to determine how they will drive their automobiles. **Minor Premise:** People driving on carefully regulated streets and roads often make bad decisions that hurt others. **Conclusion** If drivers are not held accountable for their behaviour they will drive more and more dangerously. Pass/Fail for this test?	**THE NEW CASES TEST** A moral principal can only be acceptable when it is acceptable in a different situation where someone is faced with a similar moral decision for similar reasons. *The rule of thumb:* Check your thinking by looking at other similar situations to see if it your principle is acceptable there.	**Major Premise:** Society determined that alcohol was a very dangerous and damaging substance which should be regulated for the protection of people **Minor Premise:** Bread winners who could no longer spend their wages on alcohol tend to spend it an their families, resulting the improved wellbeing of their families. **Conclusion** Dangerous substances like alcohol do need some regulation for the wellbeing of people who cannot protect themselves. Pass/Fail for this test?
SYLLOGISM A: Developing a moral judgment. **Major Premise:** People have the right to decide how to live their lives? **Minor Premise:** Most people are intelligent, have a clear sense of what is good for them, and are capable of making correct decisions for their own lives. **Conclusion** People have a better understanding of what is good for them than does government.	**THE SUBSUMPTION TEST** *The rule of thumb:* Is the moral principal we are working with part of a larger, acceptable principle?	SYLLOGISM A: Developing a moral judgment. **Major Premise:** Governments have a duty to protect the interests and wellbeing of their citizens. **Minor Premise:** There are many people who lack the knowledge, ability, and will to look for their best interests. **Conclusion** Governments must pass laws that protect people from dangerous situations.

cont'd

cont'd

SYLLOGISM B: Testing the moral judgment. **Major Premise:** Governments must pass laws that protect people from dangerous situations. **Minor Premise:** People use the law as criteria (guidelines) to guide their behaviour in positive and constructive ways. **Conclusion** The rule of law is necessary in the formation of a safe and constructive society. Pass/Fail for this test?	**The Subsumption Test** (*cont'd*) *The rule of thumb*: Is the moral principal we are working with part of a larger, acceptable principle?	SYLLOGISM B: Testing the moral judgment. **Major Premise:** People have a better understanding of what is good for them than does government. **Minor Premise:** It is people, not governments, who do the day to day decision making societally and personally that makes society work. **Conclusion** Society can only be as good as the people who do the day to day running of society. Pass/Fail for this test?

Fig. 11.10

DIALOGICAL THINKING

If students are encouraged to write their own syllogisms, and most importantly share and critique them, then they are likely to realize that the factual information chosen to represent the minor premise is very critical to the direction the conclusion will take. Joint discussions between the two groups are necessary to the process of developing definitive syllogisms for each moral test. The groups collectively need to decide which minor premises are valid factual tests for each major premise. Once the minor premise phase has been completed and evaluated, then students need to consider, also in a dialogue, whether the conclusions selected for each syllogism logically and validly represent an acceptable conclusion to the syllogism.

Once students complete the evaluation of all syllogisms to their satisfaction, they should decide whether and where the moral principles passed or failed the moral tests. On the basis of these tests, they should try to come to some conclusion about the legalization of marijuana, which is where they started.

The word 'dialogue' has been used throughout this exercise, rather than the word 'debate'. There may be a fine line between the two concepts, but the important objective underlying the term dialogue is a collective search for truth. The dialogue about whether governments should allow people to have freedom or whether governments should care about the wellbeing of its citizens is not about right and wrong. In like manner, it is important to emphasize to students that the dialogical process is not about winners and losers, but about everyone winning. Society does better when both freedom and caring exist in the society. Students should be helped to understand that moral issues are not about upmanship, but rather about finding the best way to live together. The dialogical process is a methodology intended to help people achieve seemingly contradictory but true goals.

Education is about learning to be good citizens. Humans are social creatures, and as such want to live in groups. Learning, therefore, has to be about leaning to live together. Moral education has to be about good ways and bad ways of living together. As pointed out earlier, it is sometimes difficult to understand, appreciate and empathize with the needs, wants, and points of view of others. One way of accomplishing this difficult process is through dialogue.[37] Dialogue is the process of listening, sharing and respecting other points. It is only through an honest, respectful dialogue that we discover those things that really matter to us and find ways of accomplishing and reconciling needs one to another.

Let us give part of the last word to heuristics and fast and frugal thinking. When students encounter a situation where they have to confront someone who is holding a contrary point of view, they will turn to fast and frugal thinking for a response. What will their heuristics discover for them? Will they discover the winner takes all, win at any cost examples we see modeled so often in society? Or, will they see an opportunity to grow with others in their moral reasoning? Will they have some dialogical models of discourse to use, which they learned by participating in moral reasoning activities within a mentored environment? Then their heuristics may come up with something other than "Gotcha!"

END NOTES

1. Jean Piaget. *The Moral Judgment of the Child.* 1932. Reprint. New York: Free Press. 1965.

2. L. Goldman. "Warning: The Socratic method can be dangerous". *Educational Leadership*. 1984. V 47 pp. 57-62.

3. Neil Postman. "Critical thinking in the electronic era". National Forum. 1985. 65:4-8.

4. A. Bandura, "Self-efficacy: Toward a unifying theory of behavioural change." *Psychological Review*. 1977: pp.191-215.

5. B. B. Brown, S. L. Lamborn, N. S. Mounts, & L. Steinberg. " Parenting practices and peer group affiliation in adolescence". *Child Development.* 64 (1993): 467-482.

6. Paul A Klaczynski and Gayathri Narasimham "Development of Scientific Reasoning Biases: Cognitive Versus Ego-protective Explanations". *Developmental Psychology*. 1998. Vol. 34. No. 5. p. 177.

7. Malcolm Gladwell. *Blink: the power of thinking without thinking.* New York: Little, Brown and Company 2005.

8. Gladwell suggests that people draw conclusions from a large amount of information using a technique he calls thin slicing. Thin slicing is the ability to select the few factors that really matter from what may be a very large number of variables available in a situation. People with this ability are able to draw conclusions about reality quickly and accurately.

9. Peter M Todd and Gerd Gigerenzer. "What We Have Learned (So Far)." *Simple Heuristics that Make Us Smart.* Ed. Gerd Gigerenzer and Peter M. Todd. New York: Oxford University Press 1999. p. 365.

10. Peter M Todd and Gerd Gigerenzer. "Fast and Frugal Heuristics: The Adaptive Toolbox." *Simple Heuristics that Make Us Smart.* Ed by Gerd Gigerenzer and Peter M. Todd. New York: Oxford University Press. 1999: p 9.

11. Paul Sniderman, Richard A Brody, Philip E Tetlock,. Reasoning and Choice: Explorations in Political Psychology (Cambridge: Cambridge University Press 1991): 15.

12. Sniderman p. 19

13. Sniderman p. 59

14. Sniderman p. 67

15. Sniderman p. 70

16. Sniderman p. 73.

17. Sniderman p. 70.

18. Sniderman p. 71.

19 Simon 1985. p. 301. As quoted by Sniderman. p. 90.

20. Ralph Hertwig, Ulrich Hoffrage, Laura Martigon. "Quick Estimation Letting the Environment Do the Work". *Simple Heuristics that Make Us Smart.* Ed. Gerd Gigerenzer and Peter M. Todd. New York: Oxford University Press. 1999. p. 218

.

21. Peter M Todd and Gerd Gigerenzer. "Fast and Frugal Heuristics The Adaptive Toolbox." *Simple Heuristics that Make Us Smart.* Ed. Gerd Gigerenzer and Peter M. Todd. New York: Oxford University Press. 1999. p. 27.

22. Daniel Goldstein and Gerd Gigerenzer, "The Recognition Heuristic: How Ignorance Makes Us Smart" *Simple Heuristics that Make Us Smart.* Ed. Gerd Gigerenzer and Peter M. Todd. New York: Oxford University Press. 1999. p. 41

23. Gigerenzer, Gerd and Goldstein, Daniel G. "Betting on One Good Reason: The Take the Best Heuristic." *Simple Heuristics that Make Us Smart.* Ed. Gerd Gigerenzer and Peter M. Todd. New York: Oxford University Press. 1999. p. 80.

24. Gigerenzer Goldstein p. 80.

25. Sniderman p. 93.

26. Sniderman p. 4

27. Patricia R. Palmerton and Yvonne Bushyhead. "Its Not Getting at Real". Exploring Alternative Approaches to Critical Thinking.. Paper presented at Annual Meeting of the Central States Communication Association.
ERIC: ED 374 483.1994.

28. See *Chapter Eight.* p. 290.

29. Palmerton and Bushyhead.

30. C Wright Mills. *The Marxists.* New York: Dell. 1962.

31. C Wright Mills.

32. Jerrold R. Coombs. "Validating Moral Judgments By Principle Testing". *Development of Moral Reasoning Practical Approaches.* Ed. Donald B. Cochrane and Michael Manley-Casimir. New York: Praeger. 1980. p 38.

33. Coombs p. 31.

34. Coombs p. 34.

35. Coombs p. 41.

36. Coombs p. 41.

37. M. Scriven. "Critical for survival". *National Forum.* 1985. 65. pp 4-8.

EPILOGUE

Life is always small. It is always vulnerable. It never shouts or screams. It always needs protection and guidance. Saying "yes" to it means being willing to look at the small life that seeks to be born in your heart, in your body, in your mind, among people. Death is always glamorous. Death shines; it is always big and noisy. Death goes bang, bang! Because life is very small, you can never see it happening. Have you seen a tree actually grow? Growth is too gentle, too tender. Life is basically hidden. It is small and begs for constant care and protection. If you are committed to always saying "yes" to life, you must become a person who chooses it when it is hidden.

Henri J.M. Nouwen

In *Chapter One*, I began this commentary on high school education with a class of grade nine students who were just beginning their high school careers. I would like to end with students as well. Despite the rhetoric we hear about education for students, the student voice is easily lost in any serious discussion of the purpose and future of education. As Nouwen so cogently points out in his comments quoted above, incipient life is extremely vulnerable. So it is with students. It is true they are limited in their ability to construct a rationale that defends their point of view on education, but that does not mean they do not have one. Nor does it mean their point of view is irrelevant to any discussion about good education. They are concerned about the quality of their education, but our concentration on information to the exclusion of thought limits their contribution.

Contribution requires intellectual involvement. It also depends upon feeling that one's contribution is welcomed, and that it matters to the institution in which you find yourself. In education, the critical core institution is the classroom. For students, classrooms are the place where decision making occurs that matters. Whether students are allowed to play a meaningful decision making role in their education makes a significant difference to their intellectual lives. Students drop out of school every day, even though they remain physically present in classrooms. Let me give you an example.

I remember meeting a young man in a grade ten class I was teaching at the time. He had transferred in from another school, where he had been having problems. He was a towheaded, pleasant young fellow who was not a discipline problem in any way. He would occasionally participate in class discussions, but otherwise he was uninterested in any kind of schoolwork. He would promise to do his assignments, but they seldom appeared. By the middle of the second month, he was on his way to failing the class. Upon a little investigation, I discovered this was typical behaviour. He had politely and firmly dropped out intellectually. His *modus operandi* was to keep teachers off his back by being friendly and polite, but doing as little as possible.

One of the activities we were doing at the time was examining some important historical debates. We were simulating a trio of trials: Galileo, Martin Luther, and John Scope. The class was divided into teams who would role play either the prosecution or the defence in one of the trials. Students were responsible for preparing and presenting their cases. They assigned people to role play witnesses who would testify in court under oath. These witnesses would be cross-examined by the opposing teams.

The young man became a prosecution lawyer in one of the cases. Initially he was somewhat reticent about playing a lead role in the simulation. He was particularly concerned about having to cross-examine a witness who was female and a very good student. He doubted his ability to be an intellectual match for her in the give and take of cross-examination. The day came for the battle of wits, and he started out somewhat slowly and hesitantly; but as the interview went on, he gained confidence and was able to more than hold his own. When the bell rang to signal the end of class, I went to congratulate him and his face was glowing. That class was an epiphany for him. Somewhere in the class that morning, he discovered something about his potential that he had not realized up until then.

If one thinks about education from the perspective of life long learning, these kinds of epiphanies are critical. Many times epiphanies are internal and ancillary to the direct instruction an individual is receiving. Rather, they are personal responses to a learning situation where the student discovers something meaningful and relevant to connect to his or her life. Those responses are emotional, and often manifest themselves as likes or dislikes, which are too easily discounted. In future years, they have the potential to become the personal heuristics or intellectual shortcuts of students, and they send signals about whether one should or can become involved in learning activities of one kind or another. Those heuristics can last a lifetime.

The story of the young man is a metaphor for transcendence and reductionism. This young man, try as he might, could not play the game of reductionistic education. He just could not 'get' learning reduced to its bare essentials. Being an obedient kid, he could not formally drop out, but he could not find any point to it either. So, high school had become something for him 'to endure, grind out, and eventually be free'.

Then transcendence came along one morning, and he did not see it coming. At first, it looked like another hokey school exercise, but somewhere along the way it got to him. What does transcendence look like to grade ten kids? It looks like being an adult, where you are in charge and where you are responsible and accountable. This is important, because without independence, responsibility and accountability, there can be no meaning. Meaning is a cycle:

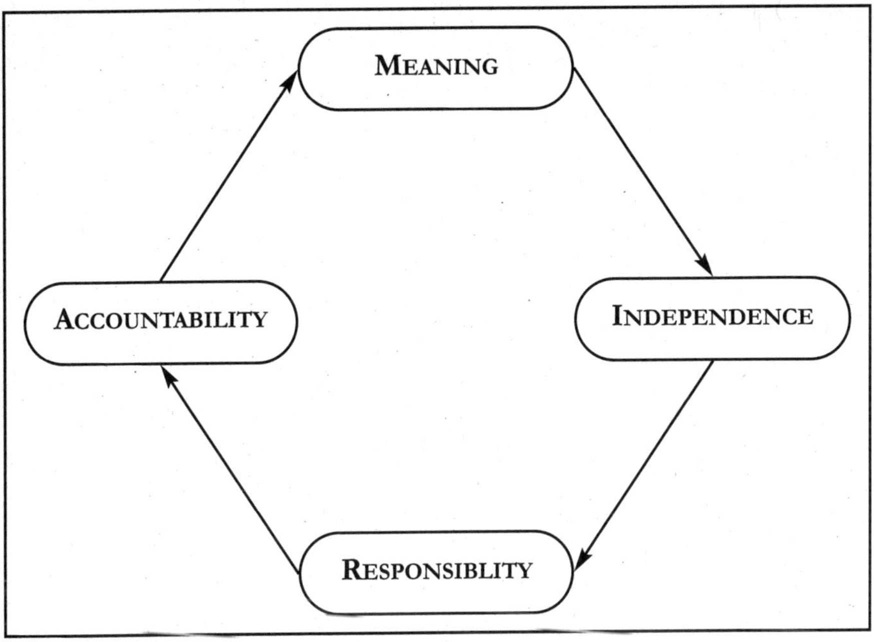

With transcendence, a bell signalling the end of the class is irrelevant to what the students are experiencing. I remember a chemistry teacher asking: "What in the world is going on? Kids come into my class arguing about this history stuff, and I can't get them to stop!" For those students, the issues had become too large and too important for a mere school bell to interfere with their thinking about them. Transcendence in the classroom is what we should be aiming for.

BIBLIOGRAPHY

Arkes, Hal R. and Garske, John P. *Psychological Theories of Motivation.* 2ed. Monterey: Brooks/Cole Publishing Company. 1982.

Bandura, A. "Self-efficacy: Toward a unifying theory of behavioural change." *Psychological Review.* 197.7

Bandura, Albert. *Principles of Behaviour Modification.* New York: Holt. 1969.

Beyer, Barry. "Improving thinking skills: Defining the problem". *Phi Delta Kappa.* 1984 Vol. 65 No.7 .

Baron, J. "Intelligence and general strategies". *Strategies for Information Processing.* G. Underwood Ed. London: Academic Press. 1978.

Bolt Beranek and Newman Inc.. *Final Report, Project Intelligence: The development of procedures to enhance thinking skills* Cambridge, Mass: Bolt Beranek and Newman Inc.

Boyer, E. "High school: A report on secondary education in America". New York: Harper and Row. 1983.

Brainerd, C. J. and Reyna, V. F. "The Memory Independence Effect: What Do the Data Show? What Do the Theories Claim?" *Developmental Review.* Vol. 12. 1992.

Brainerd, C. J. and Gordon, L. L. "Development of Verbatim and Gist Memory for Numbers". *Developmental Psychology.* 1994. Vol. 30 No. 2.

Brainerd, C. J. and Kingma, V. F. "The Memory Independence Effect: What Do the Data Show? What Do the Theories Claim?" *Developmental Review.* Vol. 12. 199.

Brown, B. B., Lamborn, S. L., Mounts, N. S., & Steinberg, L. "Parenting practices and peer group affiliation in adolescence." *Child Development.* 1993.

Bullock, Alan. *Hitler: A Study in Tyranny.* New York: Harper & Row Publishers. 1962.

Carr, E. H. *What is History?* London: Penguin. 1961.

Carraher p. Carraher, T. N., Carraher, D. W., & Schliemann, A. D. "Mathematics in the streets and in schools". *British Journal of Experimental Psychology.* 1985. Vol 3.

Chi, M., Feltowich, P. and Glaser, R. "Categorization and representation of physical problems by experts and novices". *Cognitive Science.* 1981. Vol. pp. 121-152.

Chi, M. T.H. Hutchison, J. E. and Robin A. F. "How inferences about novel domain-related concepts can be constrained by structured knowledge". 1989. *Merrill-Palmer Quarterly.* Vol. 35.

Chi, M. T. and Rees, E. "A learning framework for development". *Contributions to Human Development.* 1983 Vol. 9.

Cochrane, Donald B. and Manley-Casimir, Michael. *Development of Moral Reasoning: Practical Approaches.* New York: Praeger. 1980

Chomsky, Noam. Various interviews and journalists. *http://www.chomsky.info/interviews/1992----02.htm.*

Conanat, James B. *The American High School Today: A First Report to Interested Citizens.* New York: McGraw-Hill. 1959.

Conklin, Kenneth R. "Theory and Practice as Viewed From the Classroom." *EDUCATIONAL FORUM. XLIV*, 3 March, 1980.

Conway, M. A., Cohen, G. and Stanhope, N. "On the very long memory of knowledge through formal education: twelve years of cognitve psychology", *Journal of Experimental Psychology.* Genera.1991 Vol. 120:395-409.

Damasio, Antonio. *Descartes' Error: Emotion, Reason and the Human Brain.* New York: Grosset/Putnam. 1994. As referenced in Golelman, Daniel. *Emotional Intelligence.* New York: Bantam Books. 1995

Damon, William. *Handbook of Child Psychology.* New York: John Wiley & Sons, Inc.

DeGroot, A. "Perception and memory versus thought: Some old ideas and recent findings". *Problem Solving*. Ed. B. Kleinmutz. New York: Wiley. 1966.

Dewey, John "My Pedagogic Creed" *The School Journal* .Vol. LIV No. 3 January 16, 1897.

Homer-Dixon, Thomas. *The Ingenuity Gap*. Toronto: Alfred A Knopf 2000.

Eisner, E. *The Educational Imagination: On the Design and Evaluation of School Programs*, 3ed. New York: Macmillan College Publishing. 1994.

Eysenck, H. J. "Introduction". *A model for intelligence*. Ed. H. J. Eysenck. New York: Springer-Verlag. 1982.

Farr, Marshall J. *The Long-Term Retention of Knowledge and Skills: A Cognitive and Instructional Perspective*. New York: Springer-Verlag. 1987.

Festinger, L. *A Theory of Cognitive Dissonance* Evanston Ill.: Row, Peterson, 1957

Festinger, L. and Carlsmith, J. M. "Cognitive Consequences of Forced Compliance". *Journal of Abnormal and Social Psychology*. 1959. Vol. 58.

Friedenberg, Edgar Z. *The Vanishing Adolescent*. Boston: Beacon Press, 1964.

Friedman, Thomas L. *The World Is Flat*. New York: Farrar, Straus and Giroux,.2005.

Frost, Joe L. *Revisiting Early Childhood Education*. New York: Holt, Rinehart and Winston Inc. 1973.

Gigerenzer Gerd and Todd, Peter M. *Simple Heuristics that Make Us Smart*. New York: Oxford University Press 1999.

Gigerenzer, Gerd and Goldstein, Daniel G. "Betting on One Good Reason: The Take the Best Heuristic." *Simple Heuristics that Make Us Smart*. Ed. Gigerenzer Gerd and Todd, Peter M. New York: Oxford University Press. 1999.

Goldman, L. "Warning: The Socratic method can be dangerous". *Educational Leadership*. 1984. 42.

Goldstein, Daniel and Gigerenzer, Gerd, "The Recognition Heuristic: How Ignorance Makes Us Smart." *Simple Heuristics that Make Us Smart.* Ed. Gigerenzer Gerd and Todd, Peter M. New York: Oxford University Press. 1999.

Gould, Stephen Jay. *The Mismeasure of Man.* New York: W. W. Norton & Company. 1981.

Gladwell, Malcolm. *Blink: the power of thinking without thinking.* New York: Little, Brown and Company. 2005.

Glaser, E. M. "Critical Thinking: Educating for responsible citizenship in a democracy". *National Forum.* 1985. 65

Goleman, Daniel. *Emotional Intelligence.* New York :Bantam Books. 1995.

Goodlad, J. I. *A place called school: Prospects for the future.* New York: McGraw-Hill 1983.

Hayes, J. R. *The Complete Problem Solver.* Educational Resources Information Center (ERIC): ED234995.

Hembrow, Vern. "A Heuristic Approach Across the Curriculum". *Language Arts.* Vol. 63, No. 7, Nov. 1986.

Hertwig, Ralph. Hoffrage, Ulrich, and Martigon, Laura. "Quick Estimation: Letting the Environment Do the Work." *Simple Heuristics that Make Us Smart.* Ed. Gigerenzer Gerd and Todd, Peter M. New York: Oxford University Press. 1999.

Klaczynski Paul A and Narasimham Gayathri. "Representations as Mediators of Adolescent Deductive Reasoning". *Developmental Psychology.* 1998. Vol. 34, No. 5.

Klaczynski, Paul A. and Narasimham, Gayathri. "Development of Scientific Reasoning Biases: Cognitive Versus Ego-protective Explanations". *Developmental Psychology.* 1998. Vol. 34, No. 5.

Kuhn, Thomas S. *The Structure of Scientific Revolutions.* Chicago: University Of Chicago Press. 1968.

Larkin, J. H. "The role of problem representation in physics". *Mental Models.* Ed. D. Gentner and A. L. Stevens. Hillsdale, NJ: Erlbaum. 1983.

Maxcy, Spencer J. "John Dewey and American Education" *History of American Thought: Exploring the Diversity of American Intellectual History*. Bristol: Thoemmes Press. Chicago: The University of Chicago Press (U.S. Distributor.)

Mckay, John P. Hill, Bennett D. and Buckler, John. *A History of Western Society Volume II: From Absolutism to the Present.* Boston: Houghton Mifflin Company 1987.

McKenzie, Helen. *Education in Canada: Current Issues.* Government of Canada: Political and Social Affairs Division. May 1994.

Middlebrook, Martin. *The first day on the Somme : 1 July 1916.* Harmondsworth: Penguin. 1984. c1971.

Milestone, Lewis. *All Quiet on the Western Front.* (film)
http://us.imdb.com/title/tt0020629/ 1930.

Mills, C Wright. *The Marxists.* New York: Dell 1962.

National Commission on Excellence in Education. *A Nation at Risk: The Imperative for Educational Reform.* A Report to the Nation and the Secretary of Education. United States Department of Education. April, 1983.

Nickerson, Raymond S. "Why Teach Thinking". *Teaching Thinking Skills.* Ed. Joan Boykof Baron and Robert J. Sternberg. New York: W. H. Freeman and Company.

Novak,Joseph D. and Gowin, D. Bob. *Learning How to Learn.* New York: Cambridge University Press 1986.

Null, J. Wesley *A Disciplined Progressive Educator: The Life and Career of William Chandler Bagley.* New York: Peter Land Publishing 2003.

Palmerton, Patricia R. and Bushyhead, Yvonne. "It's Not Getting at Real". *Exploring Alternative Approaches to Critical Thinking.* Paper presented at Annual Meeting of the Central States Communication Association. ERIC: ED 374 483.1994

Pauls, Richard. "Critical Thinking and the Critical Person". ERIC: ED 273 511

Paul, Richard W. "Dialogical Thinking: Critical Thought Essential to the Acquisition of Rational Knowledge and Passions" *Teaching Thinking Skills*. Ed. Joan Boykof Baron and Robert J. Sternberg. New York: W. H. Freeman and Company.

Perkins, D.N. "Knowledge as Design: Teaching Thinking Through Content". *Teaching Thinking Skills*. Ed. Joan Boykof Baron and Robert J. Sternberg. New York: W. H. Freeman and Company.

Piaget, Jean. *The Moral Judgment of the Child.* 1932. Reprint. New York: Free Press. 1965.

Plato. *The Last Days of Socrates.* Ed. Hugh Tredennick. Penguin. 1995.

Postman, Neil. "Critical thinking in the electronic era". *National Forum.* 1985. 65:4-8.

Saskatchewan Learning. *Grade 10 History Activity Guide, Unit Five, Activity One.* Web site: *http://www.sasked.gov.sk.ca/docs/history10/activity/unit5/u5index.html.*

Quellmalz, Edys S. "Developing Reasoning Skills". *Teaching Thinking Skills.* Ed. Joan Boykof Baron and Robert J. Sternberg. New York: W. H. Freeman and Company.

Remarque, Erich Maria. *All Quiet on the Western Front.* New York: Trade Paper Back. 2003.

Rousseau, J.J. *Emile.* Tr. B. Foxley. London. 1963.

Ruscio, Ayelot Meron and Amabile, Teresa M. "The Effects of Instructional Style on Problem-Solving Creativity". *Creativity Research Journal.* 1999. Vol. 12, Issue 4.

Scriven, M. "Critical for survival". *National Forum.* 1985. 65.

Semb, G. B. and Ellis, J. A. "Knowledge taught in school: What is remembered?" *Review of Educational Research.* 1994. Vol. 64: 253-286

Simon, H. A. "Invariants of human behaviour". *Annual Review Psychology.* 1990 Vol. 41.

Sizer, Theodore R. and Schen, Molly. *Educational Wastelands: The Retreat from Learning in our Public Schools* 2ed. with retrospectives by Clarence Karier and Foster McMurray. Urbana: University of Illinois Press. 1985.

Sizer, T. B. *Horace's compromise: The dilemma of the American high school today*. Boston: Houghton Mifflin. 1984.

Smith, Adam. *An Inquiry into the Nature and Causes of the Wealth of Nations.* Library of Economics and Liberty. Retrieved November 29, 2006 from the World Wide Web: *http://www.econlib.org/library/Smith/smWN13.html*

Sniderman, Paul, Brody, Richard A., Tetlock, Philip E. *Reasoning and Choice: Explorations in Political Psychology.* Cambridge: Cambridge University Press. 1991.

Schmuck, Richard A. and Schmuck, Patricia A. *Group Processes in the Classroom.* Dubuque: Brown Company Publishers. 1983.

Schwartz, Steven. "Heuristics and Biases In Medical Judgment and Decision Making". *Applications of Heuristics and Biases to Social Issues.* New York: Plenum Press 1994.

Shoenfeld, A. H. "Explicit heuristic training as a variable in problem-solving performance". *Journal for Research in Mathematics Education.* 1979 Vol. 10.

Schoenfeld, A. H. "Measures of problem-solving performance and of problem-solving instruction". *Journal for Research in Mathematics Education.* 1982 Vol. 13.

Schoenfeld A. H. and Herrmann, D. J. "Problem perception and knowledge structure in expert and novice mathematical problem solvers". *Journal of Experimental Psychology: Learning, Memory, and Cognitions.* 1982 Vol. 8.

Starkes, J., Deakin, J., Allard, F., Hodges, N., & Hayes, A. "Deliberate practice in sports: what is it anyway?". *The road to excellence: the acquisition of expert performance in the arts and sciences.* Ed. K. A. Ericsson. Erlbaum. 1996.

Sternberg, Robert. "How Intelligent Is Intelligence Testing?" *Scientific American Presents: Exploring Human Intelligence.* Vol. 9, no. 4. Winter 1998.

Szasz, Ferenc M. *History News Network.* George Mason University *http://hnn.us/articles/1328.html*

Tesconi Charles A. and Morris, Van Cleve. *The Anti-man Culture: Bureautechnocracy and the Schools.* Urbana: University of Illinois Press. 1972.

Tillyard, E. M. W. *The Elizabethan World Picture.* New York: Vintage Books. 1963.

Todd, Peter M and Gigerenzer, Gerd. " Fast and Frugal Heuristics The Adaptive Toolbox." 1963 Todd, Peter M and Gigerenzer, Gerd. "What We Have Learned (So Far)." *Simple Heuristics that Make Us Smart.* Ed. Gerd Gigerenzer and Peter M. Todd. New York: Oxford University Press. 1999.

Todd, Peter M. and Gigerenzer, Gerd "Précis of Simple heuristics that make us smart". *Behavioral and Brain Sciences.* Vol. 23. 2000.

Tuchman, Barbara. *The Guns of August.* Presidio Press: Reprint edition. 2004.

Tyler, Ralph W. *Basic Principles of Curriculum and Instruction.* Chicago: The University of Chicago Press. 1949.

Wadsworth, Barry. *J. Piaget's Theory of Cognitive Development.* New York: David McKay Company, Inc. 1971.

White, R. W. "Motivation Reconsidered: The Concept of Competence." *Psychological Review.* Vol. 66. 1959.

Wittrock, Merlin C. "The Learning by Discovery Hypothesis". *Learning by Discovery: A Critical Appraisal.* Ed. Lee S. shulman and Evan R. Keislar. Chicago: Rand McNally and Co. 1966.

Yero. Judith Lloyd. *Teaching in Mind: How Teacher Thinking Shapes Education.* Hamilton, MT: MindFlight Publishing. 2002.

Yudkin, Jeremy. *Understanding Classical Music.* 3ed. Prentice Hall: Upper Saddle River. 2002.